Transportation Economics and Public Policy:
With Urban Extensions

Transportation Economics and Public Policy: With Urban Extensions

ALAN ABOUCHAR
University of Toronto

A WILEY-INTERSCIENCE PUBLICATION

JOHN WILEY & SONS, New York • London • Sydney • Toronto

Library of Congress Cataloging in Publication Data:

Abouchar, Alan.
    Transportation economics and public policy, with urban
extensions.

    "A Wiley-Interscience publication."
    Includes bibliographies and index.
    1. Transportation—Finance. 2. Transportation and
state. 3. Urban transportation policy.   I. Title.

HE196.5.A26   380.5   76-51828
ISBN 0-471-02101-6

Printed in the United States of America

10 9 8 7 6 5 4 3 2 1

77-9669

To

ANN

Preface

Behind the apparent agreement in the transport sector on such funda-mental goals and principles as social welfare maximization and the theoretical characteristics of optimal pricing there has long lain disorder and inconsistency. They are critical because of transportation's perva-sive role in the economy. Moreover, they are hard to see because the many aspects of transport analysis tend to be treated in isolation, the pricer not being his investment brother's keeper and the finance ministry unconcerned with the concepts and approaches to cost measurement. Too often, we agree on principles while inferring polarized policy recommendation. On the other hand, some who agree on policy trace their views to quite opposed principles. Clearly, this makes attempts to generalize policy recommendations extremely hazardous, and reasoning by analogy, very suspect.

One example of the different paths diverging from the same clearly stated principle is the variety of recommendations based on marginal cost-price equalization. This principle leads some to want higher prices and others to prefer lower prices, even for the same transport activity, because they do not stop to define marginal cost in clear and consistent operational terms. Conversely, higher prices or user charges may be recommended by some policymakers simply on the basis of a com-parison between expenditures and revenues that are ascribed to some activity according to an accounting convention; others may reach the same conclusion by way of congestion considerations. In doing so, the former do not consciously care about welfare optimization, while the latter start from this goal with no concern for bureaucratic constraints. Or, to consider another dimension, optimal short-run congestion theorists often neglect the long-run effects of a particular analysis or pricing device, and vice versa.

Indeed, the situation is worse; often we do not even recognize that there *is* a problem, that there *is* disagreement on what is being said and recommended. Thus the same article submitted to a journal may be criticized by one referee for its exasperating negligence of theoretical and empirical fundamentals and by a second referee for being a tiresome restatement of received truths.

I believe that the problem is rooted in the too frequent formulation of rules with regard to one aspect of transport decision-making in isolation of others. To remedy the situation, this book tries to integrate the three main aspects of public sector transportation analysis and decision-making—pricing theory and policy, cost theory and measurement, and investment choice—and to develop policy guidelines on the basis of welfare maximizing principles and real world complexities and constraints. Numerous empirical examples and case studies are provided to illustrate applications and suggest ways to bridge the gap between everyday data limitations and the theory and concepts presented. Extensions to some aspects of urban transport economics and general urban economics are contained in Part 4.

The book is intended for three groups: (1) field economists working in transportation and urban analysis, as well as finance and planning ministry workers confronted by the demands of sectoral investment organs; (2) academic economists interested in the applied problems of this critically important sector; and (3) students in transport and urban economics or project evaluation courses.

The book is based on my lectures on transport economics and public sector investment evaluation developed over an eight-year period. Many debts have been incurred during the course of its production. I have been fortunate in having had the opportunity to present part or all of the series of lectures at the Brazilian Ministry of Transport, the University of Toronto, and the Canadian Federal Treasury Board. I am also very grateful for the recurring opportunities to test theories on empirical anvils in a wide range of countries, economic systems, and levels of development, and I thank the various transport and planning agencies where I have had the opportunity to serve. I also thank the World Bank, where I spent one year on leave from Toronto. Comments from anonymous referees on earlier drafts, and on some portions published in journal articles, have been helpful and are hereby acknowledged, as is conversation with Rodney Dobell and Mel Fuss on some specific points of theory.

My debt to other empirical investigators, especially members of the American Association of State Highway Officials road test group and Matthew Betz, George Borts, Jan de Weille, and George Wilson, will be evident through Part 2 on cost analysis, though my interpretation of their work need not be assumed to agree with theirs. I am grateful to their publishers for permission to include some of the results (The National Research Council, The Brookings Institution, *Econometrica,* Johns Hopkins University Press, and the University of Wisconsin Press), as well as to the *Canadian Journal of Economics, Canadian Public Policy,* the *Eastern Economic Journal,* and *Economic Analysis* (Belgrade) for permission to include some of my own earlier results. My greatest debt is to my students who have patiently listened and sharply criticized, forcing me to extend, qualify, and clarify, thus resulting, I hope, in a consistent and self-contained work. Two students whose interrogation I remember as being among the more vexatious are Lok Sang Ho and Gilles Martin, and I would like to thank them and others. The responsibility for any errors that may remain is my own.

I also extend my appreciation to the Treasury Board for assistance in manuscript preparation and distribution and to the departmental secretaries at the University of Toronto for their always excellent typing and attitude—Monica Bristol, Amy Chan, Mary Colaianni, Vesna Marjanovic, and Julie Vittoz. Whenever I was in doubt about whether to request typing from a particularly messy draft or about retyping one more page for the "last" time, their cheerful disposition always persuaded me that the time and nuisance cost of the job would be negligible.

ALAN ABOUCHAR

Toronto, Ontario
December 1976

Contents

             Financing Policy   32

             1 Introduction, 32
             2 Homogeneous Output, 34
             3 Heterogeneous Output, 39
             4 Interregional Transfers and Pareto Efficiency, 41
             5 Conclusion, 43

             PART 2   ANALYSIS OF COSTS

Chapter 4   Introduction to the Analysis of Transport Costs   47

             1 Reasons for Studying Transport Costs, 47
             2 Objectives of Part 2, 50
             3 The Transferability of Cost Information, 51

Chapter 5   Road Transport Costs   58

             1 Vehicle Costs, 58
             2 Way Costs, 66
                References, 75

Chapter 6   Railroad Costs   76

             1 A Theory of Railroad Costs, 76
             2 Empirical Analysis: Long-Run Cost Behavior, 80
             3 Empirical Analysis: Short-Run Cost Behavior, 84
                References, 89

Chapter 7   Shadow Prices   90

             1 Objectives of Shadow Prices, 90
             2 Shadow Prices as Dual Solution to a Formal
                Optimization, 92
             3 Shadow Prices as Adjustments for Fiscal
                Distortions, 95
             4 Distortions in the Labor Market, 99
                References, 101

Chapter 8   Using Cost Analysis to Evaluate Pricing Policies   102

             1 Introduction, 102
             2 Pricing in the Motor Transport Sector—
                Yugoslavia, 103

Transportation Economics and Public Policy: With Urban Extensions

The General Welfare and Financing and Pricing Policy

1

Theories of Public Expenditure

1 THE NEED FOR A THEORY OF PUBLIC EXPENDITURE

Governments play a larger direct role in fields such as transportation and urban services than in most other economic activities. Usually they are directly responsible for infrastructure investment decisions in motor transport, civil aviation, coastal and maritime transport, inland navigation, and, in many countries, railroads. They frequently are, by design or default, the owners and operators of railroads and merchant shipping lines, and they determine pricing policies with respect to the infrastructure investments that they undertake or the operations that they conduct. It will be useful to designate these three forms of activity (investment, operation, and pricing of infrastructure and government transport operations) "direct government participation." In addition, in a somewhat different vein, governments regulate to a greater or lesser extent the private sector firms that perform transport services.

It is best to examine the justification for direct government participation and pricing and regulatory policies in terms of a general theory of public expenditure. But unfortunately, in spite of the efforts of the last

20 years to establish a rigorous theory of what goods and services the public sector should supply, and its implications for pricing policy, agreement on the classification and criteria for public expenditure appears still to be far away. We have today five or six competing theories and concepts, often used or defined inconsistently, even by the same author.

It is more than a nice academic objection that the theory of public expenditure "has not yet attained rigid orthodoxy," as Buchanan has put it (1967, p. 115) and has failed to develop into a unified whole. The fact is that policymakers and economists in actual fields of endeavor have no basic standard by which to judge their recommendations on specific issues, such as the pricing structure for urban transport or rural roads, or to evaluate the petitions of special interests. Among the many public expenditure theories holding that the public sector must undertake certain activities and charge for them in a way unrelated to consumers' use of them a pressure group is almost sure to find one that justifies public provision at public expense of any particular service that it happens to need at the moment. For example, education is justified by reference to income distribution objectives; related activities like rural roads to permit physical access then follow with their implied exemption from full cost recovery from beneficiaries. The income distribution argument is then applied by highway lobbies to the development of the road network in general. Marginal cost pricing of decreasing cost activities is invoked to justify large railroad deficits. And so on.

We have said enough to indicate the need for a theory of public expenditure to provide a framework to guide direct public sector activity. It is the aim of this and the next two chapters to develop a theory to guide pricing decisions.

In Section 2 we discuss Musgrave's three-way classification of the public sector, which can serve as the fundamental guide to public sector policy. In Section 3 we treat the Bowen-Samuelson apparatus, which has been advanced as the most demanding classificatory test for public expenditures undertaken for allocation (rather than distribution). We will see that this apparatus by itself is inadequate even to define a public good, although it can be put to an alternative and more compelling service elsewhere in analysis; additional conditions are necessary to use it as a criterion for public sector participation. Section 4 considers externalities as a public expenditure criterion. In Section 5 we look at cost-based criteria, presenting an alternative, more realistic theory of costs later (Chapter 3), which obviates the implications for optimal pricing and financing arising from the traditional simplified model.

Finally, Section 6 contains a theory of public expenditure in which the resource allocation justification for public sector activity is based on administrative, legal, and institutional factors.

2 MUSGRAVE'S THREE-WAY CLASSIFICATION OF PUBLIC SECTOR ACTIVITY

Perhaps the most fruitful contribution to the understanding and analysis of the public sector is Musgrave's three-way classification of public sector activity made in his seminal treatise on public finance (1959). His illuminating insight provides a very useful compass for the public sector analyst or policymaker confronting the myriad conflicting ideas and theories that condition the policy of the public sector.

Musgrave classifies the reasons for public sector activity under three headings: stabilization, income distribution, and resource allocation. Stabilization is concerned with maintaining employment objectives, and relies on various fiscal and monetary levers, such as tax policies (such special incentives as investment credits or differential unemployment insurance contributions by employers), interest rate policy, and control over the money supply.

Income distribution policies are designed to influence the income shares that accrue to various socioeconomic classes. Welfare payments, progressive personal income taxes, and progressive excise taxes represent specific income distribution policies. Education, although not always recognized as an income distribution objective, also falls in this rubric, since it enables children of low-income families to aspire higher than they could if education were to depend solely on their parents' ability to purchase education.

Resource allocation objectives, that is, the efficient use of resources, also may justify public sector activity. For, although the principles of perfect competition lead under certain conditions to efficient resource allocation, various obstacles to the fulfillment of these conditions do arise in practice, which public sector activity may help to overcome. The question that remains to be answered is: "What circumstances give rise to such obstacles?"

For the policymaker, resource allocation activities are the most difficult to define. Stabilization and income distribution may be taken as political mandates—if the electorate so wills, its representatives must respond in conformity. If officials are elected on the promise of more income equality, their target is fairly easy to define. If some maximum

unemployment rate is accepted as part of society's creed, the public
official must design fiscal and monetary policy to achieve this goal. But
what does society's commitment to efficient resource allocation imply
for decisions to undertake activities in the public sector and for their
pricing? Evidently, further criteria must be formulated, and it is this
goal that has dominated the public expenditure debate of the past two
decades.* In this debate at least three seemingly independent criteria
have evolved—vertically additive demand curves, externalities, and
declining costs. In reality, however, they are not independent, as we
shall see.

3 ANOPROSTHETIC DEMAND AND JOINT PRODUCTS

The Bowen (1948) and Samuelson (1954) vertical addition of demand
curves restricted this approach to "public goods"—indeed, *the* public
good was defined as a good whose demands could be summed vertically.
However, the apparatus has a much wider applicability, as was first
perceived by Steiner in his treatment of peak pricing (1957), and subsequently by Samuelson who used it to handle joint products wherever
they might occur, though arguing that public goods could be distinguished from joint private goods through their equilibrium welfare conditions (1969a). To divorce the concept of vertical additivity from the
notion of public sector expenditures, with which it has been almost
exclusively associated in the literature in the past, and give it a life of
its own, we call such demand relations "anoprosthetic" or upward additive.† It may be worthwhile at the same time to denote by "para-

* It would not be unreasonable to view the stabilization function as part of the efficient
resource allocation objective, since the former might be construed simply as the goal of
using, to their fullest, all the primary factors in the economy. The three-way distinction
seems preferable, however, since stabilization instruments are of a different nature from
other resource allocation instruments. If we insisted in including them under resource
allocation, we would have to subdivide this heading.
† The ambiguity in the use of the term "public good" can be illustrated most clearly
through a single article of Samuelson (1969b). After first stating emphatically that the
term should be taken as a neutral technological term devoid of political or ethical
overtones, implying nothing for public expenditures, Samuelson continued to use the term
interchangeably with public expenditure. Thus: "For the $(n + 1)$th time, let me repeat
the warning that a *public good* should not *necessarily* be run by the public sector rather
than private enterprise" (1969b, p. 108); "A public good—call it x or x_2 or x_{n+m}—is
simply one with the property of involving a 'consumption externality'..." (p. 102). But
on page 118 decreasing cost phenomena are treated as "public goods," which in this
context seems to refer to an expenditure that the public sector should undertake. This
ambiguity also characterizes other writings in the field. The only way to neutralize the
term would seem to be through the introduction of the neutral expression proposed here.

prosthetic" those demand relations that are laterally added in the customary manner.

Typical examples of "public goods" cited in the literature include flood control, police activity, defense expenditures, and television broadcasting. In all of these the quantity available to one person is not diminished by availability to others. The value of some given amount of the good is equal to the sum of the prices that people are willing to pay for that quantity, in distinction from the horizontally additive case in which a given quantity represents the sum of the quantities that each person would wish to consume at that price.

In distinguishing between private joint good production and public good production, Samuelson used the example of mutton and wool.* For individuals the demand curves for mutton are summed in the usual horizontal way. Similarly for wool. But the demand for sheep is derived by vertical summation of the wool and mutton demand curves (the product curves are assumed to relate to the amount of product per sheep). The demand for sheep in Samuelson's illustration is an anoprosthetic combination of product demand curves. The demand for products is a paraprosthetic combination of individuals' demand curves for each product.

Evidently, then, the anoprosthetic demand curve has much wider applicability than was originally thought. As Steiner showed by example and Samuelson showed pedagogically, it can be used to analyze pricing and output in many situations in both the private and public sectors. Clearly, additional conditions must be invoked before it can be used to classify goods into public and private—the construct is powerless by itself to do so. Samuelson attempts to circumvent the impasse through a set of optimality conditions whose essence is that private joint goods can be ultimately resolved into paraprosthetic demand relations and public goods cannot. The pioneer multipurpose water resource project, the TVA, for example, can be resolved into joint products (national defense and flood control), since each activity is *itself* anoprosthetic. But this is still not enough, since many goods whose privacy would never be questioned, such as a symphony concert or a

---

* Sheep production is an inappropriate activity to use for illustration in the first place, since it is really an example of variable proportions in production, as Arthur Lewis observed many years ago in answer to criticisms of his distinction between variable and fixed proportions (such as cottonseed and lint) when discussing power pricing (1941, p. 399). Any herd can be fed longer to yield more wool per animal, or slaughtered earlier to yield more meat relatively to wool. The output, hence price, of each is determined not only by the cost of breeding the animal and by its own demand, but also by the demand for the other product through the opportunity cost mechanism. It is more complicated than the fixed proportions case that Samuelson was discussing.

baseball game, also have anoprosthetic demands not further reducible into paraprosthetic curves! Rather, the ultimate reason, why some goods with anoprosthetic demand must be publicly provided in the Samuelson pure theory, we must conclude, is that the subdemand curves will never be revealed, making it impossible to know what prices should be charged to individual users. Therefore, they should be paid out of centrally collected funds.

Two objections can be raised to the Samuelson pure theory:*

1. *Internal consistency.* If the subdemand curves (Samuelson's "pseudo demand curves" (1969a, p. 28)) cannot be known, it is not possible to know the total demand. Therefore, no public agency would know the right amount to supply, and we would never know whether the actual provision attained an allocative optimum. Is public sector overprovision superior to private sector underprovision and monopolistic price discrimination? How much over, how much under, and how much better? Since we do not know the answer, there is no reason to introduce a public activity in this area. This difficulty has been acknowledged by Samuelson ["If you know enough to use the Lindahl pseudo prices, you don't have to use them" (1969b, p. 117)].

2. *Descriptive adequacy.* As a descriptive device the classification breaks down when we try to apply it. Consider the case of television broadcasting, one of the most often cited examples of pure public goods. The demand is certainly anoprosthetic. But it is, of course, privately supplied in a wide range of countries.†

4 EXTERNALITIES

Since public sector activities often are observed to give rise to external economies in production or consumption, many writers believe that they necessarily involve externalities. These writers view externalities as something more basic than the adventitious consequence of an imperfect pricing mechanism, which is what the externalities usually turn out to be on close inspection.

---

* We should really refer here to the "Samuelson pure theory of allocative-efficiency-related public expenditure." Income-distribution-related expenditures have been exempted from the discussion since early in the debate. See Samuelson, 1955.

† We have not intended an exhaustive analysis of the criticisms that have been made to various aspects of Samuelson's approach. Some of the most important criticism has dwelt on the polarity issue, questioning the importance of the extreme cases (Margolis, 1955; Breton, 1965) and on the usefulness or appropriateness of the allocation-distribution distinction (Musgrave, 1969).

Consider, first, production. A reasonable definition of a production external economy is a downward shift in an industry long-run average cost curve and of a diseconomy, an upward shift.* The curve will shift downward whenever an input in the production process falls in price. For example, construction of an improved highway in a region might permit lower costs for some input materials and for export shipment. As long as the industry is asked to pay, per unit use of the road, anything less than the amount of the downward shift in the cost curve, it will be beneficiary to the externality. If it pays just that amount it will not be. All these downward shifts should be considered in building the road in the first place; if they exceed the annual cost of the road, we may say that a net externality has been achieved. If they fall short, the road should not be built. In the first case, all users should be asked to pay up to the extent of their downward shifts; an attempt should be made to impose a pricing mechanism that can discriminate among beneficiaries (direct users and abutting landowners) in a way which, while it may permit externalities to some users, will cover the cost of the road. If it is not possible to recover the cost directly from the beneficiaries, the authority must be content to allow some net transfer from society at large to the road using sector, that is, abandon the attempt at full-cost pricing and allow externalities to be extended to some users from general tax revenues. But regardless of whether full-cost pricing is actually realized and a subsidy need be extended, highway systems are, in fact, the creature of the public sector—they *are* a public expenditure. Why? We will return to this in Section 6.

The case of consumption externalities may best be regarded within the framework of anoprosthetic demand.† We may define the case of pure consumption externalities as an intersection of the supply curve and the anoprosthetic demand curve at some point where the latter is coincident with the demand curve on only some subdemands.‡ The situation is shown in Figure 1.1. The two individual demand curves (labeled D_1 and D_2) intersect the X-axis at different points, Q_1 and Q_2.

---

* A shift in the cost curve seems the most general way to define external economies. It includes Scitovsky's two concepts—pecuniary and technological external economies—as special cases (1954). This is also Mishan's interpretation (1965, p. 6).

† Many apparently different formulations of consumption externalities may be cast into this form. For example, the Buchanan-Kafoglis (1962) case of nonreciprocal consumption of health day inputs (Figure 1B) is a variant of the Lindahl 100-percent diagram, (1919), which is similar in spirit to the anoprosthetic demand curves—both approaches involve vertical addition of prices.

‡ By an extension of this logic, one could also argue that under either kind of demand curve, any inframarginal demand is beneficiary to an externality. This lessens further the external economy justification for public expenditures.

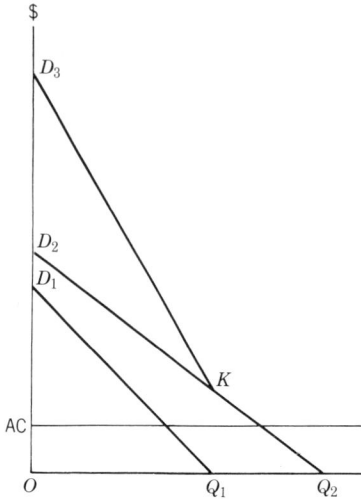

Figure 1.1 Creation of externality in consumption.

The anoprosthetic demand curve D_3 is the vertical summation of the component curves. In this case, it has a bend when the demand price for the first component becomes zero at K, and coincides thereafter with the demand curve D_2 until intersecting the X-axis. As drawn, the demand function D_1 is everywhere below D_2 but this is not necessary. D_1 could just as easily intersect the Y-axis at a point higher than the D_2 intersection.

If the supply curve intersects D_3 to the right of K, the total cost of the product could be paid by the demand represented by D_2. In this case D_1 will be satisfied at zero price. This follows in straightforward manner, either from the diagram or from the Bowen-Samuelson analytic conditions for public goods. On the other hand, a price mechanism might be found to recover part of the cost through the first component. From an allocative standpoint it makes no difference as long as the average cost curve is horizontal. If the average cost curve is declining, allocative efficiency requires that part of the cost be recovered from the first user and that the activity level be at the intersection of MC and D_3, which will, of course, occur farther out and, as before, in the range of coincidence of D_2 and D_3.

Now, what we have just said for public goods applies with equal force to joint private goods. This may not be immediately apparent, since in Samuelson's example the diagrammatic treatment shows the supply-demand intersection at positive prices for both joint products (1969a, p. 28). But it is an obvious possibility and one that has prevailed at various times in many industries. For example, precisely this situation existed in the meat market in our parents' generation, when some consumers were regular beneficiaries to the externalities implicit in the demand structure for liver and other meat by-products (which had much less demand than did meat). The market solution was simply to permit this to continue; a butcher would only forfeit the meat trade of liver customers who could simply walk up the street to the next butcher shop if asked to pay for it at the first shop. Eventually, as demand for liver and other by-products caught on, a positive price came to be feasible.

The existence of the foregoing externalities in the meat market was due to the inability to impose a positive price on some of the subcomponent demands. This was simply a private market manifestation of the "nonexcludability" principle that is often invoked today as justification for public sector activities without specific charges. Roads, for example, are said to be nonexcludable, that is, it is difficult to devise a low-cost price mechanism that could discriminate among the users. In the same way, television is said to be nonexcludable because it is difficult to charge in proportion to benefit, and so externalities arise. But the point should be emphasized that these externalities are adventitious. They are not inherent in the activity. And as we have just seen, under certain demand configurations it can also be very difficult to devise a properly discriminating pricing system for goods such as meat, the propriety of whose supply by the private sector is almost self-evident. The problem is to find the right pricing mechanism. Until this is done some sacrifice in social welfare is implied if (1) the marginal cost curve is falling (see the next section) and (2) efficient discrimination cannot be practiced. But the reason is to be found in the decreasing cost and not in the vertical additivity of the underlying demand curves. If the cost curve is horizontal, it does not make a difference. Therefore, whether resource allocation can be made more efficient through the influence of the public sector will depend, not on the generation of externalities in itself, but on the slope of the cost curve. We now turn to decreasing costs as explanation for public goods. We defer to Chapter 3 the demonstration that this reasoning depends on extremely oversimplified assumptions. The assumption of negative slope usually relates to only a single dimension of the cost structure, and the moment the analysis is made more realistic by introducing other dimensions, many of the problems disappear and efficient policy, that is, provision of the optimal quantity, may well be consistent with recapture of the investment expenditure from users.

The fact that pricing in the private sector frequently gives rise to consumption externalities is frequently overlooked in discussion of nonexcludability. Conversely, that public sector activities are not all that nonexcludable is also neglected. Police protection is a good example. If this were to be provided on a benefit payment principle, by the day, say, it is argued, some homeowners on a block would say they were not interested, knowing their neighbors' subscription would bring some police presence and thereby afford the nonparticipating homeowner some protection. However, it seems reasonable to assume that demand for police services is a function of wealth and income, which are important determinants of real estate purchase price and home valuation, on the basis of which property taxes are determined. In this case demand *can* be discerned and we may conclude that people actually are paying according to their own demand function through their property taxes (see Section 6).

5   DECREASING COSTS

The traditional explanation for public sector involvement in various economic activities stems from the assumed decreasing cost nature of the activity. This is usually associated with the names of Dupuit (1844) and Hotelling (1939) and reduces essentially to the following argument. Activities with large capital outlays usually have relatively low average variable costs, which, moreover, decline with rising output (e.g. road maintenance), so that short-run marginal costs are below average total cost (variable cost may even be zero). Assuming inability to discriminate among consumers, total cost recovery implies pricing at average total cost. This means that consumers whose valuation is below average total cost but above short-run marginal cost will be kept out of the market. Society as a whole suffers a loss on each one of these consumers equal to the difference between his forgone total utility per unit and short-run marginal cost.

The essence of the matter is shown in Figure 1.2. Beyond consumption of X_1 units per year, consumers value the activity at greater than marginal cost, but at less than average total cost. A reduction in social welfare is then suffered if output is held to X_1. Assuming that the firm is unable to discriminate, if it provides service to consumers beyond X_1, it must charge less than average total cost and it will lose money. Hence a public subsidy to users is required. Therefore, it is probably best to provide it in the public sector and incur a subsidy to be covered out of general tax revenues.

Although the argument appears persuasive when couched in the

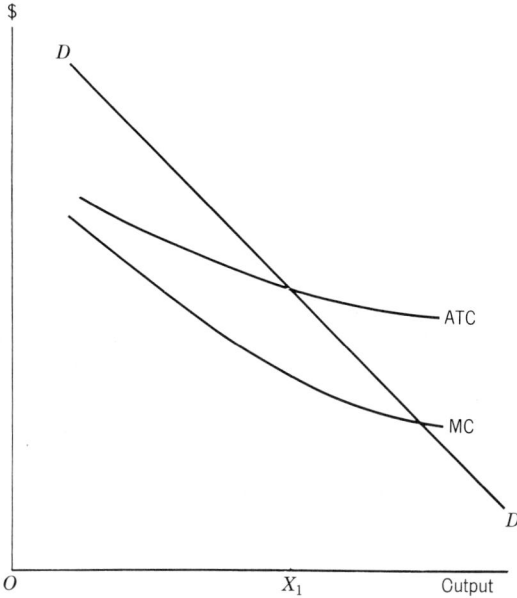

Figure 1.2 The problem of decreasing cost.

terms of Figure 1.2, which is the usual method of presentation, it cannot withstand the attempt to answer the most basic question: how should the output, with respect to which costs are said to be marginal, be defined? In the simplest case (with zero variable cost), we could imagine the activity to be construction and operation of a bridge and pedestrian crossings, which was the illustration of Dupuit's much quoted analysis, or, to take a somewhat more complicated problem, a highway of given length and vehicle-miles of uniform traffic upon it (this would have declining average maintenance cost). But to generalize from this simplistic situation does gross violence to reality. First, there is an infinite range of road designs, and the choice of one rather than another will itself condition traffic patterns.

How, then, is output to be measured? By the number of vehicles, of indeterminate and changing size? In ton-miles, the demand for which depends on ton-mile cost, which depends on the road design choice? Chapter 3 analyzes this much more complex issue and shows that when these dynamic factors are taken into account, and construction costs are interpreted more realistically than is the practice, subsidies are not necessarily needed for optimal activity levels. Moreover, owing to collection costs, pricing decisions in highways rarely can or should be made within the framework of individual roads—it is growing networks that must be priced. For the network, the simplified traditional analysis cannot help, as we will see in the Chapter 2. We will consider the mechanics for determining highway user charges in Chapter 5 and give case studies in Chapter 8.

There are still other difficulties and ambiguities in the prescription for marginal cost pricing. First, there is the question of what inputs are variable, or what is the time period within which certain inputs are to be taken as fixed. We return to this subject in Chapter 3. But there is another kind of ambiguity as well, for it turns out that two pricing rules are commonly labeled "marginal cost pricing." The Dupuit-Hotelling rule (most recently applied to the analysis of highway economics by Walters, 1968) is the more traditional interpretation among economists, but some writers and highway officials interpret marginal cost pricing to mean the assignment of administratively determined design increments to the vehicle classes for which they are undertaken (although this policy is probably more honored in the breech than in the observance). (AASHO, 1962, pp. 393–398; Ferguson, 1962.) Obviously, if increments are to be averaged over the relevant traffic groups, there will be full-cost recovery, so that these two rules will lead to two very different implications for outside support of highways!

6   A LEGAL-ADMINISTRATIVE THEORY OF PUBLIC SECTOR EFFICIENCY-RELATED PARTICIPATION

We have examined the major arguments commonly advanced to explain or justify public sector resource allocation activities and concluded that none of these furnishes an unambiguous descriptive or normative criterion. But this does mean that public sector activities must be restricted to only two of Musgrave's three branches, those that discharge income distribution and stabilization functions. Public sector resource allocation activities can also be justified on grounds that, for want of a better term, we call "legal-administrative efficiency." In such cases we usually want to impose full-cost pricing. That we have not referred to a traditional economic-theoretic notion suggests that it is easier to explain this viewpoint by reference to individual examples rather than through a theoretic generalization. The following examples might be considered.

1. Highways may be viewed as a proper resource allocation activity in the public sector because land assembly is much easier for the public

sector than for private developers, thanks to eminent domain rights. Any controversies regarding individual parcels of land can be settled in court if they cannot be decided by direct negotiation. But the prospects of early solution and early project completion are much better when the public sector manages the assembly. Spoilers cannot then prolong negotiations by holding out for high prices, artificially inflated by the belief that the assembler has already put together a ribbon of lots and is willing to purchase the missing lots at almost any price. This enables the public sector to execute the whole project relatively fast, reduce the period of resource immobilization, and minimize social costs. But the fact of public sector participation should not of itself imply anything other than a full-cost user pricing approach, which should be pursued unless there is some reason for wishing to redistribute income, such as providing access to rural schools as part of an indirect income transfer.

We note that the right of eminent domain can be and often is delegated by the public authority to a private firm. However, some economies of scale are involved in road network construction and administration, making it unnecessarily costly to delegate parcels to different firms. On the other hand, no single firm is likely to wish to take responsibility for the whole network, so that it is administratively more convenient and less costly for the public sector itself to retain responsibility for this activity.

2. In Section 4 we argued that many public services commonly thought not to be susceptible to benefit-taxation principles could indeed be paid for in this way. For example, the greater the value of the house, the greater, on the whole, is the demand for police protection and the more do people, in fact, pay for this protection through property taxes. Public sector provision of police services, therefore, could not be justified on the grounds of "nonexcludability."

Why, then, should police services be provided publicly instead of by a private army contracting its services to all members? The problem of pricing is essentially a matter of determining the demand functions of individual homeowners, which, we argued above, need not represent a formidable obstacle. In this case a private police force could simply be given the right to bill each homeowner for its services each year (according to real estate value) and to take whatever legal remedies were necessary to ensure compliance. However, public sector provision of policy services can be justified on several other grounds.

First, public provision is an administrative convenience. Public buildings must be protected, public functions supervised, and certain laws enforced that are less obviously related to home and personal protection. It is more convenient to handle these through a police force directly responsible to the government than through a private force. Once it is decided to have a public sector police force, some efficiencies may derive from a larger single force. But it is not the fact of the scale economies that determines the public sector subordination of this activity—scale economies do not lead inexorably to public sector subordination of, for example, water works, electric power, or gas supply, although in some instances these are provided by the public sector.

Second, greater care can be exercised over weapons.

Finally, even though in principle it would be easy for a private firm to receive a mandate to levy police charges, collection costs upon refusal to pay might be high. The private police force would have no resort comparable to that of an electric utility whose explicit threat of discontinued service and turn-on charges reduces its collection costs. There is no immediacy to the service provided and all that the police firm could do is threaten not to provide the service when the occasion arose. Legal action to ensure payment is costly. All these legal-administrative arguments thus support the consolidation of the police charges with other charges, all of which are then imposed through the central tax collection system.

3. A similar argument could be made about many other goods and services furnished in the public sector. Consider fire protection. May not we assume that the lesser risk of closer proximity to the station is reflected in a higher property value, which then yields a higher tax revenue? We do not suggest that an exact relationship must exist (just as private sector insurance premiums are scaled stepwise to belts rather than continuously to distance), but we would certainly expect to find the principle applied that people pay according to their expected utility from the service.

What of scale economies of fire protection? That fire protection should be provided by a single company is undoubtedly consistent with the scale economies of this activity, just as a single electric utility usually services an area. But why should the fire station monopoly not be a private monopoly just like the power company if, as we claim, both services can be paid for according to demand? The explanation is to be found in administrative convenience of collecting payment. As noted, the power company can turn the power off to delinquent customers without serious consequence. The private fire company, even when given the mandate to tax individual homeowners, might incur serious collection costs from some recalcitrant individuals. Not that they would dissemble about whether or not they really want the service, as in the usual game-theoretic approach to public allocation theory—they would simply refuse to pay. But unlike the power company, the fire company has nothing to turn off until the need actually arises, and legal remedies are costly. And ethical norms would not permit society to withhold the services of the fire station from the recalcitrant homeowners and their families, in case of fire. When the state provides the service, however, the scale economies of collection can again be exploited, and the firefighting charges consolidated with taxes intended to cover other activities. The cost of legal remedy on refusal to pay the entire consolidated tax would be small in relation to the amount which would now be involved.

7 CONCLUSION

This survey of the main principles advocated for public sector activity shows that economic theory does not provide unambiguous descriptive or normative criteria for deciding (1) whether the public sector should participate and (2), when it does participate for resource allocation purposes, what the pricing structure should be. In particular, we shall keep the following guidelines clearly before us in the rest of the book.

1. Following the clear distinction made by Musgrave, and generally agreed upon by writers in public finance, the public sector may participate directly for stabilization, distribution, or allocation (efficiency). However, many applications of "public goodness" in resource allocation activities actually are attempts to redistribute income either through "in-kind" transfers or through subsidized pricing. Accordingly, whenever considering an activity for public sector undertaking or pricing, planners must first inquire what the distributional aspect of the activity is and whether society does in fact wish to make such a transfer.

2. The resource allocation justification for public sector participation may cover a wide range of activities, depending on many aspects of the development, background, and demand conditions of society (many of these aspects are discussed in this book, but others must be left for definition according to individual circumstances). The unifying characteristics justifying such participation are primarily legal and administrative. When such activities are undertaken by the public sector there must be no presumption that anything other than full-cost recovery be accepted as the basis for pricing them. Since this guideline conflicts

fundamentally with the traditional view, one variation on which, as we have seen, is that some activities should be performed in the public sector precisely because full-cost recovery is not possible, we must start with a review of the arguments for less-than-full-cost pricing. This is the subject of the next two chapters.

REFERENCES

American Association of State Highway Officials (1962), *The AASHO Road Test, Proceedings of a Conference, 1962.* Highway Research Board Special Report 73 (Washington, D.C.: National Academy of Sciences).

Bowen, Howard R. (1948), *Toward Social Economy.* (New York: Rinehard.)

Breton, Albert (1965), "A Theory of Government Grants," *Canadian Journal of Economics,* May, pp. 175–187.

Buchanan, James M. (1967), "Breton and Weldon on Public Goods," *Canadian Journal of Economics,* February, pp. 111–115.

———, and M. Z. Kafoglis (1963), "A Note on Public Goods Supply," *American Economic Review,* June, pp. 403–414.

Dupuit, J. (1952), "On the Measurement of the Utility of Public Works," *International Economic Papers* (originally published in *Annales des Ponts et Chaussées,* 1844).

Ferguson, Allen (1960), "A Marginal Cost Function for Highways," *American Economic Review* May, pp. 223–238.

Hotelling, Harold (1938), "The General Welfare in Relation to Problems of Taxation and of Railway and Utility Rates," *Econometrica,* pp. 242–269.

Lewis, W. Arthur (1941), "The Two-Part Tariff: A Reply," *Economica,* November, pp. 399–408.

Lindahl, Erik (1919), "Just Taxation—A Positive Solution," in Musgrave and Peacock (1964).

Margolis, Julius (1955), "On Samuelson on the Pure Theory of Public Expenditure," *Review of Economics and Statistics,* November, pp. 347–350.

———, and H. Guitton, eds. (1969), *Public Economics,* Conference on the Analysis of the Public Sector, Biarritz, International Economic Association (New York: MacMillan).

Mishan, E. J. (1965), "Reflections on Recent Developments in the Concept of External Effects," *Canadian Journal of Economics and Political Science,* February, pp. 3–34.

Musgrave, Richard A. (1959), *The Theory of Public Finance* (New York: McGraw-Hill).

Musgrave, Richard A., and Peacock, Alan (1964), *Classics in the Theory of Public Finance* (New York: St. Martin's Press).

Samuelson, Paul A. (1954), "The Pure Theory of Public Expenditure," *Review of Economics and Statistics,* November, pp. 387–389.

——— (1955), "Diagrammatic Exposition of a Theory of Public Expenditures," *Review of Economics and Statistics,* November, pp. 350–356.

——— (1969a), "Contrast Between Welfare Conditions for Joint Supply and for Public Goods," *Review of Economics and Statistics,* February, pp. 26–30.

—— (1969b), "Pure Theory of Public Expenditure and Taxation," in Margolis and Guitton (1969), pp. 98–123.

Scitovsky, Tibor (1954), "Two Concepts of External Economies," *Journal of Political Economy,* Vol. 62, April.

Steiner, Peter G. (1957), "Peak Loads and Efficient Pricing," *The Quarterly Journal of Economics,* November, pp. 585–610.

Walters, Alan A. (1968), *The Economics of Road User Charges* (Baltimore: Johns Hopkins University Press—International Bank for Reconstruction and Development).

CHAPTER

2

Justifications for Less-Than-Full-Cost Pricing: A Critical Review

1 INTRODUCTION

In Chapter 1 we showed that the fact of public sector involvement in any activity does not itself constitute a justification for less-than-full-cost pricing (LTFCP). However, a number of theories have been advanced over the years to support such a view, which, in its strongest form, is that efficiency requires that full cost *not* be paid by users. (The proposition has sometimes been applied to total expenditure for all users and sometimes to the cost shares imputed to individual user classes or subclasses, where cost shares are taken to be proportional to some measure of use such as vehicle-miles or ton-miles.)

In this chapter we develop the principles for efficient user charge policy by analyzing the traditional arguments for less-than-full-cost pricing. Since these arguments are very relevant for restrained access (when ownership of way is separate from ownership of motive power, as in highway use or air navigation), owing to the nature of the pricing mechanisms that can reasonably be hypothesized, we evaluate them within the context of the highway sector. The implications for other areas are self-evident.

The traditional arguments for less-than-full-cost pricing can be classified under six headings: (1) income distribution, which would be directly frustrated by seeking full-cost recovery; (2) national security; (3) declining average cost of highways, requiring a subsidy from society; (4) the joint nature of the highway facility, requiring disproportionately large contributions from automobile users; (5) the inability, caused by prohibitively high costs, to discriminate among users, creating externalities in land rents which can subsequently be tapped for road contributions; and (6) timing—road investment is made today, but the road lasts a long time. Analysis of these arguments will show that the ton-mile share or vehicle-mile share approach for the road as a whole and for most components will indeed be inefficient, since neither ton-miles nor vehicle-miles reflect the road cost structure or the demand patterns of the user classes. On the other hand, it will be possible to define the principles for allocating most of the expenditure components according to discernible cost and demand relationships. These will be called "true cost shares."

2 EVALUATION OF TRADITIONAL ARGUMENTS

2.1 Income Distribution

Many income distribution goals can be handled through the road sector. The most obvious example in developed countries is the complementarity to school provision in rural areas, permitting the next generation an income advantage over what it would otherwise be given. In underdeveloped countries and in low per capita income regions of advanced economies income distribution aims are more direct. Here, for example, road construction enables the present generation to grow an exportable surplus that could not itself cover the cost of a road over its lifetime. A government may wish to pursue such a policy in preference to resettlement and retraining. In these two cases, the part of the road program in question should be isolated for separate support from the central budget. In North America many writers handle school support income distribution by deducting some percentage (say 30%) from the cost of the secondary or rural road system, and imputing the balance to the account of the transport sector. The second case can be allowed for simply by omitting from the road account to be charged to road users in general those expenditures that are known to relate to poor areas.

2.2 National Security

A road network permits more rapid military mobilization; in fact, some, such as the prewar German autobahn network, have been built with little else in view. Therefore, it is argued, road construction costs should be recovered at least in part from society at large, since the entire population benefits. An alternative is to price all users, including the military, according to the same standard principles, as students of public finance have frequently urged (e.g., Brownlee-Heller, 1956, p. 236). The public then knows better what it is spending for national security and can vote more intelligently at election time.

2.3 Declining Cost

Declining cost is undoubtedly the justification that economists invoke most often to obtain general public sector support of the roads. It is based on a single, isolated road, however, and cannot be readily generalized to include a growing network and dynamic and heterogeneous traffic patterns. What is marginal cost in the network framework? The cost of an additional ton-mile per year? The cost of allowing larger trucks to use the present network (which may or may not involve higher ton-mileage)? The cost of improving the network for use by larger trucks? The cost of building a new link on some given arc in a network? The cost of allowing an extra automobile to travel on the existing network? An extra truck (big, small, medium)? And so on. Output, obviously, has no simple definition.* The marginal cost of output is an extremely ambiguous concept in regard to network and multidimensional output, and the invocation of marginal cost-price equalization gives the spurious impression that agreement on what

---

* Of course, there are many marginal costs in the single road framework as well, but, as suggested, this problem can be resolved by a discriminating monopolist using a multipart tariff with variation of each part according to different use dimensions.

should be done can easily be reached once we are given the accounts of any particular highway authority. Moreover, we shall see in Chapter 3 that even on single, isolated roads or projects, the traditional two-dimensional framework fails to take account of congestion costs, which are a source of *rising* marginal cost.

One recent attempt to define marginal cost in the highway sector is that of Walters (1968). Here the operational definition of marginal cost is taken to be the vehicle-incremental maintenance cost that is assigned to users, with the annual "invariate" maintenance cost, as well as construction cost, coming out of the general budget. The annual "invariate" maintenance cost is the intercept in a linear regression in which annual expenditure is taken to be a function of average daily traffic (ADT) and variable maintenance cost is the slope. Maintenance costs are believed not to be a function of traffic composition, that is, the incremental maintenance cost is taken to be the same for small and large trucks. We shall see in Chapter 5 that this assumption is invalid—it is inconsistent with the findings of the major study done by the American Association of State Highway Officials to determine empirically the size-damage relationship. Estimated under controlled conditions, the basic relationship shows increasingly severe damage per ton-mile with increasing weight (AASHO, 1962, p. 962, pp. 415–425); the burden imposed, as measured by the number of repetitions to achieve a given unserviceability level in most situations, rises to 20 times when doubling the axle load from 5 to 10 tons. (The precise relationship depends on type of pavement and number of axles.) We return to the AASHO test results in Chapter 5.

The AASHO test is undoubtedly the most extensive controlled experiment to determine the relation between pavement deterioration and road traffic. Various rigid and flexible pavement designs were subjected to repetitive impacts of vehicles of various sizes and designs to derive road performance curves, relating traffic to terminal serviceability. The AASHO relationship is difficult to determine by observation of actual everyday situations, however, owing to the great variability of climate, traffic mix, and road type. Analysis of state highway accounts would also fail to uncover this kind of relationship, since no roads are used exclusively by homogeneous traffic classes. Moreover, being expenditure data, state highway accounts may not even reflect the cost of maintaining given standards. Thus although a calculation of relationships such as Walters' estimated relationship between traffic and state expenditures appears to be based on firm empirical data, it is in fact a very weak basis for determining the true functional relationships of vehicle size and road design and damage.*

Although the marginal cost-pricing rule cannot be applied unequivocally to a network, we can realize the spirit of marginal cost-price equalization. The marginal cost-price dictum is based on the notion that output should be increased as long as the extra cost imposed on society is less than the utility that some member of society receives from consumption of one more unit, less the disutility to other members of society. This pattern can be realized by pricing the incremental wear according to the AASHO coefficients and the joint fixed costs according to demand. In the next section we argue that each incremental component of a highway technology, such as the reduction in maximum grade from 8 to 5%, should be paid for by all the user groups according to their demand for that component. It should not be paid for just by the vehicle classes whose expected use of the network prompts the move to the more stringent standards in the first place. Correspondingly, maximum grade should be reduced as long as the benefit arising in grade reduction exceeds the cost of reduction. If a budget constraint is imposed, the highway authority can discriminate among users to recover all of this cost, or, if perfect discrimination is not possible, it will be argued in Section 2.5, the shortfall should be borne by local sources.

2.4 The Joint Nature of the Network Components

Many writers have argued that the road network is a joint product that should be priced according to demand elasticities of the various user

---

* Even the statistical results could be made to vary significantly simply by disaggregating or aggregating the data. Suppose that instead of the annual state highway expenditure accounts, one went to the original field accounts. Maintenance on any road would actually be performed in a month or two (if it were performed continuously throughout the year one could hardly speak of a fixed annual component). Suppose, for simplicity, that maintenance on any road in the network is all performed in a single month. On each road, there will then be 1 positive expenditure observation and 11 zero expenditure observations (with traffic fluctuating seasonally and stochastically about the annual average daily traffic for the road). A regression line fitted to these observations would then have a correlation coefficient of near zero, and the slope, while positive, would yield a nonsignificant t-value. In this case we would have to conclude that the marginal cost was zero. Obviously, however, this fluke arises simply through reorganization of the data and can say nothing about the underlying technological or economic relationships.

classes. They call for more- or less-than-proportional cost imputation to individual user classes, without implying advocacy of less-than-full-cost pricing for the facility or network as a whole. This argument is valid as it applies to the fixed portions of the project, such as land acquisition and basic grading. The demand for these components is anoprosthetic, and the relevant components should be priced among the several demand classes in a discriminatory way. This rule can even apply to some portions of the investment that are nominally undertaken for certain specified classes of traffic only. Thus low maximum grades may be imposed by engineering rules in recognition of the heavy traffic expected, though cars too benefit, and a greater social benefit can usually be achieved by discriminatory pricing and execution of such components of the project.

There are two main obstacles to the efficient pricing of joint components: (1) determining the individual subdemand curves and (2) deciding what components are joint.

Even the most hopeful optimist could not expect to find sufficient data to reconstruct the subdemand curves. But we can do better with regard to minimum estimates of the demand prices of various user groups, that is, estimates of marginal demands at the hypothesized output levels. Case study details are given in Chapter 8. Deciding which components of the project should be treated in this manner depends on many factors. In mountains a 1-meter subbase may be required for a road to offset the effects of ground freezing, making discriminatory pricing efficient, while elsewhere the subbase thickness may depend primarily on the expected load. Evidently no absolute classification of components can be given. Any part of the road should be considered to be a joint component for those user groups whose demand for those components is positive. In Chapter 8 we attempt to define such components empirically. Inevitably, any such attempt is bound to be less than perfect. The irony of public finance is that while such attempts are frequently criticized, traditional practice implicitly tolerates assumptions that have no basis at all for allocating general public sector funds *on efficiency grounds* to the highway sector, airports or public transit, since the demand curves at this level are just as hard or harder to estimate! The sum of this demand-related component and the specific costs (need for special design features and AASHO damage-related costs) will be called the true cost imposed by the vehicle on the system. This cost, multiplied by the volume in the class, will be called the "true cost share" (e.g. the "true large truck cost share").

2.5   Inability to Discriminate

Inability to discriminate among users is another frequent justification for less-than-full-cost pricing. Thus even if the relationship between vehicle damage and weight can be determined, it would be very costly to determine the precise charge to each vehicle. Constant supervision, scales, toll booths, and limited-access roads would be necessary, all imposing costs in terms of personnel, capital, and driver and vehicle delay. Even to charge each vehicle on the basis of its average load (to allow for empty returns) would be difficult, since a use charge would have to be keyed to each vehicle, or, if a grosser tax is accepted, to each vehicle class. Thus price-cost deviations begin to intrude already at this point, although even this scheme would be too costly to administer. On the other hand, an annual tax would encourage heavier utilization and cause distortions. Ultimately, therefore, one accepts the notion of a fuel tax coupled with an annual fee as a tax structure that does not impose too high collection costs and follows the basic cost patterns of vehicle use—the fuel tax proportional to the mileage of any given vehicle class and the license fee proportional to size. Moreover, since vehicle size and mileage tend to increase together, this combination of taxes properly designed, could yield a rising user charge per ton-mile as size rises.

With such a combination of taxes, units of some kinds of traffic may be unable to pay the price demanded by the average relationships for the traffic class. For example, if a high annual fee for large trucks is based on an assumed 100,000-kilometer annual run, it could not be paid by a truck driving 50,000 kilometers a year. To charge the higher rate would force some of the traffic out and might reduce the benefit substantially. To allow for this, the unit charge may have to be lower than the average true truck-related cost for the class in question. For other truck classes, such as small trucks carrying valuable cargoes that benefit through reduced congestion or higher-grade roads, the price may be higher. That is, it may be efficient to allocate some of the true truck-related cost discriminatorily among the truck classes. For some large truck users—especially in minerals and building material—the user charge will be almost equal to the benefit originating in the traffic while for others—some farmers, manufacturers, and marketing organizations—external benefits will develop, that is, they would be willing to pay more than the price being charged them directly for their use of the road. In the absence of the higher prices, their incomes are higher. Part of this externality could be tapped to close the revenue gap through voluntary or compulsory contributions, which can be imposed by the abutting communities in which the external beneficiaries live. This argues, then, for local rather than centralized supplementary contributions.

2.6 Timing

A sixth justification to support less-than-full-cost user charges is timing. The facility will last for many years. Why should it be paid for in a single year?

Evidently, this argument applies to the question of annual expenditure, not cost. That is, a proponent of this view could agree that users should pay their true cost shares (cost being the investment expenditure transferred into an annual amortization steam, plus annual maintenance, evaluated in terms of variable and joint component principles presented here rather than their share of the investment expenditure as it occurs). This could be acceptable, if a way could be devised to generate the revenues in later years. Apart from toll roads, we know of no case where such a financing policy has been implemented, and popular attitudes regarding road investments are so "sunk-cost" oriented that it is very difficult to imagine that transport users would ever organize themselves to repay such loans.

There is, on the other hand, one persuasive argument that justifies the current investment expenditure as the target revenue to be recovered from users. Consider the following.

When the investment is used to expand the existing network through the construction of parallel roads on congested links, realignment or grade amelioration, or additions of lanes, users on the entire network benefit. There will be benefits to users on the network who are not using the new road or road increment itself, since some of the traffic will divert to the new or improved link (or, at least, traffic will not increase as fast on the unmodified links). The benefit can be assumed to decrease with distance from the expanded segment.

Owing to transaction costs, the pricing mechanism is necessarily somewhat gross, as discussed earlier, and it is impossible to price precisely according to all of the demands on the various segments of the network (although some approximation to it is possible through regional differentiation of fuel and registration tax rates). All users on the network will therefore contribute toward the construction of the new facility. This should create no problem, since in some future year even if not immediately, the trucker on today's old road will have a new road that he can use, paid for in part by the tax contributions of the trucker who is the immediate beneficiary of the road being built today. In other words, we can imagine "loans" within the highway sector, from users in one area to those in another, both in a fairly homogenous region, as the road program develops. This, of course, is very different from a penetration road policy, where roads are built by fuel tax transfers from local areas to regions far removed, or a policy of general budget support of penetration roads, such as that in Brazil several years ago which had a road program at the federation level that included a large mileage of penetration or "development" roads. It is also very different from the United States Interstate Highway System where a large part of the financing of high-grade roads originates in a nonrelated use—fuel consumed in cities.* In our view, the latter funds should be used as an income distribution vehicle (e.g. for education, health) or treated as a congestion charge and used to help pay for infrastructure of new cities to maintain existing cities in equilibrium. (The relevant cost theory behind this view is presented in Chapter 3 and the relevant, more general aspects of urban economic analysis, in Part 4).

To approach pricing in the manner just described does not guarantee that the current expenditure will be covered—the "intranetwork loans" that are related to the demands of the various user groups for roads should cover cost shares over time but not necessarily the expenditure in each year. If the road network is mature and the annual construction program is small in relation to the network, it will probably be covered. If the network is growing much faster in some individual regions, the existence of administrative subdivisions can allow for some user charge variation to recover current outlays.

If the network is growing faster in some regions than it is deemed desirable to cover through intranetwork loans, and if the local region does not wish to cover all its outlays from current user-charge generated revenues, how is the annual subsidy to be covered? Many writers on project evaluation argue that in principle general tax revenues could be used. But this presupposes a level of skill technique in project evaluation that is far beyond what is possible today, as we shall see in Part 3. In spite of the recent advances in project appraisal many problems remain in comparing, for example, an irrigation project in Macedonia, an aluminum plant in Serbia, and a road project in Slovenia; or a

* To incorporate other nonrelated tax revenues, the United States highway lobby in 1971 tried to get Congress to earmark a portion of the alcoholic beverage tax. The Senate approved the Bill, which was later killed in joint House-Senate Conference (*New York Times*, 1971).

second airport in Toronto, the Mackenzie Valley pipeline in the north, and a heavy water plant in Nova Scotia.

Although detailed discussion of the methods and controversies is deferred to Part 3, an idea of the continuing problems in project evaluation may be conveyed now in order to help show the reasons for preferring a sectoral budget constraint for activities like highway transport in the first place, with project optimization within this sector and subject to this constraint following. One major problem is the irreconcilability of the benefit measures that are usually employed—a consumer surplus measure in a road investment versus national income generation in an export industry. To put the latter on an equivalent basis would require that a labor supply or disutility function for the new employment be introduced into the calculation. Moreover, even comparison between two roads may rely on different criteria, since penetration roads are usually evaluated in terms of national income generation.

Finally, discrepancies arise in the comparison of consumer surplus measures between full-employment and unemployment regions. While this problem is generally acknowledged, lack of consensus on how to deal with it in practice raises serious doubts about the ability of a central planning board to allocate investment interregionally. Coupled with the inherent frailty of all intersectoral comparisons, this suggests that local jurisdictions are in the best situation to assess their investment needs, since they can draw on supplementary nonmarket, ballot box information from the local constituency, whereas this information could be transferred to the central planning board only with considerable accompanying noise.

3 SUMMARY OF PRINCIPLES

The following principles emerge from this review of pricing theories:

1. Support for roads from outside the road sector may be based on income distribution considerations. In this case no attempt is made to recover the expenditure from users or beneficiaries. Ideally, such transfers should be made from the general national budget to the poor region in question for subsequent efficiency-evaluated allocation within the poor region. They should not emanate from a national earmarked road fund. Such road projects should be isolated from the road program more narrowly defined (i.e. the part of the network in settled regions that is improved incrementally each year).

2. A joint component is a component for which several classes have a positive demand. This is a general classificatory criterion that will have very different implications in actual application as we showed by the following examples:

(a) It is most probable that the incremental design specifications associated with heavy vehicle classes, such as low maximum grades, will have joint demand, since the lighter vehicles will also benefit through their execution;

(b) It is possible for a component to be joint in some geophysical situations while size variable in others (e.g., the subbase);

3. User classes should contribute to the road according to both their demand elasticities for the joint components and the specific costs that they impose.

4. Although automobile demand might be inelastic enough to pay for the entire road expenditure, it should not be asked to do so because many parts of the road are truck variable, that is, they deteriorate differentially under use by different vehicle sizes or, conceivably, are demanded exclusively by trucks. If trucks are not made to face this price, they will clearly overuse this service, in the sense that they will impose a social cost in excess of the social benefit, as measured by their own demand price.

5. What has been said of costs can be applied to the annual expenditure for the road program (i.e., that part of total road activity that is viewed as improvement of the network in built-up areas). This probably relates to most of the road activity.

6. Outside support of the road program may be justified when discrimination is inefficient, that is, when discrimination would imply a foregone benefit of unrealized traffic. Outside support is likely to be more efficient when provided by local communities rather than by centralized sectoral or regional transfers, owing to the imperfections of project evaluation techniques.

REFERENCES

American Association of State Highway Officials (1962), *The AASHO Road Test, Proceedings of a Conference, 1962,* Highway Research Board Special Report No. 73 (Washington, D.C.: National Academy of Sciences).

Brownlee, O. H., and W. H. Heller (1956), "Highway Development and Financing," *American Economic Review,* May.

"Light in the Tunnel," *New York Times* (1971), December 20.

Walters, Alan A. (1968), *The Economics of Road User Charges,* (Baltimore: Johns Hopkins University Press—International Bank for Reconstruction and Development).

CHAPTER

3

The Theory of Marginal Cost and Optimal Price and Financing Policy

1 INTRODUCTION

Decreasing average cost (with decreasing or constant marginal cost) has provided the main traditional theoretic justification for less-than-full-cost pricing in transportation and other activities. However, most transport activities are too complex to fit easily within the traditional analytical framework from which the optimality of marginal cost pricing is derived. In the highway network, for example, there are a great many possible ways to define marginal costs, and theoretical considerations do not lead unambiguously to the choice of one or another. On the basis of the principles elaborated in Chapter 2 and the empirical investigation of costs presented in Part 2, we present a case study in Chapter 8 where the criteria used to evaluate user charges are believed to be consistent with welfare maximization objectives in the network situation.

The applicability of marginal cost pricing in individual, separable projects, such as a water treatment plant, a subway, or an individual toll road, is another matter. However, we will see that even here, in the usual case, the major conclusion that if optimality is to be achieved, the total investment and operating cost of the project should not be recovered from users is not necessarily correct. This usual result derives from special assumptions, which are implicit rather than explicit, concerning the behavior of costs. When other cost assumptions are made, which are in fact more realistic as far as the public sector is concerned, the standard results do not follow.

The chapter proceeds as follows. In the next section we consider a single road activity and a homogeneous output—vehicle trips where vehicles are of the same weight and design. Here we distinguish between two situations—continuously divisible plant scale and discrete plant size. In the first case, even with optimization, it is possible that enough revenue will be generated through user charges to cover total investment and operating costs, contrary to the standard conclusions. This happens because congestion costs are included. In the second case, we will see that strict logical analogy to the continuous case again may result in total revenues, generated through user charges, great enough to cover total operating and investment costs.

In Section 3 we consider heterogeneous and interdependent demands and, again, discrete jumps in technology. Again, strict logical analogy to the pricing rule of the continuous case may generate a contribution to the investment cost, possibly enough to cover all of it.

When optimality considerations do justify nonuser supplementary contributions to the construction and/or operation of some activity, the question arises of where the funds should come from; this issue has been somewhat neglected in the literature though, the discussion usually ending with the demonstration that some form of outside support is necessary. In particular, should the local region provide this nonuser support or should it come from a broader region? In Section 4 we present the diagrammatic solution to this question, which depends on the project's economies of scale in welfare maximization. In Chapter 17 we present a study of one urban project—the Toronto subway— within this framework and evaluate the governing provincial financing procedures. We conclude that the 75% provincial contribution is inefficient in terms of welfare maximization.*

---

* In this chapter we restrict ourselves to contributions to projects whose undertaking by the public sector is justified by efficient resource allocation rather than income distribution objectives. If outside support is designed to attain distributional objectives, it should of course go from the wealthier to the poorer, which sometimes may be manifested in flows to certain types of region or to cities or towns of some given size.

2   HOMOGENEOUS OUTPUT

2.1   Infinitely Divisible Plant Scale

We consider first the case of infinitely divisible scale, starting with some minimum size. We suppose that the cost function is of the form $TC = a_i + b_iX$, where i is a scale subscript ($i = 0, 1, \ldots, n$), X is output, a_0 is the capital cost of the minimum size, and b_i are all equal to 0. In this case, the short-run average cost curve for each plant size is a rectangular hyperbola. The long-run average cost curve, defined, as always, as the locus of points of minimum average total cost per unit at different output levels, would in this case be coincident with the short-run average cost function $AC = a_0/X$, that is, the short-run average cost curve of the smallest plant size. In this case, the marginal costs are all the same and all lie on the X-axis. The result is essentially the same if a_i is allowed to increase and b_i to decrease with increasing i. In this case, Case 2 in Figure 3.1, we would have a series of horizontal marginal cost curves that, when added to the nest of average investment cost hyperbolas, would leave one function below all the others for all levels of output. Again, therefore, we would have a long-run average cost curve coincident with some particular short-run average cost curve. These two cases are shown in Figure 3.1.

For the long-run average cost curve to be tangent to a *series* of short-run average cost curves it is necessary that the latter intersect. For the latter to intersect, it is necessary that the short-run marginal cost at any scale not be constant; it must start to rise in order that the short-run average cost of the higher plant scale start out higher than the short-run average cost of the smaller scale but intersect it and fall below it. The marginal cost curves will then rise as shown in Figure 3.2. How can this happen if variable operating costs are constant? (Variable costs include private sector costs such as fuel and tires, as well as public sector costs such as maintenance). This can happen if congestion starts to take place, so that at some output level at a given facility size the cost imposed on others starts to rise (the cost to the new user will also start to rise, but not as fast). (A more extended discussion of congestion cost theory is in chapter 16.)

Figure 3.2 shows the series of rising short-run marginal cost curves caused by congestion. Also shown are the average total social cost curves. These are derived as the sum of the short-run marginal cost curves (which include marginal congestion costs), plus the average fixed cost curves [only the average fixed cost (AFC_0) of the smallest plant is shown]. It should be stressed that the curves are only representative

Case 1

$b_i = 0$

$
Average fixed cost–average total cost: ATC of smallest plant size is same as CRATC curve

a_0/X

O Trips X

Case 2

$a_i < a_i + 1$

$b_i > b_i + 1$

$
a_2/X
a_1/X
a_0/X

O Trips X

$
Average variable cost curves

b_0
b_1
b_2

O Trips X

$
Average total cost curve

$\dfrac{a_0}{X} + b_0$

$\dfrac{a_2}{X} + b_2$

$\dfrac{a_1}{X} + b_1$

Lowest average total curve is the LRATC curve

O Trips X

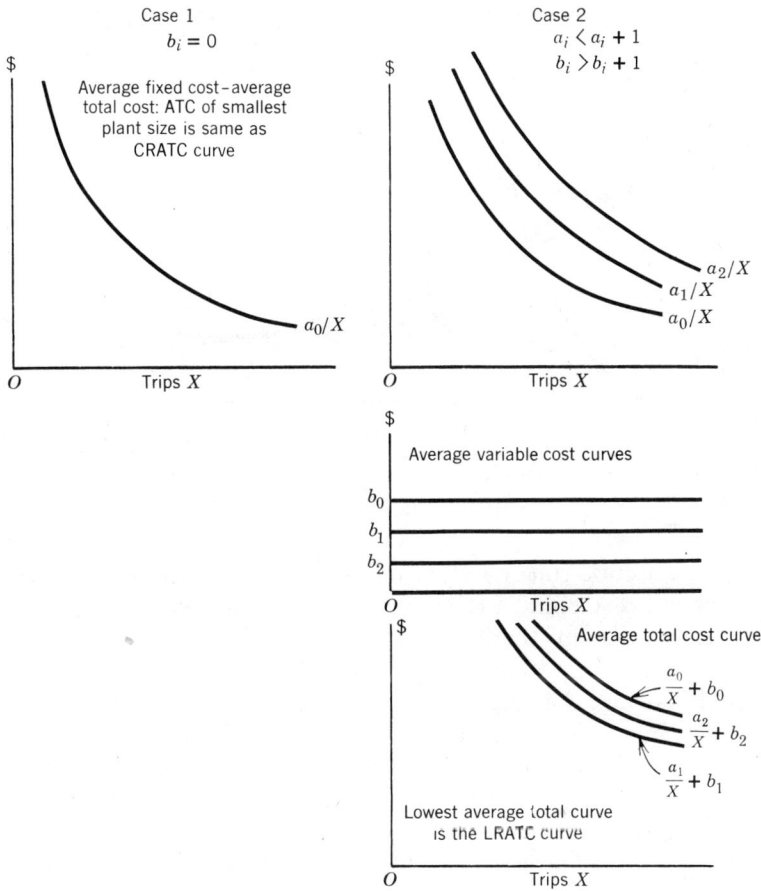

Figure 3.1 Relationship between short-run and long-run average cost curves when total cost function has the form TC $= a_i + b_i X$ (output measured in trips by homogeneous vehicles).

curves from an infinitely divisible family of curves. Also shown is the long-run total cost curve, tangent to the SRAC curves, which is continuous, since there is an infinite family of SRAC curves.

The long-run marginal cost is defined, as always, as the rate of change of total cost, assuming that all variables may be varied. This will lie below the long-run average cost curve as long as it is declining, which is the portion that is of interest from the viewpoint of marginal· cost pricing. Since the scale is infinitely divisible (from some minimum

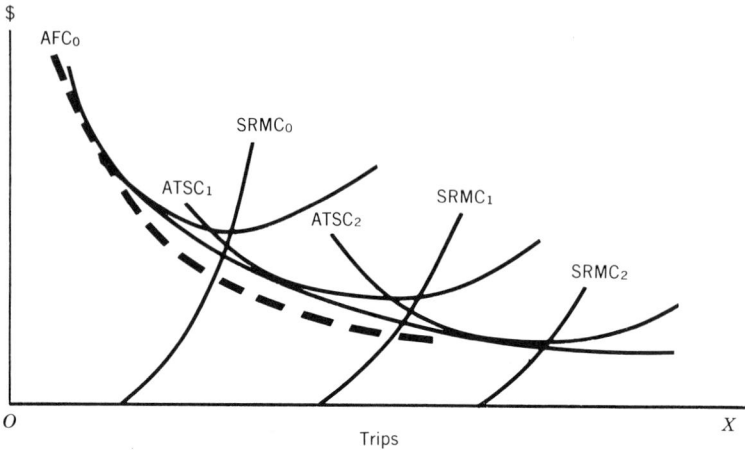

Figure 3.2 Short-run average total social cost, short-run marginal cost, and long-run average total cost (output measured in trips by homogeneous vehicles).

point on), the long-run marginal cost curve cuts a short-run marginal cost curve at every point. LRMC is shown in Figure 3.3.

We next draw in the demand curve in Figure 3.3. Traditional optimization considerations lead to an output at the intersection of the demand curve and the long-run marginal cost curve, that is, at the point $\hat{X}$. At this point, we have equality between price and long-run marginal cost, on the one hand, and price and short-run marginal cost, on the other. Thus the question whether it is short-run or long-run marginal cost that should be equated to price, which often is not faced squarely, does not arise. In the usual literature there is always a certain ambi-

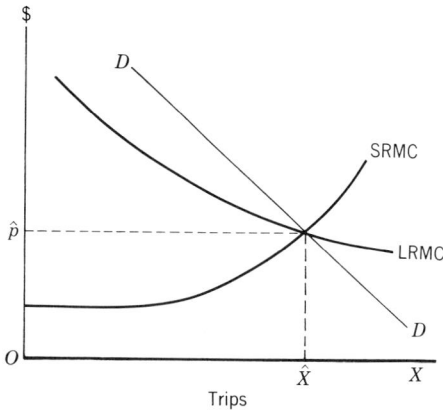

Figure 3.3 Long-run equilibrium, showing simultaneous short-run equilibrium: demand price = long-run marginal cost = short-run marginal cost (output measured in trips by homogeneous vehicles).

guity concerning this matter. (Short-run marginal cost-price equalization is frequently the point of departure, implicitly if not explicitly,
since it is consistent with both the private sector behavioral rule and
much observed behavior: lenders *do* renegotiate if a delinquent bor-
rower can earn enough to repay in amounts exceeding the alternative
return through foreclosure; producers *do* sustain operations in periods
of difficulty if their revenues exceed variable cost.)

With the cost curves assumed here, however, the question of which
marginal cost is meant does not arise—long-run marginal cost is equal
to the cost given by some short-run marginal cost function at every
point. The fact that short-run marginal cost includes a congestion
component does not really change the logic of optimization, although
the notion of charging anyone a price greater than zero when the
original cost function includes a variable cost of zero is probably hard
for most people to accept. Since in this case it does equal long-run
marginal cost, however, most people would probably be prepared to
accept it. Thus the first departure from traditional analysis is that price
should be positive even when short-run variable cost, as usually
defined, may be zero (or, more generally, the price must be greater than
average short-run variable cost). This is also at variance with standard
congestion theory which leads to congestion charges (price greater than
variable cost) on existing facilities rather than on new facilities, the
assumption being that new facilities are large enough to avoid congestion, at least in the early years. According to our analysis, facilities
should be built to operate at optimal congestion levels, which are positive. From this result follows the second important conclusion: since the
price will exceed short-run variable cost, revenue (including congestion
charges) will exceed operating costs. This difference, accumulated over
the years, *may* exceed the investment cost (including a capital charge).
It will in any event make a contribution toward it, either explicitly or
implicitly. This contrasts sharply with the usual notion that the investment cost in decreasing cost situations should be paid for by society at
large.

2.2 Discrete Plant Size Variation

The situation just discussed is somewhat artificial, since the design
alternatives that people really do work with are not infinitely divisible.
For example, when considering road construction the project analyst
usually thinks of a dirt road, a gravel road, a high paved road, and a
superhighway, perhaps with one or two variations on these possibilities—four to seven design alternatives in all. We observe in passing,

however, that the fact that we generally tend to restrict ourselves to a few choices is not inherent in the technology: in principle we could imagine an almost infinite range of design modifications. The fact that we do not indicates not technological constraints, but the traditional preference for not devoting great resources to the analysis of every conceivable possibility. This is probably a reasonable approach, on the whole, provided that the attitude does not close our minds to new possibilities in nontraditional situations.

We now drop the assumption of infinitely divisible technology and assume that there are three design possibilities, retaining our assumption of homogeneous output, the demand for which is measured by a single demand curve.

The three short-run average and marginal cost curves are shown in Figure 3.4. The LRMC curve is, as before, the rate of change of total cost as all inputs are permitted to vary, but it is no longer smooth. There are kinks at the points at which a higher numbered technology yields lower average cost. This is formed by the lowest sections of the successive SRMC curves.

The solution output now, as before, is the intersection of the demand and LRMC curves. Whether this will permit recoupment of part or all of the investment cost depends on what goes into the average cost curves. If these average costs rise, not because of congestion but because of rising variable costs of the technology itself, such as higher maintenance expenditures under greater traffic on gravel than on paved

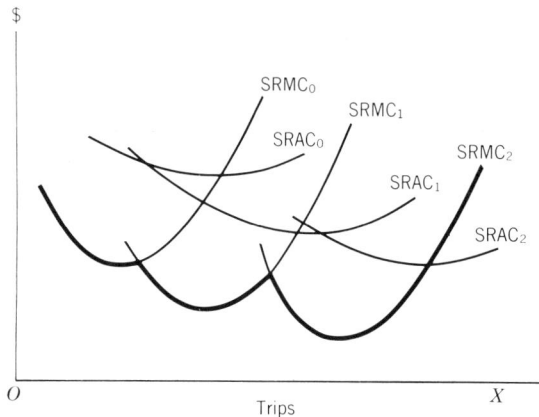

Figure 3.4 Derivation of long-run marginal cost curve in case of three discrete project alternatives; LRMC curve consists of dominated portions of three short-run marginal cost curves (output measured in trips by homogeneous vehicles).

roads, there will be no contribution to the investment recovery. If the source of rising cost is a pure congestion effect, the investment may be recovered, as in the infinitely divisible situation. It is even possible that the initial investment cost would be recovered in a way consistent with optimal pricing even when it is a "decreasing cost," privately provided activity to the extent that the value of the capital facility reflects the potential profit generated as an economic rent; that is, the capital facility even when it has zero salvage value (and is so carried on the books) will reflect the value of the annual excess profit that is figured on the current costs alone. (See footnote on p. 114.)

3   HETEROGENEOUS OUTPUT

A frequent oversimplification in transport analysis, and one whose implications are seldom confronted, is the assumption that output can be treated as a homogeneous variable such as vehicle trips, as we have done up to this point. In fact, vehicle size will depend on the technology adopted and there will be consolidations of some kinds of traffic load and shifts between the demand curves of different truck sizes. In this section we modify the traditional approach to allow for this heterogeneity. We again assume there to be just three technologies— light bituminous, high flexible, and four-lane arterial roads. Each of these will generate a different kind of traffic structure *and* location pattern. The light bituminous road will permit only small vehicles, implying high vehicle costs (i.e. gas, vehicle wear) and a location pattern different from that of a high paved road with its attendant low vehicle costs per ton-kilometer. Each design will then be associated with a different demand curve, and each will have a demand price—SRMC intersection. There is no LRAC curve—simply a series of nonintersecting SRAC and SRMC curves. In this case what is optimal output?

Evidently, each intersection of cost and SRMC defines optimal output in the particular situation to which the corresponding demand curve applies. The *optimum optimorum* can be defined only with reference to information not contained in the diagram, regarding residential patterns, business location, and so on, which are themselves determined in part by the choice of road technology. For this kind of decision, economic efficiency criteria are almost unattainable. That is, once the road is built and the location pattern adjusts, there will be an optimal output determined by the intersection of SRMC and the demand curve. But this is at variance with the basic principle of price-LRMC equalization, which, as we have also agreed, is rational.

To resolve the foregoing inconsistency, we could proceed by analogy with the spirit of marginal cost pricing and consider as long-run marginal cost the average incremental cost between design variants (average incremental investment cost plus marginal operating cost). There will be such a cost curve for each design variant above the basic one. Figure 3.5 shows the curves for the three variants, the curves for the heavier-duty roads being labeled LRIC (long-run incremental cost). If present traffic is $\hat{X}_1$, and truckers advocate a move to design 2, the long-run marginal cost would be $\Delta C / \Delta Q$ or, in this case, $(\hat{C}_2 \hat{X}_2 - \hat{C}_1 \hat{X}_1)/(\hat{X}_2 - \hat{X}_1)$. This should be imposed on all vehicles. Thus each vehicle pays the "average marginal" or "average incremental" capital cost plus the short-run marginal cost.

The traditional objection to this proposal is that it prices out of the market those valuing the service at less than average cost. Here, for example, it would be argued that the users now paying $\hat{C}_0$ would be forced off. This view is completely mistaken, since those users will be among the first to reorganize into larger trucks for which the better road has a greater value, equal to the higher demand price per vehicle, which will be lower per ton-kilometer.

There is another traditional objection to this policy. The SRMC curve for the heavier-duty design variants will of course lie below the LRIC

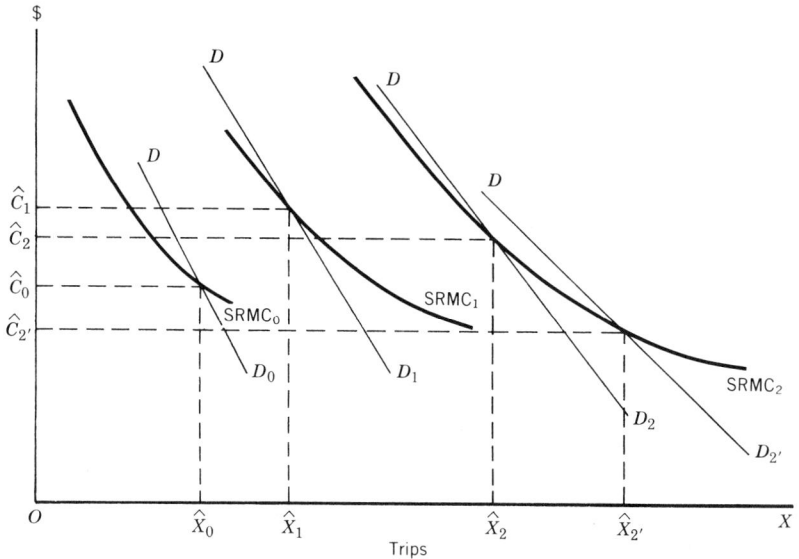

Figure 3.5 Cost, demand, and equilibrium for three technologies (output measured in trips by *heterogeneous* vehicles).

curves, and would also be downward sloping. This means that those potential users on the new demand curve between $\hat{X}_2$ and $\hat{X}_2'$ will not come into the traffic stream, although the cost that they impose will be less than their demand price *once the facility is built*. To avoid this social loss, this loss of consumer surplus, it is argued, a price of C_2' should be charged, with the resulting deficit provided from general tax funds. In this case, where should the supplementary funds come from? One of the main aspects of this question is the regional dimension— should the funds be local or should they be based on interregional transfers? We turn to an analysis of this question.

4 INTERREGIONAL TRANSFERS AND PARETO EFFICIENCY

Interregional income transfers are not at issue. When it is desired to transfer income to poor regions, or when transfers among income classes have an implicit regional aspect, sociopolitical criteria rather than economic efficiency are involved. However, part of the issue of regional transfers can be analyzed on the grounds of welfare and efficiency. For example, formula financing of urban expressways and subways in Ontario may be evaluated within the framework of welfare maximization objectives (75% of the investment cost of a subway is provided by the Province). If these grants are to be defended on grounds of economic efficiency one must argue that the rural population also benefits, and, since there are scale economies, it is best to provide various amenities, have them paid for by everyone, and then let all enjoy them. Since people are frequently seen to move to the cities where these developments take place, such propositions appear to be vindicated.

But it is an easy matter to show that such financial transfers may lead to Pareto inefficiency. More strongly, one can show that the person's selection of city—"voting with one's feet" in current parlance—is itself meaningless, since the "vote" is prejudiced.

The problem is shown in Figure 3.6. Money is plotted on the Y-axis and urban amenities on the X-axis. The indifference curves show the points of consumption of urban amenities, on the one hand, and all other expenditures between which the consumer is indifferent. At present, this consumer lives in the countryside, and has very low consumption of urban amenities. Assuming no trips to the city, he will devote the entire income to other expenditures, that is, $\hat{Y}_1$, his entire income will be spent on other goods and services. The price of urban amenities is so high that the price line (not drawn here) would be

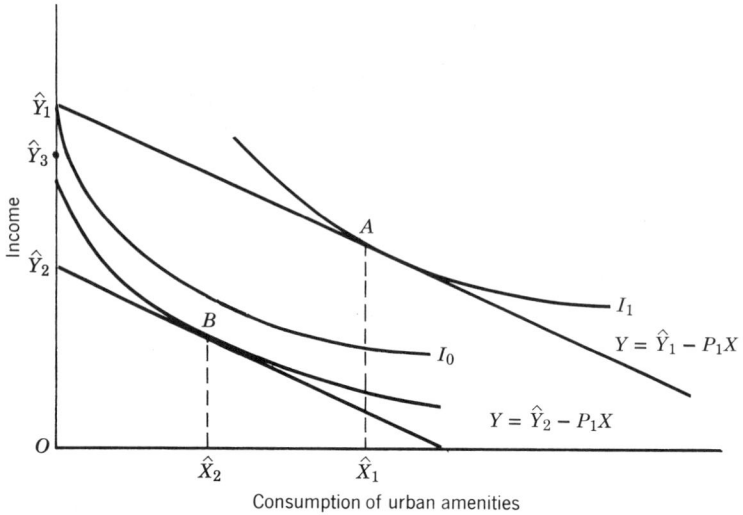

Figure 3.6 Welfare loss to rural resident under regional income transfer to pay investment cost of urban project.

tangent to the indifference curve I_0 at zero consumption. He could move along I_0 either by moving into the city and consuming some urban amenities, or simply by staying where he is and beginning to go into the city occasionally to take advantage of various city activities. This he would do if the price of urban amenities fell and simultaneously some of his income were taken from him; if the price fell and income were not taken from him, he would consume some urban amenities but rise to a higher indifference curve.

Suppose now that a large investment program is undertaken in this city—construction of water facilities, subways, and numerous other urban infrastructure needs. The price (i.e. the market price to the consumer) of urban amenities falls, as indicated by the price line P_1. The tangency to the new indifference curve is at point A. The consumer would begin now to consume $\hat{X}_1$ units of urban amenities if his income were unchanged at $\hat{Y}_1$. In fact, to pay the capital costs of the investments he is now taxed an amount that lowers his income to $\hat{Y}_2$. His consumption of urban amenities actually becomes $\hat{X}_2$. And, more importantly, he is on a lower indifference curve, I_2. Therefore, he is worse off than he was before, that is, his contribution to the change in total social welfare is negative. Furthermore, it will be seen that at his new income, $\hat{Y}_2$, he has no choice but to move to the city and consume the amenities there if he is rational, since this is the only way he can maximize his welfare subject to the tax constraint. As drawn, then, the consumer suffers a welfare reduction.

It is possible, however, for the consumer's welfare position to rise if on moving to the city employment opportunities were such as to raise his income to a level that would yield an indifference curve-budget line tangency higher than his original tangency on I_0 at $\hat{Y}_1$. For example, income level $\hat{Y}_3$ would result in a net increase in welfare. The income level should be a net income level, however, which abstracts from the income earning expenditures that are necessary in the city, such as higher food costs per capita due to the higher consumption of "convenience" foods for working couples or one-person households and costs for air conditioning to offset the greater discomfort of dense living conditions. Note that if he were taxed nothing at all he *would* move to a higher welfare level with indifference curve-budget line tangency at A on I_1. In practice, of course, it will be very difficult to distinguish the higher expenditures related to income production from those that do yield a welfare gain (e.g. purchase of certain higher priced foods not available in small towns), hence to answer the question whether any given project will lead to a higher or lower total social welfare. In Chapter 16 we investigate the effects of the Toronto subway and evaluate the Ontario subsidized financing policy, mentioned above, and conclude, on the basis of somewhat rougher information on migration, that the argument for a net increase in welfare of new migrants is tenuous in this case. Therefore, the subsidy cannot be justified on grounds of efficiency.

5 CONCLUSION

In this chapter we have considered the short-run versus long-run consistency of the marginal cost pricing rule, and its consistency with real world relationships. We argued, first, that it can be applied only within the single project case rather than the network framework. Next, perfect consistency between the implied outputs under long-run and short-run marginal cost-price equalization requires infinitely divisible scale. In this continuous case, roads will be designed to operate at some optimal level of congestion, and marginal social costs, including congestion charges, will therefore generate some excess revenues that may cover the investment. In any event, the usual rule, that all of the investment should be contributed from outside, does not hold. This "usual rule" is the policy prescription that, in most people's minds, follows from the marginal cost pricing rule.

Now, an infinitely divisible scale may be possible but is not, in fact, usually recognized owing, among other things, to the added administrative cost introduced by the complexity of considering an infinite range of project designs as well as the need to allow capacity for later growth. When just a few designs are considered, optimization logically requires the discrete analogue of the long-run marginal cost-price equalization rule of the continuous case, in which the average marginal or incremental investment cost is added to the short-run marginal cost. The users of the heavier-duty facility will be willing to pay the higher cost as they consolidate their demands from the lighter facility. However, there will be some new demands that exceed short-run marginal cost, and efficiency requires that these be met. The important implication of this analysis, however, is that these demands are likely to be much smaller in the aggregate than the total demand, much of which represents a consolidation of demands from the lighter-duty facility, such as, in this case, small trucks into large truckloads. Meeting these added demands, however, requires some way of discriminating, which may be very difficult in practice. Accordingly, general tax revenues could be called upon, but these should be *local* tax sources rather than interregional transfers unless it can be shown that the nonlocal external benefits, such as migration to the project area *together with* higher welfare for the new migrants, will result. In general, migration cannot be presumed to yield higher welfare unless a sufficiently higher net income also follows. A case study of the Toronto Subway in Chapter 17 shows one very large project in which interregional transfers appear to have been unjustified from a welfare point of view.

The Analysis of Costs

CHAPTER

4

Introduction to the Analysis of Transport Costs

1 REASONS FOR STUDYING TRANSPORT COSTS

Although the reasons for studying transport costs may seem self evident, we review them here in order to focus on the kinds of cost information needed. It is analytically useful to distinguish four objectives that cost information can serve: (1) pricing, including analysis of existing price patterns; (2) evaluation of intermodal traffic allocation in the short term when price patterns are distorted; (3) long-range traffic allocation; and (4) project evaluation, including projects outside the transport sector.

1.1 Pricing

One of the economist's most useful theoretical and empirical criteria for efficient resource allocation—profit—is not very helpful for transport sector analysis unless supplemented by a great deal of additional information. Economists are trained to view a zero-profit situation (zero profits after due consideration is made for the payment of proper managerial wages) as an indicator of efficiency, but in many transport activities this is not the case. Thus when a transport firm is a monopoly, zero profit may be caused by inefficient traffic allocation if the monopolist cuts back supply and holds prices above the competitive equilibrium level. Or the monopolist may be attempting, under the coercion of regulatory authorities, to perform at the perfectly competitive output level. Due to the absence of the chastening effects of competition, however, his internal operation may be marked by sloppiness and waste, thus leading to a zero-profit situation, but one that is inefficient as compared with the perfectly competitive zero-profit situation.

A second aspect of the monopolistic structure of some transport industries, especially railroads and in some countries air transport, which obviates direct inferences about welfare, is the possibility that even with zero profits, with all joint capital costs recovered, and with proper allowance made for managerial wages, a readjustment of transport rates could lead to a higher social welfare. Without the extensive experimentation that would take place in a perfectly competitive industry a monopolistic transport company simply does not have an opportunity to learn about customers' preferences. Higher prices for some traffic and lower prices for other traffic might lead to a rearrangement of total volume in which the value of the increased traffic more than offsets the value of the eliminated traffic, with a net benefit to society. For example, might a reorganization of Canadian railroad rates, with higher grain rates and lower rates on manufacturers from the prairies and on intermediate inputs to the prairies, with their effects on traffic, raise or lower social welfare? The cumbersome rate-making process is not sufficiently flexible to experiment in this regard.

Moreover, in some transport activities a strong tradition of state provision of transport service has developed over the years, for a number of reasons, and in these cases pricing policy is molded by several considerations other than allocative efficiency, as was argued in Part 1. We must learn to take account of such considerations—mainly income distribution objectives—in formulating criteria to evaluate the efficiency of transportation activities, since they would preclude the use of a zero-profit performance as an approbation of the firm's operations. At the same time we must guard against the frequent assumption that simply because it *is* done in the public sector, there *must* be some sound reason behind a particular LTFC pricing policy.

Therefore, we cannot use the profit of transport firms as an efficiency criterion by itself. This does not mean that we should go to the other extreme and never pay attention to profit, but, rather, that we must learn to recognize situations in which it is useful to look at profits in addition to, or instead of, other cost criteria. (The tendency sometimes arises of neglecting profit in the analysis of transport policies and patterns on the ground that all transport activities are inherently different from those in the other sectors of the economy.) We must be aware of the cost components or patterns that are useful for the evaluation of traffic patterns as a supplement or substitute for reliance on profit data.

1.2 Analysis of Traffic Allocation in the Presence of Price Distortions

If prices are correctly set, that is, if they are set correctly in terms of the relevant cost information, the user patterns *will necessarily* be the right ones. On the other hand, even if prices have been wrong, present traffic allocation, as well as the relationship between transportation and the other sectors of the economy, may be correct anyway. Accordingly, the analyst must choose the right criteria to be used for these purposes. The criteria must be based on information on true costs, which requires us to define the true cost relationships of transport activities.

1.3 Long-Range Intermodal Traffic Allocation

What costs should be used for long-range intermodal traffic allocation? The problems introduced by this kind of consideration are not merely the problems implicit in the economist's traditional distinction between long-run and short-run cost functions, since capital costs are also an important component of the evaluation of price policies. The critical issue, rather, is how costs will evolve in the future and the extent to which they can be foreseen. This will frequently require us to adapt the information on cost behavior in one country to the conditions evolving in another country.

1.4 Project Evaluation

It is not only transport projects that require analysis of transport cost information, but also other projects in which transport plays an important role—land penetration–agriculture projects, mineral development and exploitation, suburban manufacturing complexes, and so forth. If income distribution factors make full-cost recovery less than certain or if efficiency considerations call for a local contribution to cover a deficit, the costs used for pricing purposes and for investment decisions will be different.

2   OBJECTIVES OF PART 2

It is against the background of the foregoing questions that the cost analysis is presented in this and the next four chapters in Part 2. The first thing we must do is recognize possible limitations to the applicability of specific cost data: what limitations on the transferability of information on costs between different situations are imposed by different relative factor prices, exchange rate disequilibria, different shipping patterns, and similar factors?

Cost transferability is discussed in this chapter. The two chapters that follow analyze costs of the motor ´vehicle and railroad sectors, always with an eye to, or caution about, the transferability of cost information. In our empirical analysis of transport costs we, for the most part, abstract from congestion, except for its influence on transferability of cost information. The theoretical analysis and optimization of congestion appear in Part 4 in connection with urban economies, to which it is most relevant.

In Chapter 5 we consider the behavior of identifiable cost elements, including the cost of basic structure (way costs), the vehicle deterioration cost, the operating costs of individual vehicles, and functional relationships of distance and weight to vehicle operating costs. The following chapter, on railroads, first discusses the meaning or significance of various empirical data and evaluates available information. We shift focus in Chapters 7 to 9, stressing the handling of new, peculiar situations in which cost data may have to be analyzed from scratch, even in the face of insufficient information, and other adjustments made. Chapter 7 treats the theory of shadow prices. Here we consider the most important cost categories for which the question of shadow adjustments arises and examine the evidence bearing on the direction or mechanics of the necessary adjustments. While it is not possible to prescribe final, universally applicable solutions the principles and main factors to be considered are presented.

Cost analysis serves many purposes, such as the evaluation of pricing and rate-making policies, the efficiency of present traffic patterns, and long-term traffic allocation and intermodal investment plans. Chapters 8 and 9 present case studies taken from diverse economies to illustrate the approach to these problems even when inadequate information puts constraints on the analysis.

3 THE TRANSFERABILITY OF COST INFORMATION

To analyze the issue of transferability and the obstacles to it often encountered, we consider some specific problems that involve cost comparisons. Suppose that we have two situations, A and B, representing two regions or countries. We know that the cost of moving a ton of iron ore in A is 0.3 cent per ton-mile. Is this datum transferable to situation B? We consider the obstacles to transferability under increasing complications and see what qualifications must be made before such information can be used for decisions in situation B. The first three examples involve interregional comparisons. These together with the fourth assume that a single commodity is being transported.

1. Before the information of situation A can be applied to situation B we must know whether their traffic levels are similar and, if they are not, the transport cost *function* rather than the cost at a single output point. Suppose, for example, that there is a new iron ore discovery in northern Alberta and it is suggested that the ore be shipped to a proposed steel plant in Calgary. Could this ton-mile cost be compared to the ton-mile cost in, say, Labrador?

2. What about the geophysical environment? A different fuel consumption coefficient is implied if climates differ, as well as if grades differ.

3. Suppose that the foregoing questions have been resolved—the tonnages, climatic conditions, and geophysical situations are reasonably similar, making it unnecessary to examine the cost-volume function. Do the distances being traversed matter? If the ton-mile cost is invariant with respect to distance, substantial variations in trip lengths will also not matter. If the ton-mile cost does vary with distance, however, we must know something about this cost relationship.

4. Suppose now that we wish to use the information to estimate the cost in a different country. For example, could the cost observed in Labrador be used to gauge the cost for a new operation in Brazil? Assume the distances and tonnages to be equal. The grades are similar and the climates, while different, are found to have only a negligible effect on fuel or other input coefficients. We continue to assume that only the iron ore will move on the line. What other obstacles may arise to cost transferability?

Two major problems are present here. At a superficial level they both stem from the fact that different currencies are used, but at a more fundamental level they arise from the possible distortions and frictions in the economic relationships between the two sovereign nations. The obvious solution is simply to convert the Canadian cost datum, expressed in dollars—0.3 cent per ton-mile—into 2 Brazilian centavos (according to the 1973 exchange rate). But grave problems are risked if this approach is followed—it may be acceptable in some cases and fall wide of the mark in others:

(a) There may be distortions in the foreign exchange market, with one of the two countries pegging the exchange rate in order to achieve certain purposes. For example, it was argued by some observers in 1970 that the equilibrium United States/Canadian exchange rate was appreciably higher than the observed market rate of about $1.00 U.S./ $0.90 Canadian = 1.11, which purported to be a free market equilibrium rate. The Canadian government, it was alleged, artificially depressed the price of the Canadian dollar to make Canadian exports more attractive in the United States markets. In this case the official rate is not an equilibrium rate and many people would object to its use as a conversion coefficient to translate the transport cost observed in one country for use in a second country.

We will see in Chapter 7 when discussing the theory of shadow prices that the correct procedures here cannot be prescribed in a black-and-white manner. Sometimes the preferences of the government, which may find expression in a short-run disequilibrium exchange rate, should be used as a measure of cost; at other times they should not. For now we merely point out that this is a hazardous area.

(b) There is a more fundamental problem, however. Even if there were a completely free foreign exchange market with no state intercession, it might nevertheless be inappropriate to convert at the existing exchange rate. Why is this? To understand the problem, let us review the meaning of exchange rate equilibrium.

With no state intercession to raise or lower the value of one country's currency in relation to that of a second country, the equilibrium rate of exchange between the two currencies depends on the demands for them. The demand for a nation's currency in turn depends on the foreign community's wish to invest in that country (which we neglect here to simplify the discussion), as well as on the world *market's* demand for that country's goods and services. The demand for these goods and services in turn depends on their prices in relation to the prices in the importing countries. These in turn depend on the relative costs of producing them in the importing and exporting countries.

The costs of producing the goods and services that are exported may have little or nothing to do with the costs of transport in a country, since internal transport services are not exported and can affect the costs and prices of exports only indirectly as an intermediate input. On the other side of the coin, import costs, determined by the exchange rate, will have little influence on domestic transport costs in those transport modes that require small imported inputs (they will have greater influence on more import-intensive modes, however). All this is similar to the often observed result that the prices of labor-intensive activities such as haircuts or restaurant meals are much lower in developing than in developed countries, since these are not traded and have no influence on the exchange rates. For example, a haircut might cost $3 in Canada and 7 cruzeiros in Brazil. If haircuts could be exported, and if the foreign exchange rate depended perfectly on supply and demand for the currencies, the exchange rate would fall as people strove to buy Brazilian haircuts and demanded cruzeiros for this purpose. If only haircuts were traded and no demand for foreign exchange existed for any other purposes, ultimate equilibrium would find the cruzeiro/dollar exchange rate at 7/3. Instead it is 7/1.

Thus transport cost estimates translated from country A to country B by the exchange rate will be the more unrealistic, the less the transport industries of country B depend on goods that are traded. Relatively labor-intensive modes of transport, such as trucking, will have relative true costs that depend very little on foreign exchange rates. Railroads, if most of the equipment—steel, bridges, construction equipment, and rolling stock—is imported, will have costs that are more closely indicated by the exchange ratios.

Consider the example shown in Table 4.1. We can see that it would be much more accurate to use the exchange rate to convert Canadian cost experience to Brazilian conditions for the railroad sector than for the trucking industry even in the best of circumstances—even if we were

Table 4.1 Illustration of Inconsistencies and Errors in Translating Foreign Transport Costs by Exchange Rate[a]

	Rail	Road
Canada (Canadian currency)	$0.003	$0.009
	Cr$0.021	Cr$0.063
Brazil (Brazilian currency)	Cr$0.025	Cr$0.14
Ratio: line 2/line 3	86%	45%

[a] Brazilian cruzeiros converted to Canadian dollars at the rate of Cr. 7.00/$1.00.

using the correct cost datum to start with. The reason for this is that railroads, especially heavy duty lines, would be expected to be more foreign-equipment oriented than road-transport. For the former it would be a reasonable procedure to convert at the official rate. As we see in line 2 of the table, the estimate for Brazil, based on Canadian data, would be Cr$.0.021 just 16% below the actual Brazilian cost of Cr$.0.025 assumed here. But if we try to translate truck costs by the exchange rate we get a Brazilian cost of Cr$.0.063, which is less than half of the actual Brazilian trucking costs assumed here.

The lesson of the foregoing is that we can more safely translate cost data across international borders if the inputs in the transport activity more clearly reflect international trade flows. For trucking, which has a relatively high labor component, we may get very misleading answers if we compare the cost experience of one country to that of another through the exchange rate. This is simply the problem of nontraded goods, which recurs throughout economic comparisons among nations.

5. We now relax the assumption that only a single commodity is being shipped and assume that many commodities are involved in at least one of the two situations. Suppose that we have many commodities in situation A and just iron ore in situation B. How do we determine cost? We cannot simply adopt the cost of shipping iron ore in situation A, as measured by the rate quoted to shippers, since this rate will reflect, among other things, the differences in demand by shippers of different commodities in situation A and the corresponding allocation of joint costs among the different commodities. Iron ore shippers may be asked to pay a smaller part of the total joint costs involved in the railroad's operation. In situation B, on the other hand, since there are no other commodities being shipped, the iron ore will have to cover all of the costs.

Assuming that there are many commodities being shipped in situation B as well as in A does not relieve the problem of data nontransferability. The joint costs—signaling equipment or power lines, for example—must continue to be priced in a discriminatory way. These costs must be distributed over the various traffic classes according to the intensity of their demands. Typically, low-value goods will be assigned a smaller part of the joint costs per unit moved. But the same commodity may have *different values* in different circumstances. For example, coal in Pennsylvania is immensely more important for steelmaking than for home heating and at the margin it has a very low value. A diagram of the demand for coal, as in Figure 4.1, would start out falling steeply after the home heating demand was satisfied and

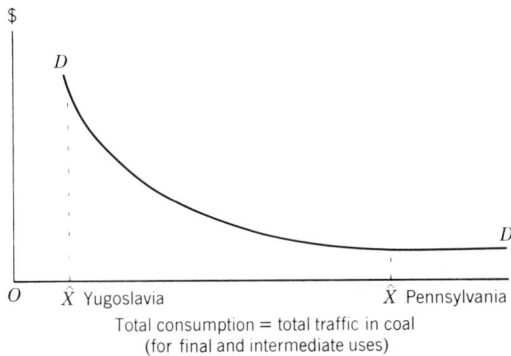

Figure 4.1 The demand for coal transportation (large steel-producing countries or regions are to the right).

would then tilt very slightly, at a low price, with increases in quantity. At the margin it has a low value. Coal in Yugoslavia, on the other hand, is used much more, relatively speaking, for heating purposes and so has a relatively greater value, that is, it is at the low volume end of the curve. Coal in Yugoslavia, therefore, would and *should* be assigned a larger amount of the joint costs per unit. Thus one cannot look at one or even a few rates of a railroad tariff schedule and, implicitly comparing them to those in another country, reach conclusions about the rationality of the rate schedule or the cost of transporting a given commodity.

6. The next obstacle to transferability is the variability of relative input prices. For example, suppose that it has been determined that the traffic to be expected in situation B will probably require electrification. (At very large traffic volume, electrification is usually the cheapest source of rail power so that we know that, if it is to be constructed, the railroad will probably have to be electrified.) We must still determine what the cost will be in order, say, to compare the railroad option with a maritime option. To do this we must know whether electrification costs will be the same in situation B as in situation A. The analyst must learn to distinguish those inputs whose costs will be relatively similar in different situations from those whose costs will differ.

7. A different kind of problem in cost analysis is the question of knowing when to accept, for purposes of analysis, the market prices or costs that are observed in a given situation and when to adjust them. Adjusted prices are usually referred to as shadow prices. A shadow

price is a price used in making planning calculations but not on the market—it is not the price to which market forces react. Its use represents an attempt to overcome the kinds of distortion that develop over time in the market. We may also apply shadow adjustments to prices that, though characteristic of a given level of development, may be expected to change with further economic progress. One example of a market price distortion, which might be obviated through the use of a shadow price, is the labor cost in Brazilian port operations. The stevedoring unions in Brazil have long been very strong; this, together with the conscious policy of wage increases pursued by some governments during the 1950s and 1960s, has led to a pattern of high wages in the ports. These wages are totally out of proportion to most of the criteria by which wages are determined, such as the disutility of labor, training costs, and the opportunity cost of labor. They do not represent a real cost to the economy in the sense that if a laborer's day were saved, the economy would benefit to the extent represented by the wage: the worker does not have an alternative activity whose real benefit for the national economy would be equal to his wage. In this case, the real cost to the economy is less than the wage of the worker. We must find some measure of what this real cost would be. More generally, we must learn to recognize situations in which market prices do not represent opportunity costs for the economy. As we will see in Chapter 7, however, the issues are quite complex and require careful analysis. Generalizations in the area are extremely tenuous.

One final point. Many readers will be asking why, when money prices are so uncertain and it is far from agreed which ones should be used, we do not turn instead to physical measures. For reasons mentioned above as well as for other reasons, it might seem advisable to rely more on physical data rather than price data to estimate costs. One important problem not yet mentioned is the effect on prices of inflation, which has been characteristic of a number of developing countries historically and is increasingly characteristic of the situation in advanced industrialized countries as well. How relevant, in this case, would a 1965 price be for analysis today? Would it not be better to estimate costs in terms of vehicle wear and to evaluate wear in terms of the wear of components— tire wear per mile on different grades and at different speeds, fuel input per mile at different speeds, and so on?

There are two problems with this approach. First, we would ultimately have to sum the factors into some single yardstick to aggregate vehicle costs, road costs, maintenance costs, construction costs, administration costs, and so on. This is true for most purposes of investment decision-making and pricing policy. The second problem, of course, is that some things simply cannot be estimated in terms of wear. A good example is the question of the cost of coal transport mentioned above. The cost of coal transport will depend on what other traffic classes are being shipped and the demand curves for them, which we must know in order to apportion joint costs. But demand curves are given in terms of one yardstick. This could in principle be anything—lint cotton, bread, or soap. But the same problems would continue to arise as do when money is the yardstick, and since money has the advantage of tradition, it might as well be used.

5

Road Transport Costs

This chapter surveys the empirical evidence on the most important functional relationships in the motor transport sector. Actual applications of the cost data are deferred to Chapters 8 and 9, where we adjust and apply them for some of the major purposes indicated in Chapter 3: evaluation of a country's user charges, evaluation of the efficiency of existing traffic distribution patterns, and analysis of future transport needs and provision.

The present chapter is divided into two sections. Section 1 deals with vehicle costs and Section 2, with way costs.

1 VEHICLE COSTS

One of the most useful studies of motor vehicle costs is that by de Weille (1966). It is based on an exhaustive analysis of the literature, including field studies, on motor vehicle costs. De Weille estimates the operating cost per kilometer for four different truck sizes and three passenger cars. He provides prototype vehicle designs for easy reference and estimates the costs of eight vehicle inputs—such as fuel, engine oil, tires, depreciation—for three road surfaces and four speeds for each surface. De Weille's basic results are summarized in a large table in his

handbook, an indispensable tool in every transport analyst's toolbox.*
Table 5.1 presents de Weille's data for representative speeds.

De Weille's estimates are based on what he calls "indicative prices,"
which apply to the early 1960s. As de Weille puts it, "These prices are
indicative only, and will no doubt differ from the specific prices the
analyst will encounter in a specific situation. Nevertheless, it seems useful to incorporate them in this study and mainly for two reasons: first in
order to provide the analyst with some basis for price comparisons when
a specific road project is considered, and secondly, to make possible an
overall view of vehicle operating costs and savings (see Chapter III of
main paper)" (p. 73). The indicative prices are, by and large, United
States prices for the early 1960s. The major exception is the value of
labor used for maintenance and the value of passenger and driver time.
Here the prices ($0.40 for maintenance and $0.25 for passengers and
drivers) are taken to be those appropriate to developing countries.

Two points of de Weille's analysis require special attention: his treatment of depreciation and his implicit assumption that average costs are
independent of distance.

De Weille's treatment of depreciation runs counter to much of the
analytical tradition in applied highway economics. According to this
tradition, depreciation charges are either very low or zero. For example,
the 1964 report of the Metropolitan Toronto and Area Rapid Transit
Study, which investigated the alternatives of a large new motor corridor
penetrating Toronto versus a rapid transit facility, assumed zero depreciation charges. This is symptomatic of a more general use of zero or
near-zero depreciation charges for purposes of analysis of the transit-
versus-private vehicle decision. The traditional approach seems to be
based on either of two considerations:

1. Many people assume that the consumption of a vehicle is a function
only of time, and whether it is driven 2000 or 10,000 miles a year makes
no difference. In this case, driving additional mileage does not consume
the vehicle faster, hence no charge should be imputed on this account.
Marginal mileage vehicle consumption costs *are* zero. A less extreme
view is that while mileage may be of some consequence, most of the loss
in the vehicle's service life relates to time rather than to mileage. For
example, especially in northern climates, the passing of the seasons
takes a tremendous toll on the vehicle—summer heat on its appearance,
and winter ice, snow, and salt on both appearance and moving parts. If

---

* Note, however, the increasing need to apply inflation adjustments to the different
inputs.

Table 5.1 Representative Motor Vehicle Operating Costs by Type of Vehicle and Road (U.S. $/1000 km)[a]

Type of Vehicle:	European Car			Average Car			American Car		
Road Surface:	Paved	Gravel	Earth	Paved	Gravel	Earth	Paved	Gravel	Earth
Speed (km/hour)	80	64	56	80	64	56	80	64	56
Fuel consumption	3.14	3.38	3.80	4.31	4.73	5.31	5.48	5.98	6.80
Engine oil consumption	0.09	0.11	0.15	0.19	0.23	0.28	0.28	0.34	0.42
Tire Wear	1.16	2.32	4.08	1.34	2.67	4.70	1.52	3.04	5.34
Depreciation	4.93	6.52	8.98	7.41	9.80	13.50	9.85	13.04	17.97
Interest	3.04	3.77	4.35	4.57	5.65	6.25	6.09	7.53	8.69
Maintenance (parts)	1.59	2.03	2.75	2.39	3.04	4.13	3.18	4.05	5.51
Maintenance (labor)	0.26	0.34	0.47	0.26	0.34	0.47	0.26	0.34	0.47
Occupants' time	5.63	7.02	8.01	5.63	7.02	8.01	5.63	7.02	8.01
Total	19.84	25.49	32.59	26.10	33.48	42.65	32.29	41.34	53.21

Trucks (Capacity)

Type of Vehicle:	1 Ton			3.5 Tons			Tractor-Semitrailer Combination					
							15 Tons			18 Tons		
Road Surface:	Paved	Gravel	Earth	Paved	Gravel	Earth	Paved	Gravel	Earth	Paved	Gravel	Earth
Speed (km/hour)	72	56	48	72	56	48	72	56	48	72	56	48
Fuel consumption	6.02	6.17	6.88	10.92	12.94	15.25	17.89	23.38	30.32	8.11	10.46	13.36
Engine oil consumption	0.25	0.34	0.43	0.30	0.43	0.62	0.45	0.64	0.91	0.83	1.17	1.66
Tire wear	2.26	4.51	9.07	5.68	11.43	25.69	15.23	30.45	68.59	20.18	40.36	90.75
Depreciation	12.46	17.38	26.66	12.32	18.84	31.16	17.10	25.65	42.75	21.36	32.06	53.44
Interest	6.67	8.69	10.14	6.16	7.97	9.42	5.70	7.12	8.55	6.52	8.69	10.87
Maintenance (parts)	3.48	4.93	7.82	10.87	16.30	27.17	17.10	27.07	44.17	15.22	23.91	39.12
Maintenance (labor)	0.30	0.43	0.63	0.94	1.40	2.35	1.50	2.26	3.76	1.40	2.09	3.57
Occupants' time	4.14	5.34	6.24	4.14	5.34	6.24	4.14	5.34	6.24	4.14	5.34	6.24
Total	35.58	47.79	67.90	51.33	74.65	117.90	79.15	121.91	205.29	77.76	124.08	219.01

Source. From Table 11 of Jan de Weille, *Quantification of Road User Savings*, © 1966 by The Johns Hopkins University Press, Baltimore Reprinted by permission.

[a] Input prices measured in "indicative" United States costs; all indirect taxes excluded.

this approach is followed, of course, a portion of the vehicle wear should be ascribed to time and a portion to mileage. There is no scientific basis for determining how much to each, but it is probably safe to say that those writing in this field who have exerted the greatest influence tend to ascribe a relatively greater amount to time than to distance.

From the viewpoint of most transport decisions, however, it is reasonable to use the average cost, that is, the annual cost divided by the total annual mileage. The reason is that major transport decisions about instituting bus lanes, constructing subways, and introducing other controls on urban transport, will all affect automobile ownership. Even if the loss in service life were solely and completely a function of time, public transit decisions may influence commuting patterns and cause people to buy additional cars, in which case the purchase costs of all the automobiles required over time should be considered as one of the major costs of the automobile commutation mode, just as are replacement subway cars or buses for the transit alternative. Similar considerations apply, of course, to intermodal comparisons for intercity transport.*

2. The second justification for using low depreciation rates is the common observation that a vehicle loses about 60 to 70% of its market value within three years of its life. This is probably an accurate statement of North American reality owing to peculiar consumption patterns there. This tells us something, not about technology potential, but about consumer preferences. To the economist this poses a dilemma: for whatever the source of these consumer preferences, whatever the advertising or status consciousness of consumers that generates these preferences, if this is how vehicle values do behave, the economist must accept them as a statement of consumers' relative valuations.

---

* It is often alleged that such uses as commuting involve "marginal" uses of the vehicle beyond its main functions. But if long-term patterns are involved and the breadwinner must drive, a second car is usually purchased. Thus it is not tenable to regard the breadwinner's use as the marginal use of a single vehicle.

The tendency to regard much of the car's use as marginal beyond the main function is undoubtedly influenced by the recognition that there are certain fixed annual costs, such as registration. Annual insurance premiums are another cost often invoked for support of this hypothesis, but there are very few others. Indeed, even insurance premiums *do* vary with annual use—if a commuter chooses to travel to work by car his premium is higher, that is, it is a function of use! Some people would still insist, though, that the marginal cost of insurance is zero, since once it is paid for the year, the cost is unrelated to additional use, just as, once a plant size is selected, short-run marginal costs exclude a plant consumption component. By the same token we would have to argue that marginal fuel costs are zero once the gas is in the tank and tire wear is zero once the tires are mounted and paid for!

There is an easy way out of this dilemma, however. If the vehicle in fact does last 8 to 10 years, the final 5 to 7 years are virtually "free," that is, about 35–40% of the original purchase price of the vehicle is associated with about two-thirds of the vehicle's life. Thus additional use of a vehicle that is older than 3 years really *does* impose little additional depreciation to the owner—too little, surely, to try to take into account in refined calculations. The logical objection to this view is immediately apparent. If a vehicle does depreciate disproportionately more in the early years, then the younger automobiles should have a *higher* than average depreciation component, even while we allow that the older ones have a below-average depreciation component. If the vehicle stock is growing, the stock of young cars will be growing faster than the stock of older cars, which, combined with their disproportionately great depreciation per mile, will more than counterbalance the lower depreciation of the older vehicles. (If there were a constant stock of vehicles, new ones just replacing old, the higher depreciation of the new vehicles would just offset the lower depreciation of the old).*

De Weille makes several calculations of depreciation on the basis of different assumptions. His most realistic approach is, essentially, to determine the total years of service as a function of annual speed and mileage, allowing for faster vehicle wear with higher average speeds. He also computes depreciation by two other procedures. The first alternative reduces the effect of higher speeds on shortening the lifetime; the second alternative assumes that there is no effect at all of annual mileage on lifetime, that is, service life is purely a function of time, which is a very unrealistic assumption.† The results under the various assumptions are all fairly close to the basic depreciation calculations for the realistic speed ranges of 25 to 55 miles per hour: the difference between maximum and minimum at the ends of this range is 10 to 20% (p. 64).

The other point that merits further discussion at this juncture is the cost-distance relationship. That this issue is not discussed by de Weille implies that his data are applicable only if ton-mile costs do not vary

---

* We note in passing that no proponents of the early depreciation school advocate that this approach should be followed. The reason probably is that doing so would mean increasing the cost imputed to motor vehicle transport, making it apparent that it represents a less attractive transport mode from the social point of view. In addition, it would tend to undermine new car sales, since it would recognize that a car can provide many years of useful service after three or four years of age.

† It is not clear why de Weille includes this calculation. If one really accepts such an assumption it is logically inconsistent to impute a depreciation per mile to the total operating cost per mile.

with distance, a condition which must be verified. The question of distance-cost behavior is illuminated by the study by Wilson (1959). Wilson examines cost data for Class I motor common carriers in the Eastern-Central Territory filed with the ICC for 1956. The data show decreasing average, but almost constant distance-incremental, costs. According to Wilson's study average cost declines for any vehicle size up to a distance of 1,000 miles (the highest distance tabulated by Wilson). Decreasing average cost, of course, is consistent with either a fixed cost in any shipment and a constant-distance incremental cost or with a falling distance-incremental cost. Accordingly, we translate Wilson's data into distance-incremental costs in Table 5.2. Evidently, starting at very short distances, the distance-incremental cost for the large trucks becomes virtually constant, so that the total cost function approximates the form TC $= a + bD$. The same is true of the very lightweight shipments.

Three policy implications follow from Wilson's study. The first is that since average costs are not constant, they should not be assumed so in

Table 5.2   Distance-Incremental Costs for the United States Trucking Industry, 1956 (cents/ton per incremental mile)[a]

Distance (miles)	Weight of Load (lb)									
	100	200	300	598	1458	3178	7132	16,808	25,904	38,265
1000										
900	7.0	2.9	2.9	2.8	2.8	2.8	2.8	2.6	2.6	2.2
800	7.5	2.8	2.9	2.8	2.8	2.8	2.8	2.8	2.6	2.4
700	6.5	2.8	2.7	2.8	2.8	2.6	2.6	2.6	2.6	2.4
600	7.0	2.6	2.7	2.6	2.6	2.8	2.4	2.4	2.6	2.2
500	6.5	2.7	2.7	2.8	2.6	2.6	3.0	2.6	2.4	2.2
400	6.5	2.7	2.7	2.6	2.8	2.6	2.6	2.6	2.4	2.4
300	7.0	2.7	2.7	2.8	2.6	2.8	2.6	2.6	2.4	2.2
200	7.0	2.8	2.7	2.8	2.8	2.8	2.8	2.6	2.4	2 4
100	6.5	2.5	2.6	2.4	2.6	2.4	2.4	2.6	2.4	2.2
50	8.0	3.4	3.3	3.6	3.2	3.6	3.6	3.2	2.8	2.4

Source. Calculated from Tables I and II of George Wilson, "On the Output Unit in Transportation," *Land Economics*, Vol. 35, No. 3, pp. 266–276. © 1959 by the Board of Regents of the University of Wisconsin System.
Used by permission.
[a] Small interclass aberrations are not significant (they are due to rounding and bookkeeping conventions).

intermodal comparison, as is frequently done, between rail and road. On the other hand, since the line haul cost, that is, the distance-incremental cost, is constant (the extra cost of each ton-mile of shipment at distances of 200 or 600 miles is virtually the same), de Weille's data *can* be used for the line haul portion of motor vehicle cost calculations. A third conclusion, which also follows from the evidence of the cost functions, is that linear programming solutions of highway routing problems are realistic and useful models after all since the *incremental* cost structure is linear: given a certain quantity of supply at certain origins to be distributed to a given group of destinations, the same fixed cost will be involved regardless of the routing pattern. Accordingly, the property of decreasing average ton-mile cost (with respect to trip length) can be disregarded for programming solutions.

Finally, the nature of the fixed cost requires further exploration in any given situation. There is more involved here than merely the loading of the cargo. Other sources of decreasing average cost are the higher cost associated with the first 20 or 30 miles of the trip, which are performed in the city or in a relatively more built-up area. These miles will be slower and, therefore, will involve higher driver time cost. The importance of this factor as a source of decreasing cost in any empirical situation will naturally depend on the importance of driver time, as measured by wages, adjusted as necessary for distortions between wages and opportunity cost. In developing countries, these will be low relatively to the materials input costs and so will provide a much less consequential source of decreasing average cost than they will in a developed country. To some extent the reduced significance of this factor in developing countries is offset by the higher material costs and the greater depreciation that we would expect to be associated with driving in heavily built-up areas, although these costs are probably not great enough to serve as a source of sharply decreasing average costs with increasing trip length. This situation will change as countries industrialize, however. It will change more rapidly in countries with severe geophysical constraints on urban expansion, such as Brazil, than in countries without such serious obstacles to urban growth, such as Iraq (see Chapter 9). But for the near future, for developing countries de Weille's data can probably be safely assumed to apply as the average cost even at very short distances, perhaps with an adjustment upward by 5 to 10%.

2 WAY COSTS

"Way costs" are road maintenance cost, construction cost, and the functional relationships between vehicle size and road damage. We consider first construction and maintenance costs and then turn to damage relationships.

2.1 Construction Costs and Maintenance Costs

Construction costs vary enormously with topography, soil conditions, road geometrics, surface, and other natural factors, on the one hand, and labor and equipment costs, on the other. Moreover, even when all the foregoing conditions are constant, the cost may vary greatly between two countries if they are in different climatic zones—a greater depth of the subbase will be required in temperate zones than in the tropics, for example, and so on. Thus construction cost experience is extraordinarily difficult to translate from one country to another, or even from one region to another within countries. Moreover, land acquisition costs require special consideration.

This environmental variability makes tabulation of construction costs uncertain. As a rough idea of the order of magnitude of construction costs per kilometer of different road types in the mid-1960s (excluding land costs) we may take $125,000 for a high-surface, two-lane road with flexible pavement, $60,000 for long-distance, heavy-duty dirt roads, $6000 for low-grade unsurfaced roads (bulldozed pathways might be a better term), and $5000 for gravel surfacing.

In any particular situation, the analyst should beware of the limitations on cost estimation by adding up components. For example, the cost of a high-surface, two-lane road cost cannot be estimated as the sum of the costs of constructing a dirt road and the costs of paving roads (existing or new dirt roads). The paved road will go over hilly or mountainous as well as flat terrain, while the dirt road will typically be restricted to flat terrain. To build the basic right-of-way in the mountain region would require tremendous upgrading of the basic specifications—better support for the substructure, more bridges to increase minimum turning radius, and so on.

Just as construction costs vary enormously, so do maintenance costs. A study by Mathew Betz (1965) attempted to tabulate maintenance expenditures per kilometer in a number of states in the United States. The essential details are summarized in Table 5.3. Evidently, there is a wide range of variation in highway maintenance expenditures. This reflects, among other factors, problems of definition and of traffic

Table 5.3   Annual State Maintenance Expenditure in the United States, 1960–1962

Type of Road	Number of States	Length of Road (miles)	Maintenance Expenditures Minimum	Average	Maximum
Dirt	1	627	$306	$821	$1077
Gravel	10	9,283	386	785	1005
Bituminous surface treatment	8	19,228	638	1264	2648
Asphaltic surface (intermediate)	9	9,389	391	1040	1480
Asphaltic concrete	2	2,924	1264	1310	1387
Portland cement concrete	10	17,927	398	1085	1485

Source.   Betz (1965), pp. 1–27.
Cited by permission.

measurement. There is also the very likely possibility that the expenditure may not correspond to the theoretically optimal level (if we could only determine what that was!) necessary to maximize social welfare, but may simply be the amount that can be spent because of the availability of maintenance funds. Nevertheless, these ranges of maintenance expenditures do provide a useful starting point for analysis of maintenance programs in various countries. Since the range reflects the interplay of numerous factors, and since many of these factors may be at work, some of them in contradictory directions, most countries' maintenance programs ought to be covered by these ranges, the prices adjusted of course for local market conditions (and the economist's final judgment being based also on the need, if any, to consider shadow prices). The probability is slight that in any country all of the factors causing maintenance expenditure variation will be operating in a given direction, which would lead a country beyond the observed ranges. Therefore, if a country's maintenance expenditure program is observed to lie far beyond the observed ranges, explanations should be sought in factors such as adequacy of weight supervision of vehicles, and corrective action taken.

The cost data discussed so far have been proposed mainly to begin to evaluate modal selection, to analyze investment projects that may include road components, and to maintain operations. From the viewpoint of user charges, we recommend a completely different approach based on a demand-related component, figured as the demand of a vehicle class for the joint cost components (new construction in the network and fixed annual maintenance), together with a component reflecting the deterioration that the vehicle imposes on the network for each mile it travels. A case study of such calculations is presented in Chapter 8. These are based on the functional damage relationships to which we now turn.

2.2   The Relationship between Vehicle Size and Road Damage

The relationship between vehicle weight and road damage was studied in the late 1950s by the American Association of State Highway Officials (AASHO). The AASHO test is the best known and most intensive controlled experiment ever conducted to study this relationship. The study project director, W. B. McKendrick, said with quite justifiable enthusiasm: "The AASHO Road Test looms as a milestone in [the study of highway performance and capability]. It is the largest and most comprehensive highway research project in the annals of highway history and it added greatly to what is known about highway pavements" (AASHO, 1962, p. 4). McKendrick's contribution to the volume provides a general description of the mechanics and procedures of the AASHO Road Test.

In the AASHO test, the number of passes of different-size vehicles required to reduce a road pavement to a specified level of deterioration was determined by experimentation. Six test loops were constructed, each with two lanes. One loop served as a control; 2000- and 6000-pound axle weights were run on a small loop, and on the four large loops were run tractor-semitrailers with single-axle loads of 12,000, 18,000, 22,400, and 30,000 pounds and tandem-axle loads of 24,000, 32,000, 40,000, and 48,000 pounds. The deterioration levels ("final present serviceability" levels) were specified by experts in terms of cracks (occurrence, intervals between cracks, width), potholes, and so on. Each loop contained representative sections of rigid and flexible pavements. Flexible pavements were given SN numbers, which reflected different combinations of design features, such as surface or subbase depth. Equivalence factors were calculated for different vehicle types and sizes to relate the damage imposed by each vehicle to that of a single-axle 18-kip load (i.e. 18,000 pounds). An equivalence factor of 10, for example, means that one pass of the vehicle in question does as much damage as 10 passes of the 18,000-pound single-axle load.

The equivalence factors for a wide range of vehicle sizes and pavement designs and two final serviceability levels (denoted by p) are shown in Tables 5.4 and 5.5, which are taken from the volume of conference proceedings that presented the results of the test. For any given rigid pavement slab thickness (or SN number) and final serviceability level, the norm is taken as the 18-kip single-axle load for that thickness and that final serviceability.

Study of the tables of equivalence factors shows that the relationship between damage imposed and vehicle weight is an exponential function.* For example, a 10% weight increase at 18 or at 36 kips results in an increase of about 50% in the value of the coefficient. This leads to the very high damage coefficients of the heavy vehicles. The largest tabled vehicle sizes have coefficients that exceed the 18-kip norm 30 to 40 times (single axles) and 4 to 7 times (tandems). At the lower end, axle weights half of the 18-kip standard (i.e. 8 to 10-kip loads) inflict less than 10% of the damage of the single-axle 18-kip load and less than 1% of the tandem 18-kip load.

Evidently, the equivalence factor patterns are fairly insensitive to pavement design. Thus while there is some variation with pavement design in the coefficients for any given weight, the difference between coefficients within weight classes is much smaller than the difference between the corresponding observations of that weight and the 18-kip standard. For final serviceability of 2.0, for example, for the 40-kip single-axle loads, the highest coefficient (for single-axle loads on flexible pavement, SN = 1) is just under one-third greater than the lowest coefficient (SN = 5). But this is a far smaller difference than the between-class variation, all of the 40-kip factors being more than 20 times greater than the 18-kip load! Similar relationships hold for other weights and other serviceability levels. Moreover, in practice, whether through administrative regulation or the higher private costs suffered through such loads, truckers do not run high loads, preferring tandem-axle designs at such weights, so that the effective relative difference within coefficients becomes smaller in relation to the between-coefficient factors. Thus at 30 kips—which is still higher than would occur in practice except in very rare circumstances—the highest coefficient for serviceability level 2 is only 25% greater than the smallest, while all coefficients exceed the 18-kip norm nearly eight times at least; on the 2.5 serviceability level, the maximum difference within coefficients is 50%, while all coefficients exceed the 18-kip norm seven times or more.

---

* The basic equation used to generate the equivalence factors is $\log W_t = \log \rho + G_t/\beta$, where ρ and β are parameters calculated for the relevant pavement design and axle layout under an 18-kip load, W_t is the equivalence factor, and G is a function of relative serviceability reductions under the load in question and the 18-kip load. Observations on relative serviceability reduction at critical points, and on variables used to calculate other parameters, were derived from the empirical experiment.

Table 5.4 AASHO Equivalence Factors; Flexible Pavement

Axle Load (kips)	$p = 2.0$ Structural Number, SN						$p = 2.5$ Structural Number, SN					
	1	2	3	4	5	6	1	2	3	4	5	6
SINGLE AXLES												
2	0.0002	0.0002	0.0002	0.0002	0.0002	0.0002	0.0004	0.0004	0.0003	0.0002	0.0002	0.0002
4	0.002	0.003	0.002	0.002	0.002	0.002	0.003	0.004	0.004	0.003	0.003	0.002
6	0.01	0.01	0.01	0.01	0.01	0.01	0.01	0.02	0.02	0.01	0.01	0.01
8	0.03	0.04	0.04	0.03	0.03	0.03	0.03	0.05	0.05	0.04	0.03	0.03
10	0.08	0.08	0.09	0.08	0.08	0.08	0.08	0.10	0.12	0.10	0.09	0.08
12	0.16	0.18	0.19	0.18	0.17	0.17	0.17	0.20	0.23	0.21	0.19	0.18
14	0.32	0.34	0.35	0.35	0.34	0.33	0.33	0.36	0.40	0.39	0.36	0.34
16	0.59	0.60	0.61	0.61	0.60	0.60	0.59	0.61	0.65	0.65	0.62	0.61
18	1.00	1.00	1.00	1.00	1.00	1.00	1.00	1.00	1.00	1.00	1.00	1.00
20	1.61	1.59	1.56	1.55	1.57	1.60	1.61	1.57	1.49	1.47	1.51	1.55
22	2.49	2.44	2.35	2.31	2.35	2.41	2.48	2.38	2.17	2.09	2.18	2.30
24	3.71	3.62	3.43	3.33	3.40	3.51	3.69	3.49	3.09	2.89	3.03	3.27
26	5.36	5.21	4.88	4.68	4.77	4.96	5.33	4.99	4.31	3.91	4.09	4.48
28	7.54	7.31	6.78	6.42	6.52	6.83	7.49	6.98	5.90	5.21	5.39	5.98
30	10.38	10.03	9.24	8.65	8.73	9.17	10.31	9.55	7.94	6.83	6.97	7.79
32	14.00	13.51	12.37	11.46	11.48	12.17	13.90	12.82	10.52	8.85	8.88	9.95
34	18.55	17.87	16.30	14.97	14.87	15.63	18.41	16.94	13.74	11.34	11.18	12.51
36	24.20	23.30	21.16	19.28	19.02	19.93	24.02	22.04	17.73	14.38	13.93	15.50
38	31.14	29.95	27.12	24.55	24.03	25.10	30.90	28.30	22.61	18.06	17.20	18.98
40	39.57	38.02	34.34	30.92	30.04	31.25	39.26	35.89	28.51	22.50	21.08	23.04

TANDEM AXLES

10	0.01	0.01	0.01	0.01	0.01	0.01	0.01	0.01	0.01	0.01	0.01	0.01
12	0.01	0.01	0.02	0.02	0.02	0.01	0.01	0.01	0.01	0.02	0.02	0.02
14	0.02	0.03	0.03	0.04	0.04	0.03	0.02	0.02	0.03	0.03	0.03	0.03
16	0.04	0.05	0.06	0.07	0.07	0.04	0.04	0.04	0.05	0.05	0.05	0.04
18	0.07	0.08	0.09	0.11	0.10	0.07	0.07	0.07	0.08	0.08	0.08	0.07
20	0.11	0.12	0.14	0.16	0.14	0.11	0.10	0.11	0.12	0.12	0.12	0.10
22	0.17	0.18	0.21	0.23	0.20	0.16	0.16	0.16	0.17	0.18	0.17	0.16
24	0.24	0.26	0.29	0.31	0.27	0.23	0.23	0.24	0.25	0.26	0.24	0.23
26	0.34	0.36	0.40	0.42	0.37	0.33	0.33	0.34	0.35	0.36	0.34	0.32
28	0.47	0.50	0.53	0.55	0.49	0.45	0.46	0.47	0.48	0.49	0.46	0.45
30	0.63	0.66	0.70	0.70	0.65	0.61	0.62	0.63	0.64	0.65	0.62	0.61
32	0.83	0.86	0.89	0.89	0.84	0.81	0.82	0.83	0.84	0.84	0.82	0.81
34	1.08	1.09	1.11	1.11	1.08	1.06	1.07	1.08	1.08	1.08	1.07	1.06
36	1.38	1.38	1.38	1.38	1.38	1.38	1.38	1.38	1.38	1.38	1.38	1.38
38	1.73	1.70	1.68	1.69	1.73	1.75	1.74	1.73	1.72	1.73	1.75	1.76
40	2.14	2.08	2.03	2.06	2.16	2.21	2.18	2.16	2.13	2.15	2.19	2.22
42	2.61	2.51	2.43	2.49	2.67	2.76	2.70	2.66	2.62	2.64	2.73	2.77
44	3.16	3.00	2.88	2.99	3.27	3.41	3.31	3.24	3.18	3.23	3.36	3.42
46	3.79	3.55	3.40	3.58	3.98	4.18	4.02	3.91	3.83	3.92	4.11	4.20
48	4.49	4.17	3.98	4.25	4.80	5.08	4.83	4.68	4.58	4.72	4.98	5.10

Source. The AASHO Road Test: *Proceedings of a conference held May 16–18, 1962, St. Louis, Mo.*, Highway Research Board Special Report 73, p. 409, National Academy of Sciences, Washington, D.C., 1962. Reprinted by permission.

Table 5.5 AASHO Equivalence Factors: Rigid Pavement

Gross Axle Load (kips)	p = 2.0 Slab Thickness, D_2 (in.)						p = 2.5 Slab Thickness, D_2 (in.)					
	6	7	8	9	10	11	6	7	8	9	10	11
SINGLE AXLES												
2	0.0002	0.0002	0.0002	0.0002	0.0002	0.0002	0.0002	0.0002	0.0002	0.0002	0.0002	0.0002
4	0.002	0.002	0.002	0.002	0.002	0.002	0.003	0.002	0.002	0.002	0.002	0.002
6	0.01	0.01	0.01	0.01	0.01	0.01	0.01	0.01	0.01	0.01	0.01	0.01
8	0.03	0.03	0.03	0.03	0.03	0.03	0.04	0.04	0.03	0.03	0.03	0.03
10	0.09	0.08	0.08	0.08	0.08	0.08	0.10	0.09	0.08	0.08	0.08	0.08
12	0.19	0.18	0.18	0.18	0.17	0.17	0.20	0.19	0.18	0.18	0.18	0.17
14	0.35	0.35	0.34	0.34	0.34	0.34	0.38	0.36	0.35	0.34	0.34	0.34
16	0.61	0.61	0.60	0.60	0.60	0.60	0.63	0.62	0.61	0.60	0.60	0.60
18	1.00	1.00	1.00	1.00	1.00	1.00	1.00	1.00	1.00	1.00	1.00	1.00
20	1.55	1.56	1.57	1.58	1.58	1.59	1.51	1.52	1.55	1.57	1.58	1.58
22	2.32	2.32	2.35	2.38	2.40	2.41	2.21	2.20	2.28	2.34	2.38	2.40
24	3.37	3.34	3.40	3.47	3.51	3.53	3.16	3.10	3.23	3.36	3.45	3.50
26	4.76	4.69	4.77	4.88	4.97	5.02	4.41	4.26	4.42	4.67	4.85	4.95
28	6.59	6.44	6.52	6.70	6.85	6.94	6.05	5.76	5.92	6.29	6.61	6.81
30	8.92	8.68	8.74	8.98	9.23	9.39	8.16	7.67	7.79	8.28	8.79	9.14
32	11.87	11.49	11.51	11.82	12.17	12.44	10.81	10.06	10.10	10.70	11.43	11.99
34	15.55	15.00	14.95	15.30	15.78	16.18	14.12	13.04	12.94	13.62	14.59	15.43
36	20.07	19.30	19.16	19.53	20.14	20.71	18.20	16.69	16.41	17.12	18.33	19.52
38	25.56	24.54	24.26	24.63	25.36	26.14	23.15	21.14	20.61	21.31	22.74	24.31
40	32.18	30.85	30.41	30.75	31.58	32.57	29.11	26.49	25.65	26.29	27.91	29.90

TANDEM AXLES

10	0.01	0.01	0.01	0.01	0.01	0.01	0.01	0.01	0.01	0.01	0.01	0.01
12	0.03	0.03	0.03	0.03	0.03	0.03	0.03	0.03	0.03	0.03	0.03	0.03
14	0.05	0.05	0.05	0.05	0.05	0.05	0.06	0.05	0.05	0.05	0.05	0.05
16	0.09	0.08	0.08	0.08	0.08	0.08	0.10	0.09	0.08	0.08	0.08	0.08
18	0.14	0.14	0.13	0.13	0.13	0.13	0.16	0.14	0.14	0.13	0.13	0.13
20	0.22	0.21	0.21	0.20	0.20	0.20	0.23	0.22	0.21	0.21	0.20	0.20
22	0.32	0.31	0.31	0.30	0.30	0.30	0.34	0.32	0.31	0.31	0.30	0.30
24	0.45	0.45	0.44	0.44	0.44	0.44	0.48	0.46	0.45	0.44	0.44	0.44
26	0.63	0.64	0.62	0.62	0.62	0.62	0.64	0.64	0.63	0.62	0.62	0.62
28	0.85	0.85	0.85	0.85	0.85	0.85	0.85	0.85	0.85	0.85	0.85	0.85
30	1.13	1.13	1.14	1.14	1.14	1.14	1.11	1.12	1.13	1.14	1.14	1.14
32	1.48	1.45	1.49	1.50	1.51	1.51	1.43	1.44	1.47	1.49	1.50	1.51
34	1.91	1.90	1.93	1.95	1.96	1.97	1.82	1.82	1.87	1.92	1.95	1.96
36	2.42	2.41	2.45	2.49	2.51	2.52	2.29	2.27	2.35	2.43	2.48	2.51
38	3.04	3.02	3.07	3.13	3.17	3.19	2.85	2.80	2.91	3.04	3.12	3.16
40	3.79	3.74	3.80	3.89	3.95	3.98	3.52	3.42	3.55	3.74	3.87	3.94
42	4.67	4.59	4.66	4.78	4.87	4.93	4.32	4.16	4.30	4.55	4.74	4.86
44	5.72	5.59	5.67	5.82	5.95	6.03	5.26	5.01	5.16	5.48	5.75	5.92
46	6.94	6.76	6.83	7.02	7.20	7.31	6.36	6.01	6.14	6.53	6.90	7.14
48	8.36	8.12	8.17	8.40	8.63	8.79	7.64	7.16	7.27	7.73	8.21	8.55

Source. The AASHO Road Test: Proceedings of a conference held May 16–18, 1962, St. Louis, Mo., Highway Research Board Special Report 73, p. 414, National Academy of Sciences, Washington, D.C., 1962. Reprinted by permission.

The picture is similar in the tandem-axle tables, although there are more marked differences between the rigid and flexible pavements, coefficients for the former being 60 to 75% higher. However, the differences between tandem-axle loads and the 18-kip single-axle norm remain much more sizable, the largest loads imposing deterioration 20 to 75 times greater.

One very valuable consequence of the patterns just examined is that the coefficients can be applied, on an average basis, to the country's road stock to allocate maintenance expenditures to the several traffic classes. This is important since, in fact, there is never sufficient information available on the makeup of a country's road network or on traffic composition to apply the equivalence factors in the detail in which they have been calculated. Indeed in many countries a paved-gravel-dirt classification is the most that one can hope for. That is, all roads with any kind of paved surface at all are lumped together. But since the rate of deterioration to reach specified levels follows a rather consistent pattern for any road design and axle layout, it would seem that the errors made by using an average coefficient approach would pale beside the errors in cost imputation that would follow from using a ton-mile or vehicle-mile approach, as is frequently recommended by writers on highway pricing policy. In Chapter 8 we apply the AASHO coefficients to evaluate the user charge structure in Yugoslavia as an illustrative case study.

The AASHO test results have been accepted by a number of state highway departments for their road design and construction activities. On the other hand, they have not been generally accepted as a basis for highway pricing. While the reasons for this policy can only be guessed at, it is probably conditioned in part by the United States highway commercial users' lobby, although whether these users' costs would rise if AASHO coefficients were to be used as a basis for pricing is an open question that cannot be answered without considerable study.

Some critics of the AASHO coefficients claim that they are invalid because they cannot be verified by reference to actual highway expenditure accounts. This is not a legitimate objection, however, for the following reasons. In practice roads are used not by single classes of vehicles but by many classes simultaneously, so that it is not possible to isolate the physical damage done by vehicles of any given size even on individual roads. Indeed the problem is even worse—not only are roads not used by homogeneous traffic classes, but on most roads we do not even know the *distribution* of vehicle weights. Moreover, most state highway departments do not report expenditures in sufficient detail to analyze individual roads. In face of all these flaws in the data base, it is not surprising that we are unable to confirm the AASHO findings—the fact is that we cannot even begin to test them. But this is not an indictment of the AASHO test, which was a carefully controlled experiment, but, rather, a reflection of the inadequacy of state highway accounts for the analysis of weight-damage relationship.

REFERENCES

American Association of State Highway Officials (1962), *The AASHO Road Test, Proceedings of a Conference, 1962,* Highway Research Board Special Report No. 73 (Washington, D.C.: National Academy of Sciences).

Betz, Mathew J. (1965), "Highway Maintenance Costs—A Consideration for Developing Areas," *Highway Research Record* No. 94 (Washington, D.C.: Highway Research Board).

De Weille, Jan (1966), *Quantification of Road User Savings,* (Baltimore: Johns Hopkins University Press–International Bank for Reconstruction and Development).

Wilson, George (1959), "On the Output Unit in Transportation," *Land Economics,* Vol. 35, No. 3.

6

Railroad Costs

1 A THEORY OF RAILROAD COSTS

The discussion of cost data in Chapter 4 showed numerous obstacles to the transferability of information on individual rates and costs, or even average costs, from one region or nation to another. For railroads, the least transferable cost information is that concerning basic investment costs, which depend heavily on local physical conditions and foreign exchange considerations. For this reason, analysis has usually focused on operating cost information, information that is obviously necessary even when project investment decisions rather than pricing of existing lines are the objective. However, widespread inconsistency and ambiguity remain in the definition and use of terms and cost concepts, such as marginal cost, variable cost, and out-of-pocket costs, although some of the most basic railroad cost relationships do show sufficient regularity to be transferable (of course, the data may not be transferable interregionally or even intertemporally if inflation is serious in the countries being analyzed). But as we shall see in Chapters 8 and 9, frequently even the correct basic cost patterns are violated in pricing applications, even though there are unexpected exceptions.

The major difficulty in railroad cost analysis is the problem common to all attempts to move from the simple two-dimensional analysis of costs to the complexity of the real world. For example, some inputs treated as investments for some purposes (by virtue of the fact that they form a part of capital), such as locomotives, are treated by others, or for other purposes, as a variable input as a function of output. Conversely, some items would be classed as variable costs according to characteristics such as their labor intensity (e.g., administration, which includes the large variable input of labor), but since they do not bear a direct relation to output, they are at least partially fixed costs, and for some analytical purposes they should be thought of as such. All this makes it very difficult to deduce optimization rules for pricing from a single two-dimensional analysis, although it does not so much hamper the optimization of investment.

We now set up a three-dimensional cost model, in which total cost depends on output (X) and technology (Y). We distinguish five kinds of cost: (1) fixed capital cost; (2) periodically recurring variable cost; (3) short-run marginal cost; (4) short-run average variable cost, consisting of the sum of short-run average periodically recurring cost and short-run marginal cost; and (5) long-run average variable cost, which is given by the functional defining short-run average variable cost at the technologies corresponding to the minimum average cost for any level of output. This cost theory is then integrated with the empirical results of George Borts' analysis of railroad costs, the most notable analysis that has so far been conducted, to derive general rules for the evaluation of railroad rates and traffic allocation. In Chapters 8 and 9 this analytical framework is applied in case studies of the Iraqi rate structure and certain aspects of other nations' rate and traffic patterns.

Figures 6.1, 6.2, and 6.3 contain the basic diagrammatic analysis. Volume, in carloads, is shown on the X-axis, size, as measured by some engineering design variable, is indicated on the Y-axis, and average cost appears on the Z-axis. Figure 6.1 shows three cost functions. Varying with the design indicator are (1) the total capital cost converted to an annual basis (financial depreciation and interest) and (2) the annual administration and fixed overhead (the periodically recurring inputs— PRC). These are the lowest and middle surfaces respectively. (It does not matter whether the PRC has actually been made or merely provided for; rent is of course paid monthly, for example. But the railroad firm decides periodically on a certain staff, service organization, etc.) The uppermost surface adds in the costs that vary with output *once* the basic plant size has been chosen *and* the periodically recurring costs have been allowed for. These costs are, of course, the short-run

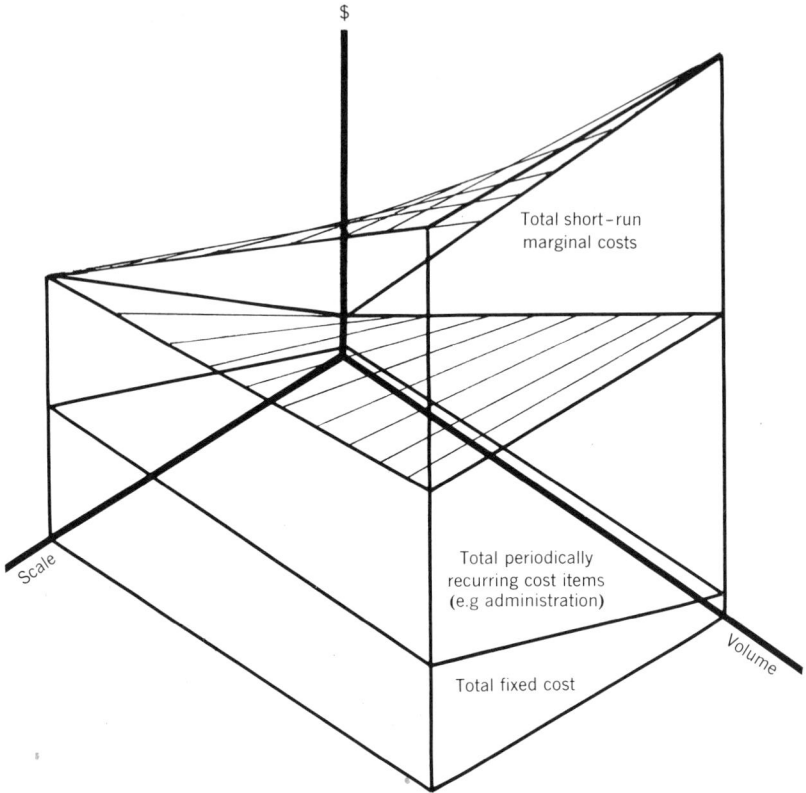

Figure 6.1 A model with continuously variable scale (basic technology): total fixed costs, total periodically recurring costs, and total short-run marginal costs.

marginal costs. They take in all cost inputs varying with use: rail wear that part of maintenance of rail bed which depends on use, fuel, physical depreciation, and similar factors.

Figure 6.2 shows the variable costs only; it is Figure 6.1 with the fixed cost function removed and the slopes of the upper surfaces adjusted accordingly. The top surface gives total variable costs (the sum of PRC and SRMC). The bottom surface gives the variable costs that vary with size of firm but not output, that is, the periodically recurring costs.

Finally, Figure 6.3 shows average variable costs. These fall and then rise with rising volume when plant is small. But as plant size increases, the slope changes, and after some point is reached, the average costs cease to rise with rising traffic but, rather, decline throughout.

The behavior of the average variable cost surface depends, obviously, on the short-run marginal cost surface. This would be expected to start to rise in smaller plants earlier than in large plants, and it is drawn accordingly (the surface is indicated by the broken line).

In this three-dimensional framework the *long-run average variable cost will be the curve traced out on the total variable cost surface through the points that minimize long-run average total cost.*

The terminology and some of the concepts adopted here differ from the lexicon now in use, which itself varies greatly from one user to the next. No great purpose would be served by an exhaustive etymological exegesis at this point, but the reader should at least note that some writers use the term short-run marginal cost to refer to what we have

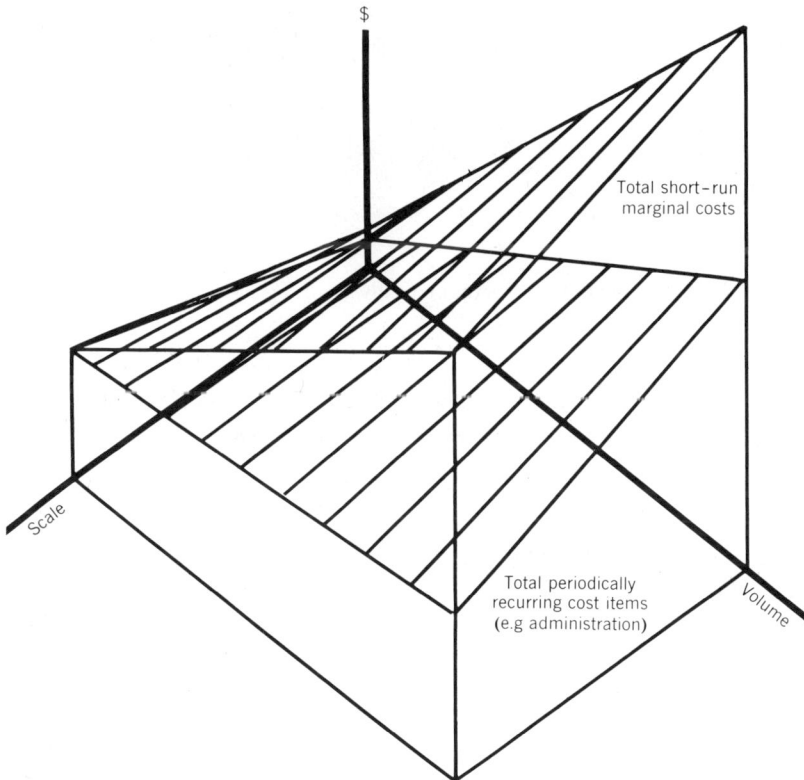

Figure 6.2 Model with continuously variable scale (basic technology): total variable cost components only (periodically recurring costs and short-run marginal costs).

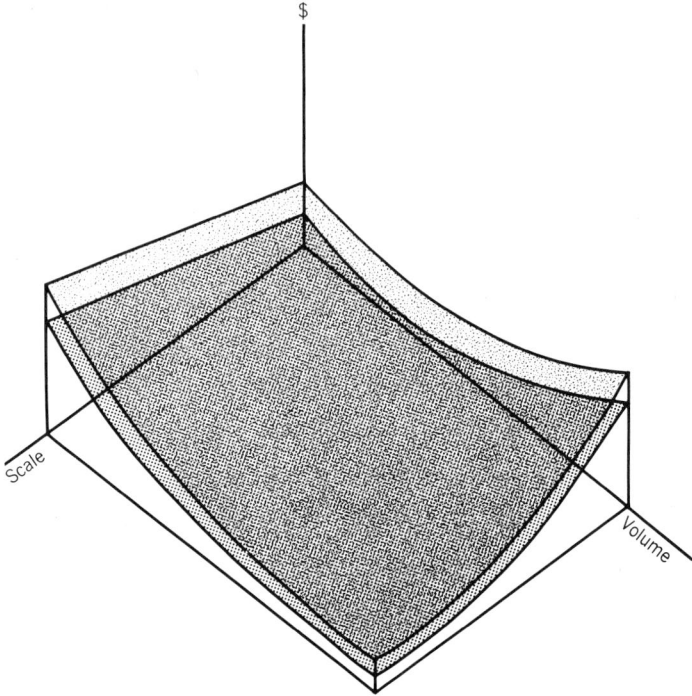

Figure 6.3   Average variable costs (periodically recurring costs and short-run marginal costs).

called average total variable cost. Others *notably* the Interstate Commerce Commission, rely on the term "out-of-pocket cost." The ICC concept "percent variable," proposed as the minimum price for new freight, is the ratio between what we have called short-run marginal cost and average total cost. In Section 3.1 we argue that a different elasticity—the ratio of SRMC to LRAVC—is the relevant criterion.

We now use the cost framework developed here to analyze empirical evidence on cost behavior. We first consider long-run cost relationships and then costs in the short run, including cost relationships of various specific operations.

2   EMPIRICAL ANALYSIS: LONG-RUN COST BEHAVIOR

Long-run average cost is the cost relationship that is relevant to intermodal technology choices, such as building a railroad or highway on a given arc. The effect of network interconnection on cost would also then have to be considered, such as sources of unit cost reduction through scale economies in administration. Alternatively, although it is much less likely to be the situation, if we are thinking in terms of a decision between a rail network for the whole country and a highway, both to be built from scratch, it would be the long-run average network costs that are relevant. In this case, all the interconnections are internal and the question of external economies, such as these originating in spreading the administrative burden already existing, do not arise.

For reasons given in Chapter 4 we would not expect to find an existing situation whose cost data might be transferred to the situation for which the modal mix decision is being made. Among the obstacles to transferability, you may recall, are topographical and factor price differences and possible misinterpretation of costs due to deferment of such projects as rail replacement or other heavy line maintenance work. In any particular situation an important aspect of the modal choice decision will be the behavior of costs as volume changes, which might justify a different decision if large traffic growth is expected.

The cost concept relevant to the investment decision is the long-run average cost function. The foregoing reflections also suggest the approach to follow—a regression analysis of different size lines, in which the existence of numerous observations would ensure that random responses to, for example, traffic conditions, maintenance deferment, and rolling stock acquisition are mutually offsetting. Unfortunately, such an analysis would require data on the initial investment in the lines included in the analysis. Since in any actual situation the investments would have been made over a period of years, major problems arise in apportioning the investment costs and adjusting them for historical price changes according to their annual breakdown.

The most that the constraints of theory and practice would permit us to do in this case would be to estimate the *long-run average variable cost*, that is, the cost of everything but the basic facility—annual maintenance costs, administration costs, fuel costs, rolling stock, marshaling yard labor, and so on. Once this is done, however, we will have a very useful input to specific project investment decisions: all that would remain would be to estimate the investment cost necessary in the actual conditions to construct facilities of different size to combine with the long-run average variable cost function.

We note that even following this approach, problems do arise in the interpretation of long-run variable cost for project investment decisions. For example, how should we compare average variable costs for two railroads if they were built at different times under different relative factor prices? Average variable costs experienced today may simply reflect the best technological choice under today's conditions; if the line were to be built today for that volume, it might use a different combination of fixed technology and variable inputs. One way to eliminate or minimize the gravity of the problem is to segregate the observations regionally to ensure similarity of time and conditions of construction, as was done in what is undoubtedly the best study of the subject so far attempted—that of Borts (1960).

Borts' study is based on the accounting data of Class I railways in the United States for 1948. Class I railroads at the time were those whose annual revenues exceeded $1 million (In 1965 the definition of Class I was changed to require $5 million of annual revenues). Class I railroads include 96% of total mileage operated by all United States line-haul railroads and account for more than 99% of total rail freight and passenger traffic (Association of American Railroads, 1965, p. ii). His basic equation is $C = \alpha X_1 + \beta Z / X_1 + \gamma$, where X_1 is total (loaded and empty) car-miles and Z is carloads.

Borts does not explicitly work within the framework of costs outlined in Section 1 of this chapter, but a careful reading shows that the average cost estimates in the 1960 study *do* correspond to the notion of long-run average variable cost described above. What he calls "marginal cost of carloads is defined as the change in cost accompanying an incremental change in car-miles and carloads such that the average length of haul remains constant" (p. 118). Subject to this constraint, the marginal cost of carloads is equal to the coefficient (α) of X_1 (freight car-miles) in his equations (pp. 118–119). This coefficient, divided by average cost, is then the elasticity with respect to carloads (subject to the length of haul constraint). Conversely, the elasticity multiplied by average cost yields what we are calling the short-run marginal cost. His major statistical findings are summarized in Table 6.1.

The costs that Borts analyzes exclude basic capital investment costs, but include currently acquired capital items such as rolling stock; periodically recurring costs such as administration and joint maintenance; and directly variable costs such as variable maintenance and fuel (see his list of cost accounts on pp. 129–130). Accordingly, all his costs are variable costs, in our terminology. Within each region he distinguishes three size classes. The average variable cost within each size class may be thought of as an observed point on a long-run variable cost function relevant to that region (column 1). The rate of change between such points would be a long-run marginal variable cost, that is, the rate of change of variable cost with respect to changes in plant size.

Table 6.1   Summary Measures of Railroad Cost in the United States

Region and Size Class	(1) Long-Run Average Variable Cost (cents/car mile)	(2) Elasticity of LRAVC	(3) Short-Run Marginal Cost (2) × (1) (cents/car mile)	(4) Distance-Incremental Cost (cents/car mile)
East				
Large	24.8	0.992	24.6	21.6
Medium	22.9	0.930	21.3	19.2
Small	11.8	1.190	14.0	19.9
South				
Large	17.3	0.820	14.2	11.1
Medium	17.9	0.811	14.5	11.1
Small	25.6	0.820	21.0	11.2
West				
Large	18.1	0.944	17.1	14.7
Medium	17.6	0.870	15.3	13.0
Small	19.2	0.882	16.9	13.5

Source. All costs based on cost Model II of Borts (1960). (Model II uses track mileage as size indicator). Cited by permission. Column 1: Table VII, p. 127, "Average cost" estimated for average length of haul and average carloads of size class in that region. Column 2: Table VI, p. 126, "Elasticity with respect to carloads." Column 3: column 2 × column 1. Column 4: Table VII, p. 127, "Marginal cost of length of haul."

The interregional differences in the LRAVC reflect such factors as topography, input cost variation, and peculiarities in shipping patterns. The observations in the different regions, therefore, do not represent observations on the same cost function. Rather, each region has its own cost function. A remarkable conclusion emerges from Borts' study. Within each region, that is, within each "subindustry," the variable cost is approximately constant starting at medium size plants. In moving from small to medium size plants, however, there is one case of increasing cost (the east), and one case of decreasing cost (the south), with one case virtually indeterminate (the west, where LRAVC first falls a little and then rises a little).

What is the significance of Borts' findings and how should they be used? Since he observed firms with different-size plants [defined either by capital (Model I) or mileage (Model II)], the variable cost data reflect long-run, rather than short-run, variable cost functions, as noted. They are stochastic observations, to be sure, but there is no reason not to assume the usual conditions on the error term. His results, therefore, are applicable to the economic analysis of new project designs. The basic cost characteristic that he finds—constant long-run average variable cost—need only be supplemented by data on the capital cost of different project variants in a given situation.* The same average variable cost can then be assigned to each to determine long-run average total cost. If the succeedingly more costly fixed investments lead to decreasing unit fixed cost, then the long-run average total cost surface will decline.

3. EMPIRICAL ANALYSIS: SHORT-RUN COST BEHAVIOR

Knowledge of short-run cost behavior is necessary for rate analysis, investment decisions involving use of existing rail facilities, and analysis of technological decisions within a railroad firm—decisions on costs of individual inputs such as labor and fuel. In this section we first analyze short-run marginal cost behavior, which is of special importance for analysis of new traffic from the viewpoint of regulatory commissions and traffic flow evaluation, and then consider rate-distance cost relationships and other technological relations.

3.1   Short-Run Marginal Cost

The concept of short-run marginal cost that we are applying here was described in Section 1. This cost is the incremental cost imposed on a firm by a unit of output, a car-mile, once the periodically renewable costs, such as administration, are given. This cost concept is of obvious importance. It is the relevant criterion for the transport cost of new projects outside the transport sector which require an already existing line. An example is ore exploitation for export where world prices are given and it is necessary to determine whether the true domestic cost is higher or lower than the world price. Looked at from the railroad's point of view, this is the criterion relevant to the attraction of incremental traffic. Of course, in this case, the effect of a lower price offered

---

* Although in one of his formulations Borts includes a capital cost independent variable and estimates its effect on total cost (the coefficient β in his Model I), owing to the difficulties in adapting this information to new situations, it would seem preferable to use, instead, new on-the-spot engineering estimates of the capital cost of different design variants for new investment projects.

new traffic (if the short-run marginal cost actually is lower than average variable cost) on the traffic on the rest of the line must be considered. If the goods are sufficiently substitutable, and a lower price is offered to new traffic, part of the old traffic will withdraw, leaving some of the periodically renewable variable costs uncovered and requiring the railroad management to rethink its policy. From the viewpoint of the regulatory commission, this cost concept should help to adjudicate issues concerning unfair competition: rates below short-run marginal costs presumably would be designed to drive out competitors, since there can be no other immediate economic advantage to the railroad from doing this.

What is the evidence on short-run marginal costs? The best study of the subject is again that of Borts, which suggests that short-run marginal cost is about 5 to 18% less than average total variable cost, with variation depending on shipping patterns and relative input costs, as is suggested by the regional differences in cost patterns. The essential details are shown in Table 6.1, column 2. The elasticity of variable costs when multiplied by the average variable cost yields the short-run marginal cost in column 3. The reader is reminded that the costs under consideration exclude fixed capital costs. All Borts' costs are what we have called "variable costs," some cost accounts being periodically renewable costs and some being short-run marginal costs. Therefore, what he calls the "elasticity of cost" is what we are calling the "elasticity of variable cost."

Under both of his models, the elasticity of variable cost is highest in the east, lowest in the south, and intermediate in the west. The relationship for each size class under each formulation also observes this pattern. This suggests that there are differences in regional cost and shipping patterns. For example, the lines in the east may already be so overcrowded that, while an additional shipment will not ncessitate proportional increases in administration costs, it may raise marshaling yard expenses due to congestion. In the south, with lower densities, additional shipments do not have similar effects.

Although the regional patterns are consistent, there are differences in the levels estimated by the two models. These differences in some cases are sizable—as high as 28% for the smallest southern railroads and nearly 100% for the smallest eastern railroads. The fact that the difference among the largest two classes tends to be smaller suggests that, where it is a question of analyzing larger lines, it is inconsequential whether capital or length of track is used as the size indicator. Moreover, the differences in elasticity are still relatively small when compared with the kinds of rate differentials that one often encounters and must evaluate in practice, which frequently amount to differences of 100% and more—far beyond the differences in elasticity estimates derived by the two equation formulations. We consider some examples in Chapter 8.

The elasticity estimate enables us to determine the minimum justifiable price for new traffic in relation to the average cost for existing traffic by calculating the short-run marginal cost. This is given by the elasticity of variable cost multiplied by the LRAVC. To do this we must, naturally, assume that all other aspects of the comparison are constant. For example, we assume that the new traffic has the same characteristics as existing traffic with respect to type of rolling stock, percentage of empty loads, and so on. Evidently, if the new traffic is to move in the deadhead direction or requires expensive refrigerator cars, the short-run marginal costs should be adjusted downward or upward in light of the special cost effect that such movements imply.

Finally, we note that the ICC has employed for purposes of rate regulation an estimate of 0.8 as the relationship between the cost of new traffic and the average cost of existing traffic. (ICC docket no. 34013 quoted in Griliches, 1972). This measure—termed "percent variable"— is in fact an elasticity, the percent change in cost accompanying a 1% change in traffic. However, it is important to note that the costs referred to by the ICC are total costs, that is, the sum of our total variable costs *and* total fixed costs. This estimate may be quite consistent with those of Borts who estimates elasticities as low as 0.81 (for medium size southern railroads, ranging up to 1.19.) On the other hand, the ICC estimate of 80% of average cost may be too low, since the ICC average cost includes certain fixed costs that are excluded from the LRAVC, hence from the SRMC as explained in Section 1 of this chapter. The conclusion is that the ICC estimate of percent variable is not comparable with Borts' estimate of elasticity of (variable) cost discussed in this chapter.

3.2 Cost—Distance Relationships

The fact that there are certain sources of decreasing ton-mile cost associated with any shipment is sometimes mistaken for decreasing distance-incremental cost behavior. While the loading, coupling, billing, discharging, and so on are all sources of decreasing average ton-mile cost on any given shipment, it takes only a moment's reflection to see that this really tells us nothing about the cost of shipping an *extra* mile at distances of 100, 200, or 625 miles! To the contrary, once one begins to think about it and ask where the sources of decreasing distance-incremental costs may be, he quickly concludes that there are none.

The cost of an extra mile at any distance should be a linear function of the cost of rail wear, cleaning of ballast, rolling stock depreciation, fuel input, and so on, all of which are independent of distance. One could then distinguish between all of the shipment preparation charges, such as those named above that are matters either for general railroad administration or for marshaling yard operations, and the line-haul costs themselves, with the latter being a linear homogeneous function, that is, one in which there are no sources of decreasing costs.

This conclusion is borne out by empirical analysis. Once again, Borts' work is dominant. In the study already cited he computes the incremental line-haul cost for the region-size classification that he has used throughout. For each size he calculates the incremental cost at the lower bound, upper bound, and average of the average hauls of the lines represented within each region-size class. We present the results in column 4 of Table 6.1.* There is remarkable stability for any region-size class and within any region as well. This means that railroad rate schedules that involve a decreasing *incremental* rate as contrasted with a decreasing average rate schedule, are misinformed. This finding is further supported by Borts' study of microcost relations to be discussed below. (Although we observed above that, in principle, the incremental cost at any distance is constant, in fact the cost of the line-haul may be higher at short distances than at long distances because at short distances the shipments move through more congested suburban areas. Thus there would be some justification for having somewhat higher average line-haul rates for short shipments than for long shipments. But we must be careful not to confuse the *geographic environmental* effect with the pure distance effect). We review several rate schedules in Chapter 8.

3.3 Other Micro Relations

A great deal of interest for transport planners attaches to the use of different inputs such as labor, fuel, and equipment and track maintenance in order to anticipate the various factor input requirements under different design alternatives. Again the best work in the field has been done by Borts (1952). The results are summarized in Table 6.2. The elasticity of factor use, defined as the percent change in factor input accompanying a 1% change in output, for the four aforementioned fac-

* Note that in Borts' source table (Table VII, p. 127) the relevant column for Cost Equation II is called simply "marginal cost" rather than "marginal cost length of haul," as the corresponding column for Cost Equation I is headed. Also, note that in his study the term marginal cost is usually used for α, the coefficient of car-miles in the basic equation.

Table 6.2   Summary Microcost Characteristics Estimated by Borts

		Elasticity	
Activity	Adjustable Input	of Adjustable Factor Use	of Total Adjustable Factor Cost[a]
Line haul	Labor	1.15	
	Fuel	0.57	
	Equipment maintenance	0.98	
	Track maintenance	0.92	
			0.94
Switching	Labor	0.92	
yard operations	Fuel	0.67	
	Equipment maintenance	0.77	
	Track maintenance	1.61	
			1.03

Source.   Borts (1952), pp. 76–77. Cited by permission.
[a] Weighted average of the four adjustable factor use elasticities.

tors, is shown together with the elasticity of cost of these four factors for two activities—line haul and switching. Again Borts used two models; we include here the results of Model I only. This is a somewhat better formulation for both the line-haul process and the switching process, as measured by the number of significant variables determined to be present in each of the formulations. For the line-haul process in Model I, 75% of the independent variables were found to have significant coefficients, while only 60% of the variables in Model II were found to differ significantly from zero. For the switching process, the percentages were 58% (14 out of 24) versus 50%. We note that we have used the term elasticity of "total adjustable factor cost" to refer to these four inputs only (Borts uses the term "elasticity of variable cost") to avoid confusion with the "total variable cost" used in this chapter, which includes, among other things, administration and equipment depreciation.

Most of the line-haul elasticities are around unity, fuel being the exception. Unfortunately, there is not enough information in the paper to speculate on the reasons for the decreasing unit cost of fuel inputs.

Borts' equations permit the analyst to see how the factor inputs vary with different variables, thus serving as a kind of simulation of cost behavior under different design and operating assumptions. For example, in the line-haul process, the relationship between the input of labor and freight car-miles, carloads, empties, capacity, and miles of track is studied. The percentage change in cost of the respective input and a 1% change in output ranging from 1.15 to 0.57%, and the percent change in the total input of all four factors being 0.94%. The switching process uses different explanatory variables. The study represents an extremely valuable source of insight and information for the analyst.

REFERENCES

Association of American Railroads (1965), *Railroad Transportation* (Washington, D.C.: Association of American Railroads, Bureau of Railway Economics).

Borts, George (1952), "Production Relations in the Railway Industry," *Econometrica*, Vol. 20, No. 1, January.

——— (1960), "The Estimation of Rail Cost Functions," *Econometrica*, Vol. 19, No. 1, January.

Griliches, Zvi (1972), "Cost Allocation in Railroad Regulation," *The Bell Journal of Economics and Management Science*, Vol. 3, No. 1, Spring.

CHAPTER

7

Shadow Prices

1 OBJECTIVES OF SHADOW PRICES

The principles elaborated in Part 1 for covering transport costs, and the discussion of transport costs in the preceding three chapters have not yet touched on one aspect of transport price and cost analysis which is extremely important for public sector investment and pricing decisions. This is the possibility that market prices fail to reflect true social costs. Where there are differences between market prices and true social costs, it is necessary to employ shadow prices to reflect true social cost more accurately.

Even after market distortions are recognized and shadow prices are introduced, the planner must distinguish between his analysis of true social costs—hence the best technological mix from an investment point of view—and what users will do on the basis of their continuing confrontation of, and response to, market prices. Though obvious, this is sometimes lost sight of, with the result that good planning of technology mix and investment may fail to bear fruit because users respond to different market signals. For example, if the planner incorporates the marginal social cost of motor vehicle transportation, which includes congestion costs that are imposed by motorists on other drivers, into his analysis of urban transportation investment, he may conclude that public transit rather than additional road capacity is the correct direction for urban transport development. However, if the drivers are not made to confront a congestion surcharge, they will continue to behave as in the past, causing a welfare loss due to the operation at traffic levels greater than the optimal congestion level, accompanied by investment in public transit facilities that are not optimally utilized. Another example are the ports in many countries. Coastal shipping may be the most efficient transport option in the sense that the social cost of labor in ports is indeed low, even though the market price of this labor, owing to union restrictions, is high; but investment in coastal shipping may lead to increased traffic because of the high market prices that the users actually must pay in ports.

Still another example—from the recent past in Brazil. The labor force on the Federal Railway Network (REFESA) in the late 1960s was about 100,000 persons. About three-quarters of these workers were protected by job tenure legislation under the Codigo dos Leis de Trabalho, and had to be retained, even though many were clearly redundant. At that time the government was following a labor force reduction program through attrition, but there was undoubtedly a long way to go and until the efficient labor force was reached, excess workers had to be retained. Moreover, it is questionable whether they should be dismissed if dismissal meant that they would have to forgo income, since this would merely exacerbate the serious income inequalities already existing in Brazil. In addition, the government might encounter much political opposition if it attempted to retire workers early, even if pensions equal to full salary were paid, since many workers might feel humiliated and would resist such a move. In this case, the work force would have to be retained. But one should try to determine the amount of the annual railroad expense devoted to the redundant workers, subtract it from total railroad costs, and then calculate the cost per mile as a basis for traffic allocation, whether by long-range modal government decisions or by market decisions by firms. The latter should be accomplished by making the shadow price the market price itself. That is, the true social cost should be taken as the shadow cost of rail operations and should become the new market price, since the rest of the labor expenditure being borne by the railroad in this case does not reflect true social costs.* These considerations emphasize the need for the project-making

* Of course, other aspects of the railroad cost base should be sanitized. For example, the traditional neglect of rolling stock should be corrected. This and other adjustments for inflation and other factors would undoubtedly have *raised* rather than reduced rates on balance. (See Abouchar, 1970.)

agency to coordinate its activities with those of regulatory agencies, public finance organs, and other administrative organs.

It is analytically useful to classify shadow prices under five headings: (1) prices that emerge as the dual solution in the course of formal optimization procedures; (2) corrections for fiscal distortions, such as tariffs, excise taxes, and exchange rate distortions, that is, distortions introduced by the state fiscal authority; (3) labor cost adjustments required by frictions in the labor market; (4) capital market adjustments provoked by the failure of market interest rates to reflect the social opportunity cost of capital; and (5) congestion adjustments. We consider the first three types of shadow price in this chapter. Capital market adjustments are discussed in Part 3 on project evaluation. Congestion adjustments are treated in Part 4 where the theory and policy for congestion optimization are discussed.

It should be stressed that in this brief review all that can be done is indicate the major issues that must be taken account of when contemplating the introduction of shadow price adjustments.

2 SHADOW PRICES AS DUAL SOLUTION TO A FORMAL OPTIMIZATION

Shadow prices received their primary theoretical elaboration in the last twenty years in the development of linear programming analysis. In this approach, we are given a programming problem, which may be the maximization of some target function, subject to certain resource availability constraints. A typical example is the following problem of maximizing the value of the output of a vector of goods subject to input capacity constraints:

$$\max \sum_{i=1}^{m} A_i P_i = A_1 P_1 + A_2 P_2 + \cdots + A_m P_m$$

subject to:

$$A_1 c_{11} + A_2 c_{12} + \cdots + A_m c_{1m} \leq B_1$$
$$A_1 c_{21} + A_2 c_{22} \qquad + A_m c_{2m} \leq B_2$$
$$\vdots$$
$$A_1 c_{n1} + A_2 c_{n2} \qquad + A_m c_{nm} \leq B_n$$

Here P and X are the market price and quantity of commodity i, c_{ij} is the requirement of input i to a unit of output of commodity j, and B_j is the capacity constraint of input j.

The dual of this problem is a minimization problem that minimizes the inner product of two vectors, one consisting of the resource or capacity input constraint in physical terms (the B_j) and the other containing price weights (R_j) for these inputs.

$$\min \sum_{j=1}^{n} B_j R_j = B_1 R_1 = B_2 R_2 + \cdots + B_n R_n$$

subject to:

$$R_1 c_{11} + R_2 c_{21} + \cdots + R_n c_{n1} \geq P_1$$
$$R_1 c_{12} + R_2 c_{22} \qquad\quad + R_n c_{n2} \geq P_2$$
$$\vdots \qquad\qquad\qquad\qquad \vdots$$
$$R_1 c_{1m} + R_2 c_{2m} \qquad\quad + R_n c_{nm} \geq P_m$$

The price weights R_j are regarded as the economic rents or use values of the available resources under the market prices existing for the outputs. In effects, they distribute the total revenue calculated in the maximand among the various inputs. Their economic significance is twofold. First, they show the value at the margin of the various input processes to the producer under the optimal production solution and indicate, for example, the amount that a rational producer would be willing to pay to acquire one more unit of capacity of input j. Second, no product should be produced unless its market price P_i is at least equal to the opportunity cost of its production, as measured by the inner product of its physical inputs (c_{ij}) by the imputed rents (R_i). This is shown by the constraint equations of the dual solution. Incidentally, the dual valuations have the property that once they are chosen, the firm left to itself and concerned with cost minimization, in terms of the dual prices, would be led to produce exactly the same bill of goods as it would do by solving the primal problem.

Historically, these dual prices came to be associated with the concept of shadow prices, at first exclusively. However, if shadow prices were to be restricted to such a concept they would have little importance at the level of the national economy. There are several reasons for this.

First, at the national level, many products are both outputs and inputs. It is meaningful to impute input prices for internal accounting purposes within the firm for production shop control or new input (capacity) acquisitions, where the input prices are derived from their potential contributions to production. But when the same product may be both output and input, what is the meaning of having one price for the output and another price for the input, which is a clear possibility? If steel ingot is a constraint on production and is given a shadow price higher than the market price, the market price should change. In a market economy it will do so automatically; if the market is sluggish, or in a nonmarket economy, it should be changed by fiat. Once this is done, it would obviate the need for a system of double prices. This is related to the discussion in Section 1 concerning the need to harmonize the shadow prices used by planners with the effective market signals for users.

Another obstacle to the use of linear program dual prices at the level of the national economy is that the national economy consists of tens of thousands of distinct products. Making them location specific, (e.g., galvanizing capacity in western Pennsylvania) would vastly increase the number of products, and it would be further complicated, since some outputs are intermediate inputs on which other production technologies depend. The technological alternatives and complexities in the corresponding linear program would defy solution by a standard algorithm. To simplify by aggregating into a few dozen sectors would probably give meaningless results. Taking average technological coefficients might solve the problem on paper but yield a solution that is not feasible in practice. In this case, what significance should attach to the dual prices?

We point out that a problem would remain if the maximand were cast in the form of a vector of outputs in fixed proportions, with no explicit prices in the aggregate function. Presumably the fixed proportions reflect the preferences of the planning ministry, which should reflect underlying scarcities, which are what the shadow prices are supposed to measure. Again, if there were an inconsistency between market price and shadow price it should be corrected at this point, so that, again, it would be unnecessary to have two kinds of valuations for the given commodity in future.*

---

* The use of dual prices has sometimes been recommended for purposes of transport flow optimization. This is a narrower application than the one discussed above, and since it deals with transportation it is of special interest to readers of this book. However, even here there are problems that are not generally recognized. In general, discussion of dual transport shadow prices has not examined carefully the economic and institutional framework necessary for their successful application, and overconfidence in their ability to rationalize transport operations has developed from this neglect. Thus it has been argued that calculation of shadow prices—essentially a set of differential rents in the producing regions, on one hand, and surcharges in the consumer regions, on the other—could provide a basis for transport rates to permit efficient decentralized transport decision-making. In fact, however, since the market prices in the consumer region would be affected, either absolutely inelastic demand by the consuming region or other special properties for the demand relations would have to be assumed. Since, generally, these could not be assumed without serious compromise with reality, it follows that the dual shadow prices could not be relied on to achieve the desired decentralization. On the other hand, the pattern of dif-

3 SHADOW PRICES AS ADJUSTMENTS FOR FISCAL DISTORTIONS

Market prices for many products include indirect taxes, import duties, and disequilibrium exchange rate components. Many writers argue that these components do not reflect true social costs and should be deducted from observed market prices. For example, Little and Mirrlees argue that "To get the accounting price [shadow price] of the input, we would like to subtract input duties and other indirect taxes" (1968, p. 152), as well as other distorting influences, such as the excess of wages or profits over those that represent true social costs.

The solution can never be as simple or as straightforward as suggested in the quotation for two main reasons: (1) A price component, though labeled an excise tax or tariff, may in fact represent the cost of some (possibly intermediate) service provided to the consumer of the good in question. (2) The instrument in question may be applied in individual cases for two essentially different purposes—income distribution or resource allocation. Whether or not it constitutes a distortion will depend on this purpose. We will consider these in turn.

An excise tax, in principle, is a mechanism for redistribution of income. It can easily be imposed on a graduated basis, with lower rates on necessities of life, although in practice it frequently does turn out to be regressive. It may happen, however, that in a particular situation a tax, although nominally an excise tax, should be considered as a payment for some service. In the next chapter we will see that this was precisely the situation in the Yugoslav truck transport sector in the early 1970, and that what is there referred to as a "turnover tax," (*porez na promet*), a sales or excise tax, should really be construed as a user charge. The user charge that the trucks should be paying is higher than what they are nominally paying for road use (i.e., higher than what is termed the "road user tax" in Yugoslavia), but is approximately equal to the total of the two taxes combined. Truck transport-intensive goods should include this turnover tax component as part of their price, not merely because it is there, but because only by including it does the price reflect the true social cost. In this case a serious mistake would be made if we simply netted out the excise taxes to determine true social cost. On the other hand, if the combined total of the two taxes exceeded the warranted user charge, the total tax should be reduced.

---

ferential rent and consuming region surcharges (together with regional production cost information) can be used to give an indication about where to locate new capacity. This problem is discussed in Abouchar (1969.)

It is conceivable that similar situations might arise in regard to import tariffs. In some particular situation a tariff might constitute a charge for services rendered, such as state service on behalf of the importer, although this is less likely to be the situation with tariffs than with excise taxes.

The other obstacle to the formulation of a general rule concerning the treatment of these fiscal instruments originates in the function of the instrument—income distribution versus resource allocation. This is likely to be more important for import tariffs or exchange rate distortions than for excise taxes, except by chance, as in the example above, although it remains conceivable for the latter as well.

Suppose that there is a tariff of 30% on wheeled service vehicles, such as trucks, road building equipment, and cranes, and 60% on automobiles. It is frequently recommended that the tariffs on all these vehicles be eliminated when it is necessary to calculate the costs of highway transportation in developing countries. Let us look more closely. Consider first the automobiles. Obviously, the consumers of automobiles are from upper income classes. The tariff definitely does have a redistributive effect, anc to this extent might properly be deducted from market price to determine the correct shadow price. However, it may also, or instead, be the objective of the tariff to encourage domestic production to substitute for imports. In this case, a car purchased abroad represents a discouragement to domestic industry and reduces national income or national income growth below what it would have been if the automobile were produced at home. If national income growth is the success indicator for the economy (we argue in Part III that it should be), this represents a cost to the economy, since it means making national income less than it would otherwise be. Consider the following illustration.

Suppose that two projects are being reviewed for urban transit in a new city that is to be built: public transit versus an automobile option. Suppose the vehicle depreciation costs of the two are 8 million and 10 million pesos respectively, with all vehicles produced domestically. Assume, for simplicity, that the sum of labor, fuel operating inputs, and other investment costs are the same for both projects. We assume further that the same resources would be used to produce either the automobiles or the transit vehicles. In this case, we would obviously prefer the public transit alternative. This involves a net release of 2 million pesos worth of resources for use in other activities. From the welfare point of view, national income will be higher by 2 million pesos: the task of urban commutation will be "purchased" for 8 million pesos annually, as it is in other cities, and 2 million pesos worth of resources are liberated to be spent on production of other consumer goods, such as washing machines.* The total contribution to national income is 10 million pesos.

Suppose now that instead of the domestically produced cars, imports are used. Since (we are assuming) foreign productivity is 40% higher, the annual vehicle cost (excluding tariffs) is 6 million pesos. Neglecting transport costs, this is the price at the importing country's port. A tariff of 2/3 is imposed, raising the import price to 10 million pesos.

If the tariff-exclusive price is used for the investment decision, the automobile option will be selected, since it is only 6 million pesos. We will now be "purchasing" the urban transport activity for 6 million pesos. The foreign exchange needed to buy the vehicles will have to be earned by exports. Owing to the domestic productivity differential, the 8 million pesos worth of resources that are spared by not having to produce the public transit vehicles at home can be used to produce exports. Owing to the productivity differential, export prices will have to be subsidized, in this case by 4 million, to sell competitively for 6 million pesos abroad. The welfare-relevant contribution to national income in this case would be just the 8 million pesos, which is the price of purchasing the urban transit activity in other cities. National income is lower than it would have been under the public transit alternative with all inputs produced domestically.

In the foregoing comparison we have assumed implicitly that the quality of service is the same. But obviously, taking account of quality differentials does not introduce any problems of principle. Accordingly, the imported cost, including tariff, should be taken into account in deciding between private transport and public transit. In actual cases it will happen that the entire tariff should not be construed as a desire to provide incentives for the local industry—indeed, to take the extreme case, imagine that all of the tariff is an income distribution instrument. Suppose that foreign industry has no cost advantages over domestic industry so that no protection is necessary. Nevertheless, there is some demand for foreign cars simply because of differences in styling patterns or prestige value. In this case, the sacrifice to national income through the purchase of a foreign vehicle will be zero, and the automobile tariffs should *not* be included in the prices for investment decisions.

The example just given is somewhat improbable; the public authority in a developing economy would rarely have to make such a decision, since, by and large, the potential riders on the transit mode would be

---

* We are assuming that the decision is being made within the fully employed sector of the economy and that the unused resources will in fact find employment. If this is not the case the analysis is more complex, as we see in Chapter 13.

unlikely to own or be potential buyers of automobiles. Thus while the automobile tariff would be a combination of income distribution and import substitution instruments, this particular item would have little significance in evaluating any investment projects. But what is important to keep in mind is that the tariffs on vehicles are frequently set as a class, or there is some prior disposition to apply overall tariffs to all classes of some commodity and then make adjustments depending on the national "need" for particular items or subclasses. In this hypothetical economy, the wheeled service vehicles are assumed to have a 30% tariff, while automobiles have 60%. How should it be treated?

The tariff on the wheeled service vehicles should be disregarded or included depending on what we believe to be the purpose of the tariff. If it is designed as an import substitution inducement, it should be included in the price, since a purchase from abroad means a reduced output domestically, that is, a reduction in the generation of national income. The foreign selling country, to be sure, would spend the money on exports from the home country, but because of the cost differential, the amount of employment generated would be less than if the money were spent on the equipment in the home country to begin with as above (i.e., if the tariff is 30% and the import is 1.3 million pesos, the foreign supplier would get 1 million pesos to spend in the home country, generating national income of 1 million pesos, whereas if 1.3 million pesos worth of domestic production were purchased, the national income contribution would be 1.3 million pesos). If a different mode were employed (or different location pattern developed) which required only domestically produced goods, the contribution to national income would be 1.3 million pesos. Therefore, the tariff should be *included* as part of the true social cost of the road building equipment, eventually being reflected in the cost of building the road and, finally, in the estimation of transport costs in the motor transport sector.

Disequilibria in exchange rates should be treated similarly. For example, the home country's currency may be undervalued in order to stimulate exports. Suppose that the exchange rate is set at 0.5, while the equilibrium rate is 0.67, that is, $2.00/3.00 pesos. To import a locomotive costing $300,000 would then translate into 6000,000 pesos or 450,000 pesos, according to these two exchange rates. The argument for adjustment is that, since the exchange rate is undervalued by one-third in relation to the present equilibrium exchange rate, the extra 150,000 currency units do not represent a real cost to the economy, and the locomotive should be priced domestically at 450,000 units. However, to proceed in this way goes precisely counter to the objective of the undervaluation, which was to improve the economy's competitive position abroad, that is, to reduce the price of its exports and increase the price of its imports. This undervaluation and the resulting higher landed cost of the import will ideally reflect the intensity of the government's preference for domestic production. An affirmative decision to use an imported good or technology is justified only if the benefit to the decision-making authority, as measured, say, by the cost savings it is permitted to realize through use of the imported good, exceeds this premium. This can be ensured only if, in choosing a minimum-cost project alternative, it compares the exchange premium, along with all other costs, to the benefits to be generated, that is, if it uses the prices based on the market, disequilibrium exchange rate and does *not* make a shadow adjustment.

The foregoing analysis relates to exchange rate disequilibria based on allocation rather than distribution goals. If, on the other hand, the exchange rate undervaluation is designed purely to stem the outflow of domestic currency, and to penalize those who would do so, it may be regarded as an income distribution activity, and the calculation of true social cost should then be based on the equilibrium exchange rate. In practice, however, countries that have exchange premiums designed for this purpose usually have internal industrialization objectives that are enhanced by undervaluing the exchange rate, and the two motives tend to become interrelated. But if they can be disentangled for the calculation of costs in individual projects, so much to the good.

It goes without saying that the actual determination of the amount of the exchange rate disequilibrium, or the warranted industrialization-related tariff, requires careful study. This is true even in the absence of any distributional objectives. The estimate should be based on considerations of relative labor productivity at home and abroad, but it is complicated by the existence of movement in invisibles. In many cases the Ministry of Finance or the Ministry of Planning will have investigated these issues, and the rates that it sets should, in the absence of a good reason to the contrary, be accepted and used in the normal situation. Of course, in obvious situations—such as a widely fluctuating exchange rate observed over the previous few years—a newcomer to the scene might wish to question whether the exchange rate does reflect the proper amount of undervaluation, since it would be unlikely that the "equilibrium rate" itself would be fluctuating so wildly or that the productivity differential would be so mercurial.

4 DISTORTIONS IN THE LABOR MARKET

Many economists lay primary stress on labor as a source of distortion between market prices and true social costs. Minimum wage legislation in backward countries, as well as advanced economies, is commonly thought to lead to wages that are high in relation to the productivity of labor. In this case, the price of labor and the prices of labor-intensive goods are overstated: market price exceeds true social cost. Conversely, commodities and activities that are raw materials-intensive and/or capital-intensive, acquire market prices understating their value. This then leads to production techniques that are capital-intensive. For example, high-grade roads rather than more primitive designs; concrete dams rather than earthen dams; and fuel-intensive transport modes.

Other sources of distortion of labor costs in the economy include job tenure legislation or regulations of output norms which have the effect of increasing the payments to labor in given activities or institutions.

One of the main kinds of evidence that there are wage distortions is the coexistence of minimum wages and secular unemployment, that is, unemployment that is persistent rather than related to dips in the business cycle. It is argued that the unemployed workers obviously would not be able to produce for an employer an amount equal to the wage they would have to be given if they were employed, or else they *would* be employed. That is to say, the wage exceeds their marginal product and so, for purposes of investment decision, labor prices should be reduced until equality with the marginal product is reached.

Some writers have questioned whether in fact the wage is higher than the marginal product, explaining the coexistence of high unemployment and minimum wages in terms of the low productivity of the unemployed owing to their lack of skills. These writers argue that the minimum wage does in fact correspond to the greater cost of training necessary to achieve the higher skills of those who are employed. In this case it would not be necessary to adjust market wages, since they already reflect the productivity of workers and the costs of acquiring their skills.

Moreover, labor cost adjustments are a particularly delicate issue in countries with serious interregional differences in employment. If investment is allocated centrally on the basis of some agreed upon criterion, and different prices are used in different regions for what appears to be the same kind of labor, charges of regional bias are inevitable, even though the planners are motivated by the best intentions. When political pressures arise, or when the motives are less pure, this interregional wage variation will be thought still more arbitrary and may discredit the use of economic analysis in the investment allocation process.*

---

* But still other considerations are relevant. For example, we must recognize that while wages might overstate the productivity of labor, nevertheless a more labor-intensive

Obviously, the general issue is far from settled. What has been said shows the main considerations that must be made in evaluating public financial ground rules and in reviewing projects, modal split, and pricing structure. Thus the difficulty of properly calculating interregional productivity differences, together with the accompanying problems in their use, as noted in the preceding paragraph, reinforce the recommendations about regional income transfers and investment policies in federal systems that we presented in Chapters 2 and 3 and to which we return in Chapter 8.

REFERENCES

Abouchar, Alan (1969), "The Transportation Dual and Economic Planning," *The Annals of Regional Science,* Vol. 3, No. 2, December.

——— (1970), "Pricing Rationality and Deficits on the Brazilian Railroads," *Journal of Transport Economics and Policy,* Vol. 4, No. 3, September.

——— (1972), "Project Delay in the Analysis of Factor Substitution and Shadow Wages," *Canadian Journal of Economics,* Vol. 5, No. 3, August.

Little, Ian M. D., and James A. Mirrlees (1968), *Manual of Industrial Project Analysis* (Paris: OECD Development Centre).

---

technology might lead to delays, which also involve costs and may not be reflected in market prices. The cost to the economy of the delayed project completion that results from the more labor-intensive technology can be taken into account in either of two ways: (1) at the project analysis stage, by considering the effect of additional labor input on a particular construction schedule and on deferred benefits or (2) by devising a twice-adjusted shadow wage for each industry. After first being adjusted for the underemployment within the economy, it is then corrected to reflect the cost of the deferred benefit that longer project times usually involve. The second procedure provides for greater automaticity—the correct price could be given to project-makers who would then be relieved of the burden of making numerous construction technique variants for each project (Abouchar, 1972).

CHAPTER

8

Using Cost Analysis to Evaluate Pricing Policies

1 INTRODUCTION

If the underlying price structure for transport activities is rational, we can assume that people are making socially efficient decisions regarding location and transportation and are choosing efficiently among transport modes. Therefore, the first step in any survey of a nation's transport sector or of individual modes should be to review the pricing policies that are in effect. Since almost always there are insufficient local cost data, the analyst must learn to make do by reference to experience elsewhere (such as that presented in previous chapters), properly adjusted for local conditions, and by logical extrapolation. The alternative—doing nothing on the ground that perfect data are unavailable—opens the door to all kinds of distorted transport prices, with their distorting effects on the economy.

This chapter presents the results of cost and pricing studies conducted in a number of countries in widely different geographical and socioeconomic conditions. They are presented here as a guide to the translation of the theoretical and empirical cost relationships of Chapters 4 to 7, to help handle data in new situations, and to illustrate ways to overcome data deficiencies. Chapter 9 applies the cost analyses to the evaluation of modal split. Further aspects of the theory of cost behavior that are of special relevance to project evaluation are discussed in Part 3, and some relationships to urban decisions are examined in Part 4.

2 PRICING IN THE MOTOR TRANSPORT SECTOR— YUGOSLAVIA

From the viewpoint of the public sector, the main interest attaches to the charges imposed on direct road users (passenger and cargo vehicles). Prices charged by the direct users or operators to final shippers or consumers fall within the province of the state in its role as regulatory authority, rather than as executive, except when it performs an operating role through public sector transport firms. Trucking, as an essentially competitive industry owing to the absence of scale economies, can generally be assumed to have efficient pricing decisions to final shippers if the prices to the direct users are rational.

2.1 Efficiency of Yugoslav Highway Charges

Two views prevail concerning the susceptibility of the highway sector to analysis from the viewpoint of pricing efficiency. One view holds this sector to be inherently incapable of being rationally analyzed because of conflicting criteria and data inadequacy. But in Part 1 we presented a theory of efficient pricing that is reconcilable with data availability, so that this view may be rejected. The other view is that efficiency is best measured by the degree to which public revenues that are nominally generated by road users approximate the public expenditures made by the road authority. For example, the International Road Federation in its annual yearbook compares total road sector revenue to total expenditure to show that the road sector is self-paying, hence by implication efficient. Total revenue is defined to include, for example, all sales tax and automobile fuel tax revenues. Thus the possibility that many vehicle interclass and urban-interurban distortions may exist, masked by high excise revenues, is overlooked. (International Road Federation, 1971, pp. 152-171). This is clearly a defective approach.*

---

* The recent debate on highway economics in Canada stems from the notion that revenue-expenditure comparison is a good approach, with the earliest papers focusing primarily on the handling of various revenue sources and expenditure items. (See Dalvi, 1969; Conklin et al., 1970.)

The approach that we proposed in Part 1 requires first the determination of the "warranted user charge" for each vehicle class. This consists of a vehicle-variable cost and a demand-related component to apportion joint costs. The latter, in turn, requires an estimate of total annual joint cost. Finally, we compare this estimate with actual payments. For this we must estimate total annual payments and classify them into user charges and other taxes. We proceed according to this plan.

2.2 Vehicle-Variable Costs

Following the generally accepted notions of economic efficiency, the sunk cost of constructing the existing highway network will not be considered to be a current cost. That part of the investment which is subject to wear and must be replaced, chiefly the pavement and sub-base, is a current cost, however, and must be assigned to the traffic classes according to the deterioration that each imposes. The AASHO road test coefficients, which were discussed in Chapter 5, are the best measure of the deterioration imposed on different pavement designs by traffic components, and we apply them to the allocation of size-variable costs in this chapter. In our discussion truck designations refer to the payload. Three truck sizes are used in the analysis: small (4-ton load), medium (10-ton load), and large (20-ton load). The loads are converted to gross vehicle weights, which is the basis of the AASHO equivalence coefficients, by applying U.S. Department of Transport (1970) vehicle specifications. Metric-ton adjustments are made where appropriate.

We must first estimate the stock of the various vehicle classes and their annual runs, and the total annual road network deterioration. To estimate stock we proceed from the official transportation and communications yearbook (Socialistička federativna republika Jugoslavija, 1970). In 1970 there were about 850,000 vehicles registered in Yugoslavia including 720,000 cars, 120,000 trucks (and truck tractors), and 15,000 buses. The average run is 50,000 kilometers for trucks and 70,000 kilometers for buses. We here assume the average run for large trucks to be 75,000 kilometers, for medium trucks 65,000 kilometers, for small trucks 40,000 kilometers, and for cars 15,000 kilometers. A further calculation is based on an annual run of 115,000 kilometers for large trucks. We would still have to know the interurban shares of these mileages, as well as the detailed distribution of trucks. We assume that the medium 10-ton capacity trucks number 40,000 and the 20-ton capacity trucks number 30,000 (the statistics list 30,500 truck tractors). This involves some simplifications, which are unavoidable in the absence of more complete census and sample data.

There is, of course, no physical indicator of annual road deterioration, and we base our deterioration estimate on the annual financial accounts. Yugoslav road expenditure data are classified by maintenance, reconstruction and modernization, and new construction. Reconstruction is supposed to refer to improvements to existing roads, including base works, while modernization is supposed to refer to simple repaving. There is undoubtedly some overlap here, but it is unimportant because both activities vary with vehicle size in the sense used here, that is, they represent efforts to rebuild a deteriorated pavement. More important is the overlap of modernization/reconstruction and maintenance with new construction. It is very likely that new construction contains some blacktopping or upgrading of gravel roads, both of which are vehicle-size related. We will assume that half of maintenance and one-third of new construction are really vehicle-size related.

Table 8.1 shows the average annual expenditure by category for 1969–1970. It is assumed that all reconstruction and modernization, one-half of maintenance, and one-third of new construction are size variable in the sense used here. Unfortunately, however, we must work with 1971 user charge data, making it necessary to estimate 1971 expenditures, which had not yet been reported at time of analysis. To do this we project forward the 1970 expenditure by 25%, a rate that is consistent with informal estimates in Yugoslavia.

Table 8.1   Estimation of Road Expenditure Categories and Size-Variable Shares in Yugoslavia, 1971[a]

	Average Annual Expenditure, 1969–70		1971		Percent of Estimated Expenditure in this Category
	Billion D	Percent of Total	Estimated Expenditure (Billion D)	Size-Variable Cost Share (Billion D)	
Reconstruction and Modernization	1.3	54	1.690	1.690	100
New construction	.5	21	.660	.220	33
Maintenance	.6	25	.780	.390	50
Total	2.4	100	3.130	2.300	

Source.   Data as presented in Abouchar (1974).

[a] Total 1971 expenditure assumes a 25% annual growth over 1970. (1970 assumed to be D 2.500 billion.) Annual five-year plan calls for average 1971–1975 expenditure of D 5.2 billion.

To determine the size-variable cost per unit, we must first convert total traffic into equivalent traffic units (ETU) by applying the AASHO coefficients to the estimated traffic. The ETU calculations are shown in Table 8.2. Backhauls are assumed to be half-loads; other procedures are explained in the footnote. Total ETU of 5687 million units is then divided into the total size-variable cost of D 2.3 billion from Table 8.1. This gives a variable cost of 40.4 paras per ETU.* For each class, this is then multiplied by the average of the loaded and backhaul coefficients, divided by the total gross vehicle tonnage, and adjusted to a metric ton basis. For example, for the 20-ton capacity trucks we get: 40.4(1.92 + 0.42) 0.5 = 47.3 paras per vehicle-kilometer. This gives 47.3/(36 + 25) 0.5 = 1.55 paras per ton-kilometer, or 1.7 paras per metric ton-kilometer. (See Table 8.4.)

2.3   Demand-Related Component

The balance of maintenance and new construction should be priced according to demand. For new alignments, the differential price that a truck should be willing to pay is equal to the cost reduction from the new road. This can be appproximated by the saving in driver time. We assume that route rectification, combined with faster hourly speeds, doubles the hourly mileage calculated in terms of the old route (i.e., the 4000 kilometers between points A and B, which could be traveled in 10 hours on the old route, can be covered in 5 hours on the new route). The 1970 average truck driver wage was about D 1250† or D 8.4 per hour. Dividing this by the 40-kilometer per hour effective distance saving gives an average saving of 21.0 paras per vehicle-kilometer. This saving per kilometer is then divided by the average gross vehicle tonnage as shown in Table 8.3 to get the saving per gross ton-kilometer. Since there are usually two drivers on long-distance shipments, the gross ton-kilometer saving for 20-ton capacity trucks must be doubled.

The estimated saving will be realized only by those using the new roads. If we assume that this amounts to 20% of the traffic in any given year, the saving must be divided by 5 to get the average saving per vehicle. We disregard the savings accruing to vehicles on other routes as inconsequential. Also neglected is the saving through reduced fuel con-

---

* 100 paras = 1 dinar.

† The average income for all truck drivers in 1969 was D 1173. Data for 1970 were not yet available. The 1970 truck driver wage is assumed to grow at the same rate as do other wages in the economic sector (6%). See Socialistička federativna republika Jugoslavija (1971), pp. 268, 270.

Table 8.2 Calculation of Equivalent Traffic Units for Five Traffic Classes in Yugoslavia, 1970

Description of Vehicle	Load[a]	(1) Stock (000)	(2) Vehicle Average Weight (tons)	(3) Average Annual Run (000)	(4) Ton-Kilometers (bills) (1) × (2) × (3)	(5) Percent of Total ton-km	(6) Weight per Axle (000 lb)	(7) Average AASHO Equivalence Coefficient	ETU Vehicle-Kilometers (millions) (1) × (3) × (7)	Percent of Total
Cars (medium)	3 passengers	720	2.2	15	23.4	14.2	2.2	0.0002	2	Negligible
Trucks										
Small (4-ton capacity— RUP No. 5)	Full	50	7.5	20	7.5	4.5	7.5	0.035	35	0.6
	Half	50	5.5	20	5.5	3.3	5.5	0.01	10	0.2
Medium (10-ton capacity—RUP No. 8)	Full	40	20.0	32.5	26.0	15.8	20.0	1.57	2041	35.9
	Half	40	14.0	32.5	18.2	11.0	14.0	0.34	442	7.8
Large (20-ton capacity— Tandem-axle RUP No. 12)	Full	30	36.0	37.5	40.5	24.5	36.0	1.92	2160	38.0
	Half	30	25.0	37.5	28.1	17.0	25.0	0.42	472	8.3
Buses	40 passengers	15	15.0	70.0	15.8	9.6	15.0	0.5	525	9.2
Total					165.0	100.0			5687	100

[a] Truck capacity-loaded weight relations based on data presented by U.S. Department of Transport (1970). RUP designations refer to specifications on pages 10–11.

107

Table 8.3 Calculation of Road User Contributions in Yugoslavia, 1971

Vehicle Class[a]	(1) Average[b] Vehicle Weight (metric tons)	(2) Annual Mileage (000 km)	(3) Registration fee (D)	(4) Fuel[c] Consumption (liters)	(5) User Cost[a] per Liter (D)	(6) Total Fuel Cost (5) × (4)	(7) Total User Contribution (6) + (3)	(8) Total Ton-Kilometers (000) (1) × (2)	(9) Total User Contribution per Ton-Kilometer (paras) (7) ÷ (8)
Cars (medium)	2	15	170	2,160	0.55	1,190	1,360	30	4.5
Trucks									
Small (4-ton capacity)	5.9	40	1,725	10,620	1.2	12,740	14,465	236	6.1
Medium (10-ton capacity)									
Gas	15.4	65	6,000	29,250	1.2	35,100	41,100	1001	4.1
Diesel	15.4	65	6,000	22,500	0.64	14,490	20,490	1001	2.0
Large (20-ton capacity) diesel									
Moderate use	27.7	75	13,500	33,750	0.64	21,735	35,235	2078	1.7
Heavy use	27.7	110	13,500	49,500	0.64	31,880	45,380	3047	1.5
Buses (40-passenger) diesel	13.6	70	2,000	25,200	0.64	16,130	18,130	952	1.9

Source. Data as presented in Abouchar (1974).

[a] See footnote 5 Table 8.1

[b] Average of forward and backhaul, converted to metric tons.

[c] Based on U.S. Department of Transport, 1970.

[a] For cars—*naknada za puteve* only. For trucks—*naknada za puteve* plus turnover tax.

Table 8.4 Warranted User Charge and Actual User Contribution in Yugoslavia, 1971 (per metric ton, trucks only) (paras)

Vehicle	(1) Vehicle- Variable Cost[a]	(2) Demand- Related Component[b]	(3) Total Warranted User Charge	(4) Actual Contribution (Table 8.3)	(5) Actual ÷ Warranted User Charge
4-ton capacity	1.4	0.71	0.72	6.1	8.4
10-ton capacity					
Gas	2.27	0.27	2.54	4.1	1.61
Diesel	2.27	0.27	2.54	2.0	0.79
20-ton capacity	1.7	0.28	1.98	1.7	0.85

Source. Data as presented in Abouchar (1974).

[a] Variable cost is determined from the relationship P_{ETU} (1.1) $(C_L + C_{\frac{1}{2}})/(L_L + L_{\frac{1}{2}})$ where P_{ETU} = the average cost of size-variable components (reconstruction and modernization + ½ maintenance + ⅓ new construction); 1.1 is a metric-ton conversion factor; C_L and $C_{\frac{1}{2}}$ are the AASHO coefficients for full loads and half-loads; and L_L and $L_{\frac{1}{2}}$ are the gross tonnages under full and half-loads. For large trucks, we have

$$P_{ETU} = \frac{2.3 \ (10^{11}) \ \text{paras}}{5{,}687 \ \text{million}} = 40.4 \ \text{paras}$$

Therefore, total vehicle variable cost = $[40.4(1.92 + .42)/(36 + 25)]1.1 = 1.7$ para per metric ton-kilometer.

[b] Demand-related component is determined by dividing the hourly wage—8.4 dinars—by the increase in speed permitted by the new construction (assumed to be 40 kilometers) The saving per kilometer is then divided by the average gross vehicle tonnage (Table 8.3). This is then assumed to represent the saving per ton-kilometer of 20% of the traffic in class.

sumption and vehicle maintenance. The final demand-related components for the four truck classes are shown in Table 8.4.

Although many assumptions have had to be made in deriving the demand-related charges, they do not affect our final conclusions significantly. These charges are small in relation to the variable cost component for the medium and large vehicles, and for the small vehicles the esimated present user contributions are already large enough to allow for large errors in calculating them, as Table 8.4 shows. We now consider the present user charge pattern.

2.4   Estimation of User Contributions and Comparison with Warranted User Charges

Estimation of user contributions is shown in Table 8.3. The Yugoslav data on license fees are given in terms of truck capacity. To calculate contributions per gross ton, gross vehicle weights had to be derived. This was done, as before, by applying U.S. Department of Transport specifications.

The most controversial point in the user contribution calculations is the treatment of the turnover tax (*porez na promet*). Many Yugoslav interest groups (including road-building agencies, road user groups, and manufacturers) today believe that the part of all turnover taxes in excess of the "basic" tax should be counted as a user contribution. But these views conflict with the essence of the turnover tax, as, indeed, does actual tax practice. In the past, the turnover tax has been levied almost wholly on final goods at rates which are progressive in relation to the presumed income level of the respective consumer classes: it is zero on food and books, for example, has a basic rate of 12% on some consumer goods, and then rises to about 35–40% on luxuries. Where final goods also serve as intermediate goods, the tax is, in principle, rebated. Taxation experts in Yugoslavia have expressed the belief that the rebate mechanism works effectively. In view of these characteristics of the turnover tax, it is appropriate to regard the whole of the turnover tax *paid by trucks* as a road user charge but all that *paid by cars* (about 35% of retail price) as an excise tax. In addition, of course, we consider the narrowly defined road fuel tax (*naknada za puteve*) as part of the user contribution per gallon. We must then convert this to a per-kilometer basis, which is done with the assistance of the Department of Transport fuel consumption coefficients as indicated in Table 8.3.

Table 8.4 brings together the warranted user charges and the user contributions. Column 5 shows the user contribution relatively to the warranted charge, calculated in column 3. The very large trucks fall short in their user contributions, as do the 10-ton diesel trucks, although neither class by very much. The apparent paradox of a lower variable cost for the 10-ton truck occurs because the larger truck has a tandem axle, which is relatively less burdensome on the road per ton of gross weight than is the single-axle, 10-ton truck (see Tables 5.4 and 5.5).

The discrepancies that have been uncovered are less serious than might have been expected, and it is possible that they can be explained by the roughness of the data and our need for simplifying assumptions along the way. The calculations show that all vehicle classes are paying more than their directly variable cost, as defined here, plus a demand-related contribution toward the joint component costs. Whether the excess paid is sufficient to cover the analogous costs for cities, including congestion or other external effects, would require separate study. The data for such a study in the necessary detail are, of course, lacking. It can be seen, however, that the excess of actual contribution over warranted user charge does decline with rising vehicle size. This is probably consistent with the costs that they impose in urban networks, since a higher fraction of city use consists of small vehicle traffic.

2.5 Supplementary Beneficiary Contributions

The foregoing price-cost comparisons relate to the directly variable costs and to a demand component of the true joint costs. The demand component reflects the estimated average minimum savings for each vehicle class in the entire system—on the arcs being improved (with new additions or rectifications) and on the rest of the network as well. This will not necessarily cover total expenditure in any one year and may lead to a requirement for nonuser supplementary financing, which, as we have recommended, should originate in the local communities. The analysis of the overall financial accounts of the road network shows that the communities contributed about 15% of the total in 1969. As a result, approximately three-fourths of total revenues originated in sources that we define as direct beneficiary groups—users and abutting communities.* Federal participation (including army activity, grants from the Fund for Development of Backward Regions, and some unidentified federal grants) was about 12%. Republic participation (about 10%) is a grey area between beneficiary and nonbeneficiary participation. It is not included in the estimated three-fourths of direct beneficiary share, although part of it undoubtedly should be. Whether the nonbeneficiary contributions were consistent with income distribution goals or simply constituted an attempt to close the gap between desired investment plans and the capacity of the road sector to generate user-charge revenues cannot be determined.

3 RAILROAD PRICING CASE STUDIES: IRAQ AND INTERNATIONAL COMPARISON

We turn now to analyses of railroad rate patterns in several countries. The first analysis is a detailed study of rate policy in Iraq and the

---

* In this estimate the turnover tax is treated as described in Section 2.4 for purposes of calculating present user contributions; that is, the turnover tax on automotive fuel is treated as an excise or general revenue tax, while that on estimated truck gasoline and diesel fuel consumption is treated as a user contribution.

second is a comparison of the effectsɷof a ery important aspect of rate structures—the taper—on six national systems.

3.1 The Rate Structure in Iraq

In this section we will discuss a number of important aspects of railroad pricing and traffic policies in Iraq.

3.1.1 *Overall Rate Evaluation*

As we said in Chapter 4 under competitive conditions the overall adequacy of a railroad's rate structure and operating efficiency could be measured by the ratio of total revenue to total cost (where cost includes allowance for depreciation of rolling stock and new permanent way investment and capital charges, as well as maintenance, administration, etc.). To ensure economically efficient transport and location decisions by others, inputs should be valued at replacement cost. Efficiency is implied if the ratio is equal to unity.

If competition is not perfect and there are monopolies, or administrative distortions, the revenue/cost ratio is ambiguous. The firm may be equalizing its revenue and cost by higher charges to a captive market, and there may be poor internal cost discipline. This problem is of more than academic curiosity for Iraq because there have been distortions since 1971 when state-owned companies came under the obligation to ship by the state railroad companies. As we will see shortly, this administrative distortion has not affected traffic seriously so far, however. Table 8.5 shows the revenue/cost ratios for total traffic and for freight and passenger traffic separately for three recent years. Depreciation of 521,000 ID* *was* included in the official accounts only for 1971/1972. Through an independant estimate based on present replacement costs and a 20-year life, we conclude that the 1971/1972 depreciation should have been 858,000 ID, 65% higher than the official 1971/1972 depreciation, but 70% *lower* than the official 1970/1971 figure. Our own estimate is taken here as the annual depreciation in all three years of Table 8.7. Given the usual uncertainties in relating financial depreciation to the real wear of physical assets, it would probably not be warranted to adjust it further to allow for variations in traffic levels.

On the whole, the ratios reflect favorably on railroad operations in Iraq. The freight revenue/cost coefficient has been stable over the quinquennium, with both costs and revenues rising in about the same pro-

---

* Iraqi dinars. In mid-1974, 1.00 ID = $3.40 U.S. approximately; 1 ID = 1000 fils.

Table 8.5 Operating Ratios on Iraqi Railroads, 1967/1968, 1969/1970, and 1971/1972

		1967/1968	1969/1970	1971/1972
I.	Calculated from official statements; all exclude depreciation (except 1971/1972, which includes official depreciation)			
	Freight	0.99	0.90	0.97
	Passengers	0.53	0.75	0.91
	Total	0.90	0.88	0.96
II.	Reflects realistic depreciation[a]			
	Freight	0.88	0.82	0.88
	Passengers	0.49	0.67	0.81
	Total	0.80	0.79	0.87

[a] Depreciation calculated on rolling stock and locomotives only.

portion. Moreover, since these increases reflect traffic growth that was about the same before and after the introduction of the state shipping preference, we must conclude that this artificial distortion has not been significant in the past. (A special sulfur rate was introduced later.) As Table 8.5 shows, if we allow for depreciation in all years, the ratios fall by 9 to 11%, but for freight, at least, the ratio remains high. (Since freight revenues and costs are six to seven times as high as those of passengers, the freight ratio has a dominant influence on the total ratio, which also remains high—0.87). While there is room for improvement in these ratios, they are higher than those in many, probably most countries. For example, Brazil, East Germany, Italy, Austria, and Great Britain all show substantial shortfalls between average revenue and average cost.

The foregoing analysis suggests that the freight rate structure is basically sound. The average rate should be raised by about 15% overall. The adjustments to individual rates, which are recommended in Section 3.1.4 for rates that are now substantially below short-run marginal cost, should be enough to achieve this increase. They may even permit reductions on rates that now contain a very high value-of-service component.

The cost used as a standard for evaluating the average rate does include rolling stock and locomotive depreciation, realistically estimated, but it does not include the basic capital investment in the fixed facilities. The maintenance account does seem to allow for rail replacement, however, which of course *should* be considered as part of the variable cost. Thus none of the initial capital investment is built into the cost base, which conforms to the basic incremental cost standard we have set for pricing. If the network were approaching congestion, however, a higher charge would be necessary to try to get traffic closer to the optimal level.*

The passenger ratio, while improving, remained low in 1971/1972, reflecting basic problems. This is discussed in Section 3.1.5.

3.1.2   *Estimation of Average Variable Cost and Short-Run Marginal Cost*

We apply here the cost concepts elaborated in Chapter 6. (The reader may find it useful to reread the exposition of Section 1 of that chapter.) We start with the railroad accounts. To estimate average variable cost we must adjust total reported railroad costs in two ways: (1) add a rolling stock depreciation component and (2) subtract fixed capital items. This is shown in Table 8.6 (line 5). Short-run marginal cost requires an adjustment for the periodically recurring costs (e.g. administration) to determine a minimum bound for accepting any traffic. This is shown as line 9 (for 1971/1972) and line 10 (for 1974).

3.1.3   *The Rate-Distance Relationship*

The relationship between distance and railroad rates is a major aspect of the pricing of rail services.

As shown in Chapter 6, the average cost per kilometer falls with increasing distance, because there are fixed cost components in the

---

* It is an interesting implication of congestion pricing by a firm providing a limited-access facility, such as the railroad provides, that pricing according to average total cost or fully distributed costs might lead to the optimal output level in a way that conforms with marginal cost pricing. Consider a congested facility with marginal social cost exceeding marginal private cost (average social cost), where the cost curve reflects all the imposed costs. The private firm pricing according to fully distributed cost would consider the variable costs discussed here and the capital costs. This value might normally be determined by their scrap value or transfer cost, which for most items—such as tunnels and grading— would be zero or negligible. However, since the capacity of the line restricts output to a level far below the intersection of the demand and variable cost curve in the present situation, tremendous confusion would result unless a rent generated by the market came to be included in the trip rate. In a perfectly functioning market, this rent would be equal to the rectangle between the price-marginal social cost intersection, and the average variable cost at that traffic and this would *come* to be the annual value of the fixed capital facility. Averaging this value together with variable cost would lead to a fully distributed cost solution corresponding with the marginal social cost solution. Thus, while in Chapter 3 we showed that the optimal price would recover part of the capital cost to forestall overcrowding and provide a sequence of facilities each of the optimal size, in the present case we see that even with just a single facility or complex, inclusion of a charge for the fixed component might lead to optimal use levels. For a general discussion of congestion see Chapter 16.

Table 8.6 Calculation of Average Recurrent, Average Variable, and Short-Run Marginal Rail Costs in Iraq

	Dinars (000)
1. Expenditures assigned to freight traffic (official figures; excludes depreciation, 1971/1972)	7118.8
2. Add depreciation of rolling stock and locomotives assigned to freight traffic	695.0
3. Equals total annual variable cost	7813.8
4. Divide ton-kilometers, 1971/1972 (millions)	1612.0
5. Equals average variable cost, 1971/1972	4.85 fils/ton-km
6. Adjust for inflation to March 1974 (multiply by 1.16)	5.62 fils/ton-km
7. Subtract joint administrative costs (20.6%) from line 3[a]	14665.
8. Divide by ton-kilometers, 1971/1972 (millions)	1612.0
9. Equals short-run marginal cost, 1971/1972	3.94 fils/ton-km
10. Adjust for inflation to 1974 (multiply by 1.16)[b]	4.57 fils/ton-km

[a] Calculated on the basis of the 1972/1973 budget, p. 6.
[b] Baghdad wholesale price level in 1974 (annual rate extrapolated from March 1974) = 1.49; average rate for 1971/1972 fiscal year = 1.29 (1962 = 100).

shipment such as loading and train formation. However, the incremental line haul cost is constant—the technological relationship between the total cost of a shipment and the distance shipped may be expressed by a straight line equation $TC = a + bD$, where D is distance and a and b are constants. These hypothetical relationships are confirmed by the cost study of Borts presented in Chapter 6. This means that the cost of shipping an additional kilometer is the same at a distance of 50 kilometers as it is at 500 kilometers. Therefore, the rate to shippers for an additional kilometer should not vary with distance.

The Iraqi railroad rate structure has always been based on a constant incremental rate for each commodity class and so may be regarded as correct in this respect. This is exceptional, as we will see in Section 3.2. of this chapter.

3.1.4 *InterCommodity Rate Relationships*

Rational pricing principles require that traffic be charged enough to cover its short-run marginal cost plus any contribution that it can make toward the joint costs undertaken on behalf of all traffic (both the PRC and the fixed costs). The sum of the extra contributions from all traffic should cover the total joint costs.

The extra contribution that any traffic can make will depend ultimately on the underlying demand curve for the product in question. Usually this means that a more valuable commodity can pay more than a less valuable commodity, even though their hardware and handling requirement are the same. For example, vegetable oils in tank cars have many chemical and handling properties in common with petroleum products, such as diesel fuel. But in most countries the demand for vegetable oils makes people willing to pay more per kilogram of consumption, hence to pay more in transportation charges per ton. Therefore, it is correct to charge more per ton of vegetable oils than of diesel fuel. Naturally, this does not preclude the possibility that the government may prefer *not* to collect as much of a contribution to joint cost from traffics that constitute the necessaries of life, such as grain. The railroad can then charge an amount that is as low as variable cost. If the government wishes to give a further advantage to low-income groups, it should do it directly if at all possible. However, with grain a policy of direct subsidy might be difficult owing to the large number of producers and consumers of grain and grain products.

The intercommodity rate differences can be analyzed with the help of Table 8.7. In this table the major traffic components (which account for about 85% of total annual tonnage) are classified according to value and shipping requirements. The applicable rate (fils/ton-kilometer) is indicated next to each commodity.

On the whole, the railroad's rate classification appears sound, with higher rates being charged higher value commodities within each column (shipping requirements). Of special significance are the high POL (petroleum, oil, and lubricant) rates, indicating that the sizable railroad POL traffic is not being artificially and inefficiently stimulated. (This traffic now accounts for about 30% of tonnage and 25% of ton-kilometers.) There are at least six exceptions to the overall reasonableness of the rate structure, however, and we will consider these in detail. (We also note that the present grain rate of 2.3 is around 35 to 50% below variable cost. This rate is undoubtedly consistent with national income distribution goals and should be retained.)

1. *Dates.* In Section 3.1.2 we estimated the short run marginal cost to be 4.57 fils per ton-kilometer. Owing to its huge volume (about 6% of total ton-kilometers), the variable cost for dates is undoubtedly lower, but it is not likely to be as low as the present date shipping price, 2.3 fils

Table 8.7 Classification of Rates on Major Commodities by Shipping Requirements and Values in Iraq (Commodity—fils/ton-kilometer)

Relative Value of Commodity	Shipping Requirements					
	Perishables		Flat Cars		Liquids	
Low					Petrol (gasoline)	13.80
					Bulk Fuel	9.78
					Tar	4.60
					Bulk Kerosine	9.78
Medium	Dates	2.3	Iron and steel intermediates	4.6	Fuel in drums	9.78
					Kerosene drums	9.78
					Vegetable oil	3.45
High	Dried fruit	5.75	Cars and parts	9.78		
	Fresh fruit	3.45	Machinery	9.78		
	Vegetables	3.45				

Dry Bulk	
Cement	
Imported	3.45
Domestic	2.3
Salt	2.3
Stones	2.3
Sand	2.3
Sulfur	1.0
Grains	2.3
Flour	7.48
Sugar	3.45
Fertilizers	4.60

per ton-kilometer, which is 50% of the short-run marginal cost. Perhaps this low rate was adopted to stimulate date exports. But this objective could be best performed through a direct subsidy to date growers for two reasons:

(a) It would keep the railroad rate structure from becoming a cushion to absorb the losses of other activities, with eventual losses and deterioration of internal cost control in other industries.

(b) There would be much greater flexibility in foreign trade, since the government could withdraw the subsidy when production costs fell and/or world date prices rose. It would be much easier for the government to do this on an individual commodity basis than for the railroad to revise individual rates periodically.

Incidentally, the recent worldwide inflation may have raised date consumption prices sufficiently to allow Iraq to raise its export price enough to obviate the need even for a direct subsidy to growers. Iraq's export price was not raised between 1972 and 1974, which means that the entire retail price increase is being realized by the distributors in the consumer countries. Higher railroad rates for dates during the period might have stimulated rises in export prices and higher export earnings.

2. *Sand and stone.* Statistics on tonnage and haul are not published for these products because they account for only a small proportion of total traffic. The average haul is probably short, however, as is normal in quarrying operations. The fact that a very low rate is set for these commodities suggests that the railroads are trying to compete with trucks (or barges) for this traffic. The rate now being applied is barely half the short-run marginal cost estimated above. Since there is no reason to think that the unit directly variable cost of these products could be so much lower than the short-run marginal cost based on the all-commodity average, this rate is unjustified from the national economic point of view. Similar comments apply to the rates for salt and domestically produced cement.

It also follows that the grain rate is far below short-run marginal cost, as noted previously. But this probably reflects an implicit government income distribution policy, which would undoubtedly be more difficult to pursue through direct payments to consumers or growers, since farms are small and such a policy would entail very high administrative costs.

3. *Sulfur.* The low export sulfur, rate, recently introduced, is less than half the lowest rate previously existing on comparable products, and less than 25% short-run marginal cost. Even allowing for special operat-

ing cost conditions for sulfur exports, the SRMC for sulfur could not conceivably fall below 3 fils per ton-kilometer.

The reason for the low rate is probably the desire to promote sulfur exports and diversify Iraq's foreign trade. But the same alternative policy should be applied as was proposed above for dates—direct subsidies to producers. And for the same reasons of cost discipline and flexibility. Again, it may well be that recent increases in world sulfur prices are enough to obviate the need for a subsidy.

4. *POL in containers*. Both cost and demand considerations justify a higher price for packaged than for bulk POL. It costs more to ship a ton in drums than in bulk since there may be incomplete car utilization. And since POL in drums or tins has different and higher priced end uses than does bulk POL, it can afford a greater contribution toward joint costs.

5. *High-value perishables*. High value perishables are among the lowest-rated commodities. Again, this is incompatible with both cost and demand considerations. These products were reclassified downward in the 1970 rate book, suggesting an attempt by the railroads to forestall the diversion of this traffic to truck transport. Rates should be raised. Any traffic switches to truck transport may then be taken as a rational choice from the viewpoint of the national economy.

6. *Less-than-carload (LCL)*. A final deficiency in the intercommodity rate structure is the failure to discriminate between carload and LCL freight. LCL ton-kilometer freight costs will never be less than carload and will frequently be higher. This is especially true with heterogeneous manufactures, since they may not utilize a vehicle fully (in earlier tariff schedules, "vehicle" rates were frequently used to cover such traffic). Moreover, a higher value will usually be implied by LCL shipments—such as stones in bags for home decoration versus stone for foundation construction. Thus, again on grounds of cost and value, more commodity freight rate discrimination is called for.

3.1.5 *Passenger Policies*

Passenger traffic declined sharply between 1962/1963 and the late 1960s, but has since returned to a level close to that of 1962/1963. The passenger rate/cost ratio, which was shown in Table 8.1 for the period following 1967/1968 rose with the subsequent traffic recovery. (The rates themselves have remained unchanged since 1955.)

Although total traffic has declined only about 7% from 1962/1963 to

1971/1972, sleeping car traffic has fallen 45%. Moreover, it fell 32% during the quinquennium 1967/1968 to 1971/1972 while the two coach classes rose 40%.

In view of this traffic behavior, the wisdom of continuing to provide sleeper service should be questioned. Sleeper passengers have excellent alternatives in air transport—indeed, it is probable that much of the sleeper car reduction since 1967/1968 has been diverted to air (total embark/disembarkments at Basra rose by 17,000 and at Baghdad, by 93,000 during the period). Since trip time is much shorter, and fares by air are actually *lower,* this would seem a very attractive alternative.

3.1.6 *Problems Related to Inflation*

Iraq's excellent national economic growth record since the mid-1960s was attained with very little inflation. While the annual rate of average price increase fluctuated widely—between −4.7 +9.7%—the average compound rate over the period 1962-1973 was a modest 1.54%. Starting with 1973, however, the inflation rate rose sharply, reaching 14.0% by March 1974, or an annual rate of 18.7%. This sharp rise may be a foretaste of future monetary instability resulting from the future huge increases in foreign exchange earnings from oil and the increased tempo of domestic investment. In anticipation of this phenomenon the transport agencies must start to consider the implications of inflation for transport pricing.

Inflation means generalized and continuing increases in prices (some prices may increase at different rates because of special features of the nation's development). In order that prices continue to furnish a rational basis for choices by firms and consumers, they must go on reflecting the real costs that the economy undergoes when users choose any course of action. If rail prices are correct in a country before inflation begins, and if transport input prices rise while the transport rates do not, or rise much more slowly, it is obvious that after a few years transport prices will fail to reflect the true social costs involved in transport use decisions.

Now, railroad operating cost data from 1953 to 1967/1968 are insufficient to determine whether railroad rates were too low during this period. However, we do know that freight rates were held constant between 1953 and 1970. Moreover, we did see that rates were 8 to 12% too low during the quinquennium 1967/1968 to 1971/1972, 8% too low in the latter year. Rates since then have been raised by 15%, while the rate of inflation has been held to 13% (March 1974). But with inflation accelerating, as it appears to be doing now, the new rates will soon be out of step unless the railroads learn to adjust rates with greater speed than in the past—there have been only three rate revisions in the past 40 years.

3.2   An International Comparison of Rail Rate Tapers

The notion that distance-incremental costs decline is virtually an article of faith to management, shippers, and regulatory agencies in many countries, including some of the most powerful and advanced industrial countries. Table 8.8 shows the incremental rate structure for a number of countries over a wide variety of economic systems and levels of development.

Four of the schedules, those for Canada, the United States, Brazil, and the pre-1939 Soviet Union all show very sharp rate tapers, Canada's rate falling by as much as 85% at very long distances. This may reflect a historical tradition, conditioned by the urge to hold together a country that was very vulnerable to economic and political

Table 8.8   Rate Taper on Six National Railroad Systems (Incremental Rate at 20 to 60 miles = 100)

Distance (miles)	Canada[a]	United States[b]	Brazil[c]	Soviet Union[d] Pre-1939	Soviet Union[d] Post-1939	Iraq	Yugoslavia
20–60	100	100	100	100	100	100	100
61–100	100	100	100	100	100	100	100
101–150	50	62	100	100	100	100	100
151–190	50	62	100	84	91	100	100
191–300	40	54	90	84	91	100	100
301–440	36	45	90	84	91	100	100
441–815	36	45	70	84	91	100	100
816–1250	36	45	50	68	91	100	100
1251–1500	36	45	50	51	85		
1501–1875	32	45	50	51	85		
1876–2700	32	45	50	44	85		
2701–3300	14	45	50	44	85		

Sources.   Calculated from: Currie (1967), p. 212; Locklin (1972), p. 188–189; RFFSA (1968); Kuchurin (1951); Iraq Ministry of Transport, Railroad rate books; Yugoslav Railways (1971).
[a] Rate for class 100.
[b] Rate for class 100.
[c] All general rates.
[d] Cement rate, which is typical.

pressures from the United States, but even at the very short distance of 200 miles the incremental rate falls by two-thirds. (This taper pattern only applies to 25 to 40% of total traffic, since a great deal of total rail activity is covered by negotiated and statutory rates).

Iraq and Yugoslavia stand out from the general pattern in their adherence to a constant incremental rate structure, which actually does reflect the true cost-distance patterns.

The Soviet Union provides an interesting, and unexpected, case study of an attempt to use the price mechanism for more effective decision-making even in the pre-World War II period. Russia, a country with a historical frontier tradition like the United States and Canada, also had a decreasing incremental rate structure, which carried over into the Soviet period through the first three five-year plans. But the crushing loads imposed on the railroads under these plans led the leadership to revise rates to discourage transport use. In fact, however, it was location decisions regarding new capacity throughout the 1930s that had reacted to wrong railroad cost and price signals, so that very little could be done to relieve railroad congestion through revision of rate structures in the short run. For example, new cement production capacity was implanted primarily in traditional western regions at costs 30 to 50% below production costs in the east, but transport costs raised final delivered costs to levels 8 to 10 times as high (Abouchar, 1971, Ch. 3). If the post-1939 rates had been effective earlier, they might have had some influence though.

Finally, we should observe that departures from the general principle of constant incremental rates may be warranted in certain cases. For example, if two regions originate a commodity destined for a third market, the origin that is farther away might be able to compete only if it is granted the same rate, either through a negotiated rate, a zero incremental rate for the distance differential, or a constant but lower incremental rate for all distances (which would in effect be a "paper" rate for all distances but the one actually concerned). The possibility that such considerations lie behind observed exceptions must be allowed for when evaluating a rate structure. In such cases, however, the rate must satisfy the minimum allowable rate constraint, that is, the rate for the shipment must cover short-run marginal cost as defined in Chapter 6. An example of a railroad with many paper rates designed to encourage traffic on specific runs was the Brazilian Federal Railway Network in the 1960s. These rates, however, were all well below short-run marginal cost, as were the rates of all other commodities on this network. (Abouchar, 1970.)

REFERENCES

Abouchar, Alan (1970), "Pricing Rationality and Deficits on the Brazilian Railroads," *Journal of Transport Economics and Policy*, Vol. 4, No. 3, August.

────── (1971), *Soviet Planning and Spatial Efficiency* (Bloomington: Indiana University Press).

────── (1974), "A New Approach to the Evaluation and Construction of Highway User Charges," Eastern Economic Journal, Vol. 1, No. 2–3.

Conklin, D. W., J. E. Tanner, and L. S. Zudak (1970), "Comment" [to Dalvi], *Canadian Journal of Economics*, Vol. 3, No. 4, November.

Currie, A. W. (1967), *Canadian Transportation Economics* (Toronto: University of Toronto Press).

Dalvi, M. Q. (1969), "Highway Costs and Revenues in Canada," *Canadian Journal of Economics*, Vol. 2, No. 4, November.

International Road Federation (1971), *World Road Statistics, 1966–1970*, (Geneva and Washington).

Iraq Ministry of Transport, Railroad rate books.

S. F. Kuchurin (1957), *Tarify Zheleznikh dorog (Railway Rates)* (Moscow: Transzhelizdat).

Locklin D. Philip (1972), *Economics of Transportation* (Homewood, Ill.: Richard D. Irwin), p. 188.

RFFSA (Brazilian Federal Railway Network) (1968), *Tarifa Geral (3) da RFFSA*, (Rio de Janeiro).

Socialistička federativna republika Jugoslavija (1971), *Statistički godišnjak Jugoslavije (Statistical Yearbook of Yugoslavia)* (Belgrade).

────── (1970), *Saobraćaj i veze (Transport and Communications)* (Belgrade).

U.S. Department of Transport (1970), *Road User and Property Taxes, 1970*, (Washington, D.C.).

Yugoslav Railways (1971), *Tarifa za prevoz robe (Freight Rates)* (Belgrade).

CHAPTER

9

Using Cost Analysis to
Evaluate Traffic Allocation

1 INTRODUCTION

We have stressed repeatedly that transport pricing should be based on clearly defined principles of cost behavior and cost allocation, except where specific income distribution objectives can be achieved most efficiently by departing from these principles (such as grain movement in Iraq being subsidized through low rates, thus redistributing income—a result more costly to achieve by alternative means, owing to high administrative costs). The applicability of this argument is undoubtedly much more restricted than is commonly believed, however. Thus the general approach to analysis of the efficiency of the transport sector should be to examine the transport cost structure to see how the transport pricing patterns accord with it. If prices are correctly set in the first place, the market can be depended upon to allocate traffic efficiently in conformity with prevailing preferences and costs.

The problem frequently arises, however, that we cannot collect enough data to determine the costs in individual cases, either because accounts are badly maintained, because there have been widely different trends in relative modal input prices, or because cost information

124

is regarded as confidential by the executive firms or agencies. We then cannot perform the necessary rate-cost analysis to judge efficiency in the transport sector.

When we cannot obtain the needed cost-price information, we can look directly at traffic distribution to judge the efficiency of certain aspects of the sector. This cannot be a complete analysis, of course, since the possibility remains of distortions in relative prices between transportation and the rest of the economy. But it at least provides information on the efficiency of modal split.

The need to analyze traffic is not restricted to cases of limited information. Even relatively full information, may not be as complete as we would wish, and it is useful to supplement the price analysis with direct evidence on traffic response. Moreover, with complete information about present-day operations, long-range network planning still requires analysis of the future cost structure in order to make rational investment choices about the allocation of future traffic.

In this chapter we first present a decision tree for short-run traffic allocation to evaluate existing traffic patterns. We then analyze one country—Yugoslavia—to illustrate the use of the decision tree. The final section of the chapter evaluates costs for use in programming models for future traffic allocation to orient network planning.

2 A DECISION TREE FOR TRAFFIC ALLOCATION

The optimal distribution of traffic to different modes of transport depends on a large number of variables relating to the cost and service characteristics of modes and to the nature of the goods being shipped. It can be analyzed by the scheme of the decision tree in Figure 9.1. If prices are set to reflect true cost behavior, and there are no administrative impediments or distortions elsewhere in the economy, we may assume that the existing traffic distribution is the optimal traffic allocation. If this is not the case, we must present guidelines for traffic allocation to evaluate the existing patterns. This is the purpose of this section. We restrict attention to the case of existing networks.

First, a note of caution. It would be futile to hope for a single absolute classificatory criterion for traffic assignment, or even a set of absolute criteria. The analyst must be constantly on the lookout for situations that, while in accord with the welfare maximization spirit of these guidelines, may appear to contradict their letter. For example, while one would conclude from these guidelines that bulk sulfur should move by rail, it might nontheless be reasonable to ship it by truck on certain routes where it serves as a complementary backhaul (as it does in the fruit traffic by truck from Beirut to Baghdad). Sulfur, though not nearly as valuable as fruit, nevertheless has a sufficiently high value to justify the directly ascribable costs (incremental fuel consumption and incremental vehicle wear due to the cargo only). We must, therefore, maintain flexibility—the ability to interpret individual flows in the light of general conditions and factors rather than with respect only to the particular flow itself. By contrast, salt movements by truck from the north to the south in Brazil undoubtedly do not justify the incremental cargo costs on this backhaul.

We now turn to the cost and service characteristics of main surface transport modes and then present a decision tree for traffic assignment. Comparative analysis of transport modes frequently neglects two extremely important considerations:

1. The services provided by different transport modes are different.

2. Average modal costs depend, *inter alia,* on volumes.

Both of these factors preclude direct comparison of different modes and assignment of traffic to them on the basis of observed historical costs. Although these points are crucial for rational traffic allocation and, once stated, are so obvious as to seem unworthy of special elaboration, they are too often neglected in actual discussions of traffic allocation.

We consider service first. The main intermodal service difference is speed, truck usually being the fastest on any given arc, followed by rail and then river. Truck is the fastest for several reasons:

1. The railroad vehicle—the train—is large and must collect traffic at numerous intermediate points in order to operate at low cost. Only unit trains (trains carrying a single commodity, such as iron ore) can move over long distances without intermediate collection. But even these are slowed down by the periodic stops of other trains in the system, unless there are more sidings, which raise the infrastructure cost. Trucks, on the other hand, with much smaller loads (at most 50% of the load of the train) can carry a single load over the entire arc.

2. Water is still slower. Although its shipping vehicle is smaller than the train, so that it lends itself to longer journeys without intermediate stops, its actual speeds are slow since:

(a) The speed per kilometer on water is slower than by rail or road.

(b) On any arc there are usually two to three times as many kilometers to travel due to the winding course of the river.

3. Besides having faster arc speeds (i.e. speeds between the terminal nodes), truck service usually will be faster by virtue of having fewer transloadings. For example, a 20-ton agricultural load can be moved from farm to final wholesale outlet by truck; were it to move by rail, it would have to go by truck to railhead and from the rail destination by truck to wholesaler. These extra operations require time and careful coordination of schedules.

We now turn to costs. The cost analyses surveyed and analyzed in Chapters 5 and 6 suggest that in the United States rail average variable line haul costs are 20 to 40% as high as those by truck, the percentage varying with distance. River costs are considerably lower than rail costs. Adjustment for river *length* raises the latter considerably, however, although they still remain below rail costs between most terminal pairs in most countries. Since the most difficult problems usually are encountered in the road-rail assignment, we focus on this.*

The relative railroad/truck cost of 20 to 40% is a statement of historical fact in the United States. Its transferability to new situations requires knowledge of possibly excluded costs and of traffic volumes under which the modal costs are relevant.

Regarding first the possible exclusion of costs we note that rail costs include such items as line maintenance, but we did not analyze the truck sector to determine whether user charges actually being paid were adequate to cover warranted user charges in the United States. Clearly, if they do not, rail ton-mile costs would be even further below truck costs.

The other problem is the traffic levels underlying the estimated relative cost ratio of 20 to 40%. The road costs are more sensitive to type of structure and geometrics than to density. But to some extent, density on a given arc may be taken as a proxy for construction characteristics, and we may generally expect that if road operating costs are higher on some arc because of difficult road features due to difficult terrain, the railroad will also have more difficult features, raising its operating costs. Since railroad construction has relatively more rigid requirements, however, a rail line on an arc compared with average conditions

---

* As a general rule, it is *probably* safe to assign to river traffic those shipments for which speed, resistance to hydration, and other special features do not dictate road or rail. Considering the costs of landing construction, relay facilities, and similar factors, this suggests that longer, low-value bulk hauls should go by water.

will cause less of a cost differential than will a truck, with the net effect of reducing the estimated relative rail/truck cost below 20 to 40%.

Thus we conclude that the relative line haul costs of 20 to 40% is an accurate statement of relative rail/truck costs. Combining it with the characteristics of the modes, such as line speed, door-to-door elapsed time, and door-to-door costs, we can allocate traffic between the major surface transport modes. Figure 9.1 is a decision tree showing this process. To use it requires quantification of certain variables and a few additional comments.

1. By value of commodity and distance we think roughly in the following terms:

Class 3 (low value)—below $30 per ton.
Class 2 (medium value)—$35 to $70 per ton.
Class 1 (high value)—greater than $75 per ton.

2. Length of haul (short, medium, and long) is relative to value class and density. A long haul for dense low-value commodities is 75 kilometers and up. For dense high-value commodities, it is 250 kilometers. These are indicated on the branches of Figure 9.1.

3. According to the decision tree, high-value and medium-value freight are assigned to road, except when a rail connection exists on the arc *and* the *individual commodity flows* are dense. Since for medium- and high-value commodities speed is essential, shippers should choose rail only if they can reduce their shipping times to times attainable by road. This usually requires a shipper to have his own siding and to ship to buyers with sidings. This is not likely to be feasible for producers shipping fewer than five or six carloads of 75 to 150 tons a week (4000 to 7500 tons a year), depending on size and age of cars and bulk of commodities. However, if there is one such shipper, on an arc there are likely to be more. Agricultural regions, for example, would be characterized by several such shippers, as would be regions of consumer goods production. Hence the total flow on the arc of the medium- and high-value goods would be several times as high as the 4000 to 7500 tons hypothesized for individual shippers.

4. Truck low-value commodity assignments. The two low-value truck assignments require a word of explanation. The "thin" assignment assumes implicitly that the total flow is also too thin to have justified railroad construction in the first place. The low-value, short-haul dense flow relates to commodities such as ubiquitous building materials quar-

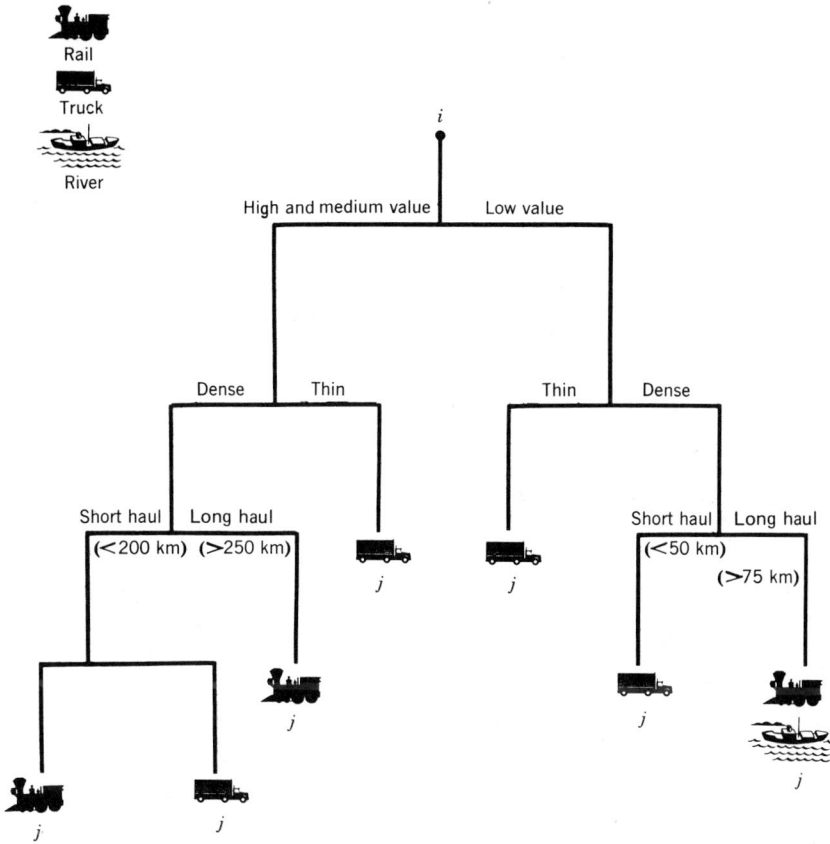

Figure 9.1 Decision tree for assignment of flow of commodity k from origin i to destination j (X_{ijk}).

ried in or close to cities or other construction sites (dams, dikes, roads, etc.). These would not typically originate at a railhead. Therefore, at least one truck-rail transfer would be required, not only introducing another cost element, but probably also requiring a longer total truck-rail journey. Direct truck door-to-door distance might be 40 kilometers while the truck-rail joint move might be 65 kilometers. When quarries are at greater remove—over 75 kilometers, say—these cargoes should be assigned to rail or barge, that is, construed as long-haul, dense, low-value commodities (on the low-value branch of the decision tree, the long haul is shorter than on the high-value branch).

3   A CASE STUDY OF TRAFFIC PATTERNS:
YUGOSLAVIA IN THE 1960

Traffic records are rarely maintained in the kind of detail envisioned by the decision tree just elaborated. The most we would normally expect to find is aggregated commodity breakdowns for railroad (which may only account for 30 to 50% of total surface transport), without an origin-destination $(O-D)$ matrix. Therefore, unless a major national transport study is to be undertaken, complete with extensive field surveys, the data on interregional flows and on flows over individual arcs are unlikely to be detailed enough to apply the decision tree to all of a nation's surface traffic or even to large regional components. It can alert the analyst to individual irrationalities that warrant closer inspection. The cases of sulfur on the Iraq-Beirut truck run (which on closer inspection turns out to be efficient) and Brazilian north-south salt movements by truck, almost certainly inefficient, were mentioned above. But besides being helpful in spotlighting individual areas of concern, the *reasoning behind* the decision tree can be applied to overall surface transport patterns. In this section we compare a number of measures of traffic distribution in Yugoslavia in the late 1960s, with the norms that follow from the traffic allocation tree.

Officially designated common carrier (ODCC), passenger and freight motor transport and railroad activities have grown between 1958 and 1970 as shown in Table 9.1. The ODCC freight by itself comprises only about 40% total truck transport, own-account and privé (small "for-

Table 9.1   Rail and ODCC Motor Transport Activity in Yugoslavia, 1958–1970 (Selected Years)

| | Passenger-Kilometers (billions) | | | | Freight: Ton-Kilometers (billions) | | | |
	Rail	Road (ODCC)	Total	Rail/Total (%)	Rail	Road (ODCC)	Total	Rail/Total (%)
1958	8.9	1.8	10.7	83	13.0	0.6	13.6	96
1960	10.4	2.8	13.2	79	15.2	1.0	16.2	94
1965	12.8	6.0	18.8	68	18.0	3.0	21.0	86
1970	10.9	14.1	25.0	44	19.2	6.7	25.9	74

Source.   Socialistička federationa republika Jugoslavija (1970), pp. 26, 108, 109.

Table 9.2   Some Measures of Rail and ODCC Road Freight Patterns in Yugoslavia, 1969

		ODCC Road	Rail
I.	Measures of trip length		
	1. ALH (Average length of haul) (all commodities (km)	98	252
	2. Maximum ALH (km)	283	329
	3. Minimum ALH (km)	29	88
	4. Number of commodity average hauls exceeding ALH of other mode	1	12
	5. Relative ton-kilometer volume of five leading homogeneous commodity classes in mode as percent of all rail and road shipment of these commodities	28%	83%
II.	Measures of density and value: number of low value goods accounting for more than 5% of		
	1. Tonnage	2	3
	2. Ton-kilometers	1	3
	3. Relative tonnage volume of five leading homogeneous commodity classes in mode as percent of all rail and road shipment of these commodities	59%	55%

Source.   Socialistička federationa republika Jugoslavija (1970), pp. 30, 113.

hire" truckers not in the ODCC statistics) activity accounting for the balance.

In general, truck transport has tended to attract the higher-value traffic, although trucks also carry many low-value goods in areas that lack good rail connections and on shorter hauls in cases where door-to-door delivery would otherwise impose a relatively high additional cost if freight were to move by rail. These are the characteristics of an efficient traffic allocation that could result from application of the decision tree analysis and can be seen in the summary measures presented in Table 9.2. (Although statistics are compiled only for ODCC transport, evidence available for the rest of the truck transport sector tends to confirm the following analysis based on the ODCC data.)

Table 9.2 presents aggregate indicators of road and rail freight traffic patterns. These demonstrate that the two principal land modes each tend to be used to their best advantage. The first five measures indicate clearly that rail tends to be used for long-haul movements, with 12 rail commodity classes showing an average haul greater than the overall road average haul, while only 1 road average haul exceeds the average haul of all rail traffic (line I.4). Moreover, the commodities comprising the five homogeneous flows that are heaviest in terms of truck ton-kilometers account for only 28% of the total rail and road ton-kilometers of those commodities (line I.5). At the same time the leading five rail traffics, in terms of ton-kilometers, account for 83% of the total rail and road movement of these commodities, again showing the tendency of rail to be used in long hauls, as well as on dense flows.

The last three measures indicate density and value patterns. These again show rational modal split. Of the five lowest-value commodities,* only one ("other mineral building materials") accounts for more than 5% of road ton-kilometers, while three rail classes exceed this share; the corresponding numbers for simple tonnage are two and three respectively.

On the other hand, that truck transport has such a heavy flow on certain commodities (59% of the total rail and road tonnage on the five densest truck flows moves by truck) at first glance seems to impugn the rationality that has been claimed for modal split; but this heavy share is in large measure due to "other mineral building materials," which accounts for 44% of total truck tonnage, but has an average haul of only 29 kilometers, and would seem to have its explanation in terms of distance from quarry to construction site or processing plant. Leaving this flow out of all calculations reduces the percentage in line II.3 to 21%. Moreover, these five commodity flows have average hauls ranging from 82% shorter (coal) to 40% shorter (cement) than the corresponding rail hauls, suggesting that higher costs would be incurred if transfers to rail and back to truck were involved.

Trucking activity outside the ODCC sector tends to specialize in short hauls. Thus the average haul in this activity can be calculated from the annual transport yearbook as 18 kilometers in 1969. A large part of this is urban traffic, although no official estimates on geographical shares are known to exist.

The apparently rational traffic patterns in Yugoslav transport are due in large part to the correct pricing procedures adopted. We considered at length the highway pricing and one important aspect of railroad pricing. (See Abouchar, 1975, for a more complete evaluation of the Yugoslav transport sector.)

---

* (1) Coal, (2) ores and concentrates, (3) nonmetallic minerals and products, (4) firewood and cellulose, and (5) other mineral building materials.

4 ANALYSIS OF FUTURE EVOLUTION OF COSTS FOR USE IN TRAFFIC ASSIGNMENT MODELS AND INFRASTRUCTURE INVESTMENT PLANNING

The objectives of long-term economic planning may require analysis of regional development and transport flows in order to allow sufficient lead time for investment in basic transport infrastructure. Formal programming models may be useful here. We caution the analyst against overly grand ideas about what programming models can accomplish in such a situation, however; they are obviously much better adapted to cope with simple unimodal optimands and given regional production and consumption patterns than with a general equilibrium planning model. This suggests that, rather than being left as complex models that simultaneously determine output levels, consumption levels, interregional flows, and modal split, the problem should be divided into several subproblems, with separate but coordinated analysis. Thus for a motor vehicle program requiring flows in certain regions some traffic flows previously believed to be logical candidates for rail might be transferred to the road program.

To decide on the assignment of a traffic to a program requires knowledge of costs on various arcs. Obviously, even if less formal planning methods are used, knowledge of relative costs is necessary for modal split and related investment plans.

The relevant cost information, however, should reflect the future evolution of costs rather than the present cost structure. We are talking not about the effects of an equiproportional inflation of all prices, but about changes in relative costs. If there is some expectation that the relative cost structure will change, it is the costs of operations in the future that are pertinent. For example, with economic development we may expect drivers' wages to rise in relation to vehicle depreciation, which *may* affect the relative rail-truck costs on individual distances or arcs. Another example is new investment. Obviously, the costs relevant to traffic allocation in 1990 will include the cost of infrastructure, which was not considered in the traffic assignment tree of Section 2 or in much of the analysis in Chapter 8 where the concern was with pricing.*

In this section we present a case study to show how the future evolution of modal costs should be analyzed. The study is based on the

---

* Actually, the cost of new construction for a highway, where this construction may be considered a marginal increment to an existing network, *was* taken into account and allocated disriminatorily among traffic components to derive the warranted user charge in Chapter 8.

economy of Iraq. We analyze rail costs, motor vehicle costs, and river costs and then compare the projected cost patterns of these modes over various distances.

The approach in all cases is the same—determine the changes in relative average total costs of modal inputs in order to determine the intermodal relative costs that may be expected to prevail in 1990. Pure inflationary influences need not be taken into account. The complete analysis *treats* passengers as well as freight, but only the latter is presented here.

The costs relevant to long-term traffic assignment decisions include all the costs that any course of action imposes on the economy. Where a transport link already exists we need consider only the recurrent future outlays, including fuel, maintenance of permanent way, and capital consumption. Provided that the permanent way is perfectly maintained, we need consider only vehicle wear as capital consumption. (Rail replacement, road repaving, and similar factors are here thought of as part of the maintenance cost.) The cost calculated in this way is the annual total variable cost. Dividing this by the traffic will give the average total variable cost.

Average total variable cost is appropriate for such decisions as whether to expand traffic on individual modes where it is not a question of undertaking permanent way investments. This is also the amount that should be recovered by the transport firms each year as payment for their shipping services. To do this, rational pricing policy requires that each unit shipped be charged an amount equal to the directly variable (short-run marginal) cost of that shipment plus whatever contribution it can make to the joint costs that are undertaken on behalf of all traffic.

Finally, on arcs or modes where there does not now exist a permanent way the new cost to the economy must include a permanent way capital cost component. This cost must reflect the social opportunity cost of capital. The opportunity cost of capital is a concept that indicates the minimum productivity a unit of capital could achieve if invested elsewhere in the economy. Therefore, it indicates the minimum sacrifice that is entailed by using it in one sector rather than another. An opportunity cost ranging between 8 and 11% is frequently assumed, but, as we see in Chapter 11, there is reason to believe it is really lower—5% or less. Five percent will be adopted in this analysis. Infrastructure capital outlays will be multiplied by this amount to derive a measure of annual infrastructure cost. Dividing this by any traffic level will give average annual capital cost for that traffic level. We add this to the average total variable cost where relevant.

4.1   Railroad Costs

Average total variable cost was analyzed in Section 3.1.2 of Chapter 8. The average calculated in Table 8.6 (5.62 fils per ton-kilometer) was based on total traffic. For analysis of future relative costs for intermodal traffic assignment we must calculate the average total variable cost at various distances and then add the average investment cost at various distances and densities.

The average total variable and short-run marginal costs in Table 8.6 may be compared with the corresponding highway costs to show the relative costs of the two modes. For traffic assignment on individual arcs, however, we must allow for the possibility that the relative average costs at short distances may differ from those at long distances. For example, even though the incremental line-haul costs are constant, railroad average costs decline with increasing length of haul because there are fixed terminal costs relating to loading and unloading. The Iraq State Railway rates allow for this, and terminal charges in relation to line-haul charges behave like terminal costs in relation to line-haul costs as determined in Borts' analyses of United States rail cost functions. In Iraq, they comprise about one-third of the average ton-kilometer cost on short distances and decline to 10% at 500 kilometers. In Table 9.3 we adjust the average total variable cost estimates of Table 8.6 to these conditions.

Table 9.4 shows the total investment costs for five new railroad projects and two large line improvement projects as reported by the Ministry of Transport in 1974. The costs include all communications, stations, and so on. For the new lines the average cost per kilometer is seen to be 160,700 ID. At 5%, the annual capital cost is thus 8040 ID.

Table 9.3   Average Total Variable and Short-Run Marginal Railroad Costs at Various Distances in Iraq

Length of Trip (km)	Average Total Variable Cost (fils/ton-km)	Short-Run Marginal Cost of (fils/ton-km)
100	8.70	7.22
350	5.78	4.79
500	5.43	4.50
800	5.26	4.36

Source.   Based on Table 8.6, lines 6 and 11.

Table 9.4　Costs of Constructing or Improving Five Railway Lines in Iraq (Projects Currently Proposed—1974)

		Cost (ID 000)	Total Length (km)	Average Cost (000 ID/km)
I.	Construction			
	1. Mussaib-Sammawa	30,000	275	109.1
	2. Baghdad-Kut-Basra	100,000	700	142.8
	3. Baghdad-Hsaibah	100,000	400	250.0
	4. Al Qaim-Akashat	23,000	154	149.0
	5. Baghdad-Kirkuk + Kirkuk-Mosul	80,000	543	147.3
	Total	333,000	2072	160.7
II.	Improvement			
	1. Baghdad-Basra	13,500	578	23.4
	2. Baghdad-Mosul	11,775	530	22.2
	Total	25,275	1108	22.8

For the reconstruction, the average kilometer cost is 22,800 ID, or 1140 ID per year.

For traffic assignment on any arc we must compare average total motor transport cost with average total rail cost, with capital costs included in both, implying an increase from the levels of Table 9.3. However, the variable costs themselves will decrease under the new conditions, and we assume arbitrarily a one-third decrease in average variable costs at all distances. This procedure is adopted in the absence of better information; although several railroad project studies have been performed, no operating cost estimates under new operating conditions have been prepared. Table 9.7 shows the calculations of the final future rail costs and compares them with river and motor transport.

4.2　Motor Vehicle Transport Costs

As before, we can divide total costs into periodically recurrent variable costs, short-run marginal costs, and capital costs. Marginal costs refer to the direct or nonjoint costs of individual operators, that is, the costs of undertaking a trip once the firm is in business and must bear certain overhead costs or joint costs in any event. Since overhead or joint costs comprise a relatively small part of trucking firms' cost structure, their short-run marginal cost (including depreciation) will be taken as equal to *their* average total costs.

To determine the average total variable cost of the trucking sector, as against the costs of the individual firm, however, we must also consider the average cost of maintaining the road network. According to calculations by the author similar to those for Yugoslavia but not presented here, most classes of properly loaded vehicles do pay enough in fuel taxes and registration fees to cover the annual recurrent road costs. (Small vehicles pay considerably more, and their excess may be thought of as a proper form of income distribution or progressive taxation.) Large buses and, perhaps, very large trucks (of over 25-ton gross weight) may be exceptions to the general conclusions *if* the highway "construction" expenditure actually includes a large part of the costs of repaving or resurfacing, which therefore is not included in the vehicle variable cost base. These conclusions seem firm enough to enable us to accept the average tax-inclusive total variable costs of properly loaded vehicles as a measure of the average total variable cost of the motor vehicle transportation activity. We now consider the more detailed functional relationships and trends.

We start with the 1971/1972 cost accounts of the Public Road Transport Company (PRTC). We first determine the company's average cost and adjust it successively for inflation to 1974 (to put it on the same basis with rail cost estimates), for directional imbalance, and for distance. The PRTC cost accounts are taken as a starting point since this company is understood to have the most balanced traffic flows and its cost accounts are assumed to be the most complete and reliable.

The basic datum for the calculation will be the Basra-Baghdad rate of the PRTC. This was 2 ID in 1972/1973. The company had a small loss in that year, but it was lower than the loss in the preceding year (the first year of operation)—the company just having started operations, its costs still had not fallen to normal. Accordingly, we disregard the loss and assume that the company's tariffs covered its total costs in that year. This has to be adjusted as indicated below.

4.2.1 *Inflation*

The 2 ID rate was for 1972/1973. Adjusting this for the annual rate of inflation between 1972/1973 and 1974 raises the basic cost to 2.4 ID. Since almost all PRTC trucks on the Basra-Baghdad route travel fully loaded in both directions, this may be taken as the average variable cost under a full load.

4.2.2 *Directional Imbalance*

Road transport in Iraq is extremely unbalanced with respect to direction. This can be seen in Table 9.5 which is based on data from recent road transport surveys conducted by the Ministry of Planning. The table shows the median percentage of empty trucks in the total interregional flows. Empty trucks accounted for more than 52% of truck movements on 8 of the 17 interregional flows originating in Baghdad. Other entries are read similarly. The overall average empty share is 50%, according to the survey.

To determine the effect of directional imbalance on costs, we must first break down average total cost into cost of load and cost of the vehicle moving empty. Unfortunately, the various controlled field studies of road transport costs, such as those of the U.S. Highway Research Board, as well as studies based on secondary sources concentrate on costs of fully loaded vehicles. There appear to be some

Table 9.5 Median Values of the Percentage of Empty Trucks in Interregional Flows in Iraq, 1972

Province	Flows	
	Terminating in	Originating in
Baghdad	52	33
Ninevah	28	56
Dubok	53	54
Arbil	50	67
Kirkuk	33	60
Sulaimaniya	38	70
Diyala	74	51
Basra	41	35
Thi-Qar	50	50
Maysan	50	46
Waset	50	50
Al-Muthanna	42	51
Al-Qadissiya	50	62
Babil	52	47
Kerbela	68	33
Al-Anbar	91	7
Foreign	36	33

Source. Calculated from Iraq Ministry of Planning (1972).

scale economies, however, so that the cost of an additional ton on a vehicle is less than the average cost per ton for that vehicle.* This declining cost relationship does not appear to be very strong, however.

The cost of the driver for the two-way trips is fixed whether there is a return cargo or not. Driver's wages constitute 7% of total cost.

Finally, we also must know the empty/gross weight ratio. Typically, the empty weight is about 45% of the fully loaded weight. Adding this to the slightly decreasing cost per ton and the invariance of driver's cost suggests that the cost of an empty is 55 to 60% that of a fully loaded vehicle. Therefore, the average total variable cost per *ton* on trips with empty backhaul in which the load restrictions are observed is higher by this percentage, since the forward direction freight must bear the whole cost of the return. For a truck on the Baghdad-Basra route the cost rises to 3.8 ID when there is no backhaul cargo.

The effect on price due to removal of all overloads will depend on the relative volume of empties and the amount of overload. We assume that (1) truck transportation proper (excluding quarry runs) contains 60% empties and (2) half of the trips with empty backhauls are overloaded by 50% on the forward run. Then the average effect of removing all overloads, if solvency is to be preserved, is to increase the average trip-ton price by 12.5%.

4.2.3   Scale Economies

To estimate average variable cost of motor transport we must know how costs vary with vehicle size and distance of travel. The PRTC Baghdad-Basra rate itself is constant—2 ID—but since the PRTC does not function under competitive conditions, this cannot be taken as a statement of the true technological relationship. On the other hand, railroads also have cost variation with vehicle size. But for purposes of intermodal traffic assignment, which relies heavily on value of commodity, distance, and number of intermodal transfers, this is not so important. The *range* of cost-size variation of one mode relatively to the other, rather than a single definitive number, is the critical factor.

The distance-cost relationship for motor transport is another matter. The best study of this aspect of road transport cost behavior is the 1959 study by Wilson, analyzed at length in Chapter 5. Wilson showed that the average cost declines with distance, rather substantially, for all

---

* We should stress that this statement refers to additional loads on vehicles of a given capacity rather than the cost/vehicle-size relationship, which decreases much more sharply.

vehicle sizes. For the future, a pattern of decreasing average cost closer to that observed by Wilson for the United States is assumed.

The major source of decreasing cost in the United States is undoubtedly the high cost associated with access to American cities where traffic is very dense. This represents a fixed cost on any given trip. The incremental line-haul cost in Wilson's study is approximately constant. City access is not now a serious problem in Iraq, so that costs here must be much more nearly linear. On the other hand, in the future, as urban traffic increases, a United States-like pattern will undoubtedly start to develop. However, since in many of the cities in the central part of Iraq there are few geophysical constraints on growth, we assume that urban growth will be extensive rather than intensive, holding down congestion and leaving access costs below what they would be in more densely packed cities. Accordingly, the average cost-distance function is assumed not to decline in the future quite as markedly as that in the United States observed in Wilson's study.

We start with the cost estimated for the Basra-Baghdad trip, 550 kilometers. The average ton-kilometer cost on that run is 2.4 ID per 550 kilometers, or 4.4 fils per ton-kilometer. This basic estimate of average total variable cost must be adjusted for different distances, network qualities, and higher relative costs of labor in the future. The estimates are shown in Table 9.7. A fairly linear average cost-distance relationship is assumed for the present situation, because city access is not now difficult.

We also assume that with economic development labor productivity and wages in the economy will rise. Thus whereas labor (including maintenance) now accounts for 8 to 10% of total truck costs in underdeveloped countries, as we noted when analyzing de Weille's cost data in Chapter 5, in developed countries it accounts for perhaps 50 to 70%. Relative capital costs are lower. Therefore, capital-intensive activities become relatively less costly with industrialization. The net effect of these influences will be to raise real truck average variable costs relatively to the level of rail average variable costs, since rail transport has a lower labor input (the final absolute levels, of course, cannot be predicted and are, in any event, unimportant, since we are analyzing the cost advantages of one mode in relation to another and here relative costs are enough for traffic assignment). We assume that the net effect is to raise truck variable costs by 50%. The results are shown in Table 9.7.

While the road data of Table 9.6 are believed to be reasonable and applicable under certain conditions, the analyst should be cautioned against using them indiscriminately without necessary adjustment. The two most important areas where adjustments may be needed are road construction costs and variable costs on unbalanced routes. To recall, the basic empirical input to the table is the PRTC Baghdad-Basra trip prices, and here the traffic of the PRTC, at any rate, is fairly well balanced. If the analyst is assigning traffic on an unbalanced flow, truck costs per ton-kilometer will rise. The amount may be easily calculated following the procedures outlined in Section 4.2.2 on directional imbalance. Note that on any unbalanced flow, average rail costs are also higher. Therefore, the traffic assignment on that link may be affected only a little *once it is decided to assign traffic* to that link. However, an optimizing solution might not assign traffic to unbalanced links if it is known that the costs on unbalanced flow are much higher due to imbalance.

The other area where adjustments may be necessary is capital cost. No capital charge is placed on existing roads, since their costs are sunk and the capital they represent has no alternative use. This assumption was also made for railroads. For new roads a construction cost of 50,000 ID will be assumed. This is higher than the historical average construction cost of 35,000 ID but is probably a reasonable reflection of inflation up to 1974 and quality differences on future roads. Therefore, we include a charge of 2500 ID, 5% a year, as the capital component to be averaged over annual traffic and combined with average total variable cost to compare with the railroad average total cost for purposes of traffic assignment. A second calculation is based on an assumed construction cost of 100,000 ID per kilometer. If higher costs are contemplated it is an easy matter to allow for them following the approach used here.

4.3   River Costs

An estimate of river costs may be calculated in the following way. First, we assume that terminal costs are about the same as railroad terminal bulk costs—say 250 fils per ton in 1970. One estimate (Podoski, 1970, p. 52) places average river barge cost at one fils per ton-kilometer in that year. For Baghdad-Basra, the distance by river is about 1200 kilometers, about twice the rail distance because of the river's winding course. Assuming that Podoski's estimate was intended to relate to this route, a "line-haul" cost of 0.75 fils per ton-kilometer is implied. We also estimate the annual river maintenance cost as 1 million ID. From this we may calculate the average variable costs as shown in Table 9.6. We further assume a capital investment of 32 million ID to improve the levees and deepen channels (annual capital cost of 1.6 million ID). This is substantially more than some recent unofficial estimates of river needs on the Tigris, which, there is reason to believe, were conservative. We can now calculate average total costs as shown in Table 9.7 (1970 costs have been adjusted for inflation in these calculations).

Three important points concerning river transport should be observed in connection with the presentation of data in Table 9.6.

1. Distances are rail or road distances; to calculate river costs we assume river distances to be 100% greater due to the winding course.

2. Average annual variable costs are not presented. To calculate them, the average annual river maintenance cost must be added to the average vehicle cost.

3. Capital cost and maintenance costs in the stub cover individual items that relate to the whole river. Average ton-kilometer costs assume that all traffic moves the distance shown in the stub at left.

4.4 Comparative Costs and Traffic Assignment

Table 9.7 recapitulates and compares the costs for the three modes studied here. When present and future costs must be distinguished, the

Table 9.6 Average Vehicle, Capital, and Total Costs by River in Iraq[a]

Distance by Rail and Road (km)	Average Vehicle Cost (fils/ ton-km)	Average Total Cost at Volume of[b]		
		1 million tons	2 million tons	5 million tons
		CC = 1,600 fils/ton MC = 1,000 fils/ton	CC = 800 fils/ton MC = 500 fils/ton	CC = 320 fils/ton MC = 200 fils/ton
100	4.50	30.50	17.50	9.70
350	2.36	9.79	6.07	3.84
500	2.10	7.30	4.70	3.14
800	1.88	5.13	3.50	2.53

[a] For explanations regarding calculations, see text. Illustrative calculations (at 350 kilometers and two million tons per year): average variable cost/ton-km = average vehicle operating cost/ton-km + average river maintenance cost = 2.36 fils + (1,000,000 ID/2,000,000 tons)/350 = (2.36 + 500/350) fils = 3.79 fils/ton-km. ATC = AVC + ACC = 3.79 + (1,600,000 ID/2,000,000 tons)/350 = 3.79 + 2.28 = 6.07 fils/ton-km.

[b] CC = capital cost; MC = maintenance cost.

variable costs are those applicable to the future situation. For river, we calculate here the average variable cost, which is the sum of the average vehicle cost, shown earlier, and the average maintenance cost (average total cost is taken directly from Table 9.6). Since for river transportation maintenance is a fixed annual sum, the average unit maintenance will depend on volume (for road and rail, it is much more nearly independent of volume). We also extended the table beyond the range of earlier tables to show cost behavior at an annual volume of 10,000,000 tons. Capital costs are as follows: rail, 0.8 fils per ton-kilometer; road, 0.4 fils per ton-kilometer; and river, 160 fils per trip (capital cost) and 100 fils per trip (maintenance cost); 260 fils per trip is then averaged over trip length, as indicated in the stub.

For the large road volumes (over 2 million tons), additional calculations are included on the basis of a construction cost of 100,000 ID per kilometer (annual capital cost of 5000 ID).

The table provides very useful and partly unexpected information on comparative transport costs as they are likely to evolve in Iraq. Perhaps the most surprising conclusions are those resulting from the very high capital costs of rail construction. These conclusions, together with the reservations concerning their use for traffic assignment, are given below. To simplify the exposition, we refer to volumes of 1 or 2 million tons per year as "low" volumes and 5 and 10 million tons as "high" volumes. Similarly, distances of 100 or 350 kilometers will be spoken of as "short" and the others as "long" distances. Also, the reader is reminded that by "costs" we always mean total social costs, not merely those to the industry or the shipper).*

1. River costs are lower at all volumes for trips greater than 100 kilometers. On shorter trips, the terminal costs, combined with the longer travel distances required by river, offset the lower ton-kilometer line-haul costs of river. Since river is lower and its cargoes are susceptible to spoilage from hydration (e.g. bulk cement), these relative costs are not a sufficient criterion for traffic assignment.

2. On low volumes, road is cheaper than rail on almost all distances. This cost comparison allows for the future development of road

---

* In hypothesizing 50,000 and 100,000 ID for highway costs we have not explicitly treated land acquisition costs. Land costs, whatever the government may actually pay, should allow for impact on employment and productivity in agriculture. Assuming 3 hectares per kilometer of a 2-lane road, and a net annual value-added to 50 ID per hectare, which seems a generous estimate, the capital cost of construction would increase by only 4% and would not affect the conclusions of Table 9.7.

Table 9.7 Average Variable and Total Costs in Iraq: Rail, Road, and River (Projected to 1990)[a]

Distance (km)	Future Average Variable Cost (fils/ton-km)	Average Total Costs at Volume of						
		1,000,000 tons (fils/ton-km)	2,000,000 tons (fils/ton-km)	5,000,000 tons		10,000,000 tons		
				Road Capacity Cost = 0.5 fils/ton-km	Road Capacity Cost = 0.1 fils/ton-km	Road Capacity Cost = 0.25 fils/ton-km	Road Capacity Cost = 0.5 fils/ton-km	
100								
Rail	5.83	13.83	9.83	7.43		6.63		
Road	13.20	15.70	14.45	13.70	14.20	13.35	13.70	
River	6.50–14.50	30.50	17.50	9.70		7.10		
350								
Rail	3.87	11.87	7.87	5.47		4.67		
Road	9.90	12.40	11.15	10.40	10.90	10.05	10.40	
River	2.93–5.23	9.79	6.07	3.84		3.10		
500								
Rail	3.64	11.64	7.64	5.24		4.44		
Road	6.60	9.10	7.85	7.10	7.60	6.85	7.10	
River	2.50–4.10	7.30	4.70	3.14		2.62		
800								
Rail	3.52	11.52	7.52	5.12		4.32		
Road	6.20	8.70	7.45	6.70	7.50	6.15	6.70	
River	2.13–3.13	5.13	3.50	2.53		2.20		

[a] Based on annual capital cost of 0.05 × construction cost. Assumed construction costs: rail, 160,700 ID/km; road, 100,000 and 50,000 ID/km; river, see text. For river, the average variable cost is given as a range; annual river maintenance cost is averaged over 1 and 5 million volumes. Road costs assume balanced traffic.

transport costs along lines of the United States, where labor costs are relatively higher and city-access costs will increase the average cost on shorter trips (due to the latter factor, the 100-kilometer haul for volumes of 2-million tons costs more by road than by rail).

3. On high volumes, railroad is preferable. However, it should be stressed that 5 million tons represents a very high traffic volume. Assuming, as we are doing, that traffic moves the whole length of the line, a density of 5,000,000 ton-kilometers per kilometer is implied. This is a high density. On United States lines in the mid-1960s the average density was 2 to 3 million ton-kilometers per kilometer of track. In the Soviet Union, the most railroad-intensive economy in the world (railroads carry about 80% of its traffic), the average density is 7 to 8 million ton-kilometers per kilometer of network.

REFERENCES

Abouchar, Alan (1975), "Transportation and Public Sector Policy in Yugoslavia," *Economic Analysis,* (Belgrade) Vol. 9, No. 3-4.

Iraq Ministry of Planning (1972), *Road Transport Survey* (Baghdad).

Podoski, Jan (1970), *Final Report on Long Term Transport and Communications Planning in Iraq* (Baghdad: Ministry of Planning).

Socialistička federativna republika Jugoslavija (1970), *Saobrácaj i veze, 1970 (Transport and Communications)* (Belgrade).

Planning and Project
Investment Decisions

10

Introduction to Transport Planning

1   PLAN OF PART 3

Transport planning covers many issues, ranging from modal and total transport sector budgets to the evaluation of individual transport projects. Writers do not always treat these topics in a unified way; techniques for project selection are seldom related to modal or total transport budget formulation. Accordingly, the field worker is frequently at a loss to reconcile project decisions with budget allocations made at a macrolevel. The relation of these topics to optimal transport pricing and the theory of costs, which we discussed in Part 2, is frequently even less evident. In Part 3 we attempt to present a unified approach to the questions of transport planning and project appraisal, relating the various aspects among themselves and to the pricing and cost analysis of Parts 1 and 2.

The plan of Part 3 is as follows. Chapters 11 to 13 deal with various aspects of project evaluation. For completeness, Chapter 11 begins with the selection of an investment criterion as the problem might arise in the private sector. We analyze the two major criteria—net discounted benefit and internal rate of return, and some variations thereon—and review problems in their application. There are many such problems, some of them being mere academic curiosa, but others constituting serious impediments to the use of these criteria. When we move to the public sector in Chapter 12, additional problems are introduced in the selection of a project decision criterion. The review of the possible private sector criteria in Chapter 11 will help us resist the temptation to view public sector decision-making as a poor relation to private sector decision-making, the former hopelessly ensnarled in unquantifiable magnitudes and the latter lending itself to the rational calculus of profit maximization.

Chapter 12, on the form of the public sector criterion, continues to probe the issue initiated in Chapter 11 of discounted benefit streams versus internal rate of return. Now the question of the correct discount rate, a final decision on which we can forestall through Chapter 11, must be resolved. This is the main issue of Chapter 12.

Chapter 13 on the measurement of benefits presents two main approaches—triangular and rectangular. The former refers to consumer surplus criteria, which, we conclude, are less satisfactory than is the rectangular approach, where benefits are measured by such categories as net national income change, cost, reduction, and profit. We trace through the logical implications of using any one of these. The state of economic development is a critical consideration in choosing among the criteria, although, if correctly calculated, some of them will amount to the same thing. For example, in a fully employed economy the change in profit accompanying an investment will be equal to the net change in national income. In fact, we will see that the net national income approach offers the clearest guidance to how the calculations should be made in any particular situation, except for projects in which large changes in relative prices may lead to an ambiguous change in national income.

When net national income change gives an ambiguous answer, it is necessary to evaluate a project in terms of a physical criterion. Chapter 14 contains a case study—the Second International Airport at Toronto. This is presented primarily to analyze the conditions that must prevail in the economy in order for a physical criterion to be rational. These conditions relate to the way in which transport demand is given expression. Possible pitfalls in estimation and assumptions are also illustrated in this chapter.

Finally, we turn to the present chapter. This is divided into three sections. In Section 2 we consider some broad issues that must be brought to bear in planning the technology mix. The key to rational behavior here is a proper view of the notion of transport demand, which is often misunderstood. A discussion of this topic shows the different senses in which the term "transport demand" is used by writers and planners. In Section 3 we consider the investment budget, a topic all too frequently left out of the analysis of transport planning or, for that matter, the planning of other public sectors also. Unfortunately, writers have devoted innumerable works to the theory of optimization of investment on a project-by-project basis, but the issue of the determination of the total investment budget is put aside, usually with the implication that it is a readily soluble issue, provided that one goes about project selection in the right way. As we see throughout this part of the book, there are not only many real world frictions, but also numerous conceptual difficulties standing in the way of the application of a project-by-project approach.

2 PLANNING THE TECHNOLOGY MIX AND TRANSPORT DEMAND

2.1 General Considerations

The best combination of technologies in an economy depends on the demand characteristics of the economy, the geophysical environment, and its resource endowment. Planners will usually have to combine more than one mode, even where it is a question of constructing the basic transport network, not to mention peripheral extensions of the basic network to cope with local requirements and conditions in individual regions. Normally, the main contenders for a combined basic network are rail, road, and water (river and coastal) transport, though the possibilities for air transport and pipeline must not be lost from view.

Even though it is sometimes thought that a country should try to reap maximum benefits from scale economies by concentrating on a single mode of transport, it will rarely be efficient to think in black or white ("road or rail") terms when resolving the basic technology issues (though it may occasionally be possible to do so). One of the outstanding examples of developing such a transportation sector is the Soviet Union where railroads have carried 85% or more of the domestic freight and most passenger traffic through most of that country's history. And this undoubtedly does represent rational technology, since most distances are great and the conscious decision to deemphasize consumption and encourage investment meant that (1) passenger motor car production would develop extremely slowly and (2) the consumption sector generally would develop slowly, forestalling the need that might otherwise develop for a one-vehicle origin-to-destination journey with the savings in labor handling, damage, and other transloading costs that such procedures can achieve for consumers goods shipment. But it is important to remember that the scale economies could only be realized because of the earlier decision to postpone the development of those activities for which a different kind of transport technology would be required. To say this is not to endorse the past joint development of road and rail everywhere, however—even in some countries that rely on the market to mold consumption and investment. In Brazil, for example, highways have developed to perform many of the functions that *could* and *should* have been performed by rail or coastal shipping; the United States analogy of "truckers-as-marginal-users-of-roads, developed in the first place for private passenger cars" has often been invoked for the Brazilian highway sector, with pricing policy artificially and inefficiently stimulating the development of truck transport.

In some countries it might have once been more rational to pose the question in "either-or" terms, for much of the network, at least, rather than expecting two or more modes to be developed simultaneously. But by now most countries have undertaken development of several modes, and the relative costs under continued operation *may be* quite different from what the relative modal costs *might have been if the several modes had never been instituted in the first place.*

The existing transport mix will generally lay primary stress on rail or road, with secondary stress on the other mode and/or water transport. In developing economies, the railroads are generally a legacy from colonial days or have been nationalized from a foreign industrial firm. Coastal steamers may also be a relic from the past, and usually are not in good condition. Subsequent investment has frequently simply enabled railroads and ports to stave off decay and replace some rolling stock or other facilities. The question that now must be faced is: how much of any mode can be salvaged and incorporated into a modern system in which the mode realizes its present-day technological efficiencies? Should investment be increased to allow it to do so, or should the mode be permitted to stagnate and continue its demise?

The broad decisions of technology should be based on cost considerations, analyzed and illustrated in Part 2, and their interplay with demand as it has evolved in the past and as it may be expected to develop in the future. However, as we saw, the analysis of cost evolution is full of uncertainties and remains inexact. So, of course, is analysis of demand. This means that recommendations regarding future technology mix will be somewhat uncertain, and the more remote the future date under consideration, the more uncertain will be the analysis. However, one should not exaggerate the need for recommendations concerning the correct technology mix in the future. Precise forecasts of a transport network's length or detailed shape or even of the amount of investment that should be directed into it at a future date are not needed. We will conclude in Section 3.4 that the most reasonable approach is to establish the budget on a year-to-year basis, with the basic budgetary magnitudes generated by the market itself in response to rationally set user charges based on the principles outlined in Part 2.

Some writers would object to this view, suggesting instead that the demand for transport as a whole or individual modes of transport should be the primary consideration in formulating the investment budget. Now, the notion of transport demand, as it is frequently used, contains many defects that obviate its use as a widely applicable category in analyzing transport investment. Indeed, some of the deficiencies in the commonly used notion of transport demand provide a compelling reason to rely instead on a budget generated by user charges. To understand these problems we now examine this critical and frequently misunderstood subject.

2.2 Transport Demand

For purposes of transport sector analysis we must distinguish among three uses of the term "transport demand." The first is the conventional relationship between quantity taken and price, all other things being equal. The other things are usually time, national income, economic structure, and so on. The relationship then shows how quantity taken will increase with reductions in price. As one of these other variables, such as national income, changes, the demand curve would *shift* to the right, as shown by successive rightward movement in Figure 10.1.

Demand is frequently also used in the sense of observed output. In this approach, we determine the historical relationship between quantity taken and, say, national income, population, or time. When one of these is plotted as the independent variable on the X-axis, we generally find the curve rising, showing greater quantities of transport consumed with rising values of the variable. Ideally, this relationship is based on successive supply-demand intersections, such as that at X_0 in Figure 10.2. Figure 10.2a illustrates the successive intersections between supply curves and demand associated with different income levels. The intersection output levels, indicated on the X-axis, are then plotted against national income (Y) in Figure 10.2b—the lower curve. For purposes of planning individual transport projects or modes, it is then a

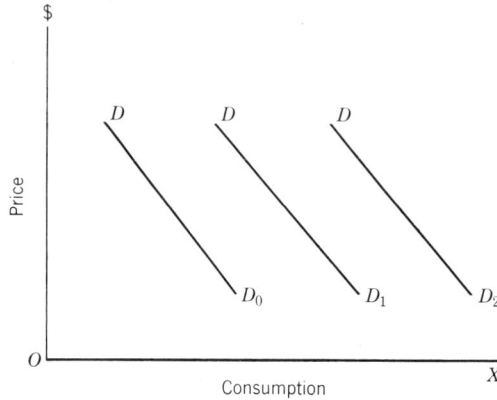

Figure 10.1 Demand schedules at various income levels [$D = F$ (Price, national income i)],

simple matter to calculate the underlying algebraic relationship, extrapolate national income at a rate based on historical trends or planned growth rates, and infer therefrom the transport growth to be expected in the near future or to be associated with the national income in any particular future year.

In the derivation of this equilibrium transport output–national income relationship, we are assuming the supply-demand intersections to be based on a supply curve that reflects the true cost structure. Essentially we have argued that this should be taken to be the average cost of a unit of output from now on, where part of the cost to be incurred "from now on" will include the average incremental investment cost.

There is a third sense in which the term "transport demand" is used. This also results from the intersection of demand and cost curves, as with the second interpretation, but it is not the welfare maximization intersection. In case 2, the supply-demand intersection was based on the true measure of social cost. (If it is necessary to include a component for external diseconomies, this is assumed to be included.) Accordingly, the supply-demand intersection is the activity level that is efficient from the viewpoint of social welfare maximization, and we are justified in using the historical series as a guide to future policy. This equilibrium represents a welfare optimum, since at any lower activity level we know that someone's utility, as measured by the price he is willing to pay; hence the social benefit, since in this case the social benefit will be equal to the private benefit, will exceed the social cost.

In the third sense in which the expression "transport demand" is used, however, while the historical output series still does represent points on the successively rightward shifting demand curves, the points of intersection give activity levels that are higher than the welfare optimization levels and, therefore are inefficient from a welfare maximization point of view. This set of intersections would take place at lower prices than the welfare optimization intersections, which means that the social benefits are less than the social costs. This is exemplified by price P^1 in Figure 10.2a. The historical output–national income

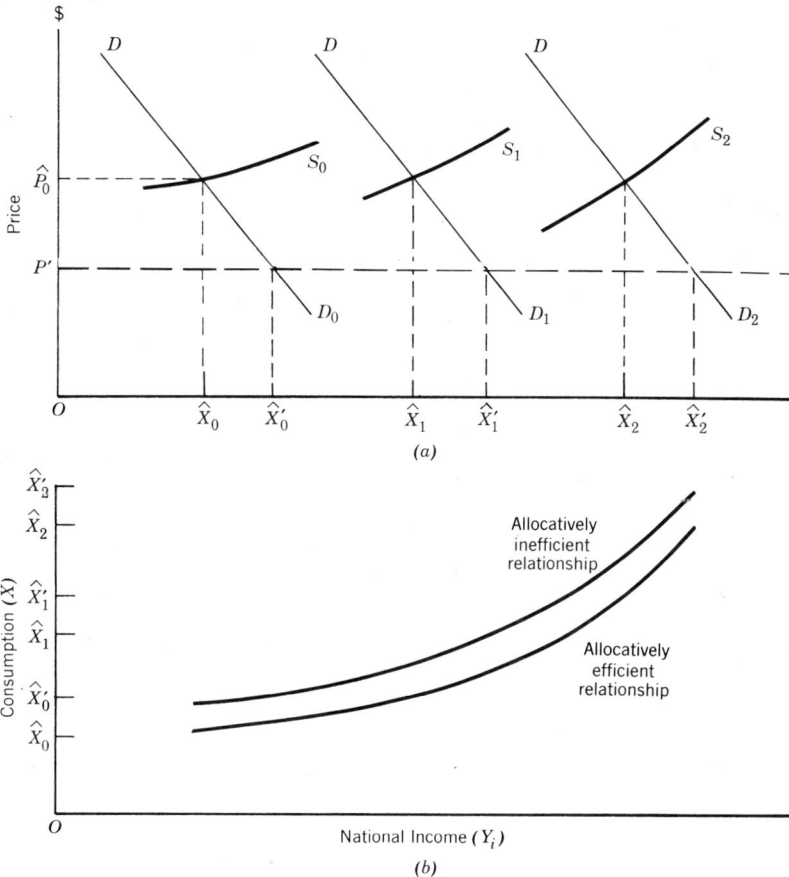

Figure 10.2 Derivation of historical demand-income relationships. (a) $D = f$ (price, income, etc.). Allocatively efficient supply-demand intersections and actual price-demand intersections under distorted market relations. (b) Historically observed demand-income relationships with and without market distortions.

curve that plots the observed historical outputs against national income, which follows from this interpretation, would then lie above the allocatively efficient curve, as in Figure 10.2b. That is, the upper curve shows the actually recorded output levels, based on the actual price policies that have been followed, while the lower curve represents the series of outputs that would be associated with the social cost-demand intersections—the socially optimal output series. Evidently, in this hypothetical example, the historical series overstates the quantity of transport that ought to be provided.

There is a tendency in many countries—perhaps most countries—to underprice transport and, consequently, to generate a historical series that overstates transport activity as compared with socially optimal levels. Such a series should more properly be called "transport output" or "traffic" rather than "transport demand." If these terms were actually used, transport investment plans based on them would probably be challenged by other public agencies or by private sector observers. Many people would question the need to provide facilities for projected traffic levels and might ask instead, "why?" Economists might argue that we should seek some sort of overall optimization, which might involve a *reduction* in traffic rather than an increase in traffic. A transport development objective, cast in the normative or welfare language of "demand," however, takes on the aura of unimpeachable prescription.

3 PLANNING THE INVESTMENT BUDGET

In spite of its tremendous importance, the planning of the investment budget is not usually treated in works devoted to transport economics and policy. Consequently, fiscal authorities are given little encouragement to improve *ad hoc* procedures. In this section we survey and compare procedures actually used or recommended for use, indicating their major problems in practice. One caution. To speak of procedures in use is not to suggest that in any given situation a given procedure is used to the exclusion of others. Nor does it mean that a given procedure actually was the basis for an investment plan at a particular time. It may merely constitute a rationalization after the fact, a justification for a (frequently) politically determined decision previously arrived at. In this case, our criticism may be even more important, since the object of the criticism is only a veil—the underlying justification for a budget is weak and would bear even less public scrutiny.

In this section we proceed as follows: Section 3.1 treats one major approach—extrapolation of measures of past performance such as historical traffic/investment ratios, usually supplemented by projections of traffic, called "demand." The reader can probably surmise on the basis of the previous argument the nature of the potential inefficiency here. In Section 3.2 we consider investment allocation based on international analogy, where there are also numerous pitfalls.

Many works have been written on the theory of optimization of investment in individual projects. But the issue of the determination of the total investment budget is left aside, usually with the implication that it is a readily soluble issue, provided that one goes about project selection in the right way. As we will see, this approach fails to reckon with many real world frictions, but there are also numerous conceptual difficulties standing in the way of application of this approach. This is the subject of Section 3.3.

Following the discussion and rejection of the project optimization approach, we turn in Section 3.4 to an approach based essentially on a user-generated revenue constraint, possibly with some supplement. This approach is admittedly less ambitious than the project optimization approach, but superior to it because of administrative and conceptual difficulties of the latter.

3.1   The "Demand Approach" (Projection of Past Activity Levels)

As we noted earlier, a common approach to investment budgeting is to extrapolate historical transport output time trends, or output-national income relationships. The discussion of transport demand in Section 22, shows the deficiency of this approach—pricing distortions in the past may have caused the actually observed activity levels to deviate sharply from the socially efficient activity levels. This is certainly the case, for example in Brazil, where throughout the 1960s railroad rates were set at levels of 40% or less of total variable cost as we defined it in Chapter 6 (i.e. reflecting all operating costs including depreciation of rolling stock). The analysis of Brazilian railroad rates in Chapter 8 and elsewhere (Abouchar, 1970) is convincing documentation that traffic there has been artificially and inefficiently encouraged through the rate policies. A similar tendency is observed in the highway sector where the prices charged to highway users (determined through analysis of the relevant tax patterns) are also far below warranted user charges. All of these stimuli almost certainly lead to total transport levels that are inefficiently high, resulting in too much interregional traffic in place of greater local production. At the very least, these distortions have provoked too much highway and railroad shipment, which could have been performed much more efficiently by coastal transport.

The inadequacy of projections of historical trends is not limited to the case of developing economies, however. The bulk of the United States interstate highway system has probably been overbuilt, reflecting not the efficient demand for intercity highway transportation, but an inefficiently high historical traffic experience. The historical trends were conditioned by political pressures of the highway lobby—oil companies, motor vehicle producers, rubber companies, and trucking firms. Investment was allocated to the highway system through an earmarking of gasoline tax revenues, generated largely *outside* the Interstate Highway System, a huge portion of it within cities.

Forecasts of historical activity levels adjusted for population or national income growth as well as more sophisticated approaches involving socioeconomic composition and determinants of trip generation are frequently used also in the analysis of individual project investments. In Chapter 14 we look at a particular investment project—the Second Toronto International Airport—the analysis of which relied heavily on such trends. We will there inquire into the welfare significance of such relationships and show that they can be accepted only if there have been no historical distortions.

3.2　Investment Allocation by International Analogy

It is sometimes attempted to allocate transport investment on the basis of international experience. As is usually the case with international comparisons, such information should be used only with great care. We consider here four obstacles to the casual use of international experience.

3.2.1　*Differences in Output Mix*

Any given economy may have special requirements for transportation. For example, it may have long distances or require shipments of special kinds of products—bulk commodities, for example. As a result, total transport output is an extremely heterogeneous concept and foreign experience cannot be assumed as a norm for the given country. Therefore, we cannot take the transport capital stock or the transport investment observed internationally as a norm for the home country. Moreover, even if output were homogeneous—if a ton-mile of transport of the average commodity were a meaningful output measure—it might still be possible to produce it by a different amount of capital in the home country as compared with international experience, implying a different investment level. In fact, as we see next, the capital/output ratio may vary very substantially among countries.

3.2.2 *Differences in Modal Composition*

International experience may relate to modal mixes that are extremely inappropriate for the home country. For example, the home country might have an excellent potential for a system of river arteries, which can usually be developed at lower cost than rail transport. If the international average experience is accepted as a norm, there is a great danger that the low-cost river transport will be neglected. This kind of problem, of course, is more serious if a country consciously patterns its development of individual modes on the behavior of other countries. Thus the need for ambitious highway expansion programs in developing economies is frequently justified by reference to the experience of Western Europe or North America. This approach fails to exploit the special resources of the home country. The neglect of coastal transport in Brazil while developing highway transport between 1960 and 1970 is an example of such an approach.

3.2.3 *Geophysical Differences*

Obviously, the home country may have special geophysical conditions that, even if the modal mix is to be the same as in other countries, may occasion a very different cost pattern. For example, a highway network in the North temperate zone, which must guard against severe winter damage, implies very different costs from those to be expected in a Mediterranean region. Railway construction costs in hilly or mountainous regions will be much greater than on flat terrain so that, even if the modal composition is the same, investment requirements would differ for the same output level.

In fact, widely different geophysical conditions would probably lead to different modal compositions, which would affect investment requirements for a given output level. More fundamentally the widely different cost patterns would probably warrant different transport intensities for the economies in the first place. In this case, it would only be the sheerest coincidence if the same amounts of investment were undertaken, providing for similar output levels. No normative significance could be attached to such a relationship.

3.2.4 *Stages of Development*

Finally, even if we did not have all of the foregoing vexations to contend with, the transport investment/national income ratio might well vary as a function of the level of economic development. Investment should not be allocated according to the relationship observed in other countries that are not at a similar stage of development. For example, total transport investment in an advanced economy, which includes a large contribution toward consumption through automobile investment and related investment in highways, would be inappropriate for a still undeveloped economy. More generally, developed economies would transport more final consumption goods, which require different kinds of transport facilities. On the other hand, countries still in the course of development might require larger threshold investment in transportation.

Unfortunately, the relationship between the transport investment/national income ratio and stage of development is not unidirectional. According to the study by Dražen Bejaković, in 1970 the share of investment going into transport and communications starts out high (27%) in the poorest five countries included in his study. It falls to 15% for the seven next poorest countries, and rises thereafter to an average of 19% for the two most developed groups of countries. These two groups include advanced industrialized countries, observed for varying periods of time since World War II. Ten socialist countries, also observed for varying periods of time since the war, show an average of 12% (Bejaković, 1970).

These results may be entirely compatible with a theory of development holding that the poorest countries have to execute tremendous threshold investments before any meaningful progress can be achieved. However, the very high Group IV average of 27% was heavily influenced by two very mountainous countries, Afganistan and Nepal, while the low Group III average of 15% was heavily influenced by the very low share in Ecuador (4%), also a mountainous country. All these differences may simply reflect the peculiar needs of individual countries, as stressed above. Here we merely note that there is room for deviation from the average performance of the relevant country group and, therefore, the significance of these averages should not be exaggerated. On the other hand, when a country does depart sharply from the average for its group, it should prompt questions about the methods by which basic investment is allocated. In this book and elsewhere (Abouchar, 1969, 1970) the author has raised serious questions regarding the pricing policies followed in the Brazilian transport sector; many

individual transport project decisions and, indeed, the overall development of individual transport modes have also been questioned. If one
found that, in spite of these reservations, the total transport investment
share in Brazil was only on the order of 12 to 15% of national income
(its group average being 19%), we might have to reconsider these conclusions. In fact, however, during the early 1960s Brazil was devoting 25
to 30% of total investment to transport, that is, 6 to 11% greater than
the Group II average. As we have stressed, such a comparison by itself
cannot be taken as conclusive evidence that too much has been invested
in transport, but is strongly suggestive when taken together with the evidence presented elsewhere.

3.3   The Project Optimization Approach to
the Investment Budget

Readers aware of the great progress in the development of project selection techniques in the past 20 years may suppose that determination of
the investment budget is a trivial matter, an exercise in paper shuffling
which can take place after the individual projects have been selected.
The apportionment of investment, according to this view, would simply
be the result of chalking up the individual investments to be made in
each mode, and then totaling the modal subtotals. The truth is that
there remain many obstacles to the unquestioned use of the recently
developed project selection techniques and, accordingly, they cannot be
relied upon as the exclusive determinant of investment allocation. These
difficulties are both empirical and conceptual.

Project selection criteria are the subject of Chapters 10 to 12. We see
that the best way to use the criteria developed for rational investment
decisions is subject to the budget constraint implied by the *prior* investment allocation decision. A number of serious problems arise in regard
to project selection criteria. The correct discount concept for comparing
differential cost and benefit streams must be specified and the rate
empirically determined. Benefits must be defined and measured in different economic sectors, such as transportation, steel production, and
education. Labor costs must be correctly measured, recognizing that the
opportunity cost of labor may vary among regions, leading to problems,
as discussed in Chapter 7. And a procedure for measuring benefits must
be established.

In addition, administrative complexities exist that impose real costs
on the economy but usually are not, taken into account, though in principle they could be, in discussions of optimal project selection. The fact
is that higher real costs *would* be involved if there were violent shifts in

the intersectoral and/or intermodal distribution of investment. Under the project-by-project optimization approach, the possibility could not be precluded that this year only highway projects would be selected while next year all would be railroad projects or at least some radical shift in the proportion of highway and railroad projects. Another year might see major shifts between, say, agriculture and education. If the administrative costs (setting up and closing down the administration) are not taken into account—and they rarely are, since projects are normally evaluated on the assumption of a frictionless bureaucratic transfer—high costs would accompany radical changes in sectoral programs from one year to the next. Investment would be more efficient if some degree of stability were administratively imposed on the bureaucracy to gain, and improve upon, its expertise, reduce the interregional transfers of equipment, and so on. Following such a procedure, we must recognize that, in some years, projects in some sectors may fail to be undertaken, even though they might have a higher payoff than projects executed in other regions or sectors. Once it has been decided to use a "satisficing" approach of this kind, the question arises of how to draw up the budget. We propose that the budget be based on a properly conceived system of user charges.

3.4   Investment Budget Based on User Charge Revenues

We have seen that there is no obvious way to translate historical traffic growth into a statement of investment needs, primarily because past growth may have been artificially stimulated through distorting, low prices. Nor can international comparisons be relied on. We also argued that for a number of reasons the investment budget could not be formulated by summing up projects showing the best payoff.

We first consider the example of the highway sector, which is usually the most important sector today in regard to investment, and then generalize the recommendations based on this sector. In Chapter 2 we developed a theory of intranetwork loans to support expansion of the highway network. We argued that if the road transport network was being expanded at the rate of 10 to 15% a year—the situation in many developing countries—or less, as in industrialized countries, a large part of the new investment expenditure *could* and *should* be generated by the traffic on the already existing network. The road transport network was defined to include roads whose principal *raison d'être* is the movement of people and goods, rather than the opening up of new areas for settlement, the purpose of which could be regarded as income distribution or national defense. The traffic would contribute to the investment only in amounts limited to the minimum cost reduction that the truckers on the new or improved roads receive, averaged over all traffic (the demand-related user charge component). This policy would ensure that no truck is forced out of the traffic stream if its movement is efficient, since it is asked to pay only an amount equal to its cost reduction, on the average, after the investment (together, of course, with its vehicle-size-related damage). This would be the case over a period of years, although in one year a truck of some region might gain more and in other years less than it paid through this demand-related user charge, as the administrative authority (the individual state)* shifted its investment from one area to another within the state.

As presented in Chapter 2, the revenue generated by the demand-related user charge was to be used to defray investment as well as the annual recurrent maintenance costs, such as snow removal. (The highway deterioration charges, measured by the AASHO coefficients, would cover pavement restoration costs.) This should go into an earmarked road fund and form the basic guide to road activity *within that administrative authority*. We recall here two important considerations. (1) This does not preclude income transfers made from rich to poor states. These should be made independently of any transport budget and their use decided upon in the beneficiary region, as is done in Yugoslavia, with all claims within the recipient state, such as roads, highways, and steel mills, competing for the funds. (2) It was recognized that individual states might find it in their interest to build additional highways, beyond those permitted by their user-charge-generated constraint, either as part of the main interstate connections or as part of their locally oriented road network. Extra amounts that states wish to subscribe in this manner should then be decided by the local state government, the funds originating in supplementary subscriptions contributed from other persons, communities, or firms or coming out of the explicit interregional income transfers. Decisions on what costs to impute to unemployed labor, or how to measure the benefit from hospitals versus roads could be weighed more meaningfully at the local level than at the federal level. These decisions would be made through public debates, legislative argument, cabinet-level persuasion, and/or local referendum, and it is likely that the apportionment agreed upon would remain reasonably stable over a period of several years. Being sensitive to local pressures, however, one department would be less likely to gain excessive power and be able to insist on maintaining its

---

* For simplicity we use the term "state" to mean the main subdivision in the country, which may in fact be called "republic," "province," "state," and so on.

investment allocation in the face of a shift in public sentiments to other sectors.

The approach just proposed can be applied in its essentials to the expansion of other modes as well. The pricing structure of the railroads, for example, should include a depreciation component that can be used for capital expansion. This relates to capital investment needs that are modest in relation to the existing network—adding 8 to 10% track per year, upgrading of track, and so on. In this case, the investment funds could be generated out of current revenues. But if the investment proposals are very large in relation to existing traffic, precluding the use of user-charge revenues to cover investments simultaneously, one cannot generalize that the principle of covering investments out of user charges should be retained. We must then know the reasons for the large investments, and we must determine why present traffic cannot generate funds to cover these investments.

If the investments are designed to upgrade track, replace and upgrade rail, put in concrete ties, electrify some stretches, and so on, and the network is a highly ramified system, the investment fund should come from the capital market, either through the banking system or in the form of bond subscriptions, with the capital integrated into the cost structure of the railroad. The same procedure should be applied to any government corporation. The argument sometimes heard in Canada and in the United States that the railroads are a "public good" or "social overhead capital" and, consequently, should be paid for from an overall public fund is meritricious. In general, railroad operation cannot be said to be an income distribution activity, and, as we saw in Chapter 1, there is no economic efficiency justification for providing such activities out of grants from general tax revenues.

Exhortation for public support today in Canada, for example, is sometimes based on the historic government support for the construction of the Canadian Pacific and the key role that this line played in confederation in the nineteenth century. This argument cannot justify public participation today. This is not inconsistent. It *was* necessary for confederation; if the people at the time believed confederation to be a good thing, this was part of the price the provinces were paying for it. What political goal would be promoted by general public sector subsidization of the main Canadian railroads today? If one *could* find some way in which all would benefit, without distorting relative prices, there might be some argument for public grant. But since this does not seem to be the case, this approach cannot be defended.

In some countries the argument can be advanced that the present system is too backward for the present traffic levels to indicate the rail demand that would be observed on a high-quality railroad system. However, here it is relatively easy to calculate the implied cost of upgrading and operating services on various major subnetworks within the system. In Brazil, for example, such a calculation would almost certainly result in the closing of 70% of the mileage. The rest of the system does have an economic justification and incorporating investment expenditure into the cost base for the remaining traffic seems a reasonable approach. Indeed, it is followed, for example, on the densest railroad line in the country, which is a subsidiary of a mining operation, and there seems no reason not to proceed this way on the rest of the system as well. We are suggesting, it should be emphasized, not to restrict capital investment to *simultaneously generated revenues,* but to build the investment into the cost base for *rate-making purposes in the future.*

We have been talking about improving the existing mileage and/or making small increments. This does not cover all possibilities for transport investment, however, and in some other instances, a different approach might be justifiable. But we should emphasize that it is justifiable because the considerations are different. Thus on an isolated project—a regional development project, for example, in which the notion of intranetwork loans cannot be applied because the project is not part of a network, as we will see in subsequent chapters—different considerations apply. We are then concerned primarily with questions of income distribution and/or generation of income through employment of slack or underutilized factors of production. In such cases we should invest in projects where the contribution to national income growth per dollar of investment is greatest. Here the national income growth that takes place will be based on presently underutilized factors, without forgoing any opportunities by attracting the factors to these uses. It is then reasonable for the government to invest in a road or railroad as readily as it might invest in an irrigation scheme or grain elevator. The essential difference is that in the case of minor additions to networks it is very important not to distort prices since, as we know, price distortions almost invariably entail inefficiency. In the underemployed part of the economy, on the other hand, where resources are being underutilized today, any investment that is not at variance with overall social and political goals and laws should be considered for public execution.

Finally, the reader should be warned against being deceived by labels. The fact that the investment fund of some transport mode is earmarked does not legitimize the investment budget of that mode. The earmarking procedure may be based on regulations that do not ensure that the amounts involved are actually related to warranted user charges. Three examples will illustrate the problem.

1. Construction of the U.S. Interstate Highway System is based on gasoline tax revenues, a very large share of which is generated outside of the Interstate Highway System—within cities and on secondary roads. Such users do not benefit from the system (except, of course, when they actually do drive on it) even indirectly, from reduced congestion on parallel roads. Traffic on U.S. 90, for example, does not relieve the traffic in downtown Cleveland. Accordingly, the revenue originating in such activities should not be taken as part of a proper budget constraint for the Interstate Highway System. (Even less justified, of course, would have been the earmarking of part of the alcohol tax mentioned in the footnote on p. 28 in Chapter 2.)

2. A second example of incorrect earmarking is the Brazilian railroad network, which, according to 1966 legislation, was to receive 9.4% of the total fuel tax revenues (Ministerio do Planejamento, 1967, p. 72). At the time annual railroad fuel consumption was 2 or 3% of total fuel consumption. In fact, much of this fund actually got into railroad operations rather than into the investment fund, but this is merely another perversity.

3. Finally, our earlier analysis of the Yugoslav highway user charge pattern showed that even the taxes that are levied must be analyzed to see whether they are actually what their names say. Recognizing that they might not be we must conclude that it is not sufficient merely to check whether the earmarking includes taxes generated within the mode. We must also see whether the taxes themselves are the correct ones to impose.

REFERENCES

Abouchar, Alan (1969), "Public Investment Allocation and Pricing Policy for Transportation," in Howard S. Ellis, ed., *The Economy of Brazil* (Berkeley, University of California Press).

———— (1970), "Pricing Rationality and Deficits on the Brazilian Railroads." *Journal of Transport Economics and Policy,* Vol. 4, No. 3, September.

Bejaković, Dražen (1970), "The Share of Transport and Communications in Total Investment," *Journal of Transport Economics and Policy, Vol. 4. No. 3, September.*

Ministerio do Planejamento (1967), *Plano Decenal de Desenvolvimento Economico e Social,* Book III, Vol. 2, *Transportes* (Rio de Janeiro).

CHAPTER

11

Investment Criteria
for the Private Sector

1 WHY SHOULD WE LOOK AT THE PRIVATE SECTOR?

Projects must be evaluated and ranked if the investment budget is formulated by the method recommended in Chapter 10, as well as under the more ambitious approach of comparing recommended projects intersectorally and interregionally and aggregating them for each sector in order to distribute the investment funds over the departments of the public sector. In this chapter we consider the theoretical advantages and deficiencies of the formulations that have been developed over the years regarding the basic decision criterion. Although our main objective is to choose one criterion for general application, examining the properties of the various criteria helps to develop the analyst's understanding of their economic significance and to teach him to recognize situations in which a different criterion may be more suitable. Many writers in the field tend to become partisans of one criterion or another and may tend to exaggerate the advantages of one criterion over another. Accordingly, to develop independent judgment, the analyst should consider the problem in depth.

The main principle behind the art of project selection is to choose the project for investment that has the greatest social payoff. The definition of social payoff involves three questions: (1) how to measure the benefits in any year? (2) how to measure the costs in any year? and (3) how to make the time streams of different projects commensurate by reducing them to single numbers that can be compared? So many difficulties can be encountered at every turn that many writers on economic organization as well as practitioners suggest that public sector criteria are inherently elusive and illusory. Consequently, they criticize attempts to rationalize public sector investment, implying at the same time that private sector criteria are based on a much firmer foundation. Therefore, we introduce this topic by reviewing private sector investment choice theory. We see that owing to real world frictions there are obstacles to the actual implementation of all of the main decision criteria and to the welfare maximization that is supposed to result from their use even for a firm devoted to pure profit maximization. In addition, of course, there may sometimes be institutional impediments to their use, further keeping the private sector from attaining an optimum. This examination of the private sector will provide a good perspective to public sector decision-making. Invidious comparisons are often made between the two sectors regarding their ability to make intelligent (read, "welfare maximizing") decisions. We do not rule out the possibility that private sector decisions are better; but if they are, it is not because they are based on inherently superior decision rules.

The examination also enriches our understanding of the role and nature of interest and its possible use as a means of comparing different time streams, to pave the way for Chapter 12.

2   INTRODUCTION TO PRIVATE SECTOR INVESTMENT OPTIMIZATION RULES

Numerous criteria have been proposed for private sector investment optimization. These criteria are not always mutually consistent. Moreover, the criteria cannot always be readily calculated, since, as we will see, the information inputs that are held constant when we explain the various criteria cannot always be assumed to be constant in real life. Thus the rate of interest that a company must pay on a project loan may depend on the projects to be selected, but the selection process may require an interest rate as an input in the first place. This is only the start of the difficulties that are encountered when we look to the private sector for guidance. It may turn out, for example, that none of the principal optimization criteria discussed in Sections 3 and 4 is in fact used and that management is heavily influenced by personal interests (Section 5). Thus there may be a divergence between the private interest of managers and the private interests of the corporation shareholders, posing an impediment to the use of procedures that optimize from the shareholders' point of view. Finally, there may be price distortions that preclude the optimality of private sector criteria even if they are used consistently and optimally from the viewpoint of the collective interests of the firm (management and shareholders).

According to the basic assumption of profit maximization, a firm should make any investment that will have a net positive return. It does not matter whether it uses its own funds or borrowed funds. Beyond this basic prescription, it is not possible to give an unambiguous rule about investment decisions, except in the simplest case—a firm borrows money and invests it in the first year, determines the annual net income flows (net of interest payments), and compares the sum of the net revenue stream with the original loan, either by repaying installments on the original loan out of current receipts or by reinvesting current receipts and repaying the loan at the end of the loan duration. In both cases we assume for simplicity that the salvage value of the project is zero, although a positive salvage value could easily be integrated into this scheme. In this simplest situation, as long as there is any positive net income (after paying all wages and salaries), the investment should be undertaken. The firm should undertake all investments that produce a positive return.

Real life does not permit such a simple criterion. To understand the problems, let us consider some of the assumptions that are implicit in the criterion just stated. First, it assumes that there is a perfect capital market in the sense that the firm can borrow all the money it wants at the going interest rate. That is, the going interest rate is assumed to be an equilibrium interest rate, which will ensure that every company will be able to borrow for all projects having a return higher than that interest rate, while projects having a lower return are automatically priced out of the market. Moreover, the interest rate is assumed to be known and stable (since it takes time to evaluate projects, this approach implicitly supposes the same interest rate to be applicable when projects are actually undertaken). Finally, the possibility that different projects will have different time streams is ignored. Since all of these implicit assumptions are open to question, a more refined investment criterion must be formed. Indeed, the only thing that may be salvaged is the assumption that the firm will be willing to borrow if it is a profit maximizer. We turn then to the three main criteria that have been proposed. These are the net discounted absolute return (NDAR), the net discounted relative return (NDRR), and the internal rate of return (IRR).

3 DISCOUNTED CRITERIA

We consider first the NDAR and NDRR. The formulas for these expressions are as follows:

Criterion	Decision Rule

(1) $\text{NDAR} = \sum_{t=0}^{T} (R_t - C_t)(1 + b)^{-t}$ Invest in all projects where $\text{NDAR} > 0$

(2) $\text{NDRR} = \sum_{t=1}^{T} (R_t - C_t)(1 + b)^{-t}/C_0$ Invest in all projects where $\text{NDRR} > 1$

where R_t = revenue in year t
$\quad\quad C_t$ = cost in year t (excluding any depreciation of original invest-
$\quad\quad\quad$ ment)
$\quad\quad C_0$ = cost in year zero, that is, the amount of the investment
$\quad\quad b$ = the rate of discount
$\quad\quad T$ = the duration of the project

How have these rules been developed? Why or in what sense will either of them lead to an optimal decision? The answer most often given is that they ensure that the discounted present value is at least equal to the investment cost. This is almost a tautology which hides more than it reveals. But the genesis of the rule is essential for our understanding of the proper role and limitations of discounting of public sector benefit streams.

Consider the absolute criterion. The net return in year t is $R_t - C_t$. Suppose that this money can be reinvested in year t at a rate of return equal to b until the end of the time horizon, which is year T. Moreover, the reinvestment in any year will itself generate returns at rate b in subsequent years, until year T. Every year's return will thus be compounded over the remaining years $(T - t)$, yielding by year T a return equal to $(R_t - C_t)(1 - b)^{T-t}$. Hence the total return at the end of T years will be

(3) $\sum_{t=0}^{T} (R_t - C_t)(1 + b)^{T-t} = \sum_{t=0}^{T} (R_t - C_t)(1 + b)^{-t} (1 + b)^{T}$ or

(4) $(1 + b)^{T} \sum_{t=0}^{T} (R_t - C_t)(1 + b)^{-t}$

We may rewrite (4) as

(5) $(1 + b)^T \sum_{t=1}^{T} (R_t - C_t)(1 + b)^{-t} + (1 + b)^T (-C_0)(1 + b)^0$, or

(6) $\qquad (1 + b)^T \sum_{t=1}^{T} (R_t - C_t)(1 + b)^{-t} - (1 + b)^T (C_0)$

The profit maximization assumption tells us to invest as long as there is a positive return, that is, as long as this expression is greater than zero. As long as this is true, we have

(7) $\qquad (1 + b)^T \sum_{t=1}^{T} (R_t - C_t)(1 + b)^{-t} > (1 + b)^T C_0$

and, dividing through by $(1 + b)^T$, we have

(8) $\qquad \sum_{T=1}^{T} (R_t - C_t)(1 - b)^{-t} > C_0$

The argument for the relative criterion is similar.

In deriving the criterion, b, was the rate of return. It is the ability of earnings to be reinvested, to be productive, that justifies the criterion. It does not matter whether the earnings are reinvested in a physical process or in a financial asset. Such an opportunity should merely be available. However the criterion makes no distinction between borrowed and own funds. Accordingly, we must also show that this decision rule leads to a positive net return in the case of borrowed funds. Suppose that b is both rate at which the firm can borrow and the rate at which it can reinvest or lend. The cost of the borrowed funds compounded for T years and then repaid will be $(1 + b)^T C_0$, while the money earned and reinvested each year will be the summation in (3) starting with $t = 1$, which is equal to the first summation in (5), which under the decision rule is seen to be at least equal to $(1 + b)^T C_0$.

With a perfect capital market, we invest in the same projects under both decision rules. However, the projects will probably be ranked differently under the two rules. This evidently does not make a difference for the selection of projects as long as the firm has access to funds to invest in every project whose value exceeds the cutoff levels, zero and unity, respectively. This presupposes a perfect capital market in which the firm has unlimited access to funds.

Now, while the discounted present value criteria seem straightforward, several problems prevent their use from leading to optimal project decisions, even in the private sector. The following four problems illustrate this feature of discounted criteria.

1. In practice, the capital market cannot be expected to operate as

smoothly as is assumed here. One can expect that there will be capital rationing, the banks deciding to allow just so much to any client, for example. Loans to a client beyond this amount may be made only at higher interest rates. Higher interest rates require recalculation of all projects, and a different set of affirmative project decisions may emerge. Questions then arise concerning the treatment of interest rates. In principle, all possible combinations and sequence of projects should be evaluated, with the funds against which higher rates are being charged being assigned to the marginal project. The projects should be reevaluated in a number of iterations, allowing each project to have a turn at being evaluated with the higher rate.

2. If capital is rationed by some device other than its price, the firm will be unable to invest in all projects down to the cutoff point. It will have to stop at an earlier project. If the projects are ranked according to the NDAR we may well get a different group of projects for investment than we would have by using the present value ratio. That the relative present value is optimal in the first place derives from the optimality of the absolute difference as a criterion, which followed from the profit maximization principle. This suggests that the absolute criterion should be given priority. However, the equivalence of the criteria was derived only under the assumption of a perfect capital market. Without such a market, the absolute criterion may lead to wrong results. This can be seen from the example in Table 11.1. If investment is restricted to eight units because of borrowing constraints, we do better to go by the relative rather than the absolute criterion.

Table 11.1 Comparison of Results with Absolute and Relative Criteria

Project	$\sum_{t=1}^{T}(R_t-C_t)(1+b)^{-t}$	C_0	NDRR $\dfrac{\sum_{t=1}^{T}(R_t-C_t)(1+b)^{-t}/C_0}{}$ Value	Rank	NDAR $\sum_{t=0}^{T}(R_t-C_t)(1+b)^{-t}$ Value	Rank
A	11	5	2.2	3	6	2
B	16	8	2.0	4	8	1
C	5	2	2.5	2	3	3
D	3	1	3.0	1	2	4
If firm can borrow only eight units						
Projects selected			A, C, D		B	
Total Net return			11		8	

3. The project rankings will depend on the interest rate used, since this will affect the size of the discounted benefit stream. But there can be no guarantee that the interest rate used when the projects are evaluated will hold up and be relevant when the actual loans are made. Normally not too consequential, this may be problematic in times of rapidly fluctuating interest rates, such as 1974 in North America (see Chapter 12). This will affect the project rankings, which must then be reviewed. We note, furthermore, that the lender may not share the view of the firm and may have a different idea of priorities. It may be unwilling to lend for certain projects because of other considerations.

4. To demonstrate the optimality of present value criteria we earlier assumed that the firm could lend at the same rate at which it could borrow. This enabled us to shift the total net present value of the stream of positive earnings to the last year of the project life (year T) and relate it to the total principal plus compound interest due the lender at the end of the term. That is, we showed that any project selected would be profitable, since $(1 + b)^T \sum_{t=1}^{T} (R_t - C_t) (1 + b)^{-t} > (1 + b)^T C_0$. Any other sequence of repayments of interest or principal could easily be accommodated, and optimality maintained, so long as the borrowing and lending rates were the same. Now, in fact only rarely or never will the project initiator be able to borrow and lend at the same rates. This applies both to borrowing the initial principal, with the returns used to repay the interest at the end of the period, and to investing his own funds and calculating the sacrifice made by forgoing the return he might earn on the money by lending it out. However, the decision criterion can easily be adjusted to accommodate differences in borrowing and lending rates, as well as more complicated modifications of the repayment stream (e.g., interest to be repaid currently and principal to be repaid in constant amounts). For illustration, we assume the simple situation in which total principal plus accumulated interest (on an annual compound basis) are repaid at the end of the period, and the borrowing rate (b_b) is not equal to the lending rate (b_e). With reinvestment, the net revenue stream from year 1 to year T is then equal to $(1 + b_e)^T \sum_{t=1}^{T} (R_t - C_t)(1 + b_e)^{-t}$, which must exceed $C_0(1 + b_b)^T$ for the project to be profitable. Therefore, the ratio of the present value of the return stream must be discounted by the *lending rate* rather than the *borrowing rate*. The ratio of present value to the period zero investment (C_0) must be greater than $(1 + b_b)^T/(1 + b_e)^T$, which is a fairly simple adjustment. (Any other assumption about the repayment stream

could be adjusted for by similar considerations, although the final rule will of course be more complicated.) However, this requires knowledge about the future lending rate, which, of course, is uncertain.

These and other difficulties in the use of discounted criteria have led some economists along other paths of inquiry. The main candidate to replace the discounted criteria is the internal rate of return, to which we now turn.

4 THE INTERNAL RATE OF RETURN

The internal rate of return (IRR) is the value of r that equates the expression $\sum_{t=0}^{T} (R_t - C_t)(1 + r)^{-t}$ to zero. We call it $\bar{r}$. The investment rule is to invest in all projects with $\bar{r}$ greater than some threshold level, which remains to be determined. Alternatively, if there are J projects the rule can be to rank them in descending order according to $\bar{r}_j$, and invest in those with highest $\bar{r}_j$ until the budget is exhausted. In this case, the budget also must be determined.

The IRR has the advantage that it can be calculated, and the projects ranked, independently of a discount rate. Thus the difficult question of what the rate of discount should be is avoided, as is the possibility that it may change, thus affecting project rankings between the time that the IRR is calculated and the time that the investments are actually made. If the market rate of interest is used as the cutoff, it is easy to verify that any investment selected with an IRR exceeding the market rate of interest will be able to repay the interest and yield some positive net profit (again, assuming equal borrowing and lending rates). To see this assume that the loan is made during the current year and the entire construction of the physical investment is performed this year. In each year for the duration of the investment after the current year the difference between the revenue and cost will be positive. Therefore, we may rewrite the expression for the IRR in the following way [Substituting V_t for the difference $(R_t - C_t)$]:

$$\sum_{t=1}^{T} V_{jt}(1 + \bar{r}_j)^{-t} = C_{j0}$$

And if, as before, we compound both sides at the market borrowing of interest, equal to the lending rate, we get

$$(1 + b)^T \sum V_{jt}(1 + \bar{r}_j)^{-t} = (1 + b)^T C_{j0}$$

for any project selected.

As with discounted present value criteria, several objections can be raised against the IRR. The six most important ones are summarized in Table 11.2. So are the answers to the criticisms, the answer consisting either of safeguards to supplement the calculations or of an evaluation of the likelihood that a situation will arise in which the criticism will be applicable. The reasoning is presented in greater detail in the following paragraphs.

1. *Inequality of borrowing and lending rates.* For many large investment projects the borrowing and lending rates may be sufficiently close for the IRR as given above to be reasonable. However, if there is a 7 to 10% difference, it need not follow that investment according to the internal rate of return will generate enough to cover the loan and interest repayments. Thus, though reasonable where certain assumptions are permissible, the criterion would not be universally valid in its raw form, but it can easily be adjusted just as we adjusted the present value criteria.

2. *Inability to choose efficiently between project variants.* This problem is illustrated in Figure 11.1. We are choosing between two mutually exclusive project variants. Project I has an IRR of 14%, and project II has an IRR of 16.2%. Project II would be chosen on the basis of the IRR. But, as Figure 11.1 shows, project I has a higher net present value for all rates of discount below 5%, the crossover rate. On the other hand, the time streams of net revenues of the two projects are such that above this crossover rate, project II has a higher net present value. If net present value is the criterion that is correct, in principle, from the welfare maximization point of view (and that this is so will be confirmed in the next chapter), we should adopt variant I if the true discount rate is lower than the crossover rate. In this case, use of the IRR will give the wrong decision.

How should we proceed? The problem is critical for a private firm in view of the uncertainty about the rate of interest discussed earlier; it is even more critical for the public sector, which cannot use the market rate of interest for its calculations at all. However, it seems reasonable here to calculate the crossover rate, which only requires a little additional arithmetic. If the crossover rate is very low, disregard it; if it is high, use the project with the lower IRR, since there is a much greater range at which this project would have a higher present value. If it is 6 to 8%, look more closely at the data.*

3. *The ranking may be wrong.* If the ranking based on the IRR may be wrong for two mutually exclusive projects, it may also be wrong for a

* For a more complete discussion of this problem see Alchian (1955).

Table 11.2 Summary of Criticisms of IRR and Recommended Treatment

Criticism	Problem	Recommendation
1. Returns may not cover repayment of principal and interest	Borrowing and lending rates may be different	Make adjustment as with discounted present value criteria (the proper adjustment for the particular repayment conditions in question)
2. Cannot choose efficiently between two project variants	If interest rate is below crossover would favor variant with lower NPV	If crossover rate is very low, need not worry. If it is in range of 6 to 8%, look more closely. If it is higher, use variant with lower IRR
3. Ranking may be wrong	True ranking (from social viewpoint) is that which follows NDAR (from viewpoint of firm, NDRR), which requires knowledge of correct discount. If we do not know, cannot know true ranking	It does not matter if ranking is wrong if cutoff is right. Cutoff will be correct if we use correctly determined budget constraint, which is better gauge of needs of sector (see Chapter 10). For projects in sectors without budget constraints, use present value criterion, trying different rates of discount
4. Not know cutoff for decision rule	We do not know market rate of interest (or, in public sector, "correct rate of discount")	Use budget constraint as in item 3
5. Multiple rates or complex rates only	Likely to occur when there are high dismantling costs.	Requires switch of signs on return stream. This is unlikely to happen unless there are high dismantling costs, which is unlikely
6. Different time horizons may preclude comparisons of projects	An IRR of .2 for short duration may actually generate lower return than project with IRR of .12 for long duration	Important for firm worried about reinvestment. But if situation changes so rapidly that the firm could not find similar investment possibilities following duration of first investment, the industry must be undergoing radical change so that under present value criterion, original calculations would not have held up. In normal industries, reinvestment possibilities unlikely to fall so far that with sequence of projects would do worse than with just one long-duration project at lower IRR

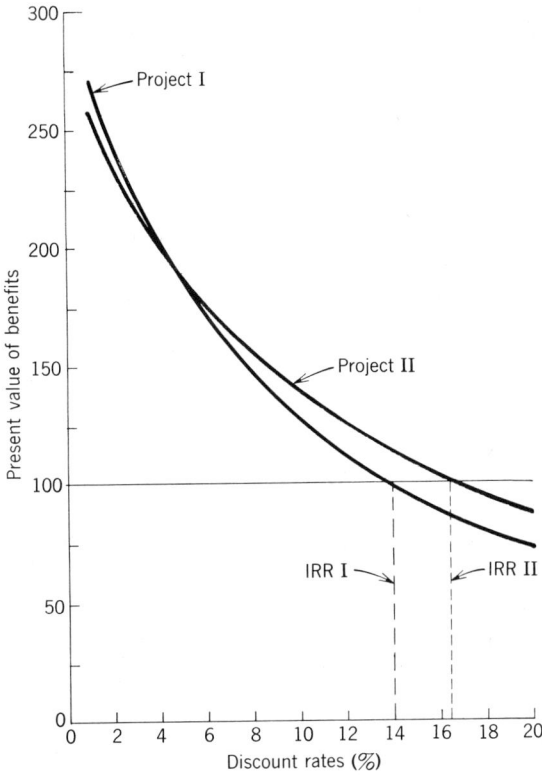

Figure 11.1   Present value of two return streams and internal rates of return.

dozen or more projects that are not mutually exclusive. That is to say, we may get one ranking by the IRR; we may get the same ranking by a rate of discount of 12%; and we might get a very different ranking by a rate of discount of 8%. Is the IRR ranking correct? That depends on whether the rate of discount of 12% is correct. What should be done? We point out that if the IRR is defective here because there is some uncertainty about what is the true rate of discount, then using the discounted present value will be equally uncertain since we would not know what rate to use as the rate of discount. What is the solution? We have argued (see Chapters 3 and 10) that the correct approach to the allocation of investment within sectors is to start out with a correctly determined budget constraint for the sector, determined according to the reasoning presented in the chapters cited. If we do this we can simply invest in projects until the investment funds are exhausted. For the projects that are chosen, it does not matter if they are misranked. For those that are misranked just below the cutoff limit, no great harm is done since they will very probably be accepted in next year's plan. If a particular project falls consistently below the cutoff limit, however, it ought to be looked at very closely to see whether there is some consistent bias in the way the benefits and costs of the projects are being valued.

For projects in sectors that do not have budget constraints generated as we have urged, a present value criterion should be used, with different rates of discount being charged, although 5% is probably appropriate. The theoretically correct rate of discount to use is the marginal productivity of capital, a concept that is difficult to define operationally. We discuss this concept and its measurement in Chapter 12.

4. *Ignorance regarding cutoff for investment decision rule.* The problem here is that in its usual formulation the IRR decision rule does not provide information on the cutoff rate. On the other hand, we point out that if we do not know the correct cutoff rate we will also not know the correct rate of discount to use in the discounted present value criterion. Again, the solution is straightforward. As long as we use an investment constraint correctly generated through properly constructed user charges, we need not know the cutoff level of the IRR; we simply exhaust the budget.

5. *Multiple rates or complex rates only.* While this problem is very interesting from a conceptual point of view, it is much less significant in actual applications, although its seriousness may rise in the future. The problem is that the IRR, rather than being unique, may have multiple values that equate the net revenue and cost streams. The problem was first described by Lorie and Savage (1955). Hirshleifer (1958) went further and showed that there might be no real IRR, but only complex roots. (The reader is referred to these two excellent papers for good overall discussions of the problem together with arithmetic examples.)

How many rates may there be for any investment? As many rates as there are changes in sign in the annual net revenue stream. Thus nine rates are conceivable in a 10-year project. For this to happen there would have to be a switch between positive and negative return in each successive year. In fact, we can rule out most such possibilities as interesting but improbable occurrences and confine ourselves to the case of at most two changes of sign, as a reasonable probability. In this case, there is first a negative revenue flow while the project is being constructed; then there is a positive return in each year until the end of the project life; and then, conceivably, there might be a negative return.

Now, it is perhaps symptomatic of the unreasonableness of the expectation of sign reversals that Hirshleifer gives no examples, and that the
example given by Lorie and Savage is somewhat artificial. (In their
example, based on two oil well pumping variants, the negative flow
toward the end of the period associated with the use of the larger pump
is due to the oil reserve being exhausted earlier. Thus there is a loss in
revenue generated in the last years because instead of pumping out the
average annual production yielded by the small pump, zero output is
produced!)

In the future we may expect a change of sign in the net revenue
stream to become more common because of the dismantling costs in
such operations as strip mining and other activities with government-
imposed restitution costs, reflecting public concern with the environment. However, the mere fact of a change in sign does not ensure that
there will be more than one internal rate of return. The final dismantling cost must be very high relatively to the stream of returns during the
project's life. It is unlikely ever to be so high in reality. Thus even when
there are two changes of sign (three different subseries during the duration of the project, in each of which a given sign will prevail), the likelihood that there will be more than one IRR is extremely small.

6. *Different time horizons may preclude project comparison.* Suppose
that a project has an IRR of 20% and a 5-year duration. A second
project has an IRR of 12% and a 10-year duration. If IRR alone is
considered, the first project is preferable. After the first 5 years, when
the firm considers reinvesting its funds or undertaking new investments, the best available project may be one with a very low IRR,
which, even combined with the earlier project having a high IRR, will
generate a lower net present value than that which would be generated
by the single project with the IRR of 12%.

Again, this problem is more interesting as a curiosum than as a
practical possibility. First, we *would* expect the firm, at the end of the
first project, to have investment possibilities with an IRR of the same
order of magnitude as the short-duration project with the higher IRR
today. If this is not the case, the firm either (1) now is aware of its
future investment opportunities and will make calculations today on
the basis of the best time path for investment (that with the highest
IRR) or (2) does not expect this to happen and is caught by surprise. In
the latter case, a large difference between the two IRR indicates that
some fundamental changes are taking place in the industry, so that
even the project with the more modest return may turn out to have a
much lower return. If, five years hence, the outlook falls so dismally,

prices of the industry's products will fall, reducing the annual return in future years; that is, the longer project with a lower IRR today will actually turn out to have a lower net present value than now hypothesized.

From this review of the internal rate of return criterion, we can conclude that (1) some problems peculiar to the internal rate of return are interesting curiosa, but are unlikely to be bothersome in practice and (2) the real problem originates in the lack of a normative return to serve as the cutoff criterion. However, whenever this represents a serious problem for the internal rate of return, it will also represent an obstacle to the use of the net present value. Uncertainty about the rate of discount for calculating net present value is greater in the public sector, as we will see in Chapter 12, than for the private firm, for which the rate to use in calculations of the net revenue stream is more clearly spelled out—it is the rate being charged for the investment funds. But this rate is unstable. As we have argued, however, for much if not most investment the correct public sector procedure is to start with the sectoral investment constraint. Where it is a matter of dealing with sectors that do not generate their own investment budget constraints, it will be necessary to approach the matter somewhat differently. For this a net present value criterion must be used. We defer further discussion of this point to Chapter 12.

5   PRIVATE SECTOR BEHAVIOR AS GUIDANCE FOR THE PUBLIC SECTOR

We have seen that the private sector optimality criteria are rather ambiguous in reality. They are supposed to lead to private optimization for individual firms, which is supposed to be consistent with social welfare optimization. We do not know, however, whether any rule can in fact do so.

Not only do the different decision rules give different answers for the optimization of the individual private firm, but the interests of different parties within the same firm may also be different, so that no explicit optimality criterion will be used at all, even an ambiguous one. Too, distortions in the private sector may cause a divergence between private and social optimization.

Are optimizing criteria used? The investment decision of the firm, it should be noted, will reflect the private interest of the firm's management, which does not always accord with the interests of the stockholders. For example, the president may have a five-year contract in which his remuneration depends on currently generated profits. He will then be more interested in projects showing an early return. The stockholders, on the other hand, are interested in maximizing present value, which in some cases will lead to a preference for a project with delayed earnings. The president, to be sure, may also recognize that contract renewal might depend on net present value maximization rather than short-term maximization, but he may not be young enough for this to matter—if he is 62, for example, the possibility of contract renewal will not entice him.

Nor should it be assumed that a company placing greater emphasis on early return will find some stockholders of like mind who will buy into this company with no welfare loss. If the net present value is higher with an investment selection having later returns, a stockholder who is more interested in early returns could sell his interest in the company to somebody more interested in later returns and buy into another company stressing early returns. Once adjustments are made, everyone owns a claim to an income stream that is more in accord with his tastes. Difficulty arises when management changes, and a shareholder, having bought into a firm with certain expectations, finds these expectations to have become invalid because of the policies of a new president. Thus it cannot be generally assumed that the interests of owners and management are consistently served by using any of the formal investment decision criteria.

Even when the interests of managers and stockholders are compatible, are the firm's interests consistent with social optimization? The answer here is almost certainly negative. There are many reasons for this. First, the revenue stream and cost stream are valued at market prices, and the market prices may systematically diverge from prices that are optimal in a social sense. Problems of pollution and congestion are the most obvious problems. Others are price distortions, such as those in most transport systems, which cause the prices facing users to fail to reflect the true cost. Finally, even if the IRR is used for the private firm, it may give a suboptimal solution. It maximizes subject to a given cutoff rate or a budget constraint. If present values are used, they maximize subject to a given discount rate. There is no way of knowing whether this cutoff rate and the discount rate used in the present value calculations are the correct cutoff point from the social perspective. In Chapter 12 we see that there is reason to believe that they are not.

We turn now to the public sector. This review of the private sector has indicated the direction that our search for a decision criterion should take, although we have seen some of the weaknesses inherent in the criteria even in the private sector. For the public sector the problems are more complex. But this review shows that those who criticize public sector decision-making as being inherently incapable of formulating good criteria and reaching sound decisions are insensitive to the frailty of private sector criteria.

REFERENCES

Alchian, Armen A. (1955), "The Rate of Interest, Fisher's Rate of Return over Costs, and Keynes' Internal Rate of Return," *American Economic Review* December; reprinted in Solomon (1959).

Hirshleifer, Jack (1958), "On the Theory of Optimal Investment Decision," *Journal of Political Economy,* August; reprinted in Solomon (1959).

Lorie, James H., and Leonard J. Savage (1955), "Three Problems in Rationing Capital," *Journal of Business,* October; reprinted in Solomon (1959).

Solomon, Ezra (1959), *The Management of Corporate Capital* (New York: The Free Press).

12

The Form of the Public Sector Criterion

1   INTRODUCTION

In moving to the public sector, we must cope with several additional problems in selecting an investment criterion. First, the public sector concern must be broader than the net return with which the private sector is concerned (although even there, as we saw, conflicts arise between the private returns of different groups with supposedly the same objective). Accordingly, we begin by casting our payoff criterion in terms of net social return. The net social return is the difference between the gross social return and social cost. Since different investments involve different time streams of returns and costs, these must be adjusted to a comparable basis. This requires a decision about a discount coefficient, which is the major concern of the present chapter. In the next chapter we examine the elements going into the measurement of the benefit of a project. There are numerous problems here with which the private sector need not contend. For example, not only are there social costs for which a private firm frequently need not take responsibility, but also there are second- and third-round effects that *may* or *may not* need to be considered in the public sector criterion, but definitely do not concern the private firm. Price changes, too, may result from individual investments, and they must be treated in a meaningful way to measure benefits. Finally, it is necessary to allow for possible differences between social and private valuations through the use of shadow prices, the theory of which was discussed in Chapter 7.

In this chapter we look at the essential form of the public sector criterion. To anticipate slightly, or to state what the reader has probably already guessed, we will conclude that the IRR is the correct criterion, when it is possible to formulate a budget constraint, because of the irreconcilability of intersectoral benefit comparisons and the uncertainty regarding the rate of discount. This will be clearer after the analysis (in Sections 2 to 4) of the different concepts that have been proposed to serve to discount differential benefit and cost streams. We conduct the discussion in some detail in order to provide a firm understanding of the meaning of the different concepts and a rationale for the concept that we propose and its numerical magnitude. The concepts may be classified into three basic groups: (1) the rate of interest; (2) the social rate of time preference (sometimes, social rate of discount); and (3) productivity of capital (sometimes, opportunity cost of capital). (The internal rate of return is also, of course, a kind of discount rate. Since it also constitutes a different criterion, it is not included, here however. We return to it in Section 5.) We now consider these three concepts for use as a discount coefficient to provide us with an optimal decision rule for circumstances in which a previously formulated budget constraint is not possible.

2   THE RATE OF INTEREST

If the rate of interest is to be used, we must first specify, which rate of interest it is to be, since many rates coexist. Frequently it is the prime rate or the central bank discount rate that is meant. Since the prime rate is given to the most substantial customers, it may be taken as a reflection of the rate on the safest investments. The public sector investment being assumed as safe (the public sector can always repay the loan), this is sometimes thought to be the appropriate consideration. Now, since we are concerned with optimization, the discount rate concept to be used should be derived from considerations of optimization. But the justification just presented for the use of the prime rate does not arise out of optimization considerations. To hold otherwise, one would have to assert that the rate of interest reflected some sort of optimum. In fact, it merely reflects some equilibrium position at a moment of time, which may or may not be optimal. This is true even if it is a full employment equilibrium. To see this, we review briefly the characteristics of the rate of interest. The following discussion is based on the traditional Hansen geometrical exposition of the Keynesian model (1953). We abstract from the questions raised by the existence of multiple interest rates and assume there to be a single rate (called henceforth "the market rate of interest" or simply "the rate of interest")—a simplification that, as we will see, does not overcome all the conceptual problems in the use of the market rate of interest. We consider four problem areas.

1. *Which equilibrium rate?* If the market rate of interest is supposed to represent some optimal configuration, or emerge in the course of some social optimization process, we would not expect the optimal economic environment to make jumps. But the market rate of interest is very variable, and becomes suspect on this account. Evidently, the observed rate depends on the level of output and employment. Accordingly, the first question that must be asked is: which rate is relevant? Only the interest rate associated with full employment or that occurring at any level that happens to be observed when the projects are being reviewed?

It will usually be said that the full employment equilibrium rate is what is implied. If there is secular unemployment, that is, long-term rather than cyclical unemployment, it would be argued that the interest rate corresponding to the secular unemployment equilibrium is the relevant one.

2. *What is the full employment equilibrium rate?* But even if we leave aside problems of isolating the full employment equilibrium interest rate from the influence of cyclical unemployment, several objections may be raised to the use of the interest rate as the discount coefficient. First, there are fluctuations even in the full employment equilibrium rate that appear to be unrelated to the considerations we should take into account when we formulate long-term investment projects. This can be seen, in Table 12.1, showing the fluctuations in the prime rate in the United States over the period 1952–1975. The rate of umemployment is also shown. Evidently, even with unemployment as low as 4%, which is usually taken as the full employment level, wide variations are observed in the prime rate, which ranges over an interval of 4% percentage points (equal to 133% of its lowest observed value, 3%). This variation is due to short-term influences of international balance of payments, international money market movements, and other factors

Table 12.1 Prime Rate and Unemployment in
the United States, 1952–1975 (January of
Year)

Year	Prime Rate (%)	Unemployment Rate (%)
1952	3.0	3.2
1953	3.0	2.7
1954	3.25	4.5
1955	3.0	5.0
1956	3.5	4.2
1957	4.0	4.2
1958	4.5	5.2
1959	4.0	6.2
1960	5.0	5.7
1961	4.5	6.2
1962	4.5	6.0
1963	4.5	5.4
1964	4.5	5.5
1965	4.5	4.8
1966	4.875	3.9
1967	6.0	3.7
1968	6.0	3.8
1969	6.875	3.4
1970	8.5	3.5
1971	7.0	6.0
1972	5.0	5.9
1973	5.875	5.0
1974	9.75	5.2
1975		8.2

Sources. U.S. Department of Commerce (1973;
various years).

that do not necessarily bear on the considerations that one must make
in evaluating a long-term investment project.

3. *How to abstract from inflation?* Inflation may be the main influence
on the behavior of the prime rate noted in Table 12.1. The problem here
is that even under less than full employment the interest rate may
incorporate an inflation hedge premium. Under inflation, the LM curve
shifts upward, since out of a given quantity of money a larger amount
must be used on the circulation of commodities (under a constant

velocity of money), leaving a smaller amount for speculative purposes and raising the equilibrium interest rate in this sector. Concommitantly, the marginal efficiency of an investment schedule moves to the right, since product prices in later years are rising so that the firm's revenues will be higher relatively to a given investment. Thus a higher marginal efficiency of capital (internal rate of return) will be calculated for any project. At the same time, the savings schedule rises for any given income level, since consumers must devote a larger share of their income to consumption. Thus the investment-savings equilibrium takes place at a higher interest rate (and, possibly, a higher volume of investment). This happens for every income level, shifting the IS curve to the right. The final equilibrium interest rate under inflation is then higher, even though the future real output stream does not change.

Now, the separation of the inflation hedge premium from the full employment equilibrium interest rate should not be too difficult if we could assume a long enough series of observations. Nevertheless, it is difficult with a statistical series even as long as that of the United States, since other forces may be at work, causing a secular change in the prime rate–full employment relationship. Moreover, the attainment of the full employment level is rather infrequent—the umemployment rate has fallen below 4% only seven times in 23 years. Difficult in industrialized economies, it is significantly more difficult in developing economies where we do not have a long series of observations on full employment equilibrium interest rates, not to speak of a series unmarked by secular change. And since inflation is so frequently a handmaiden of development, it is very difficult to separate the effects of inflation on the rate of interest from the influence of the "real" forces in the economy. An obvious possibility would be to try to distinguish the actual rate from the interest rate that characterizes the interest rate typical of the secular unemployment level; but, again, if the economy *is* developing, by definition the secular unemployment level has been changing. Accordingly, we may expect a varying ratio between the inflation hedge component and the equilibrium interest rate.

4. *Is the market rate a competetive equilibrium rate?* A fourth objection to the use of the private sector equilibrium market rate of interest is that some evidence shows businessmen's expectations to tend to underrate distance returns. For example, Shackle (1967) in his survey of the nature and role of interest points out the widespread practice of accelerated depreciation of equipment, which will actually be kept in operation longer than the accounting life. That is, if the present value of an investment were calculated under two assumptions concerning the

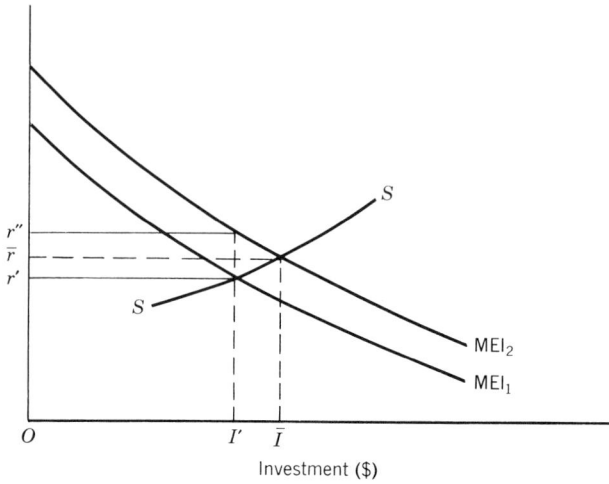

Figure 12.1 Marginal efficiency of capital schedules: true and apparent (under accelerated and under realistic depreciation).

time stream, one in which the annual depreciation was related to the true service life and the other in which the depreciation was accelerated and written off within a very short period, the first procedure would yield a higher net present value (discounted at the same rate). If, as Shackle argues, the firm undertakes the investment based on the second mode of calculation, as would be possible in a sufficiently noncompetitive economy—with net present values lower than in calculations based on a more reasonable expectation of service life, the rate of return that will actually materialize will exceed the expectations of the firm when it makes the investment decision. The problem is illustrated in Figure 12.1.

The marginal efficiency of investment (MEI) curve, based on the return under accelerated depreciation, is shown as MEI_1.* The level of investment shown on the X-axis is undertaken if the return is as indicated by the ordinate of the MEI_1 curve. However, the real return, with depreciation calculations based on a reasonable expectation of equipment life, actually results in a higher return. These "true" returns are shown by MEI_2. A given savings curve will intersect the MEI_1 at a lower interest rate and lower volume of investment then the equilibrium MEI_2 curve. If businessmen are truly myopic, they will invest only an amount

---

* MEI, Keynes' expression, is the same as the IRR.

I'. The true return here is r'', although the firm talks in terms of r', which is lower. At the same time the true equilibrium rate is given by $\bar{r}$, to which corresponds an investment volume of $\bar{I}$. All this applies to a given income level. Repeating the analysis for every income level would give a savings-investment function below the true equilibrium function, which would interesect LM at a lower interest rate. Therefore, if this is a correct description of actual behavior we should not rely on the interest rate that is actually observed, which is lower than the equilibrium rate, or the true rate of return, which is higher.

The foregoing considerations suggest that the market rate of interest is not the correct concept to use as the discounting factor. Accordingly, the value of any particular interest rate existing at any given moment of time cannot be assumed to be the correct discount criterion.

3. THE SOCIAL RATE OF DISCOUNT AND THE SOCIAL RATE OF TIME PREFERENCE

Many writers argue that the correct discount factor is the social rate of discount. This argument is based principally on the alleged myopia of private investors. They will be guided by private profit, whereas public sector investments should be guided by broader considerations. We have just investigated one aspect of this nearsightedness, which causes the market rate of interest to be lower and the true rate of return to investors to be higher than the equilibrium interest rate. Those who allege divergence between private return and social return generally allude also to the existence of substantial but delayed returns that private firms neglect for one reason or another. In addition, frequently, if not usually, the benefits are suggested to redound to society at large, with a business firm unable to capture them for itself through its market profit. For example, a water-irrigation-recreation investment will affect many people in many ways that are beyond a firm's reach through the market. However, this relates to the *measurement* of benefits rather than to their discounting. Accordingly, we defer this aspect of the alleged difference between social and private returns until the next chapter. Here we consider whether the private rate of return is a proper concept for discounting social returns.

In the preceding section we saw that the market rate of interest was an inappropriate discount concept, since it was too unstable, was not based on optimization procedures, and was distorted. But those who argue that a lower rate should be used in discounting public sector investments than private investments usually base their argument on the alleged social benefits not susceptible to market capture, although this is really a question of measurement rather than intertemporal commensuration. Therefore, a theoretical foundation must be built to determine the correct discount concept. But first we consider some of the concepts that have been put forth—on the basis of little real justification other than that they are lower than the prime rate.

The major suggested rate concepts are those of a credit granting agency of a producing country such as the U.S. Export-Import Bank, of a producing firm that sells the capital equipment to the investing country, and of some international lending agency such as the International Bank for Reconstruction and Development (IBRD). Now, while these rates may all be lower than the prime rate, there is usually a reason for it. For example, the rates of a credit-granting agency may be artifically low, since the loans on which they are given are tied to the purchase of high-profit equipment or employment-generating production from a producer in the lending country. Similarly, the terms offered by the producing firm directly may be low to compensate for higher prices being charged due possibly to the higher costs experienced in the selling country. Accordingly, while it may be true that these rates may be below market equilibrium rates, there is no reason to think that they are the correct rates to discount social returns.

A similar objection would be made to the use of the lending rate of an international institution such as the IBRD. All other things being equal, this rate could be lower than other rates because the rate at which the IBRD can borrow funds is itself below the prime rate in most countries. The reason is that there is virtually no risk whatever in making a loan to this institution, since its capital is subscribed by a large number of participant countries, and an institution that merely has to recover its loan, together with its own expenses, can do so at a very low rate.

We have been discussing why the rates charged on loans by various institutions should not be regarded as proxies for the social rate of discount. But what is the social rate of discount? If this can be deduced through an optimization process, a more enlightened course would be indicated. The social rate of discount is usually thought to be self-explanatory, requiring no elaboration, so that there is relatively little discussion of the empirical counterpart of this concept in the literature. Used interchangeably, as it frequently is, with another expression—the social rate of time preference—it conveys the idea that society has preferences among different time streams of consumption and that these can, in principle, be identified. It is usually taken to mean that, all other things being equal, society prefers a given consumption sooner than later, but this lays stress on the wrong things. We turn, then, to an optimizing approach to provide the correct discounting concept.

4 THE INTERTEMPORAL PRODUCTIVITY OF CAPITAL AND THE OPTIMAL RATE OF INTERTEMPORAL PRODUCT SUBSTITUTION

The capital productivity approach to the discount factor is the only one that follows from optimization considerations. We proceed as follows:

We assume a closed economy (a simplifying, rather than a necessary assumption). Intertemporal allocative efficiency involves choices in the distribution of consumption over time. The analysis is based on the two-period situation shown in Figure 12.2. Consumption for the whole economy in period 1 is plotted on the Y-axis and in period 2 on the X-axis. Under an existing technological regime with zero net investment the society can consume the same amount each year. Therefore, any combination of consumption bundles is possible along the 45° curve out to the maximum consumption that the economy can produce. This is indicated by the zero subscript. However, the economy could instead defer some consumption from period 1 by investing and achieving higher consumption in period 2. (Since we are assuming that the country does not have external trading possibilities, it cannot increase consumption in year 1 through imports that would have to be paid for by a reduction in year 2 consumption.)

The tradeoff between consumption in periods 1 and 2 is shown along the curved line starting at A. The diminishing returns to investment, evident throughout is especially marked at point B at consumption of $\bar{C}$,

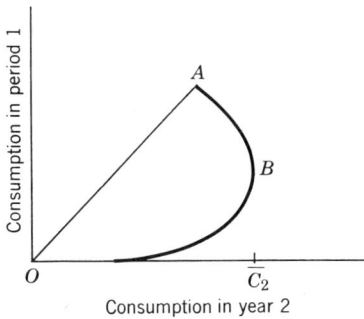

Figure 12.2 Consumption possibility frontier.

where consumption in period 2 actually begins to fall with further sacrifices in period 1. Beyond this point, further reductions in period 1 consumption in favor of investment to generate period 2 consumption cause period 2 consumption to fall below the level that could have been achieved with less investment. In the extreme case with all production in period 1 being invested we get zero consumption in period 1 and also zero consumption in period 2: the population is too weak to produce anything at all in period 2, or everyone has died.

The notion of diminishing returns to investment in the period 1–period 2 tradeoff is generally assumed in such analyses as Hirshleifer's (1958), for example. However, Hirshleifer's intertemporal transformation set is convex throughout, unlike ours, which doubles back. In Hirshleifer's presentation this is, of course, reasonable, since the individual could invest more in the physical market while borrowing on the financial market for period 1 consumption. In his example of building a house the individual could spend all his time building this capital good (the physical investment) and then borrow on the financial market for current sustenance. But while convexity is appropriate for individuals, it is inappropriate for the whole economy, since there is no one to borrow from (unless foreign trade, which we are neglecting here, is assumed to take place).

The effective consumption frontier is the part of the curve from A to B. This must be counterposed to a family of indifference curves, and the point of tangency between the frontier and the highest indifference curve defines the optimal distribution of consumption between the two periods. The rate of preference for present consumption over future consumption is given by the slope of the curve at the point of tangency. What will be the magnitude of this slope?

We observe first that any well-behaved indifference curve should be concave to the origin, which simply indicates that the less of either of the two products we have, the greater is its marginal valuation in terms of the other. Figure 12.3 shows the indifference curve family for consumption in two periods. We need make no assumptions about the natural superiority of present over future consumption, a basic psychological fact adduced by a long list of writers on the subject whose frequent reference to impatience or a positive rate of time preference of present over future consumption (i.e., MRS $- 1 > 0$) tends to predispose us to believe that this will always be so. The indifference curve analysis shows that when a unit of either product (i.e., a unit of consumption in either period) is valued at more than one unit of consumption in the other period, the consumption in that period is rela-

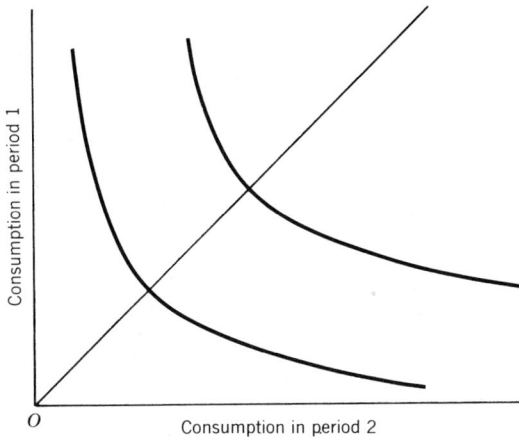

Figure 12.3 Symmetrical indifference curves for consumption in two periods.

tively less than in the other period. In particular, at high levels of period 1 consumption, the MRS (dC_2/dC_1) of future for present consumption is less than unity—we would give up *more* than one unit of period 1 consumption for one more unit of period 2 consumption. People with high current consumption potential (i.e. high current income) and low future potential (following retirement, say) will willingly put aside some current consumption for the future even without receiving a premium through the interest mechanism. This simply means that the tangency of a person's budget line and indifference curve is closer to the Y-axis. Assuming, for simplicity, that the indifference curves are symmetrical about the 45° line from the origin, the MRS of future for present consumption changes from less than unity to greater than unity at the point of intersection with the line.

The fact that we do not usually see MRS < 1—people do not behave as though they were at a point to the left of the 45° line—does not disprove this assertion. It simply means that people are to the right because their future income prospects are better than their present prospects and/or that, while the person values equally a dollar's consumption in the future and today, since some people in the economy are willing to reward him with a premium for abstaining from present consumption, he is willing to abstain thus getting more than a unit of period 2 consumption for each unit forgone in period 1. If we bring the indifference curve family and the consumption transformation curve together, their tangency defines the optimal mix of consumption in the two years. The tangency will always be to the right of the 45° line as long as it is possible to produce more in the second year by sacrificing in the first year, that is, as long as the incremental output/capital ratio is greater than unity. The observed MRS of future for present consumption will then be greater than unity.*

The slope of the production frontier at the tangency point is the optimal discount rate. Thus we have derived a discount concept from considerations of optimization over time. From the way it was derived it is obvious that this concept reflects the ability of the economy to transform consumption today into consumption in the future by means of investment, which is better expressed by "optimal rate of intertemporal product substitution" (ORIPS) than by "social rate of time preference,"* since the latter seems to lay undue stress on the inequality between the utility of a unit today and a unit in the future, which, as we have seen, need not be the case. As this analysis shows, a unit of output today is worth more than a unit of output in the future because the output today may be used to produce more than a unit of output in the future. There is no inherent systematic bias in favor of consumption today rather than in the future. Accordingly, we urge that

---

* That a positive rate of time preference does not require a premium on present versus future consumption has been stated most succinctly by Patinkin (1972, pp. 129–30): "It should also be emphasized that impatience or 'time preference'—in the sense that an individual with a two-period horizon systematically prefers (say) ten units of consumption goods today and four tomorrow to the alternative combination of four units today and ten tomorrow—is not a necessary condition for the existence of interest. For the major manifestation of time preference in this sense—in an economy in which all individuals have a finite horizon and anticipate a constant stream of income payments is that (strictly) positive savings will be forthcoming at a (strictly) positive rate of interest. Conversly, absence of time preference manifests itself in the fact that if the rate of interest is zero, then savings are also zero. Thus, the fact that individuals in such an economy insist on receiving interest in order to save is no evidence of a systematic preference for present goods over future ones. More generally, the fact that an individual will, at the margin, insist on receiving more than one unit of future goods to compensate him for foregoing one unit of present goods is not necessarily the *cause* of the existence of interest but its effect: he insists on receiving more because he has the alternative of obtaining more by lending out at interest the money that would be released from current consumption by saving."

Although greater productivity of capital-intensive production methods as the source of interest is associated primarily with Böhm-Bawerk's name (and conversely), Böhm-Bawerk was somewhat ambivalent about impatience, considering it the first reason for interest which he proposed to supplement. Had indifference analysis been available to him he probably would have reached the same conclusion presented diagrammatically here and by Patinkin. (see Böhm-Bawerk, 1959, Book IV, Chapter 1).

* Note Patinkin's careful attempt in the preceding footnote to distinguish between impatience and "time preference," in which he recognizes that, to many people, they are the same thing.

the expression "social rate of time preference" be dropped, because it seems to lay stress on the wrong things and is liable to lead astray researchers seeking to determine what the rate should be.

How should the ORIPS be determined? Frequently, authors talk in terms of the opportunity cost of capital, which, in principle, measures the return that capital will generate when invested in the next best project. Since no one tabulates such things at the level of the national economy, this merely puts the decision about what number to use one step back: we must then determine the opportunity cost of capital.

It has sometimes been argued that the rate of profit in the private sector is an adequate measure of the opportunity cost of capital. The reasoning is simply that since this is the return to capital, on the average in the private sector, any investment forgoes this return if it is put to an alternative use. A refinement over the average return is to use the lowest return on capital in the private sector on the grounds that this lowest return is implicitly presumed to be relevant to the least risky investment. The problem, here, however, is (1) that the return is given in terms of activities weighted by market prices that need not reflect social costs and (2) that some activities may be neglected altogether. Another problem that has been disputed is whether the return net or gross of income tax should be considered in determining the rate of return. Clearly, it makes a great difference, since at a 50% marginal tax rate, occurring at relatively low profit, the effect of switching from gross to net return would be substantial. If the tax is viewed as an income distribution component, the tax-inclusive return should be considered, since the economy benefits to the full extent of the return. The capital productivity would then be relatively high. Finally, we should be reminded of the distinction between the real return and the imagined return under myopic time horizon, discussed in Section 2 of this chapter.

The method of determining the productivity of capital that probably best conforms to the discount concept advocated here is the econometric macroeconomic productivity research pioneered by Solow, with major contributions by Denison, Kendrick, Jorgenson, Griliches, Arrow, Chenery, and Minhas. This methodology involves the estimation of a warranted rate of growth based on various production function estimates, and the calculation of the total productivity (i.e. the net yield) of the factors as the difference between the actually observed output and the warranted output. This differential must then be attributed to various sources, such as increased physical capital, better human capital, and better organization. Since many of these factors result from investment (e.g. labor skill levels rise with education investment), or are indirectly related to capital investment, there is a justification for attributing the total increase in factor productivity to capital investment and to use this measure as the estimate of ORIPS. What is the magnitude of this growth?

Most investigators calculate an average annual growth of factor productivity of less than 1 to 3%, variations depending on the form chosen for the production function and the variables used to measure input. For example, two major studies calculate total factor productivity of 1 to 2% (Solow, 1957) and about 1% (Jorgenson and Griliches, 1967). This implies a rate of discount and ORIPS of less than 3%, far less than the rates proposed on the basis of the other discount concepts reviewed in this chapter. Even allowing for possible errors in measurement in these studies, the rate would surely not exceed 3 to 5%. Accordingly, this is what we will recommend for discounting time streams where the present value approach must be used for project evaluation.

Since a discount rate of 8 to 10% or more is often recommended by writers on project evaluation and by policymakers, many readers will wonder whether the 5% rate espoused here will exacerbate the often noted tendency to invest "too much" in capital-intensive technology or, as some put it, to squander capital. The answer is negative. Let us see why.

First, the discount rate used will not affect the ordering of projects in those sectors whose investment projects are ordered by the internal rate of return (see below) which we advocate partly because of the uncertainty and controversy about what discount concept and rate should be used in the first place.

Now, for the project that it will affect, it is necessary to discount in order to compare the costs or the benefits, or both. We look first at projects for which we must compare costs only (i.e., project acceptance is based on a physical criterion and we wish only to minimize costs). The problem here is to choose the cost-minimizing technology. Costs must be compared between inputs in a given year and between years for a given input. The use of different discount rates will affect directly only the the second kind of comparison. The input prices for the first type of comparison will be market prices which, if the market is functioning properly, should reflect the productivity or opportunity cost of the different factors. The input price of a bulldozer will be a function of the demand for it, which in turn is a function of the productivity of the bulldozer in terms of its ability to substitute for raw manpower. In the same way, the various skill classes of labor will have wages that reflect their ability to replace less skilled labor, and so on. These productivity differentials or economic rents will help the project maker to select the cost-minimizing technology in the same way that they are expected to guide all firms in the market to promote the common good while seeking their own profit. The project maker will not choose a more capital-intensive technology unless he can thereby reduce other costs sufficiently in any given year. He will not pay the premium unless it is at least as great as the cost saving he gains by this combination of inputs rather than the next best. Thus reduction of prodigality is encouraged by economic rents in the market for all factors; it does not depend only on having the right discount rate.

For comparing benefits over time, or the different time streams of costs, the productivity of capital clearly seems to be the correct concept—we give up some today according as we may get more tomorrow; we consume a resource today rather than use it as an input to raise output tomorrow if it does not generate "appropriately" more tomorrow. The controversy surrounds the amount rather than the concept: What is "appropriately more"? Lower rates will lead to more projects that have a higher return calculated. But if correct number *is* 5% or less, and we invest in all such projects, we cannot say that we are squandering. To the contrary, if this *is* the correct number and we do *not* use it, society will be squandering its resources by investing only in projects that meet the NDRR criterion when discounted at 10%. The analyst should, however, be alert to the mispricing of capital equipment in the market and the need to introduce a shadow price premium as a correction. The difficulties in interpreting tariffs, exchange rates, market imperfections, and taxes, discussed in Chapter 7, indicate the complexity of the task. Indeed, the problem is even more complex than appeared in Chapter 7. Thus in obvious cases of market imperfection, such as a protected motor vehicle and equipment industry whose prices have not changed in the decade since its inception suggesting an increasing monopoly profit by vehicle and equipment makers as production costs fall, it seems reasonable to conclude that capital equipment costs are overstated by market prices. However, while the market price may exceed production cost owing to monopoly power, the market price may nonetheless be lower *or* higher than the opportunity cost of the particular piece of equipment which is supposed to express the ability of the equipment to replace other inputs. Clearly there are problems here—a whole range of problems—which require hard analysis, but they are not related to the rate of discount used to compare different time streams.

5 THE INTERNAL RATE OF RETURN

We return now to the IRR. In Chapter 11 we saw that the IRR was marked by some technical inconsistencies which, though interesting curiosities, do not present serious obstacles to use for choosing among alternative investments by the firm. When we move to the public sector, most of these objections are less consequential. These inconsistencies include possible nonuniqueness, possible negative values, and the inconsistency between the project ranking according to the IRR and the ranking that would follow from application of a net present value criterion, which is, in principle, the correct approach. If the discount rate is correct and we apply the competing decision rules (net relative present value: invest in all projects with net present value ratio greater then unity; IRR criterion: invest in all projects with IRR greater than the discount coefficient), the optimal project set would be the same. It thus becomes a matter of indifference which of the projects from the chosen set is ranked first. The problem remains, however, of ensuring that the correct discount rate is used. If we could know the correct discount rate a net present value approach would be possible. But the discussion of this chapter has shown the controversy surrounding the discount concept to be used, although we recommend ORIPS, as measured by total factor productivity growth. Partly because of these problems, together with a sectoral budget constraint, the IRR is the best project criterion. This preference is reinforced by other considerations. Problems of determining the discount coefficient are merely some of the obstacles to optimal project decisions. Problems in comparability of benefit measures (Chapter 13) also complicate the issue, as do other problems discussed in Chapters 2 and 7. Thus the decision rule is to run down the list of projects, arranged according to the IRR, until the available investment is exhausted. Proceeding this way, of course, means that the actual cutoff IRR, $\hat{r}_j$, will vary between sectors, and even between subsectors. For example in any given year it might be 11% in the railroad sector and 14% in the highway sector, or the other way around. At the same time, the cutoff IRR in education might be 8%, and that in steel production might be 18%. Similarly if local regional budgets are used, as has been urged, the budget in the northwest of a country might lead to a cutoff value of 13%, while that in the south would result in a value of 17%. However, we must express two reservations against too mechanical an application of this procedure.

1. If for several years some project continually falls just below the cutoff, a reordering based on net present value criteria should be

attempted. If then the project yields a value that exceeds the cutoff point, serious thought should be given to including it in the investment group. This is probably unlikely to happen, since projects that fell just short of the cutoff last year will show greater benefits this year, while those that surpassed it last year will already have been undertaken. At the same time, it is unlikely that a large number of new projects will appear that have values greater than the IRR of the project in question. To be sure, the cutoff point will also be affected by the amount available in the budget. However, since we are assuming a fairly stable budget from year to year, which is implicit in the notion of a mature network, problems are unlikely to arise on this account.

2. This approach should be restricted to situations or sectors for which a budget constraint can be devised. This covers most public sectors and transport subsectors. Sometimes, however, transport project makers will be called on to evaluate projects that are not part of the subsector network, as we have been using the term. This refers primarily to penetration projects such as the Amazon Highway project in Brazil designed to settle the region and exploit its resources. Here the present value criterion should be followed, using discount coefficients in the ranges suggested by our earlier discussion of capital productivity, that is, 3 to 5%.

REFERENCES

Böhm Bawerk, Eugen, von (1959), *Capital and Interest*, Vol. 2, *The Positive Theory of Capital*, translated by George D. Huncke (South Holland, Ill.: Libertarian Press).

Jorgenson, Dale W., and Z. Griliches (1967), "The Explanation of Productivity Change," *Review of Economic Studies*, Vol. 34.

Hansen, Alvin (1953), *A Guide to Keynes* (New York: McGraw-Hill).

Hirshleifer, Jack (1958), "On the Theory of Optimal Investment Decision," *Journal of Political Economy*, August.

Patinkin, Don (1972), "Interest," in *Studies in Monetary Economics* (New York: Harper and Row).

Shackle, G. L. S. (1967), "Recent Theories Concerning the Nature and Role of Interest," in *Surveys of Economic Theory*, Vol. 1 (New York: St. Martin's Press).

Solow, Robert M. (1957), "Technical Change and the Aggregate Production Function," *Review of Economic Statistics*, Vol. 39.

U.S. Department of Commerce (1973), *Business Conditions Digest*, November.

U.S. Department of Commerce (various years), *Survey of Current Business*.

CHAPTER

13

The Measurement of Benefits

1 THE THREE APPROACHES TO BENEFIT MEASUREMENT

In earlier chapters we spoke about a "social payoff" or "net social return", leaving the term vague pending a discussion of the items that should enter into such a calculation. We have purposely avoided such terms as "benefit-cost ratio" and "net change in GNP." It is now time to consider what this social return consists of.

Essentially three types of criterion may be distinguished: (1) rectangular value criteria, such as net national income generation; (2) triangular value criteria—variants of the consumer surplus concept; and (3) physical criteria—tons of output, passenger-miles, and so on. In this chapter we consider the first two criteria, giving preference finally to the rectangular criterion—net national income generation—at least for projects that have a relatively short life (10 to 20 years) and do not affect relative prices too violently. But over long periods, when large relative price changes can be expected, due to the project or independently of it, net national income is not a sufficiently reliable guide and physical criteria may be necessary. This is illustrated in Chapter 14 by a case study of the Second Toronto International Airport.

In this chapter we first consider the consumer surplus criterion—the measure that has been most generally accepted by theorists and practitioners in the past 15 years. In coming to preeminence, this measure has had to overcome a great deal of skepticism over the years. However, despite its acceptance, consumer surplus remains deficient in its logic and consistency of application. We then turn in Section 3 to rectangular criteria and consider the major candidates; we find net national income generation to be much more suitable as a welfare criterion than is generally supposed, and when it is difficult to measure, a number of operational proxies may be used.

2 CONSUMER SURPLUS AS A DECISION CRITERION

2.1 The Traditional Analysis and Hicks' Problem

The consumer surplus criterion is illustrated in Figure 13.1. Transport activity on some arc—trips, trip-miles, or some other indicator—is plotted on the X-axis and cost, on the vertical axis. An investment is made to improve the road—straighten alignment, reduce grade, widen it, or modify it in some other way—which reduces unit cost from C_1 to C_2. Since the demand curve for movement between the terminal points of this road is downward sloping, but not vertical, the reduction in unit cost will lead to an increase in traffic. What is the total benefit generated by this investment?

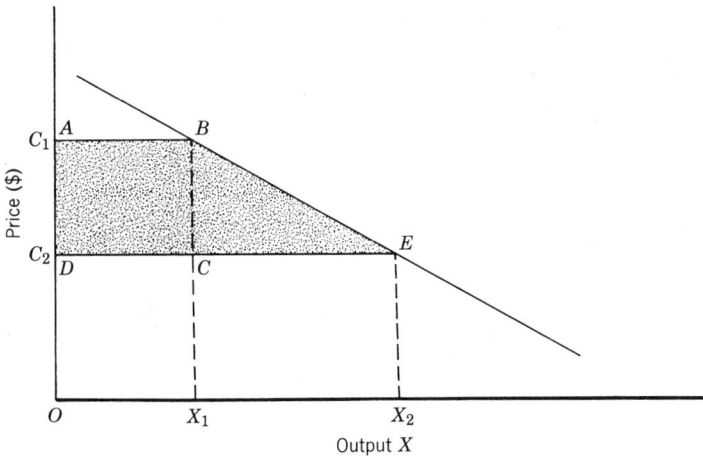

Figure 13.1 Consumer surplus: the traditional concept (as first put forward by Dupuit).

First, there is a cost reduction for each unit of current traffic of $(C_1 - C_2)$ on the X_1 units of traffic currently observed, giving a total cost reduction of $X_1(C_1 - C_2)$ on this traffic, $ABCD$ in Figure 13.1. In addition, we have an increase in traffic of $(X_2 - X_1)$. It is usually recognized that the unit cost saving on the preexisting traffic, which measures the benefit of each unit of the preexisting traffic, does not measure the benefit of the incremental traffic, since this traffic was not in fact observed earlier; it was not paying C_1 per unit before. On the other hand, this traffic *is* observed after the investment is made. It is reasonable to assume that the demand curve is linear between these two points, which means that the amount that each successive unit of traffic over this range would have been willing to pay to drive over this road is given by the price corresponding to this quantity on the demand curve. Therefore, the benefit of each unit of this incremental traffic is given by the vertical distance between the demand curve and the horizontal line at C_2. This forms triangle BCE. Therefore, the total reduction in transport cost is equal to the sum of the rectangle $ABCD$ and the triangle BCE. In addition, there may be other benefits that the analyst must take into account. More about these later.

The area $ABED$ is usually thought of as the "consumer surplus." This criterion dates to the mid-nineteenth century when the French engineer, Jules Dupuit, espoused it for the construction of a public work. It was later discussed by Marshall, and was reintroduced and further developed by Hotelling in 1938. So pervasive has been the acceptance of consumer surplus that even leading economists in the Soviet Union espouse it as the correct criterion for decision-making.[*] Nevertheless, the consumer surplus criterion suffers from several major conceptual problems. Most post-Marshallian criticism and analysis has been directed at only one of these problems. This culminated in the critical analysis of Hicks, who in the end concluded, together with other writers, that the initial objections he had raised could be overcome. However, it should be stressed that this was only one kind of criticism; there are at least four other major flaws in the consumer surplus criterion, which we consider in this chapter.[†]

The essence of Hicks' objections is that the increase in consumption following a reduction in price is made up of two effects—the income effect and the substitution effect. The problem that this leads to is

---

[*] For example, L. V. Kantorovich, the discoverer of linear programming in 1939 and a leading Soviet mathematician and economist, espoused this approach. For discussion of this and other aspects of Soviet investment decision criteria, see Abouchar (1973).

[†] An excellent recent survey of the development of consumer surplus analysis is the paper by Currie, et al. (1971).

illustrated in Figure 13.2. The fall in the price of the commodity causes the price line to swing out to the point of tangency with a higher indifference curve. There is an increase in consumption equal to $\hat{X}_1$. This increase is made up of an amount that represents the substitution of the product for other factors $(\hat{X}_2)$ and an income effect $(\hat{X}_1 - \hat{X}_2)$. The part of the increase in consumption caused by substitution does not imply a change in welfare, since it is the quantity that the person would have

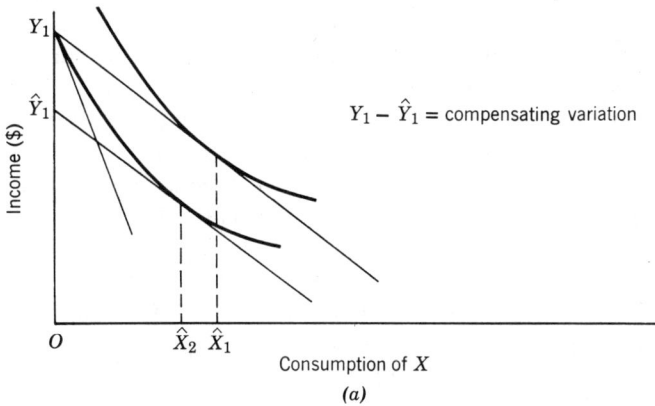

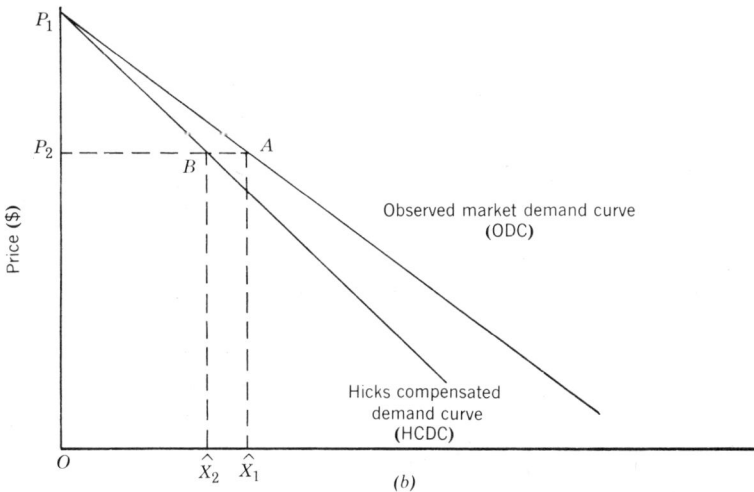

Figure 13.2 Derivation of Hicks compensated demand curve and comparison with observed market demand curve. (a) Derivation of compensating variation. (b) Comparison of Hicks compensated demand curve and observed market demand curve: area between price and Hicks compensated curve equals compensating variation associated with that price.

consumed at the new price if at the same time an amount of income were taken from him, forcing him to remain on the same indifference curve. Since he remains on the same curve, he is, by definition, no better off. He *is* better off, however, to the extent that this income is left to him. Hicks called this difference $(Y_1 - \hat{Y}_1)$ the "compensating variation." He showed that this surplus would be lower than (or equal to) the traditional Dupuit triangular measurement and showed the relationship between the two measures.

The compensating variation traces out a demand curve, which Currie and co-workers called the "Hicks' compensated demand curve," (HCDC). It is shown in the lower half of Figure 13.2. The area bounded above by the HCDC at the point of consumption that would have taken place on the original indifference curve *after* the price change $(\hat{X}_2)$ and bounded below by the price line (P_2) is equal to the compensating variation. Evidently, this will always be less than the area under the ordinary demand curve except in the special case where the income effect is zero (which means that all of the new consumption of this product which is brought about by the price reduction represents a substitute for the consumption of other commodities, and the change in real income resulting therefrom is all "net" in the sense that it can be used to consume still other goods.) Hicks put it in the following way (1956, p. 177):

> What in the light of this approach, we have been trying to do is to establish, more precisely than Marshall thought necessary, the conditions needed for the Marshall measure (i.e. the relevant area below the ordinary demand curve) to be a good measure. And so considered, the result of our inquiry is very simple. In order that the Marshall measure of consumer's surplus should be a good measure, one thing alone is needful—that the income effect should be small.

But while the Hicks problem may be solved, this is not the only impediment to the use of consumer surplus. We will consider four of the other most serious problems: (1) definition of activities; (2) intersectoral inconsistency, including a) neglect of nonmarket effects and b) neglect of triangles in market sectors; and (3) irreconcilability of indifference maps of some competing goods.

2.2   Problems of Definition of Activities

We make the standard assumptions about aggregating over individuals (essentially, that tastes are similar) and suppose that Figures 13.2*a* and

13.2*b* refer to the whole economy. Furthermore, for simplicity, we assume that the demand configurations are such as to yield a very small difference between P_1AP_2 and P_1BP_2, that is, the Marshall-Dupuit measure and the Hicks measures are practically the same. Following the conventional approach, we then estimate a consumer surplus area as $\frac{1}{2}X_1(P_1 - P_2)$. However, this could lead to a very drastic overstatement of the net benefit or consumer surplus that the project might generate. Let us see why.

Suppose that some road investment is being contemplated which appears to be in an environment sufficiently similar to a project undertaken elsewhere to justify the use of the experience of the latter to forecast the results of the new investment. After the earlier road was built, traffic rose and unit operating costs fell. The traditional calculation employs a Dupuit triangle defined by the *ODC*, which, assuming, as we are, that the income effect is small, can be used as the welfare measure. But when we look behind these cost and output observations and ask why the demand curve slopes downward in the first place, doubts arise. Why *are* the new users willing to pay to use the road? One reason is that some of them are now shipping on a competing mode or arc and paying more than the new cost will be. But since these users may already be receiving a consumer surplus, this will be lost when they switch to the new road. Therefore, what we should compare is the *change* in surplus.

The problem is shown in Figure 13.3, which illustrates a road expan-

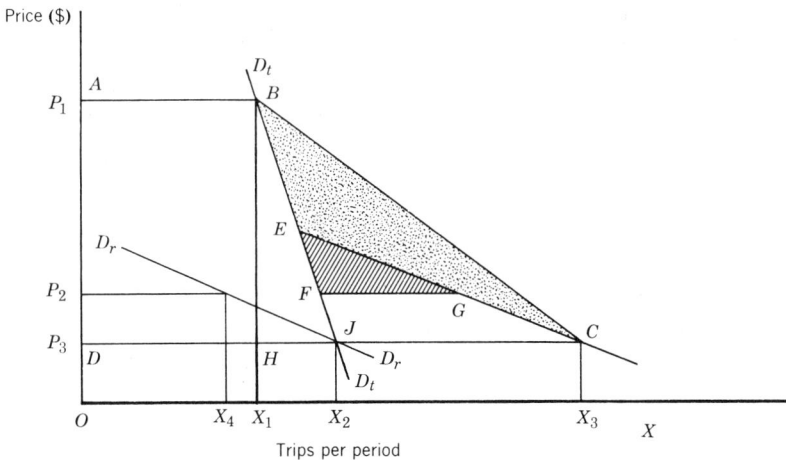

Figure 13.3 Possible overstatement of welfare change of project (even assuming that demand curves are Hicks compensated).

sion project. Present traffic on this road is X_1 at a unit cost of P_1 (we assume all traffic runs the entire length of the road). The present truck demand curve is $D_t D_t$. There is also railroad traffic on this arc: X_4 units at cost P_2 per trip. The railroad demand curve is given by $D_r D_r$.

If the road is expanded, unit costs will fall, and there will be increased traffic along the truck demand curve, as well as along the rail demand curve. The total demand curve is the horizontal sum of the two modal demand curves—the line segments BEC.

The conventional approach to consumer surplus in this case is given by BCH. The first source of welfare change exaggeration is the triangle BEC, since there are no demands along the line segment BC. In addition, the triangle EFG is equal to the consumer surplus at present being enjoyed by rail traffic (the area between the horizontal at P_2 and $D_r D_r$). Therefore, the correct measure of the Dupuit-Marshall consumer surplus triangle here is given by the sum of BJH and the trapezoid $FGCJ$, in this case an area less than half as large as the one conventionally calculated. (The rectangle $ABHD$ would appear in either case).*

2.3   Intersectoral Inconsistency: NonMarket Effects

The second major problem invalidating the consumer surplus criterion is that it provides no obvious way to take account of activities that are not priced in the market. For example, suppose that the projects being considered include a disease control project, or an education project, or something else of this nature. We will see in Section 3 that some aspects of some of these possible undertakings can be considered under the approach we will recommend. However, it is impossible to take account of all aspects of such projects.

How do we know the relationship between price and quantity demanded for disease control.

In the absence of such information, surrogates are sometimes experimented with—workdays gained (measured in wages) or output by the workers whose health is enhanced. Evidently, this approach would understate the attractiveness of such projects compared to the highway project since, in effect, we would be dealing with *a rectangular criterion* rather than a triangular criterion. In principle, if we base investment decisions on triangular criteria, we should consider the marginal utility of income for the workers concerned and recognize that some workers

---

* The inconsistency here between the correct estimate of consumer surplus and the conventional one could be resolved by defining the activities properly. If we regard the modal demands as demands for trips rather than demands for rail and road, we can easily see the correct solution. This is shown through indifference curve analysis in Section 2.5.

will put a higher value than others on the income they receive from increased ability to work, even though the number of dollars is the same. The same applies to leisure; besides the extra working days, the disease prevention program will secure greater amounts of leisure for the people affected. The value of this leisure will differ from one person to another. There is no way to measure the minimum value that anyone puts on this leisure time, or the premium over and above this minimum value, that some of those who are affected will place on their leisure. However, if the triangular aspect of the measurement of the benefits of these activities is left out of account, the result will be to yield values of the decision criterion that are systematically understated in relation to the triangular measurements of the transportation projects. If investment is actually allotted to different sectors according to this criterion, the allocation will be biased in favor of transportation projects.*

2.4 Intersectoral Inconsistency: Neglect of Triangles in Market-Oriented Sectors

Problems of intersectoral inconsistency are not restricted to activities whose outputs are not susceptible to market measurement. Even market-oriented activities such as steel production will present problems. Proponents of consumer surplus do not usually recommend that it be applied to such projects as steel mills or other manufacturing activities. The recommended procedure is to compare the discounted benefit of a public sector project, including the consumer surplus triangle, with a rate of return on alternative investments, including those in the manufacturing sector. But if the consumer surplus on the activities of the manufacturing firm is never taken into account, the comparison will obviously be distorted. Suppose that the consumer surplus triangle amounts to one-third of a total measured highway benefit and that no such triangle is included in the measurement of a steel mill, which, we will assume, has a net discounted relative present value of 1.1. If investment is allocated intersectorally in a centralized manner, investment will continue to be channeled into some highway projects that have as low a ratio as 1.11 (*including* the effect of their consumer surplus triangle) in preference to the steel mill. But if in fact some consumer surplus triangle *is* generated by the steel project, such an investment pattern will be irrational. Therefore proponents of this

---

* One study that does attempt to make a rectangular calculation of the value of time saving is the study of the Victoria Line on the London subway system by Foster and Beesley (1963, p 77). This is rarely done, however, and could in any event open the analysis to arbitrary manipulation, especially when interregional transfers are involved.

approach must be assuming that the steel project would generate *no* consumer surplus triangle. Is this reasonable?

The failure to include a consumer surplus triangle in the benefit imputed to the steel mill must be based on the following logic. The highway will have an immediate consequence on traffic, increasing the intensity of use of the facility by a great amount. The output of the steel mill, on the other hand, goes into thousands of uses—nails, washing machines, I-beams, cars, scissors, and so on. The number of additional units of any of these articles produced by the output of a single steel mill is very small. This applies in both developed economies and underdeveloped economies—while the steel mill may increase domestic capacity enormously, most of the production will substitute for imports, increasing total consumption only moderately. Accordingly, even in a developing economy the increased output of any final product will be small. Therefore the consumer surplus triangle involved in the increased output of any product will be negligible.

There are at least three criticisms of this view, depending on the assumptions made about the behavior of cost and demand. These are illustrated in Figure 13.4.

1. There is no shift in demand and no shift in the cost curve, which is assumed to be horizontal, as are the cost curves of all the final products. This is shown at left in Figure 13.4a, where the cost is unchanged at P_1. In this case there is no increase in production, since production is already taking place at the intersection of the supply and demand curves. The producer of final products can be induced to increase output only if *his* cost curve shifts downward to P_2 (at right in Figure 13.4a), which can happen because the state is absorbing part of the investment cost in the steel mill. In this case the net increase in consumer surplus is negative—it is shown by the area *BEC* between the true cost curve (P_1) and the demand curve. Thus the investment in the steel project would actually be less attractive if the consumer surplus were considered.

2. Alternatively, the cost curve shifts downward as a result of lower costs of domestic production (Figure 13.4b). The lower curve now represents the social cost rather than the cost to the manufacturers of final steel-using products, as at left in Figure 13.4a. Production costs fall for such reasons as decreased transport costs and cheaper domestic labor. In this case the consumer surplus triangle (*BCF*) *is* positive and neglecting it *will* understate the attractiveness of the steel project compared to the transport project.

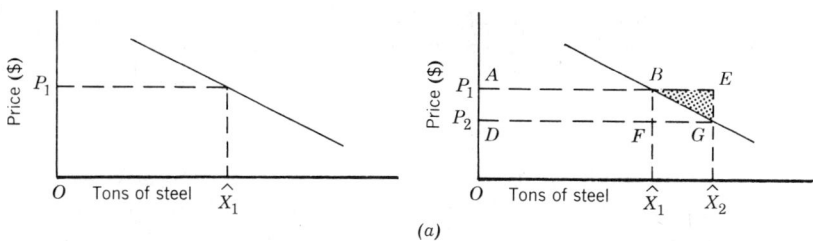

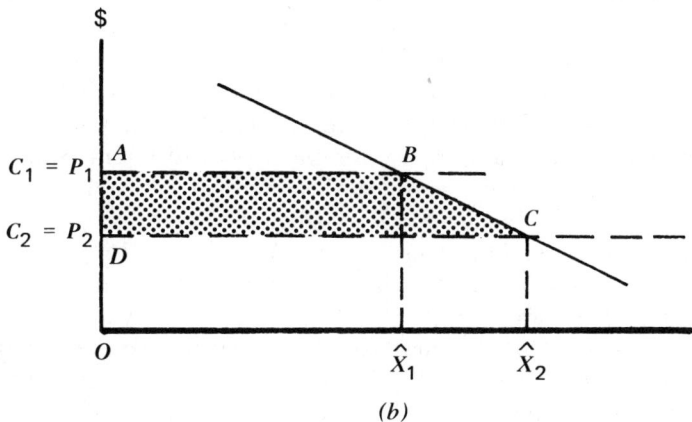

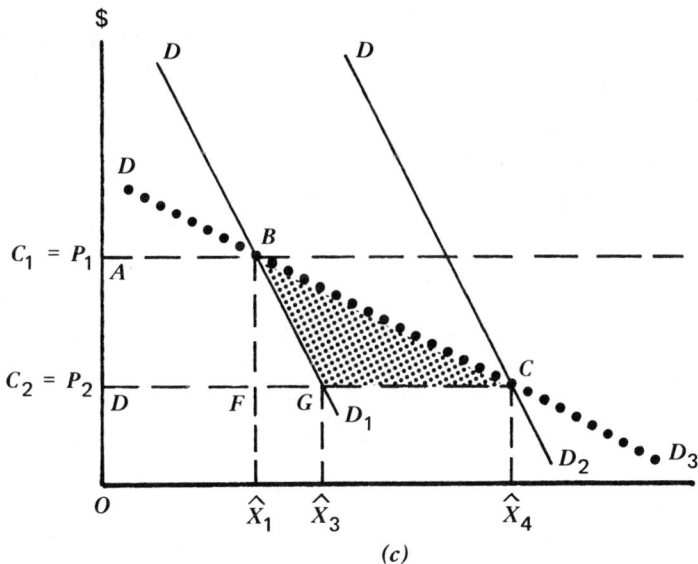

Figure 13.4 Three cases of demand and cost behavior and implications for consumer surplus interpretation. (a) No change in demand or in cost (the case on the right has fall in price). (b) Change in cost, no change in demand. (c) Fall in cost, shift in demand.

209

3. There is a shift in the demand curve (Figure 13.4c). There is also a downward shift in the private cost curve, which is the same as the social cost curve, as in case 2. Now, when examining transport investment analysts frequently project demand and determine that at the new price the traffic level of $\hat{X}_4$ will be observed, present activity being $\hat{X}_1$. This projection is based on, say, historical analogy. Now, what really lies behind this shift in consumption is somewhat as follows. The demand curve in the historical situation has shifted from DD_1 to DD_2 in the diagram. The analyst, however, perceives the situation as though there were a single demand curve as shown by the broken line DD_3. Thus he concludes that it is correct to consider the consumer surplus triangle BCF as defined by a single demand curve, different points on DD_3 being comparable. In fact, we are comparing two different points in the economy, which involves many more complications of intertemporal comparison that can be covered by a single demand curve. If we make some of the usual assumptions here regarding tastes and income distribution, a consumer surplus triangular approach would require us to consider not the triangle BCF, but the triangle BGF, which enables us to isolate the effect of the downward shift in the cost curve form the rightward shift in demand. This obviously, gives a much smaller consumer surplus triangle.

The situation just described is usually acknowledged in manufacturing activities, but not in public sector projects, such as roads. Transport project studies frequently fail to separate the shift in demand caused by increased population or increased levels of economic activity, brought about by other forces, from the effects of cost reduction caused by the road investment itself. Meanwhile, historical increases in steel production are usually attributed solely to shifts in demand curves, which, moreover, are implicitly assumed to be virtually inelastic so that even the steel industry counterpart of the BFG triangle is neglected. Thus the road project benefit is exaggerated, since a BCF triangle is used, and the steel project is undervalued, since no triangle is used (the usual criterion applied in steel production being a rectangular criterion, such as profit).

2.5 Possible Irreconcilability of Indifference Curves

The welfare levels for the various indifference curves of some activities may be irreconcilable. This problem really arises in the immeasurability of the welfare (the lack of a cardinal measure of welfare) for different activities and is similar to the problem discussed

in Section 2.4. It is illustrated in Figure 13.5. Figure 13.5*a* shows the
indifference map of a given consumer for coach travel, and Figure 13.5*b*
shows his indifference map for first-class travel *when* it becomes available. He will consume the same number of coach flights as first-class
flights, but at a lower price, as is indicated by the price line in (*a*) as
compared with (*b*). Naturally, this leaves him a larger amount to be
spent on other activities than he would have if he had bought the same
number of first-class flights at the higher price. But suppose that we
actually observe him behaving in this way when first-class flights
become available. He must prefer this situation to coach, even though it
leaves him less income for other expenditures. The welfare level

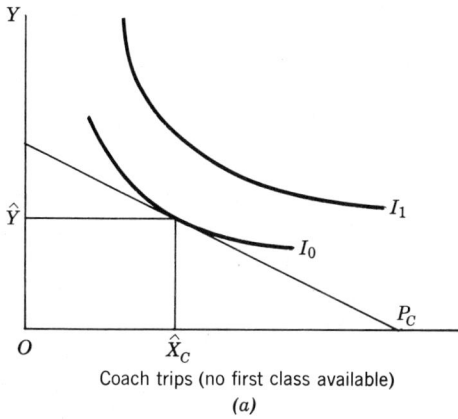

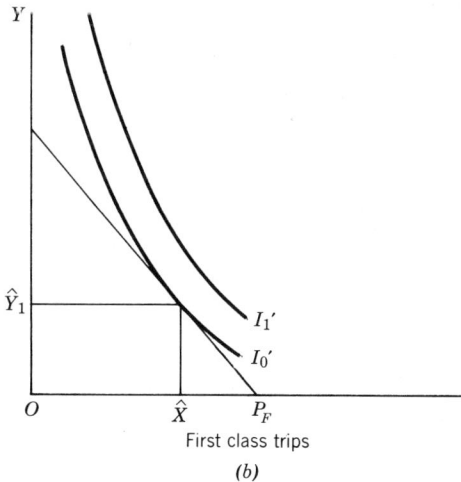

Coach trips (no first class available)

(*a*)

First class trips

(*b*)

Figure 13.5 Irreconcilability of indifference maps.

associated with indifference curve I_0' in Figure 13.5b must be higher than that in Figure 13.5a, but we have no idea how much higher, since cardinal measurement is not possible.

The situation just described is very common in transportation as well as in other activities. In essence, it means that some activities have inherently unquantifiable advantages because some consumers will perform only one of several activities. We never observe them on the same indifference map and so cannot identify the tradeoff between them. Other examples are the satisfaction derived from the use of a better built highway as compared with a low-grade road and a good road versus a poor rail connection on a specified arc. In short, any activity in which some net advantage inheres in one technology as compared with another presents this difficulty and there is no way to discern the value attaching to the advantage.*

This problem would also arise in the previously analyzed examples of the new road whose traffic consisted of two already existing modal demands—road and rail (Section 2.2). There the key to the estimation of the consumer surplus triangles was to regard rail demand as one submarket and the previously existing road activity as a second submarket. We assumed in essence that there was no difference in service—road and rail were completely substitutable, with activity by the present rail shippers rising when the cost per trip was reduced after the road was built. Without further information, we would be able to calculate the incremental consumer surplus only by assuming that there were no differences in quality. We derived this incremental consumer surplus by analyzing the submarket demand curves directly. It is also of interest to analyze them within the indifference curve framework to see how the definition of consumer surplus depends on the definition of the underlying activities. This is shown in Figure 13.6a.

Figure 13.6a,b is cast in terms of road trip demand for shippers presently using rail. (Prices and quantities correspond to the rail submarket demand in Figure 13.4.) At the present price, P_1, this market segment consumes no road trips. When the price falls from P_1 to P_3 we see a large increase in road trips. Both the Marshall-Dupuit and the Hicks consumer surplus measures are large. But if we regarded the indifference map of the present rail shippers as reflecting the demand

---

* It might be objected that we could find the consumer's own rate of substitution between the two commodities and thereby know his welfare by plotting the indifference map for coach and first-class travel. We must then know his budget constraint for air travel. But the problem arises precisely because we do not know this budget constraint; part of the problem is to determine it, recognizing that the amount he will spend on air travel in the first place depends on the quality of the service.

THE MEASUREMENT OF BENEFITS

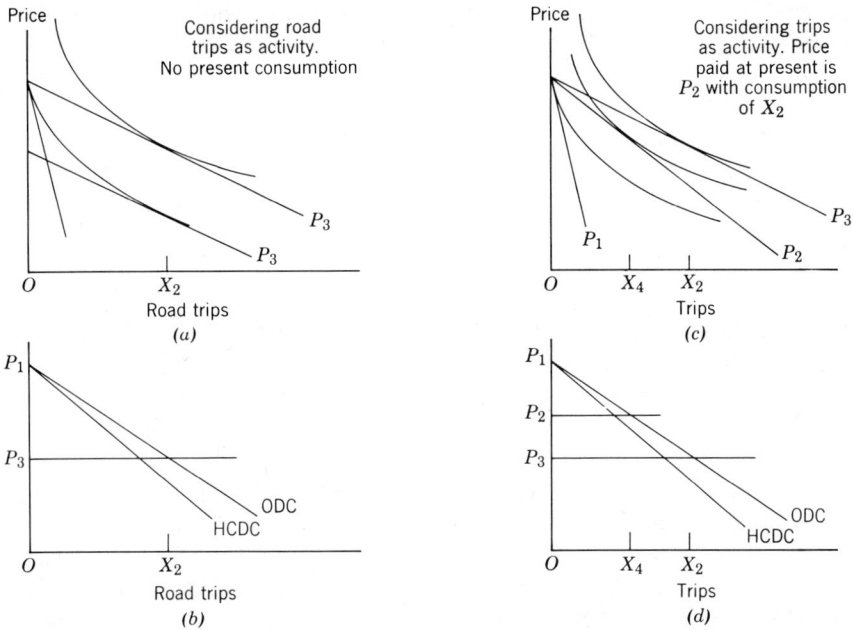

Figure 13.6 Derivation of ODC (Marshall-Dupuit) consumer surplus and Hicks compensated consumer surplus for present rail shippers when a road is built under different definition of activity (commodity).

for *trips in general* rather than *road* trips, we would get a much smaller surplus measure. This is shown in Figure 13.6c,d. Present demand for road trips is zero, but after the road is built and road costs fall, the demand for road trips by this segment of the market rises to X_2. The Marshall-Dupuit surplus and the Hicks compensating variation are shown in Figure 13.6d. By redefining the activity, we get different values for both surpluses. At present, X_2 trips are being performed by rail, with corresponding surplus measures shown by the triangles above P_2 in (d). With a fall in trip price to P_3, consumption rises to X_2, showing net surpluses given by the trapezoids between P_2 and P_3. Thus both the Marshall-Dupuit measure and the Hicks measure, if calculated on the basis of demand for road trips rather then trips in general, would overstate the true increment in welfare. Put differently, even if the HCDC and ODC coincided, defining the demand in terms of road trips would lead to a higher surplus estimate than would be derived by regarding trips as the activity.

All of the foregoing assumes, of course, that there are no differences in service. If, as is usual, differences are present, there will be higher welfare associated with truck movement. But now we are back in the coach versus first-class situation—there is a difference, but we do not know how large it is. Thus once again the triangular approach breaks down. On the other hand, it may be possible to measure the differential advantages of the road service through reduction of costs in other sectors. But cost reduction is essentially a rectangular criterion. We now turn to the analysis of such criteria.

3   RECTANGULAR BENEFIT MEASURES

The distinguishing characteristic of rectangular criteria is that any activity entering the benefit summand is weighted at a given price. Thus while many kinds of effect may be considered, all units of any particular activity are treated equally. Rectangular criteria include a wide range of approaches to benefit measurement. One example is profit of a firm, the product of quantity multiplied by price minus cost. Profit, of course, is based on the price and cost that apply to the postinvestment situation. Other examples include national income generation, cost reduction and reduction in absenteeism through disease control (days multiplied by productivity). Therefore rejection of the consumer surplus approach does not provide unequivocal guidance about what to do instead. However, considerations of overall economic welfare maximization do suggest the use of some macroeconomic (national income)* magnitude, either for use as the criterion directly, or as the conceptual framework for organizing the measurement of benefits.

Since the welfare significance of national income has often been ques-

---

* Some confusion arises in discussing investment criteria because of the ambiguity of the expression "national income," which is used in three different but related senses in economics. First, it denotes national output (occasionally called the "social dividend" in the English literature), the total output of productive activity in the economy, without recognizing any of the problems of measurement or price noncommensurability that are implicit when we speak of "national income" as a generic macroeconomic accounting term—the second use of the expression. Finally, it is used as a specific macroeconomic concept: in Canada as Gross National Product or Expenditure less depreciation, and in the United States as GNP less depreciation and indirect taxes, with a few other minor adjustments. In this book we use the expression in its second meaning, that is, with the general sense of the national accounting category. It is preferred to GNP, the highest-level macro variable in the United States and Canada, because GNP is not used in many other countries, with "national income" being better understood. The essential principles of calculation of this highest-level macroeconomic variable in all capitalist countries, whatever it is called, offer the same advantages and disadvantages as far as welfare significance is concerned.

tioned, we briefly review its adequacy in this regard (Section 3.1). In Section 3.2. we compare the relationships among the various rectangular measures, and in Section 3.3 we consider some conceptual problems in the application of national income.

3.1 The National Income Criterion

For most—but not all—projects, national income provides a suitable measure of welfare and can serve as the investment criterion. Unlike many other measures, its correct application puts disproportionate stress on lower-income groups since it is equipped to take account of sequential effects in sectors or regions with high unemployment. Therefore it is almost certainly a better welfare index than any other single measure. Nor does it require special distributional adjustments, which some might regard as arbitrary in any event, or which might provide a pretext for introducing adjustments to suit the personal preferences of policymakers in a specific situation.

National income as a welfare measure, however, has some generally recognized shortcomings. Since it is unlikely that a single perfect welfare measure will ever be attained, the question that should be asked it not whether national income is imperfect, but whether it is less imperfect than other criteria and whether its imperfections make it generally inadequate or inadequate only for certain kinds of situation. We can divide the criticisms into two groups: index number problems and problems of omission or accounting convention. Problems of the first kind may disqualify this criterion when radical changes in relative prices are likely—a subject to which we return in the next chapter.*

---

* The "index number problem" relates to the difficulty of making international or intertemporal comparisons between situations in which there are large differences in relative prices. And we hastily agree that such comparisons are *extremely* hazardous. For example, a Brazil-United States per capita national income comparison would vary depending on whether Brazilian or United States price weights were used (compare the mango/automobile price ratios, each influenced by and in turn influencing the consumption mix in the two countries). A good analysis of the severity of this problem with an empirical application is Usher (1968). Usher shows that the average per capita income in Thailand in relation to that of the United Kingdom is 6.3 when measured in United Kingdom prices and 2.8 in Thailand prices. But for project evaluation purposes, we are interested in national income change within *a given* economy so that the welfare distortions and ambiguities introduced by the need for a constant system of price ratios is absent. Thus we need not worry about the misstatement of welfare that would follow from pricing mangoes and automobiles in Brazil at the price of the New York market. However, for projects with very long life during which we can expect large differences to develop in relative prices, national income *may* be an inadequate criterion. We consider such a situation and the recommended alternative procedure in Chapter 14.

Problems of the second type would affect any criterion to some extent, and they are likely to be less serious for the national income measure for a wide range of projects. Let us look at them more closely.

It is of course true that national income is not a perfect gauge of the well-being or welfare of an economy. Indeed, given the historical reasons for the development of the national accounts, it could not be expected to be. The measurement of national income received its major modern emphasis under the force of the world depression in the 1930s, and its primary objective was to record year-to-year changes in business activity and employment as a device for the formulation of contracyclical policy. National income represents an attempt to sum all the contributions of the productive forces within a country: labor, capital, and land in all their diverse forms, the profits of final goods producers, the profits of intermediate goods producers, and the returns to the providers of primary inputs—the wages of labor—in the economy. Inevitably, certain bookkeeping conventions had to be adopted and simplifications made in such a complex system. In addition certain compromises reflecting the desire to show welfare more accurately have been introduced over the years, hybridizing the accounts somewhat.

For example, since the primary purpose is to measure business activity, a young man who is paid to cut his father's lawn makes a positive contribution to national income, even though he may have been doing the job without pay previously. Under the constant marginal utility of income usually assumed, there is no change in welfare if the pay replaces the son's regular allowance, although national income rises. To cite another example, if all renters suddenly became homeowners, national income would fall, but, again, economic welfare would not change. It is easy to exaggerate the effects of such conventions, however. Frequently the assumptions are unrealistic. For example, the boy's pay would *not* in fact enter the measured national income, and, given our institutional framework, there would *not* be an overnight shift of the hypothesized magnitude in homeownership. A recent analysis of the major distorting influences on welfare comparisons based on Canadian interregional income differences showed that they had very little overall effect. (see Abouchar, 1971).

Another anomaly frequently alleged to result from macroeconomic conventions is, for example, the failure to allow for pollution or its control: national income may rise even while people feel themselves worse off because the environment is polluted. Note, however, that if pollution is reduced, national income will rise by the amount of the pollution control investment; we will be better off *and* national income will rise. If pollution is unabated between years (continuing at the same level with respect to national income) but national income does rise (because of production of more vehicles, say), we in fact *do* have higher welfare in the second year. Some adjustment is necessary to get national income closer to the "absolute" welfare level in both years. [Further aspects of this analysis are treated in Denison's short paper (1971).] Thus although the national income accounts were devised originally to measure short-term changes in economic activity, they can also serve fairly well as a gauge of short-term change in welfare.

But there are even more compelling welfare-based arguments in favor of national income rather than, say, wages or profits within a project as a benefit measure for public investment. Since national income is supposed to measure the total output of the factors of production in the economy, it is its net generation that we would wish to consider for a project, subtracting from the project wages, profits, and other sources of value added, the reduction in value added that might take place elsewhere if the resources were redirected. Thus labor, if it has no alternative use and is brought into the stream of production, contributes to national income an amount equal to its wage. If a worker merely transfers from one occupation to another at the same wage as the result of some investment project, he makes *no net* contribution to national income. This is one of the keys to the appreciation of the universality of national income as a measure of the benefits of a project. It means that in a developing economy the labor contribution in a backward region will be treated consistently with that in a developed region in terms of its net contribution. This net contribution might be a day's wage in the backward region and nothing in the advanced region. The same principle holds in a developed economy. Newfoundland, where labor generally has a smaller alternative contribution to make, will generate a higher net national income from the same kind of project than will Toronto. Thus one can look at the future time stream of national income of a given investment. It makes a greater net contribution in a region with much unemployment than in a region with little unemployment.

3.2 Welfare Equivalence of Alternative Rectangular Criteria

In this section we consider the relation of individual rectangular criteria to one another and to the abstract notion of national economic well-being or welfare. This will serve three purposes: (1) demonstrate the superiority of the national income orientation for fully employed and underemployed economies in general; (2) clarify the circumstances under which market measures, often easier to calculate, may be utilized as surrogates for national income; and (3) teach us to recognize the activities or sectors in which decisions by market agents (private firms or government corporations) in response to market stimuli can be assumed to be consistent with welfare maximization (as distinct from situations in which it is necessary to look further or impose supplements to market behavior).

Tables 13.1 and 13.2 show the interrelationships among seven measurable rectangular criteria and welfare for the fully employed and underemployed economies. Welfare is an abstract measure and is not further defined. Real income, real costs, and real consumption are measured in terms of constant preproject prices. Income distribution is measured by some inequality measure such as the ratio of the area under a Lorentz curve (a cumulative income-population distribution curve with both income and population in relative terms on the vertical and horizontal axes) to the area under the 45° line. Profit, revenue, and nominal national income are measured in current market prices. We assume decreasing marginal utility of income.

A movement in the indicator given at left may be accompanied by a similar (plus sign), reverse (negative sign) or, without further informa-

Table 13.1   Interrelationships among Rectangular Measures: The Fully Employed Economy (or Subeconomy)

Measure of Interest	Wel-fare	National Income: Nominal	National Income: Real	Profit	Real Cost Reduc-tion	Total Rev-enue	Real Con-sump-tion	Income Distri-bution
						Effect on		
Welfare	X	?	?	?	?	?	?	?
National income: nominal	?	X	?	?	?	+	+	+
National income: real	+	?	X	?	+	?	?	?
Profit	+	+	+	X	?	?	?	?
Real Cost reduction	+	+	+	?	X	−	?	?
Total revenue	?	?	?	?	?	X	?	?
Real consumption	+	?	?	?	+	?	X	?
Income distribution	+	?	?	?	?	?	+	X

Table 13.2 Interrelationships among Rectangular measures: The Underemployed Economy (or Subeconomy)

Measures of Interest	Welfare	National Income: Nominal	National Income: Real	Profit	Real Cost Reduction	Total Revenue	Real Consumption	Income Distribution
				Effect on				
Welfare	X	?	?	?	?	?	?	?
National income: nominal	?	X	?	?	−	+	+	+
National income: real	+	+	X	?	?	?	+	+
Profit	?	?	?	X	?	?	?	?
Real cost reduction	?	−	−	+	X	−	?	−
Total revenue	?	?	?	?	?	X	?	?
Real consumption	+	+	+	+	?	?	X	?
Income distribution	+	?	?	?	?	?	?	X

tion, indeterminate movement (question mark). For example, in a fully employed economy a project *may* cause nominal income or total revenue (money flows, e.g. sales) to rise, welfare to remain unchanged, and other factors to be positively related. Since the underlying assumptions attempt to reflect the real world rather than an abstract model, the relationships hypothesized are believed reasonable; different assumptions would result in different conclusions, although it is believed that the essence would not change. For example we assume that absolute prices are inflexible downward so that an increase in profit would be associated positively with an increase in nominal income. This requires, naturally, an increase in the money supply, which the monetary authority is assumed to permit. On the other hand, real income also rises, since the increase in profit signifies an increase in market exchange (which requires monetary accommodation) or a reduction in cost (which does not). In either case, total real income, measured in preproject prices, will rise in the fully employed economy as the released resources are reabsorbed. Whether this leads to an increase in consumption depends on the sector in which costs decline.

Under our assumptions there is a great deal of indeterminacy, but there are some extremely important positive and negative relationships.

One interesting conclusion is that there are two positive relationships in the fully employed economy in the real income column, and that the two related operational measures are profit and cost reduction. Another conclusion is that in the underemployed economy, these relations are indeterminate or negative, while consumption has a positive relationship. This happens because consumption by the underemployed rises or because consumption rises in the employed sector in the first place, leading either to absorption of some underemployed resources or to imports, but not merely offsetting investment and leaving real income unchanged.

Thus in the fully employed economy we can depend extensively on profit and cost reduction, both being appropriate for government corporations, and cost reduction being suitable for highway construction and related projects. In the underemployed sector, the task is more complicated and can best be examined by way of some examples.

3.3   Some Problems in the Application of the National Income Criterion

There are two kinds of difficulty in applying the national income criterion. One is the information-analytic problem—getting statistical data, estimating behavioral coefficients, determining the offsetting changes in activities elsewhere, and so on. Much of the cost analysis presented in Part 2 and the sources cited there will be helpful here. Frequently, shortcuts and approximations must be used. It would be hard to cite a better example of imaginative handling of limited data than Bergmann's study of a major highway project in Bolivia (1966), a model for analysis in high-unemployment regions, whether in developed or underdeveloped economies. Especially to be stressed is her skillful use of approximate methods, essential in any real-life analysis.

In addition to data collection and estimation, two important conceptual problems are frequently encountered when using the national income criterion. These are the handling of transport costs and the treatment of secondary benefits.

Consider transport costs. The reader may be confused by seeing items with positive cost sometimes treated as a cost and sometimes as a benefit. A careful observer must have noticed that both approaches are followed—in the serious as well as polemical literature. For example, it is often argued that one benefit of new road project is creating jobs. But are these a benefit? Or a cost?

To decide how to treat these items, we should start with first principles. Since we are using net national income generation as the benefit measure there is no ambiguity. If we build a road in an underdeveloped region or sector, the transport activity itself will raise the national income, since it will draw into the economy workers who would otherwise be idle. Because a major goal of economic development is to promote employment and thus improve the distribution of income, this transport "cost" should be viewed positively, which is what we do when considering national income as the decision criterion. On the other hand, if we are considering a transport-saving project in a region of high unemployment, we will in fact *reduce* national income, since the released resources will have no alternative employment. This refers both to labor and capital. In this region, the reduction in transport cost would show up as a reduction in national income and since this also implies that the poor would be hardest hit, which, not being the income distribution goal, is undesirable. But if we use the national income criterion, we will make the right decision. Again, Bergmann's analysis proceeds in the right way in this regard.

In the areas of full employment, however, the reverse is true. If we reduce the total cost of transport in the fully employed section of the economy, we relieve resources that will generate national income—if the economy is fully employed, these resources will be taken up directly. On the other hand, if we create a more costly technology, the additional inputs must come from some other part of the fully employed sector, reducing the national income in that sector. However, if we are in this kind of situation, we will not actually observe changes in real national income. If there is full employment in this sector we continue to have full employment, there merely being some changes in the form it takes. With lower-cost transport we have lower prices for some goods, but the same total value added as with the higher-cost transport. Since national income is, essentially, total value added, we would get the same result with and without the project. In other words there would be no positive indication of a benefit from the transport improvement if we followed the national income criterion.

Again, first principles come to the rescue. National income comparisons presuppose price stability. If prices change, between two periods, the quantities of the two periods must be weighted by fixed price weights. The question whether to use preinvestment or postinvestment prices is one to which economic theory can provide no definitive answer (see the discussion in Chapter 14 of the ambiguity of intertemporal national income comparisons under large relative price changes). To be safe, a project might be evaluated on the basis of both sets of prices. However, we shall not usually be able to trace the transport cost effects throughout the zone of project influence and actually perform such calculations. The best we can do is to measure the cost reduction taking place each year. However, since we are in the fully employed sector of the economy we know that the released resources will be taken up and used to produce more of the goods already being produced. Under static conditions prices will have to fall. We shall then have greater consumption of the various goods being produced, but lower prices for them. In physical terms, the welfare change will vary between a minimum of $\Delta C/P_1$ and a maximum $\Delta C/P_2$, where ΔC is the amount of the cost saving and P_1 and P_2 are the prices of the consumer good whose production is increased before and after the project.

At worst, therefore, the implied increase in real national income will be proportional to the money cost saving. At best it will be greater. The cost saving, then, gives us a lower bound on national income generation and is, accordingly, recommended for use as the national income-equivalent criterion in the fully employed sector of the economy.

Another common source of confusion is the treatment of secondary and tertiary effects. Again, Bergmann's procedure is correct for the unemployed sector. She considers the effects of the road on economic activities in the region of road penetration even when these do not directly involve transportation. This conforms with the national income criterion, of course. But how should we treat such phenomena in the fully employed sector? They should not be included here. The reason is that in a fully employed economy any traceable secondary effects of the new investment will mean reduction in other activities in this sector. If we include the new activities we must also include the changes in the old activities, that is, we must subtract the offsetting reductions. Or, more simply, we can leave both effects out of account, considering as the benefit only the transport cost reduction, which will be turned into national income.*

---

* The studies by Tinbergen (1957) and Bos and Koyck (1961), which are sometimes taken as models for highway benefit calculations, include these sequential effects without considering the possibility of reductions in activities elsewhere. This procedure would only be correct in the underemployed sphere. The authors are not explicit about whether they are concerned with the fully employed or underemployed part of the economy. But since they are assuming that the resources saved from improving the transport network will be immediately taken up, it suggests that they have the fully employed sector in mind, so that other resource inputs that are reduced following the road must necessarily be taken from production elsewhere in the fully employed sector.

We note also that in the Tinbergen-Bos-Koyck, method, the change in output is calculated, essentially, according to $\Delta Y/P_2$, while each unit of incremental output is valued at P_1, in the notation used above (see Tinbergen, 1957, p. 246). Now P_1 represents one utility-cost equilibrium and P_2 another, lower one. Using P_1 distorts the welfare significance of the national income change. That is, whereas the use of national income as a welfare index implies that $\Delta W/W = \Delta Y/Y$ (the change in welfare is proportional to the change in national income), the Tinbergen measure boils down to an expression. $P_1[(\Delta Y/P_2)/Y] = (P_1/P_2)(\Delta Y/Y)$, overstating the national welfare change by the factor P_1/P_2.

Finally, we recognize that the new resources required in the fully employed sector may be provided through natural population growth or through migration from the underemployed part of the economy. In the first place we should not consider the secondary effects since under full employment, the (presumably) desired growth is taking place automatically; there is neither need for the public sector to stimulate growth nor, since in a free enterprise economy the market behavior tends to reflect the people's wishes, propriety for it to impose its preference for faster or slower economic and, hence, population growth. The case is different in the underemployed sector where there are structural obstacles to free market expression. On the other hand, when the new resources do come from migration from the underemployed sphere, the secondary effects should be considered just as they would be under project analysis in the unemployed sector directly.

4 CONCLUSION

We have concluded that the national income approach to benefit measurement is the most generally appropriate. Among other things, it ensures that the analyst focus on net benefits and distinguish those generated by the project from those that would have occurred in any event. In addition, it ensures that the same kind of consideration be given to activities in the public and private sectors, something not achieved by the consumer surplus approach. Finally, it suggests a way to take account of certain benefits usually considered intangible— disease prevention, education, and so on—by considering the impact on national income of improved health (or reduction in the days lost from work), higher educational attainments by workers, and so on. To be sure, it is usually easier to state such benefits than to measure them. How can one measure the relationship between education and improved productivity or between lower incidence of infectious disease and higher productivity in conditions in which, as is frequently the case, there do not even exist factories for the workers to work in? Accordingly, we must not overstress the advantage of national income from this viewpoint. However, it is safe to say that there has been no satisfactory alternative developed for this kind of problem.

This does not mean that national income can be applied universally, but in most cases where it cannot be applied, other procedures are given preference in any event. For example, it is virtually impossible to estimate consumers' demand for improved driving conditions on interstate system class roads or for public versus private transit and to compare these demand functions with national income measures. But if the procedures that have been urged throughout this book are followed, we do not have to. The highway development fund should be made up of revenues contributed by highway users. Their preferences can be expressed through, for example, differential taxes on the intercity part of the interstate system—when taxes stop contributing enough to develop the system further, we can conclude that no more roads should be built for the time being. The urban parts of the system can be made to depend on engineering decisions backed by local referenda and local funds—with proper allocation of the fuel tax revenues in the first place, as we have argued. Finally, some cases may defy either approach; it may not be possible to develop any kind of social payoff criterion, national income or other, owing to the possibility of disruptive structural changes. In the next chapter we consider such a project—the Second Toronto International Airport; in Chapter 17 we discuss the Toronto subway.

REFERENCES

Abouchar, Alan (1971), "Regional Welfare and Measured Income Differentials in Canada," *Review of Income and Wealth,* December.

——— (1973), "The New Soviet Standard Methodology for Investment Allocation," *Soviet Studies,* Vol. 24, No. 3.

——— (1976), "A Note on Dupuit's Bridges and the Theory of Marginal Cost Pricing," *History of Political Economy,* Vol. 8, No. 2.

Bergmann, Barbara (1966), "The Cochabamba-Santa Cruz Highway in Bolivia," in George W. Wilson, Barbara R. Bergmann, Leon V. Hirsch, and Martin S. Klein, *The Impact of Highway Investment on Development* (Washington, D.C.: The Brookings Institution).

Bos, H. C., and L. M. Koyck (1957), "The Appraisal of Road Construction Projects: A Practical Example," *The Review of Economics and Statistics,* Vol. 39, No. 3.

Currie, J. M., J. A. Murphy, and A. Schmitz (1971), "The Concept of Economic Surplus and Its Use in Economic Analysis," *Economic Journal,* December.

Denison, Edward (1971), "Welfare Measurement and the GNP," *Survey of Current Business,* Vol. 51, No. 1.

Foster, C. D., and M. E. Beesley (1963), "Estimating the Social Benefit of Constructing an Underground Railway in London," *Journal of the Royal Statistical Society,* Series A, Vol. 126.

Hicks, John (1956), *A Revision of Demand Theory* (Oxford: Clarendon Press).

Tinbergen, Jan (1957), "The Appraisal of Road Construction: Two Calculation Schemes," *The Review of Economics and Statistics,* Vol. 39, No. 3, August.

Usher, Dan (1968), *The Price Mechanism and the Meaning of National Income Statistics* (Oxford: Oxford University Press).

CHAPTER

14

Project Decisions with Physical Criteria

1 WHY ARE PHYSICAL CRITERIA SOMETIMES NECESSARY?

Generally, project benefits should be measured and the projects compared in terms of the net national income they generate. At times, however, this approach might give inconsistent results, or it might be impossible to calculate the net national income effect. A physical criterion is then used instead. In this chapter we consider the reasons for this and discuss the safeguards necessary when a physical criterion is used (Section 1). We then go on to analyze the methods used in a recent major decision—that concerning the Second Toronto International Airport at Pickering. In Chapter 17 we return to the problem within the context of a large urban investment. Toronto subway, which shares many of the problems encountered here.

The difficulties arise partly in the nature of comparisons between diverse projects—an airport and such other competing alternatives for public sector funds as flood control on the prairies, a subway in Toronto, and a heavy-water plant in the maritime provinces. Partly at fault is also

225

the ambiguity in welfare interpretations of the different intertemporal measures of inational income change. Both types of problem are much less severe when projects are being considered within a single sector, which again justifies the use of national income as a benefit measure together with the procedures of this book to generate the budget constraints.

What are these problems and why do they arise? The two most important problems are (1) the index-number problem and (2) the difficulty of determining net output.

1.1 The Index-Number Problem

The justification for using national income as a measure of benefit is that its movements reflect welfare changes more accurately than do other measures. Ultimately it is the welfare change that we are interested in, but since it cannot be measured (it involves many non-market psychological and other variables that are extremely difficult, if not impossible, to measure), we rely on national income change, which has fewer distortions than do employment and sales, for example (as argued in Chapter 13). As long as we restrict attention to short time periods, this approach is legitimate. But over longer time periods relative prices *may change* substantially, making this approach less tenable, because under relative price changes, the change in national income can be measured using the relative prices existing either before the project or after the project. The problem is illustrated in Figure 14.1.

Figure 14.1 assumes a two-commodity (I and II) economy. The economy is observed in two time periods, A and B—after and before the project is built—separated by, say, 30 years. Each situation has a given set of relative prices for the two commodities which, when tangent to the corresponding indifference curves, give the optimal point of consumption of goods I and II. These are shown by the points A and B. If the two goods are to be summed to obtain the national income for either year, they must be expressed in commensurable units. This is done by translating one good into the other according to the relative prices P_I and P_{II}. For example, in period A the national income in terms of commodity I is given by Y_{AA}, that of the period B, by Y_{BB}. Each is calculated in terms of its own prices, and the question arises how to compare the two magnitudes to determine the relative income change.

To measure the difference in welfare between the two situations, we must determine how "far apart" the indifference curves are by some measure that will be proportional to the welfare difference. The

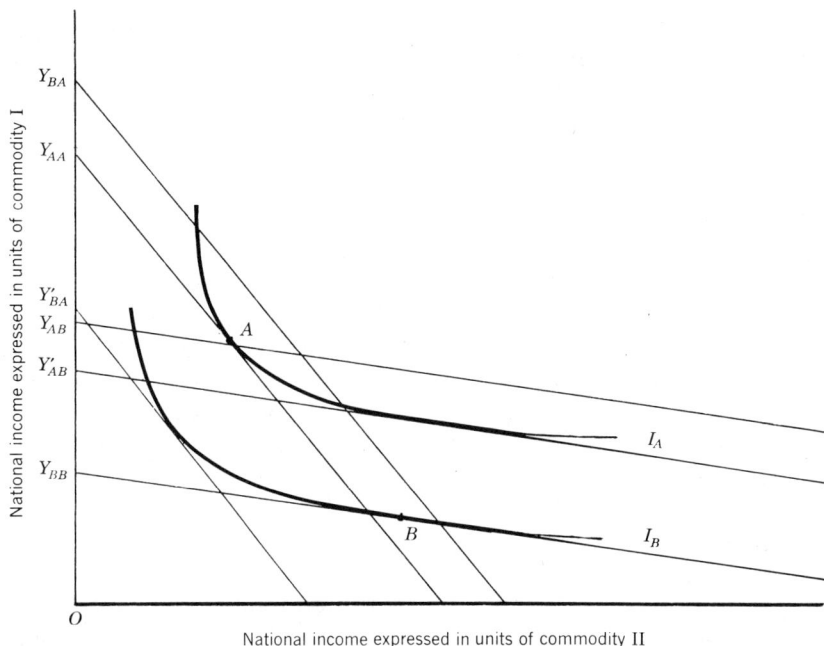

Figure 14.1 Indeterminacy of national income welfare comparisons over long time periods.

approach usually followed is to determine how much income in "after" prices would leave the "before" consumer as well off after the price change as he was before (i.e. on the same indifference curve) and compare this quantity with the income actually generated in the "after" period. (The relationship to Hicks' compensating variation income that we have already dealt with is apparent.) This is given by Y_{AA}/Y_{BA}. It is a measure of the true change in welfare, or, as it is usually called, the "true index number" of the income change between the two periods.

The comparison just made uses "after" prices, but it is just as legitimate to ask about the true change in terms of "before" prices, that is, Y_{AB}/Y_{BB}. (The relationship to Hicks' equivalent variation measure is obvious.) Thus we have two "true index numbers" to measure the change in welfare, and they are *both* true. In this case they both point in the same direction, however, so that if we simply looked for projects with a positive change in national income, it would not matter which we used.

In fact, we do need information on more than the sign of the change if the project is to be compared with others. But in general we cannot even guarantee that the direction of the true change would be the same when measured in "after" and "before" prices. Finally, we cannot even measure the true change, since we do not know the indifference curves.

What we do in practice is to weight the observed consumption quantities by the prices. In this case, we find that the change is positive when we compare the two income levels measured in "after" prices (Y_{AA}/Y_{BA}, which is less than unity, implying a egative change), while it is possible when measured in "before prices" (Y_{AB}/Y_{BB}, which is greater than unity, implying positive growth in national income).

Is it fanciful to expect relative prices to shift by so much as to complicate national income comparisons in this way? The answer, of course, depends on the problem in hand and cannot be given categorically. It depends in part on whether we attach a location subscript to any commodity. For example, if an irrigation scheme allows for consumption in a new region that would have cost a great deal in that region before and costs much less after the project, but the same as it cost in other regions before, should we regard this commodity as one whose price has fallen (i.e. should we differentiate by region of consumption), or merely as one whose price is the same (although in the situation after it is being consumed in different regions)? The same question holds for an airport or any other project.

Evidently, many assumptions would have to be made to answer these questions. They are arbitrary in the sense that, even if reasonable for some purpose, for other objectives contrary assumptions may be appropriate.

1.2   The Problem of Determining Net Output

In Chapter 13 we outlined the procedure for determining net output. This is much easier to do when looking 5 to 12 years ahead rather than 30 years. As we saw, it is essential to adjust the estimate of a project's national income generation by netting out the national income that would be realized elsewhere in the absence of the project. For an airport, we must ask what value added would have been generated elsewhere in the economy if the project were not built. This is a task so complex as to be virtually impossible to perform to general satisfaction. How many travelers would have terminated their flights in Hamilton or Buffalo without Toronto II? How many transit flights would continue nonstop without the additional capacity created by Toronto II? How many people would rely on telephone, or automobile, or bus if more capacity were not provided? What are the effects on national income of any of these actions? We have to distinguish between actions under presently existing capacity patterns elsewhere (e.g. the Calgary or Buffalo airports) and the capacity increases attainable under new investments. We would also need simulation models, demand functions, and so on, for both final use and intermediate services—clearly an extremely formidable task.

These problems are apt to be most perplexing where concern is with projects that cause major changes in the economy or in a region of the economy. Such projects are the MacKenzie Valley pipeline, the Second Toronto International Airport, the trans-Amazon highway in Brazil— projects with long life and, usually but not inevitably, extensive inter- connections as well as a wide range of substitution relationships with the rest of the economy. In these cases, criteria must be developed and applied as the situation arises, and may in some cases be more straight- forward than in others. For example, the trans-Amazon highway might be evaluated in terms of its ability to assimilate new agricultural lands, as in Bergmann's Cochabamba-La Paz highway case study cited in Chapter 13. The pipeline might be reviewed in terms of its ability to generate net national income in the form of profits from foreign earn- ings (the material and labor inputs, under the assumption of full employment relevant here, would find other uses in the absence of a pipeline).

For the airport it is difficult to conceive of anything but a physical criterion, such as originating and terminating (perhaps also transiting) passengers. However, we should as far as possible follow the spirit of national income methodology even if we cannot apply the rules themselves. This requires us to think in terms of passengers whose movement makes a net positive contribution to society. The only way we can ensure this is to make sure that traffic forecasts in the years ahead take account of costs. For example, we must avoid extrapolating a historical series in which past price distortions may have led to ineffi- cient traffic levels.

It should be stressed that this does not mean merely that we should refrain from extrapolating a historical series in a simplistic way. Even sophisticated trip generation models, which do not simply extrapolate mechanistically but attempt to uncover the underlying factors that con- dition traffic, are likely to lead to the wrong conclusions if they take no note of cost-based price.

The balance of this chapter consists of an evaluation of a major project decision based on a physical criterion, the Second Toronto

International Airport at Pickering. A few introductory words, a statement of our approach, and a summary of conclusions are presented in Section 2. The main issues are analyzed in the subsequent sections.

2   THE SECOND TORONTO INTERNATIONAL AIRPORT (PICKERING): INTRODUCTION AND SUMMARY OF ANALYSIS

After many years of discussion a decision to build a major new international airport at Pickering, northeast of Toronto, was made in 1973. Loud and widespread opposition led to the establishment of a Royal Commission which reviewed various evidence and issued its report, supporting the original decision, in spring 1974 (Royal Airport Inquiry Commission, 1974).

We review here the evaluation procedures underlying the decision and the questions that have been raised about the "where?," "why?," and "when?" of the airport. Since in any project of this magnitude many arguments are put forth that are relevant or crucial in some situations but less so in others, and since many subsidiary issues are involved, decisions concerning which are apt to be mistaken for decisions regarding the basic question, we pay special attention to the need to keep the different considerations and issues clearly in view. Our conclusions from this review are then as follows:

1. When a large new international airport is justified, building it at Pickering will be consistent with rational urbanization patterns for southern Ontario. But a decision regarding this subsidiary issue must not be confused with a decision regarding construction itself.

2. Present airport construction plans are premature. Present forecasts are overstated *very considerably*. This statement applies to three forecast concept.

   (*a*) A forecast of what corresponds to the "allocatively inefficient activity level" (the upper curve in Figure 10.2*b*) of *southern Ontario* traffic, overstated by half or more.

   (*b*) A forecast of the "allocatively inefficient level of *Toronto area traffic*. [The difference between (*a*) and (*b*) is that the traffic referred to in (*a*) would allow for accommodation of much of the traffic presently being forecast by existing facilities, rerouting, and expansion at Malton and at other cities.

(c) A forecast of the allocatively efficient level (the lower curve in Figure 10.2b), the overstatement of which is impossible to determine because of the failure to estimate price elasticities for most traffic segments.

The large new Pickering facility would undoubtedly not be required until 2000. If construction is begun now and completed by 1980, and if the net differential investment involved in construction of Pickering rather than the marginal expansions at local airports is $1 billion, the implied loss to society is given by the annual benefit that this capital would have generated between 1980 and 2000. Assuming annual capital productivity of 5%, in accord with recommendations of Chapter 12, this would amount to about $1.5 billion.

These conclusions are based on the evaluation of the evidence presented in the next three sections.

3 THE REGIONAL IMPACT OF A PICKERING SITE

Opponents of construction at Pickering point to the large quantity of high-grade agricultural land (Class I in official terminology), which will be removed from production. The rate at which such lands are being withdrawn has caused alarm in many quarters. On the other hand, Pickering Airport proponents have pointed to the high cost of land in the Malton area (where the present airport is located), to the already high levels of noise exposure in the Malton area, which would be alleviated by construction at Pickering, and, finally, to the generation of employment in the Pickering area.

All of these arguments are irrelevant or spurious. Let us consider them in reverse order.

1. The creation of jobs is an argument that undoubtedly would appeal to many local private interests in the Pickering area, but is irrelevant from a national point of view. The reason is simply that wherever an airport is built some employment will be generated. But the central Ontario region, which is usually taken as the frame of reference for the airport decision, is not a district of high secular unemployment (i.e. persistent long-term unemployment, as opposed to unemployment related to short-term cyclical swings); nor is the Pickering area in particular. Therefore, it would be wrong to consider as part of the net benefit of the construction of an airport either (a) the generation of

employment by the airport site anywhere in central Ontario or (b) the generation of employment at Pickering. We observe, parenthetically, that if an airport project were being considered in an area of high secular unemployment, such as the Atlantic provinces, we *would* wish to consider the effect on unemployment.

2. The question of land costs at Malton, as it has been pursued, is incorrect. In fact, though the extra land in the Malton area could be acquired only at great cost (according to one study submitted in evidence to the Royal Commission (Document B-27, 1973),* the area west of Malton would cost over $100 million), this might still be the most desirable way to proceed since the total cost—land plus construction—would be less. In particular, it would probably be best to acquire this land now and expand operations at Malton until about 2000. The reason is that only a runway and probably minor additional terminal facilities would be needed.

3. The exposure to noise, it is claimed, would increase to intolerable levels if Malton traffic were allowed to grow. This would be due to greater traffic over the present flyways and to enlargement of the area affected through the addition of another runway.

Before such projections can be accepted as a basis for public policy, however, we must analyze the effects of the increased noise as perceived by the public itself. The NEF (noise exposure factor) is simply a synthetic aggregation of different aspects of noise generation (number of flights, intensities of noise, number of nighttime operations) that lower personal welfare. The problem is that the dissatisfaction caused by a particular aspect of noise, is difficult to measure, and one must rely on arbitrary and unproved assumptions concerning the NEF effect. NEF 40 is probably worse than NEF 30, but that is about all that we can say. We do not really know how much worse it is.

We can approach the noise problem from a different angle, however, to get a reading on personal disutility. If the noise causes distress, house prices in the airport area should fall, compared to those elsewhere in the city (inflation and rising population would probably raise house prices in an absolute sense), as people's desire population to live there declined. Area residents would sell their homes for less and go elsewhere, and new residents would be reluctant to move in. In fact, this has not happened

---

* Documents A-2, B-27, B-39, B-48, and B-55 and the *Written Summary,* all referred to in this chapter, are documents presented in evidence to the Royal Commission during its hearings on the Second Toronto International Airport.

in the Malton area. The one study of the area that has been conducted shows that house prices south of the main runway have kept pace with those in other sections of Toronto during the 1955–1969 period (see Crowley, 1973). In addition, as the Crowley study indicates, land rezoning permits periodic revisions in land use in keeping with the advantages of a near-airport location. And the rezoning objectives—largely industrial and commercial—are very compatible with intense airport activity, since the companies have their own background noise that screens out much of the airport noise and usually do not operate at night, minimizing the nighttime effect of airport operations.*

4. The removal of Class I land from agriculture is, of course, lamentable. However, given that Southern Ontario will continue to grow and become more urbanized, the issue to face is not whether good land is withdrawn, but which land will be missed the least. It can be shown that land to the east of Metro is agriculturally the least productive. In the eastern counties the output per acre farmed is lowest in Southern Ontario and farmland comprises the smallest proportion of total land. Therefore, urbanization *should* take place toward the east rather than toward the west or the south. This is shown in Table 14.1.

The analysis in Table 14.1 is cast in terms of gross output. Gross output, of course, overstates the value of land, since it includes the input of several factors other than land—such variable material inputs as fertilizers, fuel, and equipment, labor, and capital depreciation. To measure the value of land alone we would have to know the net contribution of land—the value added by the land itself. No such series has been published by the federal or provincial governments or, apparently, estimated privately.† However, if we assume, as seems reasonable, that the net contribution of each factor is a constant share of gross output, the net value of the land will be higher in districts that have higher average gross output.

Since the net value added per acre by land is the lowest and the lands under crops are the least dense in the east, this district would seem to be the most likely direction in which to expand urbanization (though by

---

* The behavior of house prices in the south Malton area is also consistent with the behavior of the Multiple Listing Service house prices throughout the Toronto Metro area. The Metro prices rose by 66% between 1965 and 1969 (no data are available prior to 1965) compared with 62% in the south Malton area. The Malton data are from Crowley (1973); those about Metro come from Toronto Real Estate Board (1970). Metro Toronto is the municipal administrative area made up of six boroughs, one of which is Toronto City.

† One testimony presented at the Royal Commission hearings (Document B-48, 1974) does give some net value-added data for certain counties but the authors do not define the basis for their figures.

Table 14.1   Eleven Major Field Crops: Gross Output per Acre and Total Acreage Employed in Four Major Southern Ontario Districts[a]

	South	West	Center	East
Output per acre	$140	$75	$79	$53
Land under field crops (millions of acres)	2.6	2.4	0.9	1.1

Source. Calculated from the Ontario Ministry of Agriculture statistics (Province of Ontario, 1972).

[a] Districts are comprised of the following counties: *South:* Brant, Elgin, Essex, Haldimand, Kent, Lambton, Middlesex, Niagara, Norfolk, Oxford, and Wentworth. *West:* Bruce, Dufferin, Grey, Halton, Huron, Peel, Perth, Simcoe, Waterloo, and Wellington. *Center:* Durham, Haliburton, Hastings, Muskoka, Northumberland, Ontario, Parry Sound, Peterborough, Prince Edward, Victoria, and York. *East:* Carleton, Dundas, Frontenac, Glengarry, Grenville, Lanark, Leeds, Lennox & Addington, Prescott, Renfrew, Russell, and Stormont. The eleven crops are: winter wheat, oats, barley, mixed grains, beans, soybeans, shelled corn, potatoes, fodder corn, hay, and tobacco. These crops in these districts account for 98% of total Ontario field crop acreage and 99% of gross output of field crops. Field crops in turn account for 95 to 99% of acreage in the counties of these four districts, with fruits and vegetables less important in the east.

far the largest district, it has barely more land under field crops than does the central district). Other considerations may eventually lead urbanization in another direction, but until such considerations are specified, eastward urbanization would be socially least costly.

Some conclusions follow from these comparisons. A Pickering site for the airport is shown to be compatible with rational long-term urbanization goals for Southern Ontario. Furthermore, the airport noise at Malton has not had a permanently deleterious effect on local land values, thus indicating people's willingness to bear this nuisance. Too, the normal functioning of the market seems to have tended to lead to the rezoning of land for more appropriate use as necessary. Thus, while the new airport should eventually be located at Pickering, whether it should be built today or not depends, among other things, on the amount of new airport capacity required and the construction costs at Pickering and other small local airports. Though land costs are higher at Malton, the combination of Malton expansion and modifications of other local airport may be able to serve the nation's needs for the next

20 years. To see this we first review the traffic forecasts and then consider some possibilities for traffic restructuring.

4 ANALYSIS OF AIR TRAFFIC FORECASTS

Several air activity forecasts were prepared in connection with the airport proposal. These include projections of activity levels as functions of time and of GNP, civil aviation/GNP relationships over time, and air cargo activity. There was also one attempt to analyze air traffic propensities of different socioeconomic groups and project these into the future. Two kinds of question must be asked regarding any activity forecast. (1) Is it made in a way that justifies the use of the forecast activity level as a target to be provided by the public sector? That is, does it estimate the socially efficient or inefficient curve in Figure 10.2*b*? (2) Is it competently done? Is it performed in accord with generally accepted statistical-analytical practice and does it use statistical data correctly?

4.1 Traffic Projections as Social Goals

Enough has been said in Chapter 10 and Section 1 of this chapter to caution us against mistaking a forecast of socially inefficient activity levels, even when statistically competent, for a forecast of allocatively efficient activity that should be adopted as a social goal. The Pickering traffic forecasts used by the Toronto Area Airports Project (TAAP) show no recognition of this distinction. As we shall see, they make arbitrary assumptions regarding the price elasticity of demand for four out of five traffic components, which prevents an outside observer from simulating the effect on air traffic levels of higher prices to reflect the new airport costs.

Moreover, not only do we not know the elasticities, but practically no evidence has been presented on the capital costs themselves, so that even if we knew the demand elasticities, we could not simulate response. We would not know how to adjust prices to take account of capital costs, hence could not determine how many passengers would set a value on the flight high enough to cover the whole cost. Regarding the issue whether the ticket prices should be made to include the capital costs, it is in fact the stated intention of the airport project sponsors to have the users themselves pay for the airport. This is consistent with the federal policy adopted in the late 1960s, which is itself consistent with more fundamental income distribution considerations. That is, an interregional or intersectoral income transfer is not wanted here, since the beneficiaries of the airport will be middle- and upper-income, rather than poor, persons. In accord with considerations discussed in Part 4, however, there may be some justification for partially recovering capital costs from nonusers, rather than including the entire capital cost in the user changes, but in this case the nonusers should be *local*—from southern Ontario rather than from other regions in the nation. The authorities should at least know how many people *would* be willing to pay the price to fly out of Pickering, which would require a simulation model, an estimate of the capital costs that must be undertaken, and an estimate of the price elasticity of demand for air flights.

Thus the failure of the authorities to analyze such factors as the higher costs deriving from the airport construction and related further projects (rapid transit ground access, e.g.) should serve to make us question the efficiency of the whole scheme. The proposed ground access is a particulary graphic example of the failure to consider all the ramifications of this project. Though the plans for this connection have not been always consistent or fully explicit, a rapid transit ground access between Malton and Pickering has been discussed and some aspects of the operating cost have been considered. For example, the *Written Summary* (p. 146) implies a cost of about $3 per interconnecting passenger in the early 1980s. This figure can refer to no more than the variable operating cost, completely omitting capital costs. Who, then, is to pay for this investment? Assuming a construction and ground acquisition cost of $5 million per mile (split 80-20 between construction and land), a 35-mile length, a capital cost of 5%, and depreciation at 3% for the construction cost alone, we can calculate an annual capital cost of $31 per interairport trip for each of the estimated 300,000 interconnecting passengers in the early 1980s.

Our use of $5 million per mile does not seem excessive (the Yonge Street extension of the Toronto subway just completed cost about $35 million per mile). But even if one assumed as little as $1 million, the cost would still work out to $6 per passenger, which, with the $3 operating cost, would amount to nearly $18 on a two-way trip. Does anyone seriously think that the interconnecting passengers would pay for this? ("Why should I be discriminated against just because I have the misfortune of having to change air fields, while Joe down the street can fly in and out of the same airport?".) Does anyone seriously believe that the total traffic using the Toronto airport system would willingly pay for it if the cost were spread over all of the passengers? (The cost under the current traffic projection would amount to around $2 per round trip flight with a Toronto destination.) To be sure, passengers would continue to fly, for example, Ottawa-Toronto rather than Ottawa-Hamilton, but only as long as the major airlines refused to provide service to Hamilton. Probably passenger objections would turn out to be so strong that any attempt to include such a charge would soon be dropped. The result is that the national economy as a whole would bear the cost and make an income transfer to the air travelers, who, to repeat are not lower income earners.

4.2 Technical Competence of Forecasts

A detailed recapitulation of all the forecasts undertaken in connection with the airport project is unnecessary here (the *Written Summary*, pp. 14–16, gives a brief survey). We concentrate on the most recent and most important forecast documents (Document A2, 1973; Document B-55, 1974). There are a number of fundamental shortcomings in the analysis contained in these studies. Here we examine four important areas of questionable statistical practice and economic analysis:

1. The construction of a trip generation model that seems to misperform in a systematic and predictable way and the subsequent introduction of a compensating adjustment factor (termed the "calibration factor"), which accounts for 38% of the estimated traffic growth between 1971 and the year 2000.

2. The price elasticity on international travel, for which a model was employed whose only merit seemed to be that it produced a high elasticity (which, combined with the assumption of decreasing fares, greatly increases travel).

3. The assumption of zero price elasticity of demand on all domestic and transborder travel (long- and short-haul), in defiance of both basic economic axioms and generally observed airline pricing behavior.

4. To analyze general aviation, the introduction and extrapolation of exponential equations in what appear to be linear time series relationships spanning just five years.

4.2.1 *The Travel Propensity Model and the Calibration Factor*

The heart of the passenger forecasting model for 1971–2000 was a series of travel propensity or trip generation models constructed in 1971 for the five major traffic components (domestic short-haul, domestic

medium-haul and long-haul, transborder short-haul, transborder
medium-haul and long-haul, and international; Caribbean travel is
included in the transborder medium-haul and long-haul category).
Using a two-week sample survey at Malton International Airport
(Toronto I), Ministry of Transport investigators determined the income,
ethnic, and age composition of air travelers, as well as the purpose of
their trip (Document B-55, 1974, Vol. 2, Appendix A). The number of
travelers with certain characteristics was then related to the total
number of persons in the Southern Ontario region having these characteristics to determine the travel propensity of that group. These
propensities, in some cases to be adjusted for future developments,
would then be applied to the evolving future group sizes to predict traffic behavior in future years. The adjustments include the changing proportion of adults, service levels of air travel and competing modes
(vaguely defined and measured), and, for international travel only, fare
levels. The propensities were permitted to change in each decade. The
adjustments to the basic trip propensity coefficients for transborder
long-haul are shown in Table 14.2.

To assess the predictive ability of the coefficients, the model was
applied to the 1961 group sizes to simulate traffic in that year. Comparison of actual and predicted traffic for 1961 shows that the model
slightly overstated the two short-haul traffic components (3%) and
underestimated the three medium-haul and long-haul components by
almost exactly one third. These errors were then compensated for by

**Table 14.2   Growth Factors for Transborder Long-Haul
Traffic, 1981–1991**

Source of Growth	Coefficient
1–3. Income, population, ethnic origin (propensity matrix)	1.49
4. Propensity change due to change in proportion of adults	1.00 (no change)
5. Fare level	1.00 (no change)
6. Service level—air	1.10
7. Service level—other modes	1.00 (no change)
8. Travel trends	0.95
9. Calibration factor	1.35
10. Total growth	2.10

Source.   Individual factors (items 1 to 9) from Exhibit 16,
Document B-55 (1974), Vol. 1.

introducing into the model a so-called calibration factor for each traffic class, the calibration factor being in each case the relative discrepancy between the actual and simulated 1961 traffic levels. Simulations by a model with this factor included would then coincide exactly with the 1961 traffic levels.

Now, the calibration factor is intended to compensate for factors in the model that are omitted from explicit consideration. Any use of such a device must assume that the influence of the omitted factors is random. If the model systematically overestimates or underestimates a traffic component, that is, if the omitted factors operate nonrandomly, one must conclude that some important factor has been left out of the model, try to find it, and put it into the model. In the present case the differences between actual and simulated traffic levels appear to be nonrandom, the two short-haul components being overstated by 3% and the three long-haul ones understated by 32 to 35%.

Instead of searching out the missing factors that cause the model to underestimate the three long-haul and overestimate slightly the two short-haul components, the investigators assume the bias of the unadjusted model to be "permanent" and compensate for it by adjusting the predicted future traffic levels by the calibration factor for each decade in a compound manner.* For example, for the transborder long-haul traffic the final adjustment for the 1971–2000 traffic growth is adjusted by a factor of $(1.35)^3$, or 2.46; that is, the estimate for 2000 is 146% higher than it would have been if made on the basis of the unadjusted model alone!†

What is the overall impact of this device on the traffic estimates? To see this, we project traffic growth on the basis of the unadjusted model alone (including the changes in underlying variables and the future coefficients, but excluding the calibration factor) and compare it with the estimates in the study that include the calibration factor. This is shown in Table 14.3.

Table 14.3 indicates that if the calibration factor calculated for the

---

* Incidentally, this move is never explicitly stated in the study. That it is the procedure can be easily seen through analysis of Exhibit 16 (Document B-55, 1974, Vol. 2). This is shown through the Table 1 example of the 1981–1991 growth of transborder long-haul traffic which reproduces the corresponding entries from Exhibit 16 (the study is somewhat inconsistent in its use of designations, sometimes referring to transborder long-haul and sometimes to transborder medium- and long-haul). The total growth coefficient for the decade (2.10) is the product of all the individual coefficients, including the calibration factor of 1.35.

† Actually traffic forecasts are made by the formal model only through 1991. Then they are "graphically extrapolated" (log-linearly) to 2000. See Chapter 7 of Document B-55 (1974, Vol. 1).

Table 14.3   Year 2000 Traffic, with and without the Calibration Factor

Traffic Segment	(1) Traffic as Estimated in Document B-55 (Reflects Calibration Factor) (millions of origins and destinations)	(2) Calibration Factor	(3) Total Growth due to Calibration Factor 1971–2000 $(2)^3$	(4) Traffic without Calibration Factor (1)/(3) (millions of origins and destinations)	(5) $[(4)/(1) - 1.0] \times 100$ (%)
Domestic short-haul	6.0	0.97	0.91	6.6	+10
Domestic medium- and long-haul	8.0	1.32	2.30	3.5	−57
Transborder short-haul	5.0	0.97	0.91	5.5	+10
Transborder medium- and long-haul	4.5	1.35	2.46	1.8	−66
International	17.5	1.32	2.30	7.6	−57
Total	41.0			25.3	−38

Source.   Document B-55 (1974), Vol. 2, Exhibit 22, Columns 1 and 2, cited in Abouchar (1976).

1960s is not applied to subsequent decades, the year 2000 forecasts for individual traffic components will change by amounts varying from +10% (the two short-haul components) to −66% (transborder long-haul and medium-haul traffic). The total effect is to reduce the total traffic forecasts by 15.7 million passengers, or 38%. To put it another way, use of the calibration factor raises the traffic forecast by 62% over the traffic level that would be estimated without the calibration factor adjustment (41 million versus 25.3 million) and increases growth (35.7 million versus 20 million) by 78%!

Evidently, it does make a great deal of difference which approach is used. The study fails to consider the possibility that the calibration factor may simply represent some one-time change that took place during the 1960s and will not be repeated in the future. If so, it is not correct to assume that there will be similar growth on this account in the future. Alternatively, the analysts might have concluded that, since the estimating errors for 1961 are not random, some factor or factors have been neglected that might change in the future and affect the traffic forecasts (in either direction). Whatever the story, it is simply unacceptable to make a forecast of traffic growth, 44% of which is accounted for by a "calibration factor" $(35.7 - 20.0) \div 35.7!$

It is a final irony that in spite of the serious methodological flaws implicit in the use of this calibration factor, the Royal Commission should in its final report reject another lower forecast (that by John Kettle, whose year 2000 forecast was 52% lower) on the ground that "the Kettle forecast omitted the calibration factor which plays a significant role in the total forecast. The Commission cannot place reliance upon his forecast" (Royal Airport Inquiry Commission, 1974, p. 27).

4.2.2 Price Elasticity of Demand—International Travel

To estimate the future demand for air travel, an attempt was made to measure the price elasticity of demand on the traffic that was hypothesized to be sensitive to price—international travel only (essentially trans-Atlantic traffic). Most of the regression models relating travel to income and price that were tried appear to have had little explanatory power. In the words of the study: "Of the approximately 50 equations tested, few were statistically significant $(R^2 > .40)$" (Document B-55, 1974, Vol. 2, p. C-10). The elasticity finally adopted (-1.2) was estimated from an equation relating a year's traffic to the year's price and income and last year's price and income in which R^2 was calculated to be .54 (p. C-12).

Several objections to this procedure may be raised. First, no economic theory underlies the model. Rather, it seems to be a case simply of trying every conceivable formulation, as was suggested above. A second criticism is that no significance test was performed for regression coefficients (either the price elasticity α or the income elasticity β).* The price elasticity in the regressions summarized in Exhibit C3/a range from -0.4 to -1.3, with most of them being *less* than unity. Obviously, such differences would yield very different traffic response to price changes. The equation selected gave the second highest estimated price elasticity, although this particular equation has no obvious economic superiority and, indeed, its R^2 was low—.54. Since fare reductions were assumed for the future (see below), this leads to disproportionately large traffic increases.

The analysis of future price behavior was based on a historical analysis of the behavior of Pan Am and TWA passenger-kilometer costs

---

* The results summarized in Exhibits C3/1 to C3/b (following p. C-10 in Document B-55, Vol. 2) contain F ratios which bear on the significance of the entire regression rather than on the individual regression coefficients (α, a, b, β).

between 1960 and 1971, when they decreased substantially. They were projected to decline in the future, although at a much slower rate, falling by 5% by 1981 and a further 12% by 1991. These benchmark estimates were then adjusted for higher fuel costs, with basic crude estimated to rise by 60 to 140% between 1971 and 1981, and by 80 to 180% between 1971 and 1991. These assumptions may already be too low. A possibly greater oversight, however, is the failure to adjust for higher landing fees to be experienced at Toronto, as compared with the world-wide activity of Pan Am or TWA, if the new federal policy of requiring major new airports to be paid by user charges is introduced.

4.2.3 *Price Behavior and Elasticity on Domestic and Transborder Traffic*

No attempt appears to have been made to measure the cost and price behavior of transborder and domestic flights or the price elasticity of demand. Since (1) fuel costs are rising and (2) the new federal pricing policy requires that major new airport additions be paid for by users, fares will have to rise in the future for these traffic segments—indeed, they have already done so. Moreover, these increases will be *especially* significant on shorter-haul domestic and transborder flights since the landing fees would constitute a higher proportion of their ticket price. Therefore, passenger ticket prices will rise and there will be a decline on this account in these traffic components unless demand does have zero elasticity, as assumed by the study.

An idea of the change in trip price that would follow from the new airport pricing policy can be given as follows. If we assume an investment cost of $1.5 billion and an annual depreciation of 3% on the construction, which, according to testimony before an earlier inquiry commission, comprises 85% of the total airport investment cost, and if we assume a 5% capital charge, we obtain an annual cost of $100 million. Let us assume that 80% of this amount will have to be recovered from commercial aviation. In the Ministry of Transport passenger forecasts this works out to about $6 to $8 per passenger emplanement and deplanement in 1980. It would be between $11 and $12 per passenger on the basis of a traffic forecast that does not include the calibration factor. For short-haul flights, this would represent 30 to 60% of the average one-way ticket price. If the elasticity on short-haul flights is -1.2, the same as it is supposed to be on international flights, a reduction of 36 to 72% from the forecast level, of short-haul flights would be implied. If the elasticity on international flights is actually higher than -1.2 and/or the elasticity on short flights is *higher* than that on long-haul international movements, (which is very likely, since there are more alternatives—bus, train, telephone, etc.) an even larger reduction is implied. The effect of fuel cost increases must also be considered.

Actually, the preceding analysis is an oversimplification. Since we are dealing with a fixed annual cost, the final result on the ticket price will depend on the quantity involved. We used the average price calculated for a 15-million passenger volume. Since some of this traffic would not actually materialize, because of the addition of the airport charge to ticket price, the price that would have to be charged to the remaining traffic would be higher still. Considering these additional complications would raise even more the ticket price and further reduce the traffic volume. On the other hand, for subsequent years, since the traffic over which the annual fixed cost is to be distributed will be greater, the implied addition to ticket price will be somewhat lower. There would still be very large reductions in traffic on the short-haul routes.

Fuel prices, too, are rising sharply. Incidentally, there is a glaring logical inconsistency here. The Commission points out (Royal Airport Inquiry Commission, 1974, p. 27) that "Original figures [of Air Canada] were remarkedly (sic) close to those of the Ministry of Transport, Canada, but due to recent fuel and other cost increases, Air Canada was of the view that its figures should be reconsidered." This should have given the Commission pause, since it meant that Air Canada was in effect saying that there is some price sensitivity in traffic components other than international flights. The Commission at this point should either have reconsidered the Ministry of Transport forecast or else dismissed the Air Canada methodology as unreliable (as it dismissed Kettle's on the same page) because it was at variance with the Ministry's methodology, which it did accept, rather than simply allow it to be withdrawn.

4.2.4 General Aviation Forecast Equations

General aviation refers primarily to noncommon carrier aviation, ranging from the company jet to small private two-seater craft. For purposes of analysis, general aviation was broken down into local and itinerant aviation, with each type further subdivided according to the aircraft's need for the services of a major airport. Three main models are used in the study. The scatter diagrams, fitted growth curves, parameter values, and other explanatory information contained in the Ministry of Transport report (Document A-2, 1973, Figures 5.1, 5.2, and 6.3; Figure 6.3 is misnumbered) are reproduced here as Figure 14.2. A casual look

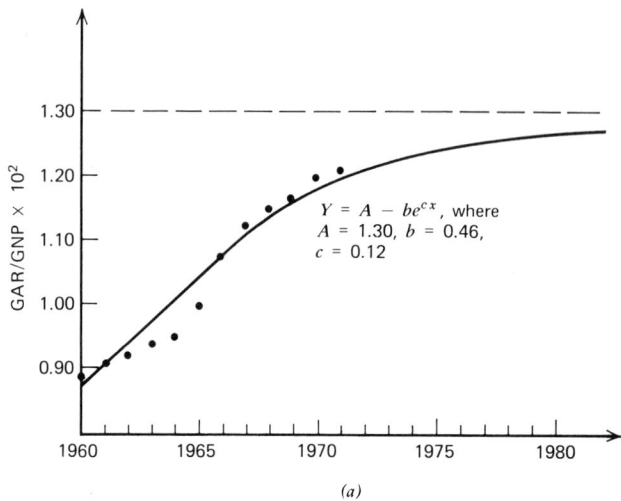

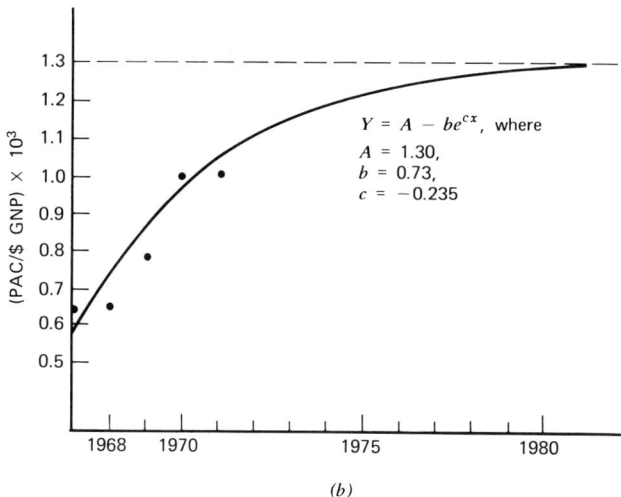

Figure 14.2 Scatter diagrams and projected growth curves for three general aviation relationships as hypothesized by the Ministry of Transport. (*a*) Relationship of general aviation registration to the Canadian GNP (1960–1971). (*b*) General aviation model (airports with towers). (*c*) General aviation model for the Toronto International Airport (private aircraft movements). PAC = private itinerant movements; GAR = general aviation registration.

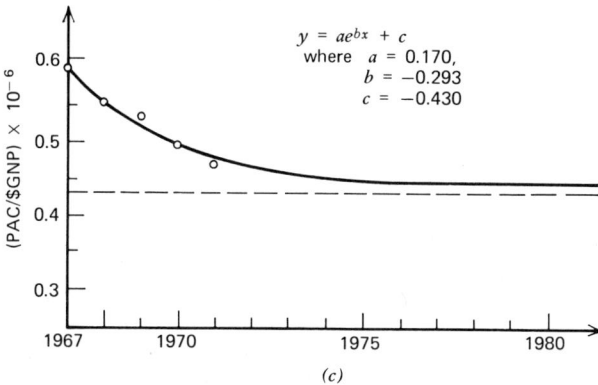

$$y = ae^{bx} + c$$
where $a = 0.170$,
$b = -0.293$
$c = -0.430$

(PAC/$GNP) × 10^{-6}

(c)

Figure 14.2 (Continued)

at all of them suggests that incorrect functional relations are assumed, but this is especially true in the models dealing with actual movements at airports with towers and at Toronto International (the first model relates only to registration). We look briefly at the questionable procedures of the models and the implications thereof.

1. *Total general aviation registrations* (Figure 14.2a). The relationship between the general aviation/GNP ratio and time is assumed to be a three-parameter-modified exponential curve. It would appear from the scatter diagram that these points would be better represented by a higher degree curve (S shape) which, in this case, would have a lower asymptote or ceiling. Obviously, if this were the case, there would be a lower registrations/GNP ratio in the future. That is to say, there would be fewer planes.

2. *General aviation itinerant movements at airports with towers* (Figure 14.2b). The ratio of total itinerant movements at airports with towers to GNP has been rising, that is, this traffic segment has been growing faster than GNP. A three-parameter formulation was also used for this activity. However, visual inspection of the scatter diagram of the past observations suggests a straight line rather than a curve. Note that if a linear relationship had been used, it would have shown greater aviation activity at airports with towers.

The motivation given in the text for this relationship is that this activity should behave like any infant industry—rapid growth at first, followed by a reduced rate of growth, ultimately stabilizing at the same rate of growth as the economy. While this is plausible, there is little suggestion in the five observations of the empirical series itself that the point of declining rate of growth has been reached. Hence it is arbitrary to assume that it has been reached; moreover, it conflicts head on with the treatment of the next general aviation segment.

3. *Total private aircraft movements at Toronto International Airport at Malton* (Figure 14.2c). The ratio of private aircraft movements at the present Toronto International (Malton) per dollar of GNP since 1967 has been falling. Although total aircraft movements have been rising, GNP has been growing at a faster rate, leading to a declining ratio. Again, a curved rather than a linear relationship is used, though here, too, the five observations are a straight-line relationship. In fact, they line up so tightly along a straight line that most textbook writers probably would be embarrassed to use this example as an illustration of a stochastic linear relationship!

Notwithstanding the linearity of the historical series, a three-parameter formulation has been used to show a fall in the rate of decline of the ratio of Toronto movements to GNP. No significance test has been performed; nor does it appear that such a test would substantiate the equation form selected.

In contrast to the preceding case where the curvilinear form led to a lower traffic forecast for all airports with towers as compared with a forecast that the straight line would have produced, here the curve leads to a higher traffic level at Toronto International than would have resulted from application of a straight line. Since the latter affects the presumed need for a new international airport, while the former does not, the errors are not merely offsetting. A definite bias is created in favor of the new airport.

Finally, we observe that the basic hypothesis that eventually the rate of growth of either of these general aviation segments will parallel that of the national or provincial economies may be reasonable. Our strenuous objection is that five annual historical observations in each series (covering the period from 1967 to 1971) give not a scintilla of evidence that the rate of growth of either of these traffic segments has moved closer to that of the national economy, that the ratio of aircraft movements to GNP plotted on the Y-axis has leveled out any at value.

5 RESTRUCTURING OF SOUTHERN ONTARIO TRAFFIC

In the preceding section we saw that future commercial traffic levels may be overstated by 50 to 65%. The general aviation forecast for

Toronto International is also seriously overstated. However, adjusting the forecast series for this overstatement would still leave traffic levels in excess of present Malton traffic levels. For example, if we decrease the year 2000 commercial traffic by 40% to 36 million passengers, we still have a peak daily volume of 800 to 900 planes per day, or about 90 planes per peak hour, if past and projected peak/total ratios are observed (the peak hour accounts for about 11% of the total. See Document B-39, 1974, p. 23 and Table A). Adding some general aviation and air cargo (that can meet the acid test of paying their correctly determined airport use charges) may result in a peak of no more than 100 planes. This contrasts with peak-hour traffic in the early 1970s on the order of 35 to 40 planes at Malton, including general aviation. However, three qualifications must be stated: (1) we are talking about the year 2000; (2) there is room for expansion of present activity by extending runway capacity at Malton; and (3) traffic can be rerouted to other airports. Let us now discuss these qualifications.

Malton today is a very large airport even by world standards. Its peak traffic, however, is far below that at a really busy airport. Part of the reason, undoubtedly, is simply that there is not so much demand to come into Toronto as there is to come into New York, O'Hare, or Washington National. That is, it is not a question of Malton's incapacity to service higher peak-hour traffic levels.

It would be very interesting to compare Malton's design, operating characteristics, and traffic levels with those of other airports. Such a comparison could be based on airport specifications as assembled and published by the International Civil Aviation Organization in Montreal. What is the present capacity at Malton? None of the statements submitted in evidence to the Royal Commission really delves into this issue. For example, from the start there has been no attempt to include the passenger-processing capacity that would be introduced by the large new second terminal at Malton, which opened in 1973. Apropos this issue, it should be noted that the first report (Parkin, 1967) emphasized that the then only existing Terminal I, being circular, would be unable to service the new generation of larger jets. Terminal II certainly overcomes this objection. What, then, *is* the present capacity of the two terminals together? Incredibly, even the government's summary (the major statement by the Toronto Area Airports Project presented in connection with the Royal Airport Inquiry Commission's hearings) makes no mention of the new terminal's addition to passenger-processing capacity. It merely describes the "inadequacy of the existing site to accommodate required facilities" (two paragraphs on pp. 23–24, *Written Summary*, no date) and the inadequacy of "road access" (p. 24).

It has not been established that with Terminals I and II and possibly some additional runway capacity Malton could not handle a peak-hour traffic of about 100 flights. If the forecasts themselves are overstated, as seems very likely, and we reduce them accordingly, and if we take into account the additional capacity that now exists or that could be achieved without too great cost at Malton, we find that the traffic levels would not exceed this number until after 2000, give or take a few years. Moreover, there are other actions that can and should be taken long before construction is initiated on a large new airport. Let us consider the possibilities for traffic restructuring.

The Toronto International airport general aviation forecast, as indicated in the preceding section, is probably exaggerated through the use of an equation that is not consistent with historical trends. To be sure, the project sponsors have not assigned all of this traffic to Toronto International, restricting themselves to aircraft of 12,500 pounds or more, starting at a future date. However, if the total forecast is exaggerated, the 12,500-pound aircraft share will also be overstated. Therefore, the general aviation activity justification for the airport will be greatly diminished on this account.

In any event, this approach to general aviation traffic allocation is dubious. When we reach the stage of great air traffic congestion, access to the limited airport capacity must be so priced as to reduce congestion to the optimal amount and ensure that the benefit to anyone imposing congestion on others is at least as great as the congestion costs that he is imposing. This can be done by way of a higher landing fee, administrative regulation of general aviation flights, or building a large new airport designed to have no congestion. In the last case, we would have to be sure, that the general aviation traffic would be willing to pay its share of the new airport costs. No study of general aviation has been performed for this project that would give a clue to how much general aviation is willing to pay for its use of airport facilities. Surely, before an airport is built, partly with the needs of general aviation in mind, we would have to know the value of airport use to general aviation.

Now, most economists would argue that general aviation should be given the right to land at an airport if it is willing to pay the proper price for the use of the facility, where the proper price includes the congestion toll. (A discussion of the theoretical aspects of this problem appears in Chapter 15.) However, determining the congestion charge and administering it would be very difficult. As noted, no TAAP submission in the evidence deals with this difficult issue. Accordingly, most economists would probably settle for an administrative rule that forbade general aviation once certain traffic levels were reached.

Thus the first thing that should be said is that general aviation should be denied access to Malton, at least during peak hours, some time in the future when traffic rises substantially from its present levels.

There are also other possibilities for traffic restructuring in the Toronto area. Comparisons are frequently made between the Toronto area and other major air traffic centers, such as New York, Paris and Washington, which have multiple airport systems. Many people infer from such comparisons that large air traffic markets need multiple airport systems. Toronto, being a large city and the center of a large conurbation, therefore, should also have a multiple airport system.

The foregoing contention is justified. However, it is also true that Toronto already *is* served by a multiple airport system. We are not referring merely to Toronto Island, Buttonville, Downsview, and other small airports in and around Toronto, but to the airports at Hamilton and Oshawa in addition to the Malton airport. Let us recall that the three airports in the New York system serve a market that is much, much larger than that dominated by Toronto or, for that matter, than any other market in North America. The Newark airport, about 25 miles and 1.5 surface hours from La Guardia, services a major subsection of the New York market—primarily passengers from the northern New Jersey area, but also some from the city itself. Kennedy on Long Island, 40 miles from Newark and about 10 miles from La Guardia, is the international airport, which also handles much long- and short-haul domestic traffic originating on Long Island and in New York City. The greater New York conurbation with a population of 16 to 20 million requires several airports because (1) traffic volumes are very large and (2) the area is large, so that travel from one part of this market to another by private automobile, public transportation, or both would take two hours or more.

Washington is serviced by three airports, and Montreal by two main airports. Even the San Francisco conurbation, although it is not generally recognized, is serviced by two main airports—the large San Francisco airport and the Oakland airport about 30 miles away—about the same distance that separates the airports in the New York system. (It might even be appropriate to include here the San José airport, since it constitutes one more link in the provision of service to the very large Bay Area market.) Thus there is an expectation that a large urban area does require more than one airport.

Having said all that, we must ask whether it is true that Toronto today does not have a multiple airport system. In fact, there are today two large airports—Malton and Hamilton—both of which, moreover, can be expanded in the future to serve large subsections of the market.

For example, according to the propensities model study conducted by TAAP itself, only about 65% of the total traffic in the Toronto region originates in the Toronto Census Metropolitan Area (CMA) (Document B-55, 1974, Vol. 1, Exhibit 2). Of the remaining 35%, about 6% comes from Kitchener and 12% from Hamilton, while the rest—17%—is not assigned to any of the CMAs in the region. Some of this non-Toronto CMA traffic, undoubtedly, originates in the north and the east, that is, it would naturally go to Malton, but some of it must be supposed to originate in the west. Since the west is much more urbanized, it is reasonable to suppose that most of it does originate here—two thirds, say—making a total of 25% of total traffic that might naturally gravitate towards Hamilton, if *given free choice* of airport. However, at present there is very little attempt to service the Hamilton market directly, although it does account for a large share of the traffic. For example, there are 16 daily Air Canada flights from Toronto to Ottawa and 17 from Ottawa to Toronto while there is not a single flight between Ottawa and Hamilton. In fact, there is no Air Canada service to Hamilton at all, according to the Air Canada Timetable for North America: Seeking such an entry in the timetable under Hamilton the passenger is told to "see Toronto/Hamilton." It seems most unlikely that there would not be a large daily contingent wishing to travel between Hamilton and Ottawa, given the industrialization of the Hamilton area. There is only one Nordair flight a day each way between Hamilton and Ottawa.*

The question of the capacity of Hamilton does not appear to have been studied in connection with the new airport. Incidentally, we observe that the distance between Malton and Hamilton, about 35 miles, is about the same as the distance between the airports within the New York and San Francisco multiple airport systems. The Hamilton CMA will continue to grow, although probably at a slower rate than Toronto, while Kitchener will continue to grow at about the same rate as Toronto, as it has done during the 1960s. The Hamilton airport could serve as the center of gravity for the Hamilton area and for much of the surrounding region from Niagara to Kitchener.

It is suggested that the two-airport system of Malton and Hamilton, about 35 miles apart, each potentially serving different large sub-markets in the southern Ontario region, is the appropriate comparison

* The fact that there are not more Nordair flights between Hamilton and Ottawa does not indicate that there are not more people who wish to travel between these cities. The Nordair Hamilton-Ottawa segment is part of the Montreal-Pittsburg run and presumably Nordair does not wish to commit more of its resources to this route, Nordair being a smaller company with operations in several other areas of the nation.

to several other multiple airport systems such as those of the New York or San Francisco Bay conurbations. Hence the frequently heard argument by analogy that Toronto, like New York, is a large urban region and so needs a multiple airport system to be built by constructing new airports is wrong. The large conurbation of which the Hamilton and Toronto CMAs comprise the major axis *already has* two airports. There are several general aviation airports within the region, including the potential capacity of Downsview. Rather than building a large new airport in the next 20 years, traffic and passengers must be correctly allocated among the existing airports. This might be achieved by encouraging connections from Hamilton to international flights in Montreal, which, with the new Montreal-Mirabel airport, will have excess capacity for a long time to come, rather than originating them at the Toronto International Airport. Now, of course, someone will raise the argument that people will be inconvenienced by this procedure. In answer, all that can be said is that some people will find it somewhat less convenient. But the number who are seriously inconvenienced will probably not be very large. A short drive to the Hamilton airport and a wait for a connection at Montreal might be preferable to a longer drive to Toronto and a direct flight. In any event, this connection would cost the passenger a lot less money—or, at least, it *would cost much less money if the announced federal airport pricing policy of users' paying for the airport is followed.* Moreover, charges at Montreal would be lower if it had greater traffic. Thus the small number of people who will be somewhat inconvenienced in the absence of Pickering, together with the other minor traffic flow improvements that might result from construction at Pickering, could not possibly justify such a project.

After the turn of the century a new airport may well be required to accommodate traffic levels that can be justifiably accepted as social goals. This distinction between traffic forecasts that are accepted as social goals and those that are not, stressed throughout this book, bears repeating once more. Such an airport should probably be put at Pickering since, as we saw in Section 2 the land costs, measured in terms of the sacrifice that society will make by withdrawing the land from agricultural use, will be lower at Pickering than elsewhere, owing to the nature of its agricultural production. Moreover, as we have noted, there will be much greater development toward the east—or at least this is the direction in which urbanization *should move,* land being relatively less productive in that direction. But there will be time enough to build the airport later. If it is not needed until 2000, initiation of construction could well be deferred until 1995. To this it may be objected that construction costs will be higher. This is true, of course. But the real issue is whether relative costs will be higher, and there is no certainty that construction costs will rise compared to other costs during the next 20 years. To argue that the cost of construction has been one of the fastest rising price series in the past six months and to extrapolate this rate to 2000 would be no more sensible than to project air traffic to the year 2000 on the basis on the air movements of late April 1973—which were far below their normal level because of the firemen's strike.

In closing, we repeat the warning sounded at the beginning of the chapter—to build an airport 20 years prematurely is to increase the social cost by about $1.5 billion. There are numerous other fine uses to which these resources could be directed—employment promotion in the Atlantic Provinces, development of fuel resources and foreign earnings, or improvement of flood control in the prairies.

REFERENCES

Abouchar, Alan (1976), "Traffic Forecasts for the Pickering (Second Toronto International) Airport: A Critical Examination," *Canadian Public Policy*, Vol. 3, No. 1.

Crowley, Ronald (1973), "Effects of an Airport on Land Values," *Journal of Transport Economics and Policy*, May.

Document A-2 (1973). Government of Canada, Ministry of Transport, Canadian Air Administration, TAAP, *Forecasts of General Aviation in the Toronto Region*, January.

Document B-27 (1973). Neil Gillis Real Estate, *Opinion of Market Value of 3863 Acres of Land in the Town of Mississauga*, July.

Document B-39 (1974). Government of Canada, Ministry of Transport, Canadian Air Transportation Administration, TAAP, *Peak Hour Analysis and Forecast for the Toronto Airports System*, February.

Document B-48 (1974). Agrology Consultants Ltd., *Agriculture and The New Toronto International Airport: an Introductory Analysis*, March.

Document B-55 (1974). Government of Canada, Ministry of Transport Canadian Air Transportation Administration, TAAP, *Originating-Terminating Passenger Forecasts for the Toronto Airports System*, Volumes 1 and 2, March.

Parkin, John B., and Associates (1967), *Master Plan for Toronto International Airport*, prepared for Department of Transport, November.

Province of Ontario, Ministry of Agriculture and Food (1972), *Agricultural Statistics for Ontario*, Toronto.

Royal Airport Inquiry Commission (1974), *Report*, Ottawa, February.

Toronto Real Estate Board (1970), *House Price Trends, 1970.*

Written Summary (no date). Government of Canada, Ministry of Transport, Canadian Air Transportation Administration, TAAP, *New Toronto International Airport, Pickering, Written Summary.*

4

Problems in Urban Economic Analysis

15

Efficiency in the Urban Economy

1 INTRODUCTION TO PART 4

Analysts working in the complex area of urban economics run two risks. On the one hand, if we insist on deriving immediately applicable policy rules, we risk oversimplification to the point where our rules are scarcely Pareto efficient. On the other hand, acknowledgment of the difficulties and even the immeasurability of many of the phenomena of concern may lead us to rules that equate marginal social benefits and marginal social costs but yet leave us hopelessly unprepared to interpret these quantities or to make the decisions that are essential in the normal course of urban policymaking and administration.

In Part 4 we do attempt to give some guidelines, recognizing the impossibility of decreeing absolute prescriptions. For example, congestion optimization is seen to be far more complex both in theory *and* in practice than is generally thought, and no absolute, welfare-maxizing decision rule can be given. When something can or should be done, however, if we recognize that *any* policy will be suboptimal, we can seek out the best of the various alternatives. Sometimes, congestion remedies may call for doing nothing in a physical planning sense and suggest instead that the best approach is a reorientation of basic tax allocation rules.

In this chapter we present an analytical framework for the definition and analysis of concepts such as "agglomeration economy" and "urban efficiency." We see that it is meaningful to speak of efficiency with respect to three different kinds of issue—growth of existing cities, design of new towns, and consolidation of contiguous cities—each requiring different considerations regarding the measurement and treatment of costs. Not enough attention has been given to this threefold distinction in the past, with the result that measurements believed to be relevant to the general question of urban size may actually be relevant to only one of these three issues—sometimes in an unexpected way. Although no new measurements of urban efficiency are offered, we consider some of the empirical literature within this theoretical framework, paying special attention to the internal consistency of empirical investigations and this theory's relevance to what the investigators have attempted to measure.

Chapter 16 discusses the theory of congestion and congestion policy and provides some insights into this question. We see that the policy prescription depends, in the first place, on whether route, network, or modal congestion is the relevant problem, a three-way distinction that is itself a new analytical approach. We also learn to recognize what other variables and considerations must condition the choice of a congestion optimization instrument in a given situation.

Finally, Chapter 17 analyzes the problems in using property value change and certain other variables as indirect measures of benefits for urban investment decisions. The theoretical evaluation is couched in a classificatory analysis of urban project decision-making criteria, supplemented by an empirical analysis of the Toronto subway. The implications for project evaluation and taxation policies are studied.

2   ANALYSIS OF URBAN EFFICIENCY

2.1   The Problem

In its most general sense, "agglomeration economy" is a portmanteau term expressing the fact that, for a host of reasons, welfare per capita is higher in a large city than in a small one. Among the reasons are production externalities of firms when indivisibilities require a large market for individual producing units; the same sort of indivisibilities in the consumption sector, requiring a large market for the provision of a wide variety of amenities; higher per capita incomes owing to the greater labor productivity arising in greater proximity to work and increased use of capital or large-scale production made possible by the larger market; and cost reductions, in public sector services. Finally, there are the intangibles resulting from the larger urban complex, such as the improved quality of work and better newspapers. Some writers intend only subsets of these effects, such as the unit cost behavior in the provision of public services. When the net result of all these factors is to lower welfare it is a diseconomy.

Obviously, it is difficult to make operational so broad a concept of agglomeration effects. Empirical research has, therefore, concentrated on some of the subconcepts, such as the relationship between unit cost and volume of individual public sector services. Most of the studies, which have been based primarily on United States data, have been statistical cross-section studies of urban expenditures by function and by total, sometimes adjusting for income and sometimes not, depending on the main focus of the investigation. Since most of this literature has been reviewed and its methodology appraised by others [see Bird (1970), Hirsch (1968), and Musgrave (1968)], we make no attempt to treat it exhaustively, simply referring to it as the need arises.

Much of the investigation of urban expenditures has been criticized for diffuseness and uncertainty about what is being measured and about the implications of using alternative formulations. It has been asked many times whether such studies of expenditure determinants measure demand or supply factors. As Musgrave (1968, p. 573) has put it:

The "service" function combines a mixture of supply and demand factors which need to be disentangled if the really interesting insights into the fiscal behavior of communities are to be obtained. To some extent, this might be accomplished by separating demand variables such as income and demographic factors, from supply variables, such as climatic conditions or wage rates. To illustrate, the cost of a range of service levels for snow removal (i.e. absence of snow on streets) will depend on factors such as snowfall, density, topography, wages and so forth. This is the cost function part of the problem. Service levels provided will then be a function of these costs *and* of demand factors, such as incomes, tastes, and other prices. The general expenditure function is unsatisfactory both because the dependent variable is poorly defined (i.e., in terms of expenditure rather than service levels) and because the independent variables combine cost and demand factors without due separation. While certain variables may bear on both sides of the picture (density reduces the cost of fire-fighting per house, but raises demand by increasing the cost of conflagration) a better separation is hardly an insoluble problem.

The same or similar point has been made by Breton (1965) and a number of others.

The dissatisfaction with past research has undoubtedly stemmed in part from the different purposes to which different observers would like to put it. For example, straightforward expenditure determinant studies may be appropriate as a predictive device, but inadequate as a normative measure. But there is another diversity of purpose to contend with in analyzing the urban economy—there is not one object of measurement, but several. Analysis must help in framing policy with respect to three quite different issues: (1) determination of optimal size for new towns; (2) consolidation of already existing neighboring urban complexes; and (3) growth of already existing cities. Analysis relevant to each of these requires a different approach. They are all important today, the last being perhaps the most critical. The following presentation, therefore, starts with the last. The necessary modifications for the others follow.

2.2   Diagrammatic Analysis for Urban Growth

2.2.1   *The Product Market*

The formulation of an urban economic model is too complex to be dealt with satisfactorily by a single expenditure determinants model. Even for a single service, there are, first of all, interrelationships between city size and demand, at the same time that demand may vary with price for any given city size.

Figure 15.1 shows market demand and cost curves for an urban public service. For the sake of definiteness, we talk about garbage collection. The vertical axis shows the price per unit and the horizontal axis, the number of pickups per unit of time, say a year. The demand curve, DD_0, slopes from northwest to southeast—at lower prices people will want to have more collections per year. Thus, as the demand curve is drawn, if price is reduced from P' to P'', the quantity demanded per year will rise by 25% from Q' to Q''.

The demand curve DD_0 relates price to quantity holding constant everything else including the size of the city, which is here N_0. More pickups are demanded at lower unit prices for essentially the same reason that more of any normal good is always demanded when the price is reduced. The specific factors conditioning demand here have the following logic: with more frequent collections people will not have to crush their refuse as intensively, objectionable odors will lessen, fly attraction will fall, and so on.

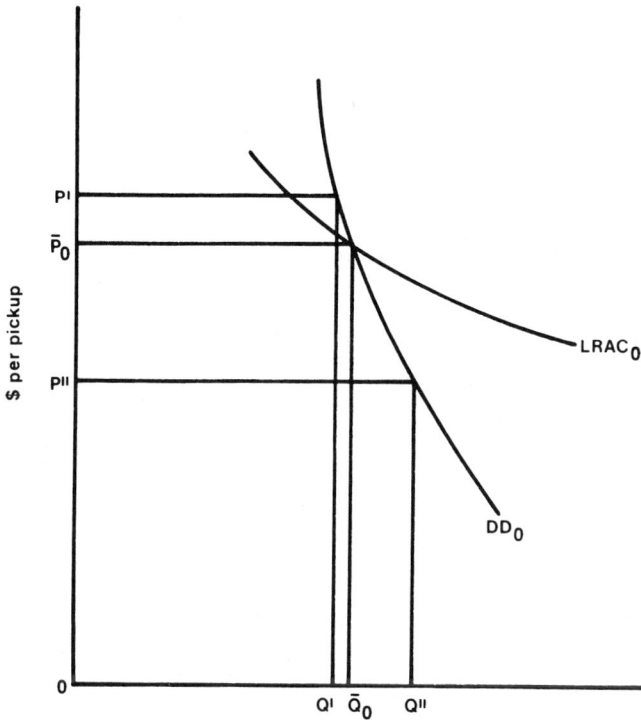

Figure 15.1 Hypothetical market demand and supply of garbage collection for a city of size N_0).

For this city of size N_0 we will also have a long-run average cost function LRAC. This curve tells us what the lowest cost is per unit at different levels of activity. Being a long-run curve each point represents the most efficient cost that might be attained if we could start from scratch in each case with city size fixed. For example, the lower cost which is secured in moving from Q' to Q'' might be based on a revised land use pattern with the city dump moved in closer, and lower labor and vehicle costs per pickup—the reduced driving distance offsets higher land costs over the range of demand but nothing critical is implied; the demand intersection at price P_0 and quantity Q_0 could easily occur over the rising range or in an interval of constancy. The LRAC is taken as the supply schedule and will be referred to as SS in the future.

The demand and supply analysis just conducted for city with size N_0 can be repeated for other city sizes. Figure 15.2 shows the relevant curves for six different city sizes with equilibrium prices denoted $\bar{P}_i$. The supply-demand pairs represent successive rightward displace-

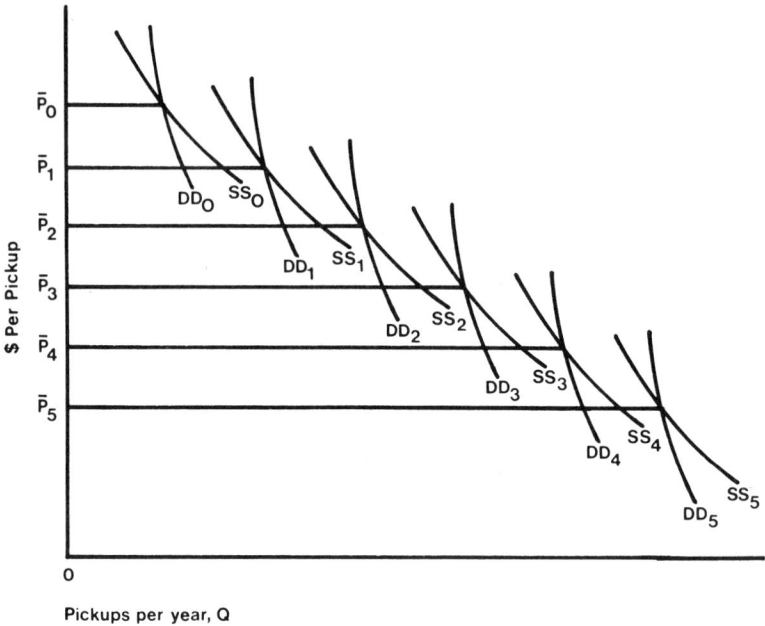

Figure 15.2 Market demand and supply curves for cities of varying size N_t.

ments, which means that people are willing to pay more per unit for the same quantity of annual pickups as city size increases, and also that it costs more per unit for the same quantity of pickups per year for larger city sizes.

The rightward shift in demand occurs for two reasons. First, individuals' utility functions change and they are willing to pay more for each pickup since greater density imposes additional health hazards. Second, the fact of a larger city implies a larger number of people who would be willing to pay more at any given level of collection activity. (In the consolidation analysis to be discussed below, by contrast, only the second of these factors enters, since the layout of the aggregated metropolitan region remains the same.)

The demand curve of Figure 15.1 and the family of curves of Figure 15.2 are based on a given income level and we should expect that an increase in income will shift the demand curve for any city size to the right, intersecting the supply schedule at a point to the southeast of its present intersection at price $\bar{P}$.

The rightward shift in the supply schedules results from increased prices for inputs, primarily land. Wages probably also rise somewhat, and final costs may be higher since elimination must be more thorough.

Several different treatments have been proposed for the input price variation which depends on city size. Breton (1965) has clarified the issue by drawing the distinction between input price variation and input quantity variation as sources of final cost variation. Musgrave (1968, p. 573) has argued that input price variation should be eliminated in expenditure studies to try to gain an idea about "service levels." But this approach would leave us ill-equipped to deal with one of the major questions at issue when the focus of study is policy with respect to existing cities: input price variation accompanying different city size is precisely the way to measure society's needs and resources, and, therefore, the welfare gain or loss to be associated with transition from one size to another. And for a policy concerned with influencing the growth of existing urban complexes, we *do* want to observe the consequences of input price variation since the very heart of the issue is the cost and benefit of changing from an existing city size to a different one, and the currently existing prices better measure the costs and benefits than would production functions based on the constant prices of some given city size.

We may formalize the foregoing as follows. First, the demand function for city size N_0 can be written as $Q_0 = f_0(P_0)$. In general, for city of size N_i it may be written as $Q_i = f_i(Q_i)$. In all normal cases we will have $Q_{n+1} > Q_n$, that is, demand will shift to the right with increasing city size. If demand shifts by a constant percentage, that is, if the quantity associated with an increase in city size is proportional to the relative size difference, we will have

$$Q_i = [1 + \alpha(N_i/N_0)]f_0(Q_0)$$

In like manner, the generalized supply function may be written as

$$AC_i = S_i(Q_i)$$

As the supply and demand functions shift to the right, the equilibrium intersection $\bar{P}_i$ will shift. The series of intersection will be termed a dynamic product equilibrium (DPE) curve.

Recalling, moreover, that there will be a different family of demand curves for each income level, we will require a DPE curve for each income. Figure 15.3 shows two such curves, denoted DPE' and DPE''. (DPE' corresponds to the situation of Figure 15.2 and the equilibrium prices $\bar{P}_i$ have, accordingly, been relabeled $\bar{P}_i'$ on Figure 15.3. DPE'' relates to a higher income level, since the equilibrium price for higher income is lower, with a higher quantity, than that of the lower income level, as indicated earlier.)

The DPE curve is a descriptive rather than an optimizing device. It

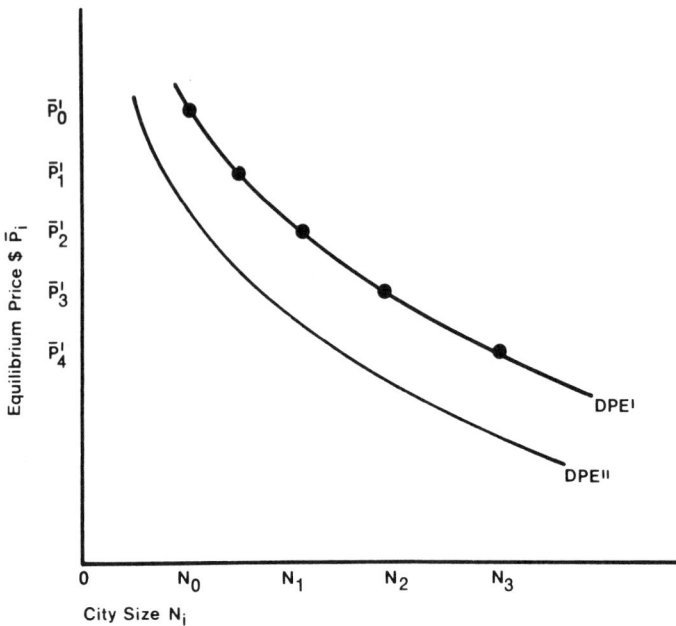

Figure 15.3   Dynamic product equilibrium curve (equilibrium price versus city size.)

merely traces out the supply-demand equilibrium prices for different-size cities. Optimization requires that this product market equilibrium curve be evaluated with respect to the benefits that are associated with different-size cities, to which we now turn.

2.2.2   Demand For City Size (Amenities)

Since cities perform different functions (serve as seaports, manufacturing cities, agricultural centres, and so on) it is first necessary to determine the function or nature of the city being analyzed. We will consider cities oriented to commerce and light industry. Their amenities will vary with their size—parks, newspapers, social life, and so on. In general it is to be expected that for any given size, the willingness to spend on municipal services is positively associated with income. Larger cities may be expected to have greater environmental diversity and advantages than smaller cities; individuals would be willing to pay more for these advantages out of any given income. The extra expenditure on the various municipal services that a consumer is willing to undertake to live in a larger city may be regarded as a price—the price of living in the larger city.

A group of expenditure-income curves is shown in Figure 15.4. Annual expenditure is shown on the vertical axis and income on the horizontal axis. The curves are labeled EE_i, the subscript indicating that the curve pertains to city size N_i. We would normally expect EE_i to move upward, though at a decreasing rate, and eventually to be displaced downward. The expenditure-income function can then be related to city size by drawing a perpendicular at any income level, say $\bar{Y}$, and plotting in Figure 15.5 the points of its intersection with the family of expenditure curves. This diagram shows per capita expenditure on the vertical axis and city size on the horizontal axis. The curve derived in this way is labeled $E\bar{Y}$. This curve will be upward sloping at first, but ultimately people will be unwilling to pay more to live in larger cities. The curves in Figure 15.4 are displaced downward when $i > 4$, and the $E\bar{Y}$ curve would slope downward.

We have considered the expenditure city-size curve for income of $\bar{Y}$. Such a curve can be constructed in like manner for any income. The curve derived for $\hat{Y} > \bar{Y}$ would lie above the $E\bar{Y}$ curve in Figure 15.5.

We can now compare the amenities or city size demand, in the form of the expenditure-income function, with a cost curve. We assume that the demand for each service, as analyzed in Section 2.2.1 is independent of the demand for others, as seems reasonable. The DPE curves are

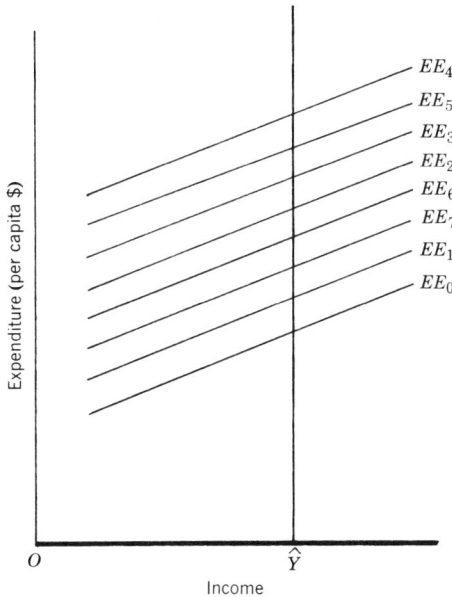

Figure 15.4   Per capita expenditure-income curves for varying city size.

given in terms of prices per *unit of service* and must be converted into expenditure terms. To do this, we multiply $\bar{P}_i$ by the equilibrium quantity and divide by city size to determine the per capita equilibrium expenditure on this service. The same is done for all other services. The resulting curves are then summed vertically to give a per capita dynamic all services product equilibrium curve for a given income level. This curve is labeled DASPE in Figure 15.5.

Following considerations of the relationship between the DPE curves for different income levels, as shown in Figure 15.3 and explained earlier, the DASPE curve for a higher income would lie above the DASPE curve in Figure 15.5.

The DASPE and $E\bar{Y}$ curves will intersect twice at $\hat{N}$ and $\tilde{N}$. The optimal city size is determined by the intersection corresponding to the large city size, at $\tilde{N}$; up to this point people's willingness to spend on city services continues to exceed the cost of providing the necessary services associated with the corresponding city size. For still larger cities, the costs exceed the willingness to spend, even though both may be falling. Thus the optimal city size is determined by four factors:

1. A family of demand functions for individual services for varying city sizes (one family for each income level).

2. A long-run average cost function for each city size.

3. The expenditure-income function, one for each city size.

4. Per capita personal income.

Let us now investigate the consequences of shifts in the curves. An increase in per capita income will shift the $E\bar{Y}$ curve upward. Since the income level is different, the DASPE curve will also move upward.* If $E\bar{Y}$ moves less than DASPE, the final equilibrium city size will be smaller, and expenditure under the higher income will be greater, than that under the lower income in the bigger city. This means that with great wealth people will avail themselves of the luxury of smaller cities (where the "physical" market supply-demand equilibrium occurs at a higher price). People will spend more per capita on urban services as well as pay more per unit of urban service while spending relatively less of their income on urban services (see the slope of the *EE* curves in

---

* The dynamic product equilibrium curve for any product will be displaced downward the less, the lower is the income elasticity of demand for the service in question (the less does the family of demand curves in Figure 15.3 shift to the right with rising income) and the greater is the elasticity of the individual cost curves in Figure 15.3.

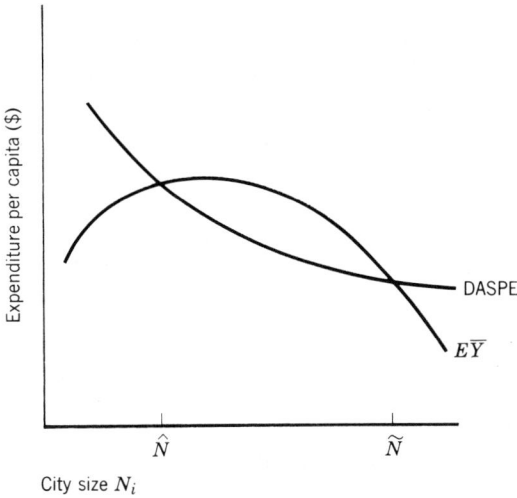

Figure 15.5 Product-equilibrium, expenditure-income equilibrium, and determination of efficient city size.

Figure 15.4). They will thus have a larger share of income uncommitted to the provision of urban services with which they can enjoy more benefits offered in the smaller city, which has fewer benefits to offer, than they could enjoy in the larger city, which has more to offer.

2.3 Analysis for New Towns Policy

Regarding new towns policy we *do* wish to abstract from the input price variation that has come to characterize relative factor costs in actually observed cities and to concentrate instead only on the scale economies of the underlying technological processes. The changes that must be introduced into the analysis of the preceding section relate first to the individual product supply curves and thence to the DPE and DASPE curves. We assume that land can be bought at constant unit price in the region in which the new city is to be founded, so that the differential effects of city growth over time have not come to be reflected in land values. In this case, doubling the size of a city dump will double land cost. Similarly, labor costs can be estimated at a given constant price, on the assumption that the workers who come to this city come from the margin in many different cities and, within the city size range being contemplated, any number can be attracted at that price.

The physical inputs underlying the cost curves of Figure 15.2 are now valued at these unit prices to calculate a single LRAC curve for each service. The family of demand curves remains as before. The series of intersections with the LRAC and the demand curve family traces out a static product equilibrium curve, one for each service, relating equilibrium prices to city size. The observation for each city size is then multiplied by the quantity provided and divided by the city size to get a per capita annual expenditure for that service. These are summed over all services to yield a per capita static all services product equilibrium curve (SASPE). Confrontation of SASPE with the expenditure-income function, as before, then defines the optimal city size.

2.4   Analysis for Consolidation Policy

Under what conditions should contiguous municipalities unite? The decision should take into account the cost reduction that may be achieved through consolidation. This is usually a managerial economy. Another main source of scale economy—price concessions—is not so straightforward; the quantity discounts offered by a supplier working with say, 40 local communities, cannot be considered as observations on a statistical supply function which would then be simply extrapolated to a larger community since the existing pricing pattern may reflect a currently existing discriminating sales pattern in which the higher average prices to some will offset the lower prices to others, overhead being apportioned, in part, inversely to the strength of the buyer. For the same reason we could not even assume that the purchases after consolidation could all be made at the price now granted the biggest user.

The main source of scale economy, then, would be management. Pecuniary economies are less certain. Other sources of cost variation such as the changing input prices or factor cost variation considered earlier would not arise in the consolidation analysis—land and labor costs in the various municipalities within the same urban region would be much the same before and after consolidation. Consolidation of 40 municipalities into a metropolitan district of one million would not witness the same stresses and price changes that would accompany the growth of a city from 25,000 to one million.

The diagrammatic solution for consolidation is illustrated in Figure 15.6. The product-equilibrium curve would be developed in the following way. A long-run average cost curve for a single municipality is given by SS_0 in the figure. A demand curve for this municipality is shown as DD_0. Consolidation of two such units would spread the managerial burden somewhat and would permit a downward shift in the cost curve to SS_0.

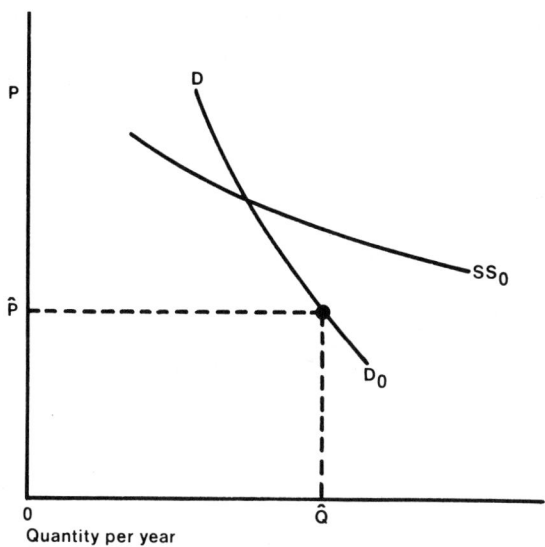

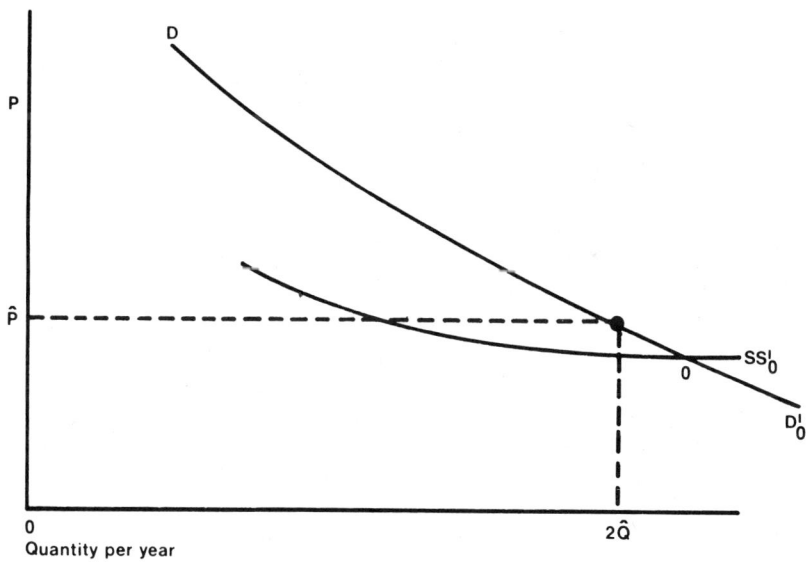

Figure 15.6 Effects of the consolidation of two municipalities.

For the two municipalities taken together a new demand curve must be introduced. It will be a paraprosthetic summation of the existing curves. This will intersect the SS_0' curve at a lower unit cost and higher output. This process continues, with the equilibrium price falling as long as there are economies causing the SS curve to shift downward. Eventually, management may start to yield diseconomies, causing the SS curves to start moving upward and raising the intersection with the successively rightward shifting demand curves.

3   EMPIRICAL ANALYSIS OF EFFICIENCY

The question of what approach should be followed to determine empirically the relations described in Section 2 is rather straightforward although any actual attempt naturally entails difficult data problems. Many of the studies that have been conducted in the past constitute appropriate formulations of some of these relations, and in this section we evaluate them in this light. A few preliminary words are in order, however.

For some services, such as police or fire protection, recourse is frequently made to expenditure to measure output. Criticism is encountered that this approach confuses demand and supply factors, as noted earlier. From the point of view of our analysis, this is unobjectionable, provided the expenditure by the public authority is in some direct way related to the final consumer through, for example, an annual property tax or an earmarked city sales tax, for in this case any expenditure observation can be construed as an intersection of the demand and supply curves relevant to a given city size. A downward-sloping demand curve can be imagined, and it would be interpreted as showing the amount that each additional person would be willing to pay for another unit of service. The intersection is the efficient product equilibrium point for a city of that size, and the series would then constitute an efficient product equilibrium curve just as would one derived from natural physical indicators. It could then be summed directly for the derivation of an all services product equilibrium curve into which services measured in physical until would also enter, but only after a transformation to an annual per capita expenditure basis.

How may the past studies be grouped within our classificatory scheme? Most of them shed light on the various modifications of a product equilibrium curve, divided about evenly between new towns and growth policy. While consolidation is the ostensible framework for many analyses, we feel that the studies done under this rubric really apply to new towns policy. Little has been done that could shed light on the expenditure-income relationship.

Examples of studies that illuminate various aspects of the dynamic product equilibrium curve (in which input prices change with changing city size) for individual services include the recent sewage disposal study by Downing (1969) or the fire protection study by Will (1965) in which the fire protection expenditures per capita may be interpreted as city-size-related, rightward-shifting, supply-demand intersections.

The gas study by Lomax (1951) also seems to be relevant to determination of the dynamic product equilibrium curve; it acknowledges the regionally related input price variability and attempts to avoid its complications by studying the cost relationships for three different regions.

Studies that relate to the question of whether and what size new cities should be include police, fire and refuse collection studies by Hirsch (1959, 1965, 1968)—St. Louis municipalities—and the Schmandt-Stephens (1960) police protection study—Milwaukee county municipalities—although many of them ostensibly relate to consolidation policy. The observations in these studies are made on municipal units within fairly uniform urban regions with boundary lines of individual municipalities being, on the whole, rather artificial. Therefore, it would seem reasonable to view determinants of land values or wages as being fairly uniform. That is, we would not expect relative land prices (ceteris paribus) in two adjacent communities of size 5000 and 50,000 respectively to show the same differences that two isolated municipalities of these sizes would show. The two adjacent cities both reflect the same factors and, but for historical accident, would probably constitute a single city of 55,000. In this case, differences in land prices would relate to different use patterns rather than to differences in demands for homogeneous land in two isolated cities of different size.

If this view is accepted, investigations of this kind really tell us, up to a constant, what the average cost of functions would be starting from scratch. That is, they yield information on the static production equilibrium curve. They do not tell us exactly, since, in a new situation, different relative prices might prevail. When starting a city from raw acreage, land prices would be lower than those in the heavily urban areas of these studies, and the labor/land price ratio might differ.

Finally, nothing appears to have been done from which inferences could be made regarding the expenditure-income function. Moreover, it is not certain just how one should proceed if he wanted to study this relationship. We could not regard the total expenditure at different city sizes as a series of product-equilibrium points without making some heroic assumptions. We could have to assume that everything that has developed in the past is as it should be. Even a small knowledge of the realities of the budgetary process precludes this view.

REFERENCES

Bird, R. (1970), "The Determinants of State and Local Expenditures, A Review of U.S. Studies," Appendix B in *The Growth of Government Spending in Canada* (Toronto: Canadian Tax Foundation).

Breton, A. (1965), "Scale Effects in Local and Metropolitan Government Expenditures," *Land Economics,* Vol. 41, pp. 370–372.

Downing, P. B. (1969), *The Economics of Urban Sewage Disposal* (New York: Frederick Praeger).

Hirsch, W. Z. (1959), "Expenditure Implications of Metropolitan Growth and Consolidation," *Review of Economics and Statistics,* Vol. 41.

—— (1965), "Cost Functions of an Urban Government Service: Refuse Collection," *Review of Economics and Statistics,* Vol. 47.

—— (1968), "The Supply of Urban Public Services," in H. S. Perloff and L. Wingo, Jr., Eds., *Issues in Urban Economics* (Baltimore: Johns Hopkins University Press).

Lomax, K. S. (1951), "Cost Curves for Gas Supply," *Bulletin of the Oxford Institute of Statistics,* Vol. 13, pp. 243–246.

Musgrave, R. A. (1968), "The Urban Public Economy," Discussion of Part III, in H. S. Perloff, and L. Wingo, Jr., Eds., *Issues in Urban Economics* (Baltimore: Johns Hopkins University Press).

Schmandt, H. J., and G. R. Stephens (1960), "Measuring Municipal Output," *National Tax Journal,* December.

Will, R. E. (1965), "Scale Economics and Urban Service Requirements," *Yale Economic Essays,* Vol. 5.

16

The Theory of Congestion and Congestion Optimization Policy

1 INTRODUCTION

Of all economic activities transportation is the most seriously affected by problems associated with congestion. It is not unique in this regard, however, since other activities, such as residential housing, are also subject to congestion effects. All have the same essential cause: the inability of the market to take account of the external cost that a late entrant into the market imposes on earlier consumers. But given its very widespread occurrence in transportation, it was natural that congestion should have been studied first within the framework of this sector.

Several types of congestion situation exist. All created by the imposition of costs on earlier entrants by latecomers, they have varying characteristics, hence require different analytical methods. For example, the problems of congestion on a single road and in an urban street network have different patterns, calling for different approaches. Analysis of airport congestion requires yet another device. In Section 2 analytical methods are presented to determine optimal output and prices for the three situations, which we call route, network, and nodal congestion, respectively. In Section 3 we apply the congestion theory to the actual implementation of congestion pricing.

2 THREE KINDS OF CONGESTION

2.1 Route Congestion

The traditional analysis of congestion, which we call route congestion, assumes that traffic travels the length of a single road. This is the traditional approach. Among standard treatments, Walters (1961) is the most explicit about demand in his graphical analysis. He shows a downward-sloping demand curve, but a horizontal demand curve would not affect the demonstration that there is a reduction in social welfare because entrants to the traffic stream beyond the optimal congestion point impose a marginal cost in excess of the price that they face, which is equal to average cost. Indeed, a horizontal curve is logically superior to a downward-sloping demand curve. We begin with the horizontal case.

Figure 16.1a shows the case of route congestion with a horizontal demand curve. Vehicles travel the entire length of the route. The price that anyone is willing to pay for the journey is P^*. The cost per vehicle trip is C^* until congestion sets in at N. At this point, owing to reduced and variable speeds, vehicle deterioration and fuel and other input costs per mile rise, raising average cost as shown by the AC curve. However, since each entrant also reduces the speeds of all inframarginal entrants and raises their average cost, the marginal social cost rises more rapidly than the average cost, as shown by the marginal cost curve. Traffic expands to N' where demand price and average social cost are equal, while efficiency calls for restricting traffic to N'' where demand price and marginal social cost are equal. The social loss is equal to the shaded area ABC. To reach the optimal traffic volume requires a congestion toll on each vehicle equal to marginal cost minus average cost at N'', that is, $P^* - C''$.

Figure 16.1b shows the same result for downward-sloping demand curves. The congestion toll, derived in the same way as in the horizontal case, is labeled $P'' - C''$. The demand curve now falls on the assumption that different kinds of cargo are to be transported, shippers of the successively less valuable cargoes being willing to pay successively lower prices to travel the length of the route.

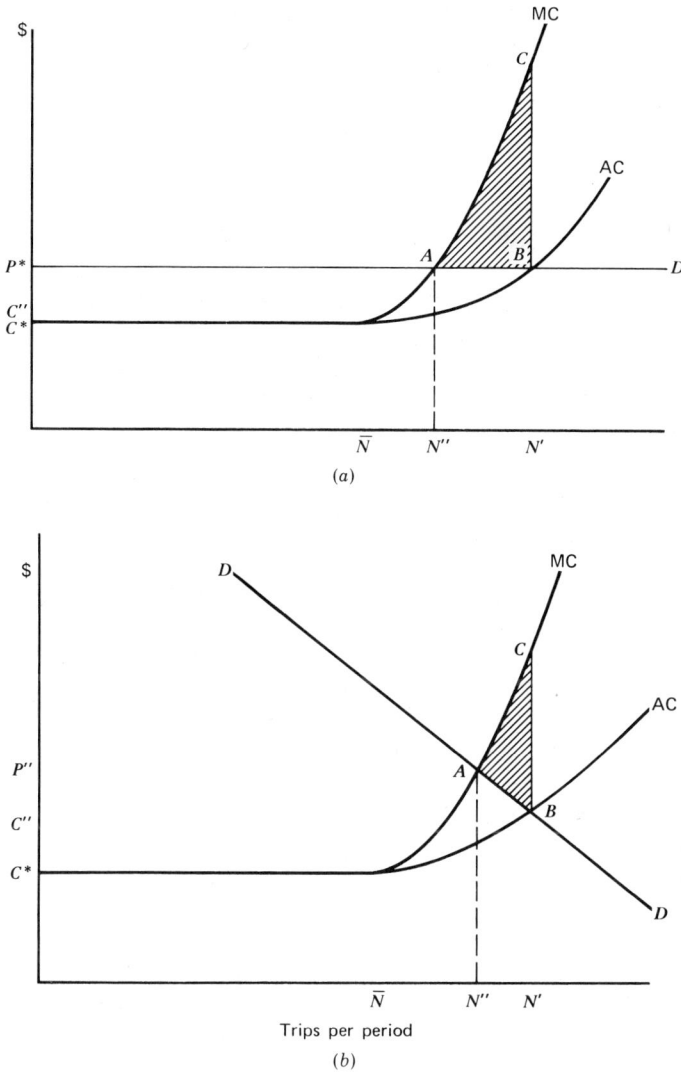

Figure 16.1   Traditional representation of congestion. (*a*) Infinitely elastic demand. (*b*) Downward-sloping demand curve.

Provided that vehicles are homogeneous, so that average trip cost is the same for every vehicle at any given traffic level, this poses no problem in route analysis. While the high-value shippers will be willing to pay more than the congestion toll plus average cost, the toll evidently will succeed in driving a wedge between average cost and the demands of the shippers whose demand price falls short of marginal social cost. Problems would occur only if the low-value cargo shippers had low vehicle operating costs—if they had smaller trucks, for example.

Problems do begin to arise, however, when demand variation stems from factors other than variation in cargo value. This will happen if vehicles are allowed to get on and off the road so that the single route actually becomes a linear network comprising a number of short lengths. More generally, it will occur in any network. If we imagine the single route AB divided into n sections a_i, a_{i+1} ($i = 1, 2, \ldots, n$), the demand of any vehicle for use of the road will depend not only on the value of the cargo being transported, but also on the total length of the sections that it runs. In this case the cost associated with any vehicle trip under uncongested conditions will be a function of the length of its particular trip. Moreover, its contribution to congestion of the entire vehicle stream will also be a function of its trip length simply because in traveling a longer distance it will affect larger portions of traffic. (The relationship between congestion and imposed cost need not, of course, be proportional to trip length.) That is, since vehicles with lower demand (i.e., those toward $\bar{N}$) may generally be presumed to use shorter sections of the route (which is one reason for their lower trip demand price), their congestion imposition will be less than that of longer-distance travelers. Moreover, since their vehicle cost will be less (per appearance on the route), the congestion charge calculated as the difference between marginal and average social cost will not be enough to keep the optimal number out of the traffic stream. Accordingly, a different apparatus must be developed to analyze congestion in networks. Because it is most applicable to problems of urban commutation, we adopt the city as an analytical framework.

2.2 Network Congestion

Figure 16.2 shows the basic demand relationships in a network congestion model. Price is shown on the Z-axis and number of trips per day on the X-axis. The Y-axis gives a spatial residential distribution measure σ^2/E (where σ^2 and E are the variance and mean of the distances to be traveled), which depends on the residential pattern, rising with increasing population dispersion. The distance may be traveled by private car, by public transit, or on foot.

The trips whose volume is plotted in the ZX-plane may be of any length. The price an individual is willing to pay for a trip will depend primarily on the distance to be traveled. People living a long distance

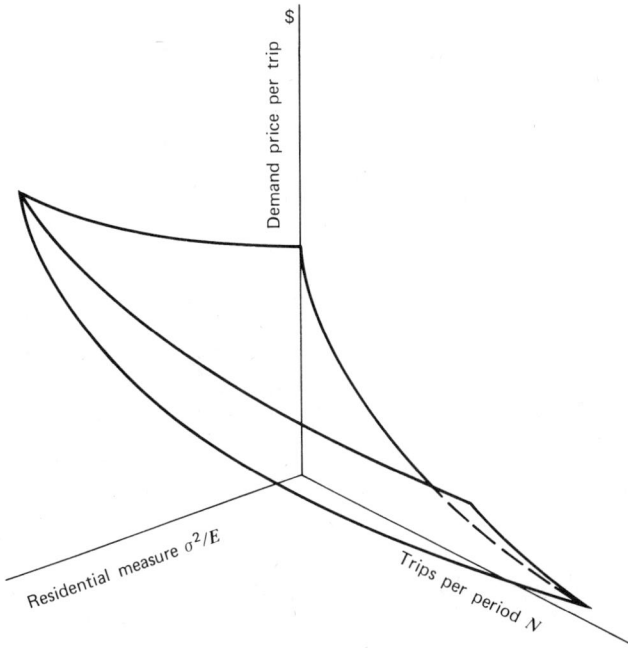

Figure 16.2   Three-dimensional demand function for trips.

from downtown would be ready to pay a high price to make the trip, while those living closer would be willing to pay less. A person living very close can walk or take an inexpensive public transit alternative. Moreover, in driving the person must cover a shorter distance, so that the price he would willingly pay for the trip is lower even if the price *per mile* is the same. This is all simply a manifestation of the tendency for property values (all other things equal) to fall with increasing distance from the core. Living far out one can buy the same amount of land for a lower price, but he then implicitly undertakes to pay a higher commuting price, that is he has a higher demand price for trips.

The schedule relating quantity of trips demanded to the spatial distribution measure in the ZY-plane is upward sloping. Each price observation is interpreted as the additional amount that some person would be willing to pay for the daily trip if he moved out far enough to increase the spatial measure between successive points on the Y-axis.

The cost relations are shown in Figure 16.3. In the ZX-plane, the average cost per trip falls as tripmakers traveling shorter distances

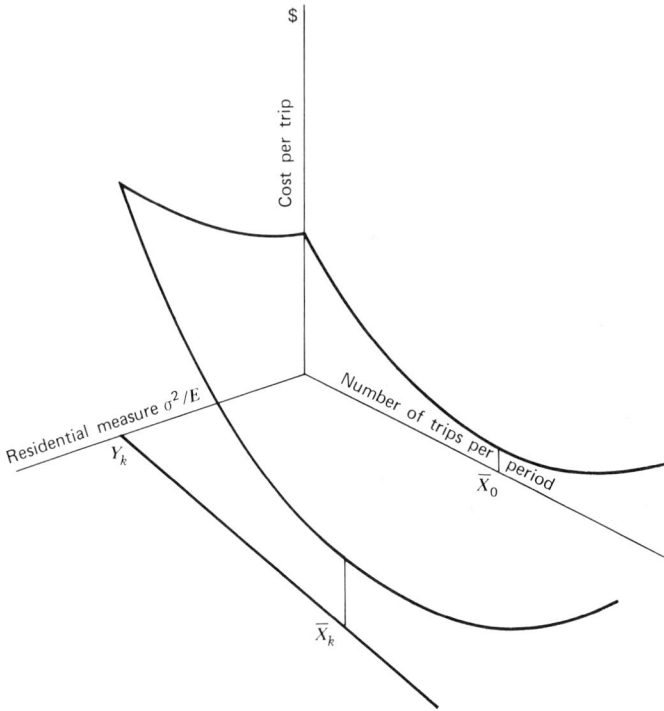

Figure 16.3   Three-dimensional cost analysis for trips.

(costing less per trip) enter the traffic stream as far as $\bar{X}$. Thereafter, since each additional unit imposes additional costs on all other vehicles, the average cost rises. The congestion point $\bar{X}$ moves out to the right with each increase in $Y = \sigma^2/E$. A representative point $\bar{X}_k$ at Y_k is shown. (The general point of inflection (congestion) is $\bar{X}_i$.) The reason is that as residential dispersion increases, there is more space over which to distribute any given traffic level, hence there is less density in the network.

From the cost and demand patterns optimal congestion levels can easily be derived by equating marginals with respect to volume for any given spatial pattern, which is fixed in the short run. But it is difficult to design a pricing mechanism appropriate to the task. For in the network analysis the average social cost is *not* the price facing each user, as in the route analysis. Rather, it is the average cost of all trips, which are of varying length. The price for those closer to the origin (making longer trips) is higher than that for those further out on the X-axis. Similarly, the congestion cost imposed by the longer tripmakers has to be greater than that of the shorter tripmakers. This, then, implies that a congestion toll should vary with distance traveled, rather than remaining uniform throughout the trip as in the route congestion case. A gas consumption related tax, for example, could be imposed, although this would lead to problems of gas fetching and competitive taxation by rival jurisdictions, as well as to the imposition of congestion tolls even in uncongested areas within the larger congestion region or at uncongested hours. The resulting inefficiencies would have to be traded off against the advantages of the gross charge in any situation. We return to this topic in Section 3.

2.3 Introduction of Personal Time Delay Cost

We have not so far explicitly treated wasted time as a cost of operation. Where time is a production input in the usual sense, such as truck delay, the time waste can be easily weighted by the driver's wage, inventory immobilization, and so on. Personal time delay is another matter. Here we encounter not only problems regarding the theoretical basis for imputing a value for time, but also problems in defining a conceptual framework within which to analyze the time valuations once they are agreed upon. In this section we consider how to introduce personal time cost logically and consistently into the congestion optimization model.

We can take account of time in three different, albeit equivalent ways, which can be more or less illuminating in different situations. First, we could consider the trip of whatever time duration (for each distance) as the service being demanded, and include in the demand price the total amounts that people would be willing to pay for all the components associated with the execution of the trip, that is the most they would be willing to pay for fuel, depreciation, tolls, and so on, together with their valuation of their own trip time. The demand curve would be higher and would have a steeper slope in the ZX-plane. So would the cost curves, since cost would include the (properly valued) trip time. These are shown in Figure 16.4a.

Alternatively, we could consider the demand curve to relate only to the material expenditures people would be willing to make on the trip, leaving aside their personal time. We *would* include, however, in the cost curves the properly valued time spent in delay from the congestion point on. This is shown in Figure 16.4b.

Finally, the demand curve could be considered to represent the demand for trips of zero delay up to the point of congestion, and thence

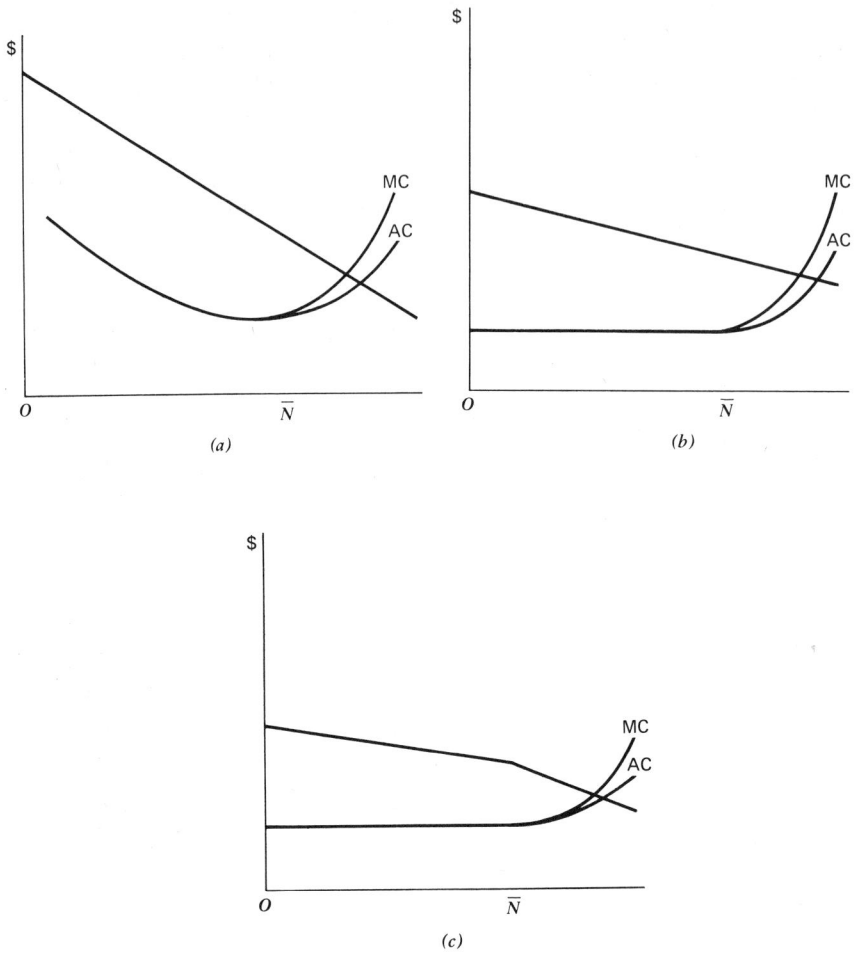

Figure 16.4 Three alternative representations of time in congestion analysis. (*a*) Demand and cost schedules include time valuation. (*b*) Time valuation included only in congestion cost. (*c*) Zero-delay and positive-delay segments of demand curve.

each point on the demand curve would represent the number of trips that have a delay defined by that level of traffic. There would be an inflection point at the congestion point $\bar{N}$, as shown in Figure 16.4c. In this case, the cost curves do not reflect the time spent in making the trip.

In all these treatments, the optimal congestion is denoted by the intersection of marginal social cost and the demand curve. Each has special advantages in individual situations.

2.4   Nodal Congestion

Congestion at such facilities as harbors and airports is independent of trip distance and requires a special analysis relating to single points or nodes. For the following nodal analysis we use a model of airport demand and congestion.

We consider first the airplane costs. We designate by ATC "technical costs," which include the cost of aircraft amortization and interest, airplane maintenance, crew and pilot costs, meals served on board, airport user fees, and other variable costs. Then the first effect of airport congestion is to raise certain technical costs, namely those reflected by the amortization for the extra hours that the plane is aloft (and the consequent extra maintenance) and the extra crew and pilot costs. (The time the pilot is aloft awaiting landing assignment reduces by an equal amount the time he may spend on other flights during the month.) The behavior of average technical cost with respect to airport activity would be like the cost curve shown in Figure 16.7. We assume all planes to be of the same size. Technical cost per plane is at first constant up to a level of activity $\bar{N}$. Then when total activity exceeds this level, the average technical cost curve begins to rise, tending to infinity as the upper physical capacity limit is reached. Marginal technical cost (MTC) is also shown in Figure 16.7.

We consider first a single route terminating at the airport and derive a demand curve for flights on this route during peak time. Our treatment of personal delay time follows the approach of Figure 16.4c, since attention here must be focused on some special aspects of demand, such as some inevitable consumer surplus on each flight owing to the inability of the airlines to discriminate perfectly. The derivation of the flight demand curve is shown in Figures 16.5 and 16.6.

We start with a passenger demand curve $P = U(X)$ showing the relationship between the price of the trip and the number of passengers wishing to make it at that price. This curve is for zero-delay flight. This is the rightmost curve, the longest curve in Figure 16.5. In this part of the analysis we assume all planes to be of the same size and have a capacity of X^* passengers. We also assume that the passenger demand on any flight is proportional to the total demand curve; in this case every flight is a cross section of the total passenger demand. For example, the curve given by $U_1^0(X)$ shows the passenger demand for zero-delay travel when just X^* passengers wish to fly. The curve denoted by $U_2^0(X)$ shows the passenger demand curve for zero-delay travel on each of $n = 2$ planes when $2X^*$ passengers wish to fly in all. The other curves are read similarly with $U_{N''}(X)$ being the curve when $n = N''$.

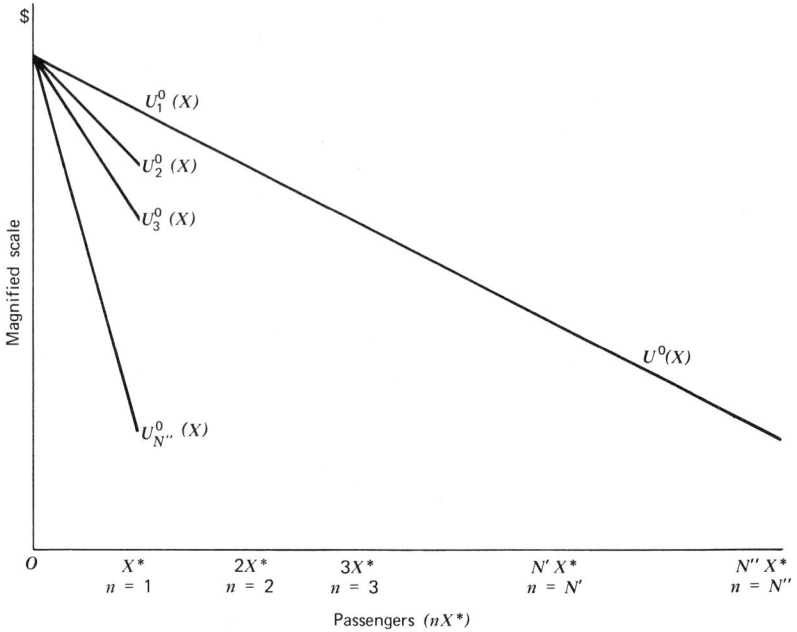

Figure 16.5   Total zero-delay passenger demand, $U^0(X)$ and passenger demand on individual airplanes, $U_n{}^0(X)$.

We have assumed that the demand for travel on any particular flight during the peak period is a cross-section of the total demand. The first effect of price increases, then, would be to reduce the number of persons traveling on each flight in proportion to the decline in total demand. However, rather than continue to fly more planes at undercapacity, the remaining passengers will be consolidated to fill fewer planes. The "fanned" demand curves in Figure 16.5 show how this occurs. $U_{N''}^0(X)$, the lowest line in this fan, represents the passenger demand on any plane when $N''(X^*)$ passengers are to fly. This number exceeds the congestion point, N', so that zero delay would not actually occur here. When price rises and the total passenger demand falls to X^*, only one plane will fly and the demand curve for that plane will coincide with the portion of the total $U^0(X)$ function that lies to the left of X^*, which is the capacity of an individual plane. This is shown by $U_1^0(X)$.

We must now construct a zero-delay flight demand curve, that is, a curve showing the relationship between the number of zero-delay flights and the price of the flight. It is easy to see that the total amount that rational passengers on the first plane should be willing to pay when X^*

is the total number of passengers is given by the area under the curve described by $U_1^0(X)$. This is a measure of the total benefit of that flight. Similarly, if $2X^*$ passengers wish to fly, they will occupy two planes, and each planeload should be willing to pay the amount under the curve given by $U_2^0(X)$. In general, the amount that each planeload of rational passengers should be willing to pay when nX^* passengers in all are flying is given by $\int_0^{x^*} U_n^0(X)\, dX$. This function, which is a measure of the social benefit per flight flown with a zero delay at the indicated level of operation, is shown by SB^0, the upper curve in Figure 16.6. The zero-delay demand curve would in reality take effect only as far as activity level N', however, since past this point flights can be made only with positive delay.

Just as we have drawn a zero-delay flight demand curve, so we may conceive of a demand curve for delays of any arbitrary length. For each such delay a demand curve would terminate at the same point on the X-axis and have a slightly smaller slope than SB^0. We show one such curve, SB'', corresponding to the delay associated with traffic level N''. However, while we may conceive of them over the entire range of

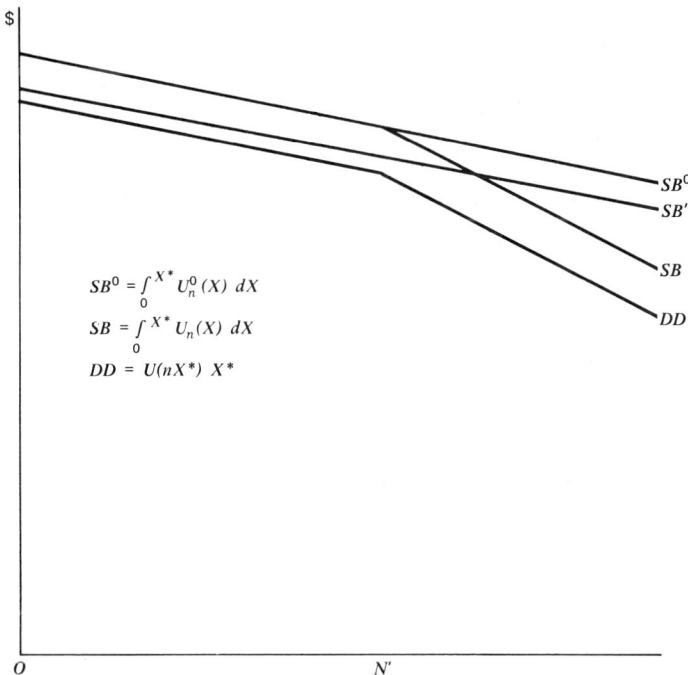

$$SB^0 = \int_0^{X^*} U_n^0(X)\, dX$$

$$SB = \int_0^{X^*} U_n(X)\, dX$$

$$DD = U(nX^*)\, X^*$$

Figure 16.6   Social benefit, apparent demand, and industry marginal revenue.

activity, any one of these demand curves would actually be observed only at the single point corresponding to that number of flights, shown on the horizontal axis, which corresponds to the delay in question. In this way there will be a single effective point for a delay of any given term greater than zero. We denote this point, in general, by ${}_0\!\int^{X^*} U_n(X)\, dX$. A single flight demand curve could then be constructed; this will consist of SB^0 up to the activity level N', and the series of effective demand points past N'. This curve is denoted by SB and is kinked at N'.

Curve SB at any point represents the total utility per flight at the given traffic level. The amount actually paid, however, will be less than SB, owing to the airlines' inability to discriminate perfectly among passengers. That is, apart from having first-class, regular, student, and similar rates, the airlines are unable to scale their ticket prices to the total benefit received by each passenger on the flight. If there were no special fares, all passengers would pay the same amount, and for each passenger but the last there would be a positive surplus. To some extent the present pricing system with special fare structure does discriminate, but only imperfectly (i.e., a surplus still arises for the first-class passengers, for the tourist class riders, and for students), since within each class a declining passenger demand curve may be assumed.

The existence of the discrepancy between total amount paid by the passengers and the total social benefit of the flight has the effect of putting the relevant demand curve facing the airlines to the left of SB; for any average revenue (planeload price) a smaller volume of traffic will be observed than is indicated by the SB curve. It will also have a kink. The curve (DD) is shown in Figure 16.6. We call this the "apparent demand curve." It is the curve facing the airline industry. For any traffic level it is the most that could be charged per flight under the existing system of price discrimination which would ensure flight demand of the given level. Perfect discrimination by the airline industry would imply a curve coincident with SB.

If, on the other hand, the airlines were unable to discriminate at all, the total revenue per plane at different traffic levels n would be equal to the amount charged per ticket, multiplied by the number of passengers on the plane, X^*. Over the uncongested activity range, this will be equal to $U_n^0(X^*)X^*$, which would be the price paid by the last passenger aboard, or, alternatively, to $U^0(nX^*)X^*$. In general it is equal to $U(nX^*)X^*$. To simplify presentation we assume complete inability to discriminate; it is evident that the limited ability that the airlines in fact do possess will change only the magnitude of the difference between planeload revenue and planeload utility.

We can now counterpose the cost and demand functions to determine the optimal level of airport congestion. Figure 16.7 shows the marginal and average technical cost curves, together with the social benefit and the apparent demand curves of Figure 16.6.

Congestion costs begin at N'. From this point on average and marginal technical cost rise, as explained above.

Output is optimal at the intersection of marginal technical cost and average social benefit per planeload, that is, at point H. Here the average gross benefit per planeload, with the benefit adjusted for the fact that congestion takes place, is just equal to the marginal technical cost to the industry. To elicit this output requires a user charge equal to the difference between average planeload revenue (C_2') and ATC, which is equal to C_2 at traffic level N_2. Industry MTC intersects apparent demand at traffic level N_2', but it continues to be below SB as far as N_2, signifying a continuing incremental net social benefit. At optimal output the net total social benefit is given by $N_2 {}_0\!\int^{x^*} U_{N2}(X)\ dX - {}_0\!\int^{N2}$ MTC dn_0. At this point traffic congestion is $N_2 - N'$.

Where output actually does take place will depend on the nature of

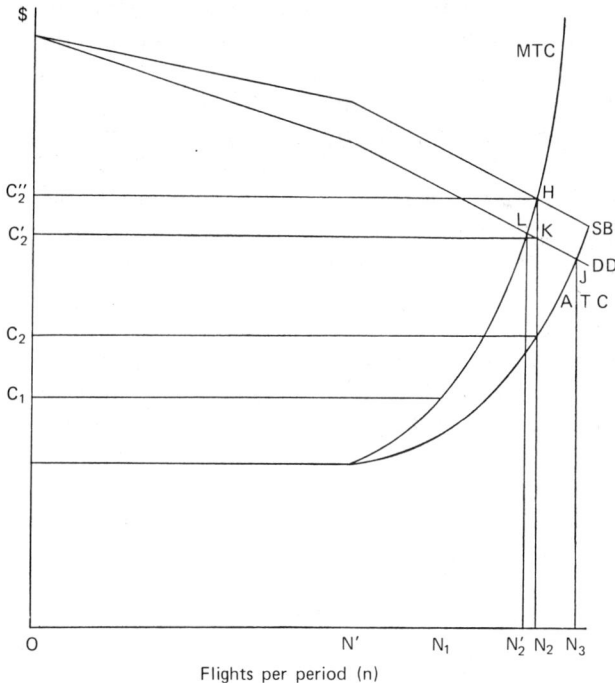

Figure 16.7   Analysis of optimal activity level.

competition in the airline industry. With perfect competition each producer would consider only his own marginal cost (which is given, very nearly, by the industry average technical cost curve, ATC) and would increase output to a level at which ATC and price were equal. This would produce an industry output at the intersection of DD and ATC at J with output N_3. The amount of the social loss in this case would be $\int_{N2}^{N3}(\text{MTC} - SB)\ dn$, the area bounded by MTC and SB between traffic levels N_2 and N_3.

Optimal output can be secured through imposition of an airport user charge great enough to raise the average planeload "revenue" to C_2' at traffic level N_2. This is the price given by the intersection of MTC and DD at which point marginal technical cost is equal to apparent demand. Efficiency requires that the charge should be paid by the airline directly in amount $(C_2' - C_2)$ rather than by each passenger as a ticket surcharge or airport entrance fee in amount $(C_2' - C_2)/X^*$. Since C_2' is based on a fare that is just sufficient to induce the last passenger aboard, an increase in fare would drive some passengers off the market. On the other hand, since C_2' is the planeload market price and C_2 is the average technical cost (including profit), the airline could obviously afford to pay $(C_2' - C_2)$ as a user charge and still operate profitably.

We now make the model more realistic by dropping the assumption that the airport is servicing a single route. It is enough to consider routes of two lengths, as shown in Figure 16.8. The long route shown in (a) has the same demand pattern as that in the previous analysis. The short route is discontinuous at some point $\bar{N}$ after congestion is reached, and actually becomes negative. The reason is that the air traveler chooses an alternative mode of transport when the delay becomes very long in relation to the air trip. People would continue to fly only if the price were negative, that is, if they were paid to do so.

One more step is required before we can sum the two route curves to derive a combined flight demand curve for the airport. As they are pictured, the short-route curve starts at a price below the long-route demand price for positive-delay flights. This means that no part of the zero-delay short-route demand curve is actually observed in practice and we must determine the positive-delay demand curves for the short route starting with the first flight on this route. This curve would look like Figure 16.8c, falling more rapidly than does the curve in (b), and then being discontinuous as before. An analogous, though less serious, adjustment is required for the long-route demand curve. Then the demand curve for flights of any given delay have a greater slope indicating that a lower level of long-route activity is associated with the given delay. These curves can then be summed horizontally to yield the total flight demand curve for the airport (Figure 16.9).

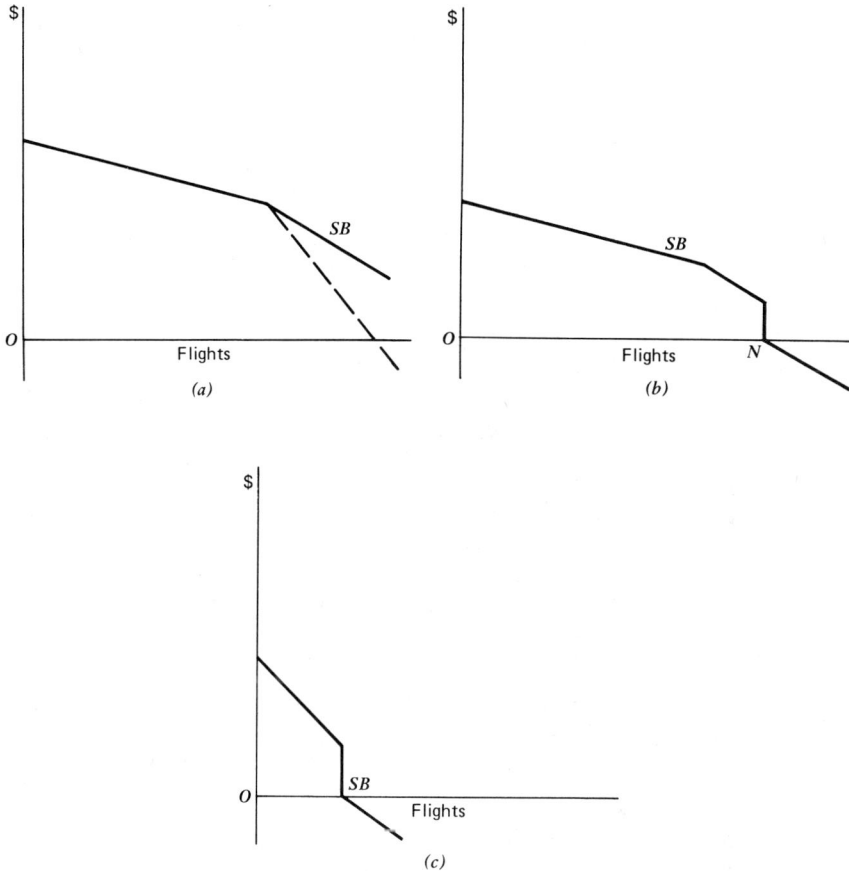

Figure 16.8 Analysis of demand on long and short trips. (*a*) Long trips. (*b*) Short trips. (*c*) Demand curve for short trips considering that long trip demand will impose prior congestion.

The total flight demand curve in Figure 16.9 shows the amount per flight that passengers would be willing to pay at any volume level. It is a simple step to move to the apparent demand curve that was used above in the single-route analysis. But since there is a difference in technical cost between the long and short routes, we must think not in terms of the apparent demand for flights by passengers, but in terms of the demand for airport landing slots by airlines. This will be a function of the difference between the apparent demand (planeload) price and the operating cost on that route, or the net revenue on each flight. A curve showing this demand is given in Figure 16.10. It is constructed by

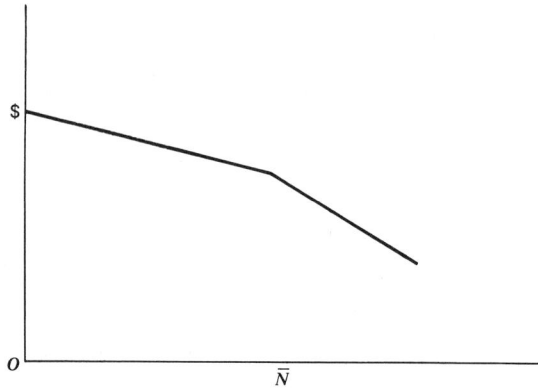

Figure 16.9   Total flight demand curve, all trip lengths.

subtracting the average cost curves from the apparent demand curves on the individual routes, and summing them as we did for the social benefit curves.

The final step is to bring together the airline flight demand curve, and a curve showing the marginal social cost of each additional flight. This is zero up to $\bar{N}$ and then starts to rise as in Figure 16.7 (it would actually be coincident with the rising portion of the appropriate marginal cost curve). This curve is drawn in Figure 16.10 and shows the optimal activity at N^*, at which point the congestion toll for the airport would be P^*.

The uniform congestion toll in this case would have a differential impact on the different sources of demand, cutting out primarily the flights on the short route. This is an efficient result, since in this case the contribution to congestion is the same no matter what the route length, while the total demand arising on each long flight is absolutely greater than that on the short flights. This contrasts with the result of imposing a uniform congestion charge per trip in the network situation. In that case, as we saw, a uniform charge had the effect of cutting out trips that contributed less congestion than did the long trips, a result that led to the search for a distance-related congestion charge.

3   CONGESTION OPTIMIZATION POLICY

A universally applicable congestion control policy cannot be prescribed. The range of available alternatives is too large. Too, there are many types of congestion, as we have just seen, in various physical settings and socioeconomic environments. The only universal statement that can be made is that we shall never succeed in reaching the optimum congestion point and that the objective should be, instead, to choose a policy that minimizes the welfare cost of congestion. This conclusion shows the need to maintain an open mind with respect to congestion control policies, recognizing that what may be extremely inappropriate in one situation, may be best in another. This will be clear from the following review, which is designed to indicate the advantages and shortcomings of alternative congestion control policies and their applications.

We distinguish four kinds of congestion control policies: (1) hardware methods; (2) fixed time charges; (3) tolls; and (4) gasoline taxes.

3.1   Hardware Methods

A wide range of hardware methods have been experimented with, primarily by the Road Research Laboratory in England. Much of the theoretical investigation has been in the framework of network congestion, but it has not yet been applied to any existing transport network. Hardware methods have been used in some route congestion situations, and it is to be expected that this will be their primary area of application in future. There are essentially two kinds of hardware method—attaching the hardware to the vehicle and attaching it to fixed points. We consider these in turn.

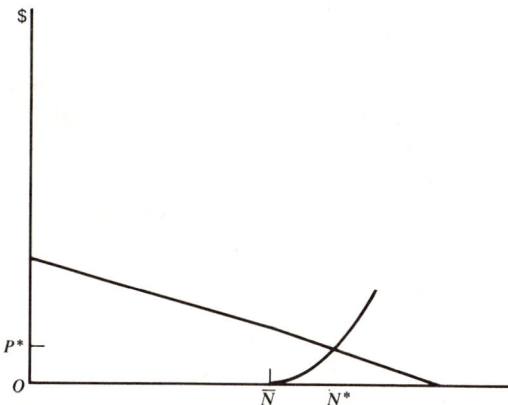

Figure 16.10   Total demand for landing slots at airport.

3.1.1 *Hardware on Vehicle*

In this approach a signal-originating device is installed on the way and a tabulating device in the vehicle. There are numerous problems here.

1. Readout may be costly in terms of time and/or money, and annoyance, which would encourage infrequent readings. But with annual readings, for example, the time of payment may be too far removed from the act of congestion and it may not provide a sufficient disincentive to congest. Moreover, the principle of having people pay after the damage has already been done (damage in which there are no lasting effects) is questionable to many observers, who would view this as an undesirable income distribution. These arguments may or may not be valid—after all, electric power, too, is paid for after it has been used, often a considerable time later.

2. Only the vehicles under the jurisdiction of the control authority would be affected. This obviously is a problem of varying importance. In London, with most of the traffic originating locally, the problem would probably not be severe. In cities with multiple jurisdictions, such as the Washington D.C. area, heavy suburban-downtown traffic and many transiting vehicles this approach would fail to catch many of the vehicles contributing to the congestion.

3. The device is subject to damage, requiring various amounts of supervision. A system of legal penalties might reduce the damage to tolerable levels.

4. Sensing devices would be required in the streets—all streets. If they were installed only on the main arteries, which are the areas where the greatest congestion is actually observed, to start with, traffic would be redistributed in other areas of a network causing congestion there as well. Obviously, a careful traffic flow modal would have to be constructed, estimates of the probable reactions to imposed congestion prices would have to be studied, and the redistribution of drivers to other streets, which would now also have to be controlled, would need to be determined to arrive at the optimal system of congestion charges. This is an extremely difficult task.

Moreover, the system would have to allow for time-variable charges. In some cities, there may be no congestion at all after peak hours, while in others social and business patterns may involve a steady high traffic density throughout the day. For example, in cities with a deep-rooted custom of returning home for lunch high traffic density is observed throughout the day. When traffic density varies, however, a way would have to be found to program the signal-transmitting devices, lowering the charges or turning the signals off at certain hours of the day. If this cannot be done, the policymaker must still consider the possibility that the welfare loss involved in having the same congestion charges imposed around the clock will be smaller than the welfare loss involved by having no congestion control devices at all. Similar judgments must be made for all the congestion control policies.

3.1.2 *Hardware Attached to Fixed Point*

In this approach, the tabulating device is at the fixed point, and the signal transmitting device is on the vehicle. This approach has many of the same problems as in the vehicle-attached hardware approach.

1. The approach requires that bills be mailed periodically to the licensee. There may be problems in collection. On the other hand, since the collection costs are lower, collection can take place more frequently, avoiding some of the problems alluded to earlier.

2. The same jurisdictional difficulties would exist as in the case of vehicle-attached hardware.

3. The approach is insensitive to time-variable congestion unless the computer is programmed to vary its charges.

4. The same problems would arise for network congestion optimization as before. Where nodal congestion is a problem, however, as in bridge toll collections, this may be an excellent approach. Such a system would allow motor vehicles to drive right through, set off a computer-recorded signal, and pay periodically. It can be applied to good advantage to all commuting traffic entering the city or any traffic that frequently uses a given facility, such as trucks traveling a regular route. Moreover, since the computer can be programmed to record differentiated charges for different vehicles, it can serve well to reduce the congestion that follows at lines which are set up to collect charges being imposed for other purposes, such as those imposed for use of the bridge itself (administration, maintenance, amortization). It could conceivably also be used merely to regulate route congestion, rather than to recover facility operating costs themselves. Such a facility could be set up on a limited-access expressway where a large proportion of users are regular users, such as the J.F.K. expressway between Baltimore and Philadelphia.

3.2   Fixed Time Charges

The general problem in the use of fixed time charges to control congestion is that the charge may be completely unrelated to the congestion
imposed—it may not get at either the distance or the time aspects of use
associated with congestion. We consider three kinds of time charges—
parking fees, annual fees, and short-term use fees.

3.2.1   *Parking Fees*

These may be either flat rate or variable. They have many problems
from the viewpoint of congestion optimization, most of them related to
the method of collection.

One problem concerns the way in which the parking charges are
imposed. Let us review briefly the general difficulties that all parking
fees must cope with. First of all, parking activity is not clearly related
to congestion imposed. Someone parking the car for the longest time
may impose the smallest congestion—a person arriving at work at 7
a.m. and leaving at 3 p.m., for example, will avoid the peak hours but,
if charged by the hour, will pay more than a person traveling during the
peak hours. Moreover, parking congestion charges that are set in a
blanket manner—say as a percentage surcharge to parking fees—would
discriminate only roughly between congested and noncongested areas of
a city, with the result that a person's fee will again be inadequately
related to the congestion that he imposes. Finally, some persons will
park their vehicles in town and use them only on weekends, again
imposing little congestion on the city during the peak user hours. But let
us consider the implications of this procedure a little more closely.

Congestion would be most easily optimized if all the parking facilities
were under the control of the single authority. This includes parking
lots, in-building parking facilities, increasingly included in new designs,
private residential on-street parking, parking in private garages, and
parking on public streets other than by local residents. Most of these
facilities lie beyond the area of jurisdiction of the city. If the city
imposes parking fees on its own lot or meters, many drivers will be
diverted to private lots. The answer is somehow to levy charges also on
private parking facilities, say by an annual real estate tax or an annual
fee per parking slot in private buildings. This would still leave private
homes. This problem will vary in importance between such cities as
Toronto, which has many private single-family residences in town, and
such urban centers as Manhattan, which has few.

Regarding the administration of the parking charge on off-street facilities, it would probably be best to impose it by way of an annual levy on the facility owners and allow them to discriminate among their users to recover this fee by a system of parking surcharges. They could charge relatively more to the drivers during peak hours if their demand were more inelastic than that of the off-peak users. However, such a blanket system of charges will also involve private garages, and since many of these car owners will not be using their vehicles during the regular working hours, an undesirable income transfer or price distortion will take place. There will be a welfare shortfall. The severity of the problem, obviously, will vary and must be considered carefully in any given situation.

3.2.2 Annual Fees

In this approach each user will be charged an annual fee beyond the other fees that he customarily pays to register his car in the district. This would constitute, in effect, an additional price that a person must pay to live in this city. It is essentially a long-term approach to the control of congestion rather than a short-term device. Discouraging newcomers or acquisition of second cars reduces the long-term growth in the congestion-generating activity.

This is undoubtedly a good approach to coping with the long-term problem. We know that it does not alleviate the problem of those already living in the city, except insofar as acquisition of second cars is concerned. It also tends to encourage residence right outside the jurisdiction of the city—in terms of Figure 14.2 it raises the residential measure and increases the amount that people are willing to pay for any particular trip. Even if there are no changes in residential patterns immediately (although there is a reduction in the rate of growth), if people within the city's jurisdiction do sell cars because of the high annual fee involved in keeping them, additional traffic will start to enter from the suburbs once the traffic originating locally is reduced.

Finally, in some cities, it may be possible for a person to avoid the annual fee altogether by registering his car somewhere else. In Venezuela, for example, it is a common practice to register cars in counties with lower license fees than in Caracas, a practice encouraged by the authorities in the communities of registration.

3.2.3 Short-Term Fees

The usual way to apply short-term fees is through some kind of sticker or coupon. For example, a dated coupon entering a slip pocket on the windscreen or a sticker fastened to the windscreen. The latter is self-destructive, but entails a periodic large cleaning job. It has the advantage that a series of stickers can be bought, with one used each day or each week. The display window requires some way of differentiating the date from month to month, which in turn implies a different series of tags each month. Either approach has high supervision costs. Moreover, if police are dishonest it is easy to get around this control device.

A monthly system is superior to a daily system, since it provides more times for catching a violator who does not buy and display the monthly tag or sticker. Any tag or sticker system will have higher payment costs (including consumer inconvenience) than the hardware-related billing system.

3.3 Tolls

Tolls best serve as a route rather than network congestion optimization device. Thus they work best on a bridge, where they can be turned off during off-peak hours (i.e., the congestion-related toll can be set equal to zero, but this need *not* imply anything about the facility-cost charge itself). On long expressways, tolls have certain problems as congestion-control devices. For example, someone getting on the New York State Thruway near Syracuse at 3 p.m. and driving to Lackawanna at 8 p.m. would pass through the entrance control gates at off-peak hours, although he would go through the most congested part of the highway, around Buffalo, at the peak. It would require a complicated program to determine the correct congestion charge at the exit gate, although this is not an insurmountable problem. Here, as in the general network case of cities, one must also consider the effect of the congestion charge on traffic congestion in other routes that were not originally being congestion priced.

3.4 Fuel Charges

Fuel charges have many advantages as congestion-control devices, although they also have many shortcomings. Probably more than the other devices, fuel taxes are subject to the geophysical and institutional environment, their suitability varying accordingly. We here list the advantages and disadvantages and point out the special source of inapplicability under certain conditions.

1. Fuel consumption varies with mileage, which in a network is more closely related to the congestion imposition than is a one-time charge.

However, it is far from perfect in this regard. It also varies, although imperfectly, with vehicle size, which is related to imposed congestion—a 20-ton truck will generate more congestion than a small car, although the congestion that it imposes is probably disproportionately more than the fuel consumed, given the problems of passing and poor visibility to which it leads. On the other hand, there will be a welfare shortfall from the fact that two automobiles of the same volume but having eight and six cylinders, respectively, would pay different amounts in fuel taxes, although they would affect congestion in the same way.

2. If the congestion charges are high, gas fetching will be encouraged. This feature probably conditions the almost automatically negative reaction of most people to the notion of using fuel taxes as the congestion-control device. People will fill up in the suburbs, and, indeed, the suburbs will compete with one another to maximize their fuel tax revenues, subject to certain profit maximization goals of service station owners. Thus wherever there are numerous jurisdictions, as in most large cities in North America, a fuel tax as congestion device would probably not be successful. However, one should be careful not to confuse the lesson that one might infer for Washington (a multi-jurisdiction complex) with the rule *for* the multijurisdictional New York area. In New York, the cost and bother for an in-town resident to drive to the suburbs to fill up would be so high as to discourage this practice, while in Washington it need not be. It must be left for empirical verification to determine whether the traffic originating in the suburbs is large enough to continue to cause tremendous congestion if a tax in the city succeeds in reducing the locally originating congestion.

On the other hand, in some cities gas fetching will be no problem at all. Caracas, for example, has very few surrounding communities, so that anyone in the Caracas area would have to buy almost all of his fuel under the jurisdiction of the city, which consists of three local governments, that is, everyone would be caught. Thus while it might not work in some cities, in others it might be the best or, to remind ourselves of the essential characteristic of congestion control, it might be the least undesirable of all the congestion-control policies.

3. Another objection to fuel taxes as a congestion-control device is that fuel consumption may not reflect congestion. Approximately the same amount of fuel is consumed at 10 p.m. as at 9 a.m. (consumption is a little higher at 9 a.m. because of the slower speeds imposed by the congestion but this would probably not be enough to generate the required congestion charge). Moreover, even in a city under a single jurisdiction there will be areas of zero congestion and we should not impose a congestion charge here since this would constitute a local price

distortion. Nevertheless, these problems may again be inconsequential, depending on the particular institutional and geophysical setting. For example, in Rio de Janeiro the congestion effects are undoubtedly much more uniform throughout the city than in Baghdad where the vehicle density is much lower because the numerator (the number of vehicles) is smaller and the denominator (area) is much larger, there being few geophysical obstacles to the city's expansion.

3.5 Conclusion; Use of Congestion Revenues

This brief summary of the features of the main kinds of congestion-control device shows us that no simple and uniform approach to congestion is possible. Almost certainly, no congestion control device will ever permit us to achieve optimal congestion. The analyst must tailor the choice of control to the kind of congestion and to the social, institutional, and geophysical factors present. The analyst must recognize that in some cases doing nothing or imposing administrative controls may be the best solution.

If a price-oriented congestion-control device is employed, the question arises what should be done with the generated revenues. Two approaches are possible here. Assuming that the city is self-sustaining financially—the economy's public finance structure contains no interregional *allocation-related* transfers and the only transfers made are income-distribution transfers—this money should go into the city's budget and be used for any amenities decided on by the city organization. It would not be theoretically justified to impose any restriction on the use of this budget. All projects should compete on an equal footing. In practice, the imposition of congestion-optimization charges would probably be followed by strong demands for various public transit facilities. By definition, optimal congestion charges (and if any congestion charge is imposed it must be one that helps the city to get *closer* to the optimum) will divert a lot of traffic from private automobile channels into the market for public transit. It does not automatically follow that the servicing of this demand represents the best use of funds generated within the city. But we can presume that if there was near-equilibrium before, the new demand will raise the economic welfare generated by investment in public transit. It any event, the important thing is that these funds should be used to service local needs.

If, on the other hand, the economy has many interregional allocation-related transfers, the use of the funds should not be restricted to local objectives. We are then closer to the position shown in Chapter 3, in which the congestion effects were the source of rising marginal costs. We can think of the city as being one of the technologies in Figure 3.5. For each "size of plant" (read, "city") we have equilibrium between demand and short-run marginal cost, where short-run marginal cost includes the congestion cost. When any city reaches this equilibrium, the "master allocator" takes the funds generated and uses them to build a new city, which should accommodate new population, which is thus diverted from the migration flow moving to the old city. The congestion charges are maintained in the old city in order to keep it in equilibrium. If growth of cities is rapid, congestion charges should be imposed immediately in the new city as well, in conformity with the analysis of Chapter 3, with the revenue contributed toward the undertaking of a third "plant" (city). If growth is slow because of low migration and/or birthrates, congestion changes may be neglected in the new city to start with.

REFERENCES

Abouchar, Alan (1970), "Air Transport Demand, Congestion Costs, and the Theory of Optimal Airport Use," *Canadian Journal of Economics,* Vol. 3, No. 3, August.

Walters, Alan A. (1961), "The Theory and Measurement of Private and Social Costs of Highway Congestion," *Econometrica,* Vol. 29.

17

Decision Rules for
Urban Projects and
the Interpretation
of Property Value Change

1 FIVE APPROACHES TO URBAN PROJECT DECISION-MAKING

In this chapter we examine the various approaches to major urban project decisions through the example of subway construction in Metro Toronto. Most of the considerations also apply to expressways, shopping malls, and even zoning regulations. They apply, of course, to most cities and city complexes.

We can distinguish essentially five kinds of criterion for deciding whether to build a subway. The criteria vary significantly in their complexity, information requirements, logical acceptability, and institutional relevance, as will be apparent.

1. Growth in assessed valuation.

2. Engineering-administrative design rules.

3. Welfare criteria.

4. Popular referendum.

5. Private enterprise profit maximization.

Section 1 describes these decision criteria and their suitability. Section 2 follows a welfare approach to analyze the new Toronto subway line and concludes that there is insufficient evidence of welfare gain to external groups to justify interregional transfers. This conclusion calls into question the present provincial practice of contributing 75% of the construction cost of subways and urban expressways and sometimes a part of the operating costs as well. Increasing pressures for such policies at the federal level in Canada and the United States are, therefore, to be resisted all the more, although personal political forces are often at work promoting them.

1.1 Growth in Assessed Valuation

The increase in property assessment that is observed to follow the construction of subway lines has often been pointed to as sufficient justification for their construction. The following statement by a former president of the Toronto Real Estate Board from recent Toronto experience is typical of this thinking (Heenan, 1966):

> If an urban rapid transit system never earned an operating profit it would still pay for itself a thousand times over through its beneficial impact on real estate values and increased assessments.

> Rapid transit creates and enhances property values like nothing else on earth. The greatest cities in the world have that essential common facility— an efficient rapid transit complex.

Such statements can be interpreted in two ways, neither of which provides sufficient justification for undertaking a subway. We consider them in turn.

1. The writers equate growth in assessment (which in this case presumably reflects rising market values) with increases in welfare. This neglects the very serious possibility that there will be offsets in market values reflecting lower welfare contribution by property outside the

subway corridor. The fact that in practice we do not usually observe offsetting declines results from the overall upward move of land prices and/or general inflationary trends. This really means that land prices would have risen anyway, but that the construction of the subway shifts the increases that would have taken place elsewhere into the subway corridor.

2. The writers are thinking primarily of the increase in tax revenues that will follow from increased assessments (this assumes that there is an overall increase in assessment—because of the land pressures and general inflationary drift the total assessment does rise but the assessment base in the subway corridor rises faster). It is a very narrow view to consider higher property tax revenue as a measure of success—the public sector must be concerned with optimization of total resource use rather than with enlargement of the role that the bureaucracy can play in the economy.

1.2   Engineering-Administrative Design Rules

One could conceive of subway construction taking place in much the same way as expansion of water mains, sewer systems, and power grids. Rough physical coefficients are worked out relating variables such as population density and area to kilometers of subway line, adding or extending old lines to accompany the extension of the city, emplacing circumferentials after certain critical size is reached, and so on. Just as one would add conveyor systems in a plant as the plant grows and becomes more complex, so would subway lines be added following the prescribed engineering-administrative decision rules.

Such an approach cannot, of course, hope to reach an overall economic welfare optimum except by chance, since it does not attempt to deal with any kind of welfare optimand. On the other hand, the other urban systems mentioned above—water supply, sewer systems, power delivery—also cannot be thought of as being optimal except by accident. A water-delivery system, for example, might minimize the water-delivery cost for a given residential and land-use pattern, but there is no guarantee that different use patterns would not have been still better. Water-delivery costs would be lower with the higher population densities of high-rise areas than with single-unit dwellings, but the latter may be a preferred land-use pattern. One can define an *optimal* water-supply system only by reference to the optimal land-use pattern; that is, a water-supply system is optimal when it gives the lowest water-supply cost under the *optimal* land-use pattern. The same holds for subways. One could always figure the cheapest way to deliver people for given origins and destination, but there is no guarantee that higher welfare would not follow from an alternative location or land-use plan.

Since we knowingly live with so many services whose optimality we can never hope to establish, however, it may not be too much to suggest that one more be added to the list, requiring only that it be done in a seemingly reasonable way. However, the unrestrained use of the passenger automobile constitutes a serious obstacle. In Moscow, modular subway construction works because people can be relied upon to use the subway (along with surface public transit). In the absence of private cars there is little alternative for city planners but to treat subway connections in the same way as other urban services, and simply provide for a subway to plug into the main network when a new suburb is assimilated or an inner area reaches certain densities.

In a modern Western city it would be difficult to follow this engineering-administrative design approach of automatically building subway links to accommodate certain densities or areas (unless extremely high levels were adopted as the critical decision densities). The reason is that there would generally not be expected to be enough riders, most commuters still preferring to travel by their own cars. If passenger cars were banned from downtown, this approach would probably be acceptable. If this idea does catch hold, the engineering-administrative design approach should be reasonable.

According to the reasoning in Part 3, we should use national income change as a welfare measure in public projects. But it is difficult, for most urban projects, to calculate the national income change in a way consistent with calculations for manufacturing activities or even highway projects, where cost reduction may frequently be employed. To be sure, since the city is usually an area of full or comparatively full employment, cost reduction might be suggested as a proxy for national income generation. Even this is difficult to measure on a basis consistent with highway cost reduction, however, because in relation to its frame of reference (the local economy of the city) the subway construction constitutes a much larger change than does the highway improvement in relation to its frame of reference. This relative size difference makes the interactions between the project and the city—migration, indirect nonmarket activities, and so on—relatively much larger than those between the highway and its region and present an insurmountable obstacle. The analysis of the national income index number problem and the problems of constructing a behavioral model and its welfare interpretation for the airport analysis of Chapter 16 are relevant here.

Moreover, many writers argue that a national income criterion would in any event be too limited precisely because some of the nonmarket activities are left completely out of account. For example, personal time savings are omitted, not to speak of activities that may not depend on the subway in any direct way. For example the more densely populated subway corridor would contain more amenities such as movies and restaurants, reducing their access time. Many trips would be made by foot. This would not show up at all in the measured transport resource saving. Some people might simply enjoy the feel of living in a busy corridor more than the relaxed pace outside the subway area, and again this welfare improvement would escape detection as long as we concentrated only on transport-resource savings. However, these welfare components should show up in form of higher housing rents (and profits to property management and development companies) and higher land values.

2 THE REAL ESTATE MARKET AND WELFARE CRITERIA

The resource-saving criterion attempts to measure welfare change by measuring the savings in resources consumed in transportation, making proper allowance for the fact that some of the transport demands arise only after the subway is built. But, as we saw, it may neglect some benefits entirely. Moreover, in the absence of agreement on the valuation of components such as time, differentiated by use, conclusions regarding a project may vary very widely. However, the flow of benefits from the subway should show up in the movement of property values— land and structures—whose prices either directly reflect the benefits to final purchaser-consumers as they themselves view them or represent the capitalized economic rent of developers. The various aspects of welfare change that can in principle be measured through the real estate market, broadly defined to include the business of all real estate participants—land developers, management companies, speculators, homeowners, and others—should be reflected essentially in two variables:

1. Real estate prices.

2. Profits of property management and development companies.*

* Property management and development companies include subsidiary firms designed for these purposes belonging to larger firms whose main activity is in other lines such as banking or manufacturing.

Unfortunately, however, these variables are also affected by factors that have no bearing on welfare, such as inflation, population growth, and rural-urban migration. These influences complicate the analysis of the property value effects that follow from the execution of any large urban investment. They create problems for the measurement of welfare change after the fact, of course, and by doing so they also create problems for preproject investment analysis and for the financing of the project. The preproject problems arise because it is only through past experience elsewhere that we can hope to develop coefficients or average values to weight many of the welfare effects in question. And in order to apportion the cost of the investment according to beneficiary groups it is necessary that they be identified.

To illustrate the difficulties, let us consider the problem of interpreting the inflation component. Suppose that the real estate rental index is found to be rising annually at 7% and the consumer price index at 4%. The extra three points *might* represent the excess demand exerted by a shifting and growing population on a fixed supply of real estate. On the other hand, the excess might also represent a quality change due, for example, to the provision of better water or sewer facilities, whose cost is included in the landlord's annual property tax and passed along through the tenant's rent. The welfare implications in the latter case (quality change) are, of course, greater than in the former.

Any one or all of the following influences on property values may accompany the construction of a subway:

1. Pure inflationary price increases of the kind that would follow from simple expansion of the money supply or changes in velocity (R_1).

2. Price increases due to the increased demand for urban land caused by total population growth (R_2).

3. Price increases resulting from the increased demand for urban land following from urban-rural migration (R_3) in the nation as a whole.

4. Price increases due to the greater increase in demand for land in this city resulting from the construction of the subway (R_4).

5. Simple increases in subway corridor property values reflecting the shift in demand for property elsewhere in the city to the area in the subway corridor. This will happen to the extent that users' demand prices, on the average, exceed the price paid to ride the subway (R_5).

6. Increases in property values arising in the shift in demand for other goods, services, and savings to demand for property along the subway

(R_6). For example, some automobile demand will be exchanged for increased property demand as people become more city oriented in their entertainment preferences. Some people may simply derive a greater satisfaction from the faster pace in the denser corridor associated with the subway, and increase their budget allotment for rent, reducing their savings, or diverting their demand from other goods and services.

7. A net increase in welfare through reductions in commuting time. Reductions in commuting time will be directly beneficial to commuters and may also lead to higher labor productivity. The latter is likely to be small; part of it will show up in the form of higher wages, of which part will be internalized into payments for housing in the form of land value appreciation (R_7).

8. Or it may appear as rents and profits to landlords (R_8).

9. The value to the commuter of reduced commuting time will be internalized in land values (R_9).

10. Or it may appear as extra profits to landlords (R_{10}).

11. Commutation materials cost reductions. Part of these savings will be internalized in property value appreciation (R_{11}).

12. Or it may appear as rents and profits to landlords (R_{12}).

13. Cost-based property value increases (R_{13}). House prices will rise in any time period if many improvements are undertaken in the house. Better maintained houses will, all things being equal, rise more (or fall less) in price than houses that are allowed to decay. If houses in the subway corridor are allowed to decay in anticipation of future zoning changes, this will introduce a negative increase in the house price.

Items 1 to 3 in this list have no welfare significance. Items 4 to 12 are relevant to welfare evaluation. (Item 13 is ambiguous.) They are not additive to materials and time cost reductions, however. To some extent they are substitutes for the capitalized (discounted) flow of market-measurable benefits—reduced consumer commuting costs, developer profits—and to some extent they reflect the future flow of nonmeasurable benefits, not necessarily discounted, such as R_6. Nor are they directly additive among themselves, since some represent flows (e.g. R_{12}) and others changes in stock values. A full-scale study would require that the individual components of value change and profit change be isolated and measured. Because of the limited reporting of profit information (a real estate firm need not report separately the relevant profits), we could not hope to isolate the profit change components. Nor can we quantify the total differential property value change in the corridor, not to speak of the individual components. Nevertheless, if these are to be large, the corridor value changes must be greater than those outside. That is, we could at least make an ordinal determination even if not a cardinal measurement. If we find no influence of the subway on property value dynamics, we would have to conclude that the welfare gains, whatever the source, are all internalized in profits or are nonexistent. Of these gains, the only ones that could justifiably be placed on the same footing with benefits measured elsewhere to compete for centrally allocated investment resources would be those that lead to a reduction in costs or increases in productivity, that is, R_7 or R_8. To evaluate others about which confidentiality of profits information fails to provide information would require a local referendum. In the exceptional circumstances of existence of nonlocal externalities, an interregional transfer may be justified. Sections 3 and 4 attempt to perform this analysis for the new Metro Toronto subway.

3   ANALYSIS OF PROPERTY VALUE CHANGES IN METRO TORONTO—1965-1972

In this section we study the dynamics of Metro Toronto property values since 1965. The data used are house sales statistics compiled by the Toronto Real Estate Board. We start with a brief description of the data and of its possible biases. Following this we explain the analytical methods employed and then summarize the results.

3.1   Description of Data

The Toronto Real Estate Board (TREB) has published since 1967 an annual survey entitled *House Price Trends and Residential Construction Costs in Metropolitan Toronto and Canada.* This publication gives the annual average house selling price for houses sold by the Multiple Listing Service in 44 districts. Thirty-eight of these districts are located within Metro Toronto. There has been no change of definition of these districts since the start of the series. The districts are shown in Figure 17.1.

The number of houses sold through MLS and included in the tabulation has grown from 13,428 in 1966 to 14,613 in 1972, with total value

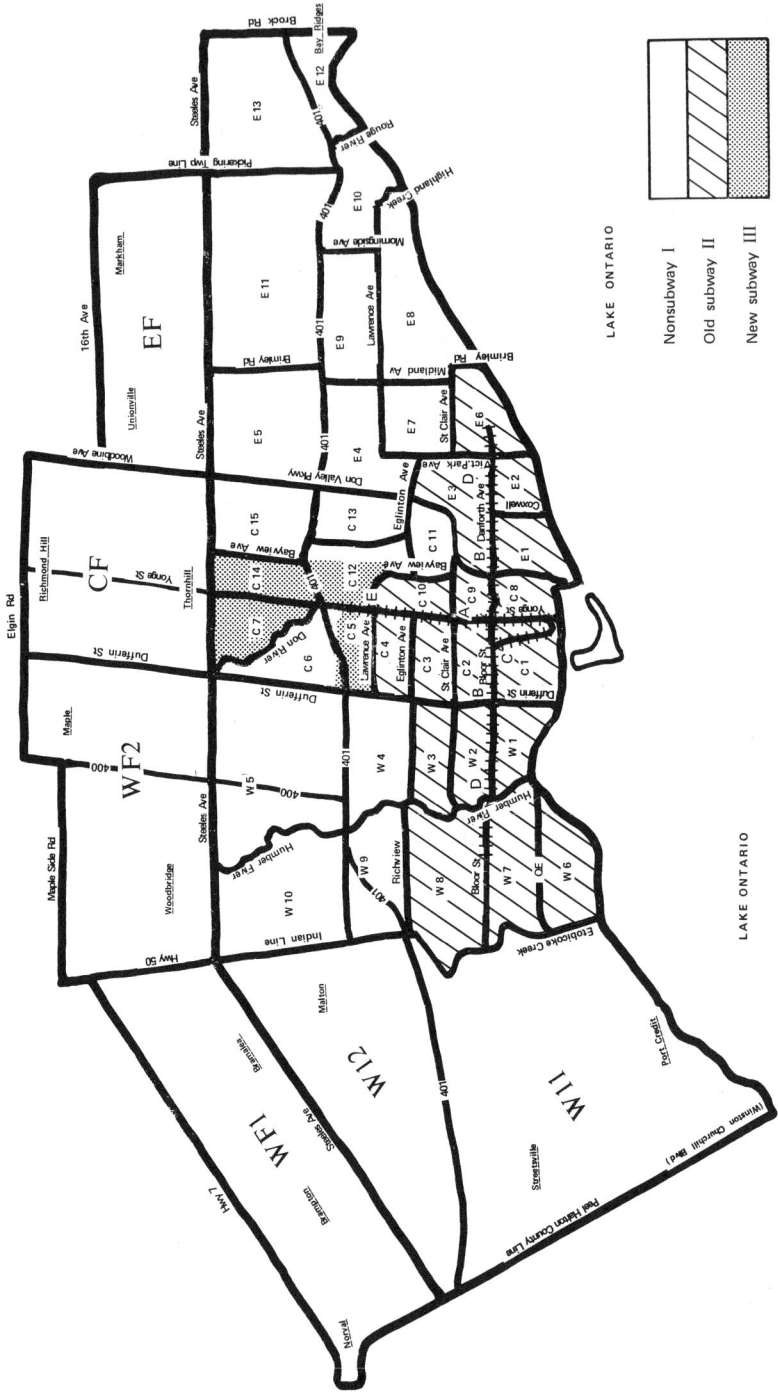

Figure 17.1 MLS reporting districts, with subway and study subareas.

Nonsubway I
Old subway II
New subway III

LAKE ONTARIO

rising from \$286.8 million to \$475.1 million. The MLS sales volume has grown from 26% of total Metro sales to 48% over the period, having reached 56% in 1971. (Toronto Real Estate Board, 1973, p. 44). This is shown in Table 17.1. The number of houses sold in each district seems to be reliably large, rarely falling under 100 (only 3 of the 38 districts in 1972 contained fewer than 100 observations), and ranging as high as 941, with an average around 300.

The most important possible bias in the data is that the total MLS share of sales in each district may vary in a nonrandom manner. For example, it has sometimes been argued that MLS sales fall off relatively in strong markets. This should affect all areas more or less similarly, unless some districts have shown particular sellers' strength, which is, of course, the objective of the study.

It is not possible to test whether the corridor districts exhibit a MLS/ total sales ratio different from those in the other districts because the total sales figures are not published by district. But Table 17.1 suggests that there may be a basis for the hypothesis that MLS is relatively less important in a strong sellers' market. In 1970 there was a decline in MLS sales in a strong market (there was an average price rise of 5% and a 5% increase in volume). The only other year of increasing total dollar volume is 1972 when there was a 13% increase in MLS sales, but a much larger increase in non-MLS sales—two-thirds. By looking at a number of different intertemporal comparisons, we should avoid the

Table 17.1 MLS Sales as a Percentage of Total Sales in Metro Toronto

	Total Metro House Sales			MLS House Sales			As a Percentage of Total Metro House Sales
	Dollar Volume	Units	Average Price	Dollar Volume	Units	Average Price	
1966	\$1,096,306,168	41,907	\$26,160	\$286,819,451	13,428	\$21,359	26%
1967	1,040,412,912	36,870	28,218	299,339,508	12,432	24,078	28%
1968	1,045,017,320	34,600	30,203	327,344,133	12,245	26,732	31%
1969	839,048,842	28,272	29,678	361,440,994	12,494	28,929	43%
1970	883,897,914	28,401	31,122	309,608,423	10,498	29,492	35%
1971	699,260,754	22,265	31,406	398,131,010	13,085	30,426	56%
1972	979,671,282	29,873	32,794	475,114,987	14,613	32,513	48%

Source. Toronto Real Estate Board, 1973, p. 44.

possible bias that might arise in these years. This does not solve the problem of individual districts responding differently; that is, some districts may have a smaller relative share of MLS sales than others. We would then expect these districts to show the same pattern over the entire period, however, so that the observed year-to-year change should be an unbiased measure of the true change (or, at worst, biased to the same extent and in the same direction as in other districts).

The foregoing considerations suggest that the MLS/non-MLS sales ratio should not bias the outcome of the experiment.

3.2 Plan of Statistical Study

3.2.1 *Objective*

The objective of the study is to determine whether the Toronto subways have an impact on real estate values in the subway corridors. To determine this we must devise a way to separate the effect of the subway from all other effects on land values. It is believed that this objective is largely realized by looking at the year-to-year relative percentage changes in property values in and out of the subway corridors. This amounts to assuming that all of Metro responds to the same basic forces of inflation, urban migration, and overall population growth. Relative differences among districts then reflect district-specific features.

3.2.2 *House Selling Prices as Measures of Property Values*

As a measure of property values, the study relies on house selling prices. These are only a subsection of property values in any district. Excluded are multiunit dwellings, commercial buildings, and industrial properties, as well as houses that are not sold (and those sold by non-MLS channels.) The possible bias originating in the third source has already been discussed and assessed to be negligible. There also seems no reason to expect any bias to be introduced by using observed sales prices in the district to measure the values of all houses in the district. As indicated above (Section 3.1), a large number of houses were sold in all districts, and there is no reason to expect these sales not to reflect competitive conditions. If many owners are holding their houses off the market in anticipation of price rises, obviously they value their houses (because of the future price rise) very much, which should be reflected in a limited supply, which forces up the price. In this case the higher price would reflect the high value set on the properties in the district.

Similarly, there would seem to be no reason to expect the selling prices to be higher than the values set on their houses by nonselling owners. If market prices were higher, these owners would be expected to sell, that is, to increase supply and reduce the selling prices.

The use of house selling prices as a proxy for the value of other kinds of real estate is more complex. There are really two possible kinds of bias: (1) house price movements may fail to reflect multiunit and commercial building (MU&CB) selling prices, and (2) even if they do, MU&CB prices may fail to reflect changes in welfare. We consider these in turn.

If a developer buys properties as part of a land assembly for a multiunit commercial development, the prices he will be willing to pay will depend on the values of similar properties now existing in the district. These in turn will derive their value from their earnings potential. Increases in the values of existing MU&CB properties should raise the ceiling on what the developer will pay to purchase properties in a tract. The purchase price for all the properties in the tract need not increase by the full amount of the increase in value of the existing buildings, but it is more than likely that the purchase price will rise.

As to deviations between MC&UB values and welfare, MC&UB values do not tell us all what we need to know to estimate the welfare effects of subways. The most important item that they leave out of account is the profit of real estate firms—developers and property managers—which arises because of the demand shifts accompanying the subway (R_8, R_{10}, and R_{12}). In addition, part of R_6 may be channeled into profits rather than into property values. To the extent that real estate firms are able to take their profits in the form of rents rather than capital gains, and can do so quietly, the market will be unable to translate the welfare gain into the value of the MC&UB properties (hence into changes in house selling prices.) The analysis must therefore allow for this item in reaching policy conclusions about subway construction and financing.

3.2.3 Summary of Subway Construction in Metro Toronto

Important dates in the development of the five subway sections in Metro are shown in Table 17.2. The subways are shown in Figure 12.1, which also contains the districts used by the TREB.

Two kinds of comparison are of interest for the study. First, before-and-after comparisons between subway and nonsubway areas are important to give an indication of the total subway impact on property values. This is especially important if the changes are once-for-all read-

**Table 17.2   Location, Start of Construction, and Opening Dates of
Five Subway Sections in Metro Toronto**

Location	Designation on Map	Start of Construction	Opening
Yonge Street	A	1949	April 1954
Bloor Street (Keele-Woodbine)	B	Early 1962	1967
University Avenue	C	Fall 1959	February 1963
Bloor Street (east and west extensions)	D	OMB approval 1964	1967
Yonge Street extension	E	March 1967	March 1973 (to York Mills)

Source. Toronto Transit Commission, *Annual Report,* various. years.

justments in relative property values. On the other hand, it is also of
interest to determine whether there are differences in the rate of change
of property values in and out of the corridor. Both kinds of comparison
can be made with the Metro Toronto data.

Construction of all subway sections except the Yonge Street extension
was started before 1965, the first year of the TREB house price tabula-
tions. This restricts us to comparisons between the nonsubway area and
the Yonge Street extension for purposes of before-and-after analysis.
However, the areas of all the subway sections can be used for inferences
concerning changes in the rate of price change. Accordingly, Metro
Toronto was divided into three areas: I, the nonsubway area; II, the old
subway area that includes the first Yonge Street line (A) with the
University Avenue extension (C) and the Bloor Street line (B and D);
and III, the new subway area of the Yonge Street extension (E). The
TREB districts are allocated to these areas as shown in Table 17.3.*

For most districts there was little difficulty in determining what
study area the district should be assigned to. The chief problems were
presented by C4 (north of Eglinton, west of Yonge) which was in the
new subway corridor. This district is at the end of the old Yonge Street
line. Since in other cases where TREB districts included the areas
beyond the subway termination points the districts were counted as
part of the subway study area, it was decided to put C5 in the old

* The fringe districts outside of the municipal boundaries of Metro (WF, CF, and EF)
were not included in the study.

subway study area (II) rather than in the new area (III). Similar reasoning was applied to C10, which overlapped into the new subway area.

3.2.4 *Statistical Design*

1. *Rates of price change.* To test whether price dynamics were different
in and out of the subway areas, the district price rises in the three study
areas over different time periods were studied by analysis of variance.
The time periods considered were the following:

(*a*) 1965–1970.
(*b*) 1967–1972.
(*c*) 1967–1968.
(*d*) 1968–1969.
(*e*) 1970–1971.
(*f*) 1971–1972.

Table 17.3   Correspondence between TREB Districts and
Study Areas

	Study Area	
I Nonsubway	II Old Subway (Yonge Street, University Avenue, and Bloor Street)	III New Subway (Yonge Street extension)
W4	E1	C5
W5	E2	C7
W9	E3	C12
W10	E6	C14
E4	W1	
E5	W2	
E7	W3	
E8	W6	
E9	W7	
E10	W8	
E11	C1	
C6	C2	
C11	C3	
C13	C4	
C15	C8	
	C9	
	C10	

The following notation will serve for each time comparison:

P_{ijT} = the average selling price recorded in district j of study area i in the later year of the comparison under investigation (i = I, II, III; j = 1, 2, ..., J_i)

P_{ijt} = the average selling price recorded in district j of study area i in the earlier year of the comparison

Denote

$$\frac{P_{ijT} - P_{ijt}}{P_{ijt}} = \frac{\Delta_{ijTt}}{P_{ijt}} = Z_{ij}$$

and

$$Z_i = \sum_{j=1}^{J_i} Z_{ij} \, n_{ij} / N_i$$

The rates of change Z_{ij} are random variables consisting of a study area component and a random component that is assumed to be unrelated to the study area or to other districts in the study area. That is, we assume that

$$Z_{ij} = \beta_i + e_{ij}$$

where e_{ij} are independently normally distributed with zero mean and have constant variance.

We wish to test whether the existence and/or the inception of the subway has any effect on the rates of price change, that is, whether price changes in districts in areas II and III behave differently from those in area I. The null hypothesis, under which the subways have no effect, may then be expressed as

$$H_0: \quad \beta_I = \beta_{II} = \beta_{III}$$

The hypothesis to be tested—that the subway does have an effect—replaces the first equality with inequality:

$$H': \quad \beta_I \neq \beta_{II} = \beta_{III}$$

2. *Once-for-all effects.* To test whether a significant rise in price could be attributed to the inception of a subway, we compared the price increases in the new subway area (III) with the price rises in the nonsubway area (I) for three time periods:

(a) 1965–1970.
(b) 1967–1972.
(c) 1971–1972.

The first two comparisons were chosen to test for significance of price change between the preconstruction period and years of advanced construction. It would also be desirable to test between preproject years and years immediately following, but data unavailability prevented this. Since 1972 was the eve of the opening, however, it seems reasonable to regard its prices as practically the same as would be expected in 1973. The third comparison—1971 and 1972—is one more attempt to measure the effect of the subway opening, to allow for the possibility that price increases might not show up in the early years of construction but only as the opening date drew close.

Using the same price notation as before, we wish to test for significant differences in the mean district price changes in study areas I and III.

3.3 Results

3.3.1 *Rates of Price Change*

The analysis of variance results are summarized in Table 17.4. No significant differences are ever found at the 1% significance level for any of the six time comparisons. At the 5% level there is only one significant difference in rate of price change (the 1965–1970 comparison) and that goes the wrong way—the average rate of price change in the nonsubway area (I) was significantly greater than that in the subway study areas (II and III).

The alternative hypothesis is that houses in subway areas show rates of price change different from those in areas without subways. There are two variations of this hypothesis: (1) having subways in the area leads to greater price increases, $(\beta_I < \beta_{II} = \beta_{III})$ and (2) having subways in the area leads to smaller price increases $(\beta_I > \beta_{II} = \beta_{III})$.

Table 17.4 Summary of Results of Analyses of Variance[a]

| | Average Percent Change in House Selling Price | | | | |
Time Interval	Area I	Area II	Area III	All Areas	$F_{2,33}$
1. 1965–1970	68.5	56.8	57.5	70.0	4.03
2. 1967–1972	38.6	31.0	37.0	35.5	1.89
3. 1967–1968	13.1	11.4	10.2	11.6	1.04
4. 1968–1969	8.6	7.6	7.8	8.1	0.32
5. 1970–1971	0.1	3.5	5.1	2.9	2.33
6. 1971–1972	11.8	7.6	11.0	10.1	1.51

[a] $F_{0.01,2,33} = 5.33$; $F_{0.05,2,33} = 3.29$.

Evidently, we cannot reject the null hypothesis in favor of the first variant of the alternative hypothesis—that subways cause greater price increases, since the increases in both subway study areas have been in all cases smaller than those in the nonsubway area.

For the second variant of the alternative hypothesis—that subways cause smaller price increases than occur in nonsubway zones—we would reject the null hypothesis at the 5% level one time out of the six experiments. This does not seem to be enough to reject the null hypothesis in general.

3.3.2 Once-for-All Effects

The results of the tests for significant difference between the mean relative price changes in areas I and III are shown in Table 17.5. Again, there were no statistically significant differences, even at the 5% level. And, again, relative price changes were in the wrong direction, that is, the nonsubway area (I) showed greater rates of price increase in all three cases than did the area in which the subway was built.

3.3.3 Interpretation of Results

The statistical experiments indicate that the subway had no differential impact on house selling prices within Metro. This is practically conclusive evidence about the subway construction effects on property values. There are two qualifications to unambiguous welfare interpretation thereof, however: (1) there may be different home maintenance and improvement patterns in and out of the subway areas that influence the rates of price change and (2) there may be differences in urbanization

Table 17.5   Results of Tests for Significant Differences between Averate Price Changes in Study Areas I and III

Time Interval	Average Percent Price Change		t
	Area I	Area III	
1965–1970	68.5	57.5	1.50
1967–1972	38.6	37.0	0.22
1971–1972	11.8	11.0	0.28

$t_{17, \alpha/2} + 2.110, \alpha = .05$

patterns between Toronto and other cities caused by the subway. We turn to these.

3.3.1.1 *Different Home Maintenance and Improvement Patterns*

While subway area house prices have risen more slowly than prices elsewhere, it is conceivable that they have risen faster in terms of non-land factor input, which would indicate a greater welfare contribution than would appear from the comparison of unadjusted house selling prices. To take 1967–1972 as an example, it was found that prices outside the subway area rise by 38.6%, compared to 31% in the old subway study area (II) and 37% in the new area (III). It is conceivable that homeowners in II and III put in much less in the way of maintenance and improvement, letting their homes run down in anticipation of eventual changes in land-use patterns with much more MU&CB construction. In this case the increase in subway area prices would be based more on shifting demand patterns than on house maintenance and repair costs than would be the case in the nonsubway area. A $1000 increase in the selling price of a $40,000 house in the nonsubway areas between 1969 and 1970 would reflect in part, this reasoning goes, the costs that the homeowner incurred in 1969 and in part the demand shift due to increased population pressure. Let us assume that the costs are $600. The same absolute and relative increase in the house in the subway area with no improvement would represent exclusively the shift in demand for subway area houses, reflecting in part increased population pressure and in part a shift in demand by city residents to more subway area housing. Potentially this represents a greater welfare than the increase in the nonsubway area. In the subway area there is an increase of $1000 in the demand price with no physical improvement in the house itself; in the nonsubway area an improvement of $600 in the house was required to generate the $1000 increase in demand price.

While the phenomenon of anticipatory decay is well known and has been observed to take place in many cities, there is no way to test the proportion in the present study without undertaking large-scale field investigations. Casual evidence suggests, however, that while in some areas one can easily find some homeowners who appear to have been influenced in this manner, it is very far from pervasive in the subway areas. Even in some areas where light industry has long existed, one finds excellently maintained houses close by. One finds homes continually being remodeled and new homes being built on the few lots still available in these districts. None of this suggests anything like a blighted condition.

3.3.1.2 *Differences in National Urbanization Patterns*

Although no differential effect on property value in and out of the subway study areas was found, it might be argued that the impact of the subway is more subtle, affecting all of Metro rather than specific areas. The subway is so appealing to people that commercial development of the city intensifies. This in turn attracts disproportionately large numbers of people to Metro—some to live in subway areas and commute to work by subway, others to live in nonsubway areas commute by bus or other means to the subway areas, and some even to live and work in various ways in the nonsubway areas to help service the needs of the more rapidly growing city. That is, if 75% of the subway investment is covered by the province out of general tax funds (implying that less was spent on other ends than would have been done in its absence, which itself implies some income-redistribution pattern to which people's settlement decisions had been made in the past), with only short-run variable costs or less paid for out of fares, there should be migration to the city. There should be consequent increases or diminutions in welfare of migrants according to whether income opportunities are great enough to overcome the initial reduction in net income caused by the tax transfer, as outlined in Chapter 3.

To analyze this question by direct observation would be difficult because to insufficiency of data on origin, time of move, expectations, and so on. Sample survey techniques would be hard put to isolate the effect of individual projects like the subway, which would be confounded with other policies and relative prices, such as differential education costs (and quality?) due to teachers' wage differences and resulting in differential property taxes. Finally, it would be hard to distinguish moves in response to the income transfer from moves independent of it, responding simply to better employment opportunities or other attractions in Toronto—moves that would have taken place anyway. It would be difficult to analyze whether the first group of moves leads to improvement or deterioration of those involved as compared with their welfare levels in the absence of the tax and the project.

Although the statistical evidence is far from definitive, it does not seem to support this hypothesis. Data on internal migration are the most relevant, since internal migration rather than births, deaths, or international immigration reveals more about a city's attractiveness. And migration data do not favor this hypothesis. Thus calculations for the 1956–1961 period, the quinquennium following the first Yonge Street subway section, show that Toronto had a net migration ratio (in-migrants minus out-migrants, aged five and over, as a percentage of total local population) of 0.5, which ranked fourteenth among the 17 Census Metropolitan Areas and compared with an overall average of 2.2 for all Census Metropolitan Areas (Stone, 1961, p. 115). This period, ending seven years after the Yonge Street line began operating, should have provided ample opportunity for the attractiveness of the subway to be felt. Unfortunately, migration data for the following decade have not yet been calculated.

On the other hand, when it comes to total population increase, Toronto ranks fourth among the 16 CMAs in the 1951–1971 period, as shown in Table 17.6, exceeded only by Edmonton, Calgary, and London. (Data for the component quinquennia are similar.) Much of the increase stemmed from international immigration, and it is unlikely that the subway was an influence here.

Finally, Toronto house selling prices between 1967 and 1972 have increased 38%, slightly less than the Canadian national average of 39%

Table 17.6 Census Metropolitan Areas: 1971 Population and the Percentage of Growth Since 1951

CMA	Population (000s)	Growth, 1951–1971 (%)
Montreal	2743.2	86.4
Toronto	2628.0	117.1
Vancouver	1082.4	92.6
Ottawa-Hull	602.5	106.0
Winnipeg	540.3	51.4
Hamilton	498.5	77.9
Edmonton	495.7	180.4
Quebec City	480.5	73.9
Calgary	403.3	183.4
London	286.0	121.8
Windsor	258.6	58.1
Kitchener	226.8	111.1
Halifax	222.6	66.2
Victoria	195.8	73.0
Sudbury	155.4	97.3
Regina	140.7	n.a.

Source. Statistics Canada, 1971 and 1961.

as reported by TREB (1973, p. 50). This was ninth highest of the 13 large metropolitan areas, which ranged from 76% in Vancouver to 1% in Montreal.

4 IMPLICATIONS FOR SUBWAY FINANCING AND PUBLIC POLICY

This study shows that the subway has had no effect on property values in the subway areas as compared with the nonsubway areas. This does not mean that the subways were unjustified economically, but only that their benefits have not been reflected in property values. There may have been enough benefits in cost savings and time reductions that did not show up in property values to justify the subway; part of these would be expected to show up in higher rents and profits of real estate firms, however. In addition, these profits might include other benefits, such as R_6, which accrue in the first place to residents but are not related to commuting cost reductions. These would further justify the subway.

We also saw that it was unlikely that the subway was having a different impact on Toronto than on other major Canadian cities. Available information suggests that Toronto has not been an outstanding magnet for migrants during the last 20 years. Toronto's net migration ratio was one of the lowest following the first subway, and total growth between 1954 and 1971 has been slow. The sharp rise in Toronto house prices has been small when compared with other metropolitan areas in Canada. While one could maintain that the subway kept Toronto from being less attractive—that it did in fact exercise a net positive attraction but this was offset by other disincentives—it would be difficult to determine what were the disincentive factors that were being offset by the subway. And in absence of such knowledge, it would be very difficult to analyze the welfare effects of such a hypothesis.

If Toronto is any gauge, then, we cannot in general expect that a subway causes significant benefits to accrue to persons other than the users (apart from pollution control, which has not been considered here). Accordingly, subway decisions would have to stand or fall on the cost reduction of users. Other factors such as changes in labor productivity (R_7) or greater environmental pleasure from the higher densities (R_6) would seem to be negligible or to be captured in real estate firms' profits.

We come now to ask what are the implications of such results for the planning and financing of subways. We note first that subways are large, long-lived capital investments, and exemplify the usual problem of decreasing average cost. Whether variable cost is constant or falling, economic optimization would require that fares be set much lower than average total cost. The following conclusions regarding the financing seem appropriate in this case:

1. If a subway is justified by cost reduction, the cost reduction will show up either in real estate firms' profits or as a pure gain by the rider. In the first case, the profits of the firms could be tapped for the investment resources. Since it would be difficult to devise a real estate firm profits tax that would be specific to the subway area, an alternative solution must be sought. The easiest way to do this would be to tax the property of real estate firms renting to users, that is, multiunit dwellings. In the second case, the riders gain all of the advantage of the cost and time savings. They could be taxed through rent increases, which could be generated by raising the taxes on properties in the corridor. This would be a more pervasive tax than that in the first case. It would have to be recognized that the tax would be somewhat gross, falling on homeowners and renters who ride the subway and those who do not. But it is unlikely to introduce any very serious distortions into housing price patterns.

In practice, much more would have to be known before one could determine which of the foregoing possibilities came closer to representing the true situation.

2. If subways cannot be justified on the basis of cost and time reductions, the most likely form that other benefits might take is profits of real estate firms beyond those increased profits that reflect riders' cost reductions and time savings. However, builders may be unwilling to discuss the profits that they hope to gain from their subway area activities for fear that a betterment tax would be imposed. This makes it very difficult to proceed. It might be that measurable cost reductions plus other benefits that might show up in real estate firms' profits could justify a subway. Thus even if real estate firms deny that they will earn profits that together with the measured cost reductions (and netting out double counting) might be great enough to justify the subway, there might actually be a benefit from an overall social point of view. In such a situation it would be very difficult for a public authority to proceed, however, since one of the principal beneficiary groups would be in the position of denying the projected benefit.

The weight of the foregoing considerations is that if enough potential benefits can be identified to justify a subway, the investment should be paid for by betterment taxes in the subway corridors.

The framework for the discussion of financing up to this point has been decision-making through a welfare criterion. Where this is the concern we must measure benefits, and, as we have seen, in the course of doing this for subway projects we also identify the beneficiaries. This enables us to recover the cost from the beneficiaries by applying standard fiscal devices such as property taxes. In the introduction to this study, however, we indicated that two other approaches to subway decisions were suitable for a capitalist democratic economy—popular referendum and private enterprise. (The engineering-administrative approach, it was suggested, might be feasible if attitudes toward administrative regulation of vehicles were to change.) The private enterprise approach has been virtually abandoned as a method for undertaking subways. If a private firm did decide to attempt it today, it would perform the engineering and market research to make its own cost and revenue calculations and we need not be concerned with it. If a referendum is undertaken, however, the question of where the resources are to come from must be faced.

The reasons why a referendum might be preferred to a welfare criterion include distrust of such approaches generally, skepticism at the notion that the benefits can be calculated, and the conviction that the externalities are significant but incalculable. In some cases this might be very reasonable. For example, even if a welfare criterion of the cost reduction type falls short of justifying a subway, pollution abatement might be important enough to do so, and the only way in which this could be made known would be through referendum. It does not really matter why the referendum is conducted, though. If a subway is decided upon by a referendum, provided that the costs are known and will be covered by local sources, enough people obviously view it as a net benefit for it to be justified. In this case many of the externalities will have been effectively quantified. The beneficiaries can be identified—they are the residents of the city—but their benefit is not related to their own use of the subway or proximity thereto, so that the subway-corridor-specific property tax approach would not work. A citywide property levy would be required.

Both of the two approaches to the financing of the subway just described—corridor-specific betterment taxes or citywide taxes—would conflict with the present approach being followed in Ontario. Today the province is prepared to contribute 75% toward the cost of subway construction. It is hard to justify this policy or understand why it came to be instituted in the first place. Possibly, it was intended to redress a balance in the distribution of highway fuel taxes—if it was felt that fuel taxes were being directed "unduly" into the rural and intercity road sector, the province could make it up to the cities by intraprovincial grants tied to various urban expenditures. Now, it may well be that there are distributional inequities and allocative inefficiencies in the present fuel tax allocation. If there are, they should be gotten at directly and the basic division of the fuel tax among competing ends decided on a rational basis. To try to correct possible distortions or inequities by intraprovincial urban grants of this type is neither logical nor efficient. It is not logical because it would be the sheerest coincidence if the subway transfer happened to be close to the amount of the fuel tax that was being unduly directed to nonurban users. It is inefficient because it only can serve to confound the public finances further, encouraging other ad hoc modifications of the future tax structure, which may be very far from optimal.

REFERENCES

Heenan, G Warren (1966), "Transit: Concept to Completion," address to workshop of the Institute for Rapid Transit and Boston College, June 15.

Statistics Canada (1961), *Census of Population* (Ottawa: Information Canada).

——— (1971), *Census of Population* (Ottawa: Information Canada).

Stone, Leroy O. (1961), *Migration in Canada, Regional Aspect.* (Ottawa: Dominion Bureau of Statistics—Information Canada).

Toronto Real Estate Board (1973), *House Price Trends and Residential Construction Costs in Metropolitan Toronto and Canada*, (Toronto).

Toronto Transit Commission, *Annual Report,*various years (Toronto).

Index

321